HYPER-
BORDER

THE CONTEMPORARY
U.S.–MEXICO BORDER
AND ITS FUTURE

FERNANDO ROMERO/LAR

PRINCETON ARCHITECTURAL PRESS, NEW YORK

Published by
Princeton Architectural Press
37 East Seventh Street
New York, New York 10003

For a free catalog of books, call 1.800.722.6657.
Visit our web site at www.papress.com.

Names, characters, places, and incidents in the "scenarios" portions
of this book are the product of the author's imagination or are used
fictitiously. Any resemblance to actual persons, living or dead, events,
or locales is entirely coincidental.

For LAR/Fernando Romero
Project director: Alejandro Quinto
Newscaster of the future: Mónica de la Torre
Researcher and writer: Brittany Tobar
Researcher and writer: Devon McLorg
Researchers: Ivonne Santoyo, Bárbara Miranda, and Jorge Espinosa
Designers: Alejandro Quinto and Peter Ty
www.laboratoryofarchitecture.com

For Princeton Architectural Press
Text editor: Scott Tennent
Project editor: Clare Jacobson

Special thanks to: Nettie Aljian, Sara Bader, Dorothy Ball,
Nicola Bednarek, Janet Behning, Kristin Carlson, Becca Casbon,
Penny (Yuen Pik) Chu, Russell Fernandez, Pete Fitzpatrick,
Wendy Fuller, Jan Haux, John King, Nancy Eklund Later, Linda Lee,
Laurie Manfra, Katharine Myers, Lauren Nelson Packard,
Jennifer Thompson, Arnoud Verhaeghe, Paul Wagner,
Joseph Weston, and Deb Wood of Princeton Architectural Press
—Kevin C. Lippert, publisher

Library of Congress Cataloging-in-Publication Data
Romero, Fernando, 1971-
   Hyperborder : the contemporary U.S.-Mexico border and its future /
Fernando Romero. — 1st ed.
      p. cm.
   Includes bibliographical references and index.
   ISBN-13: 978-1-56898-706-4 (alk. paper)
   ISBN-10: 1-56898-706-4 (alk. paper)
   1. Mexican-American Border Region. I. Title.
   F787.R57 2007
   303.48'2721009051—dc22
                                    2007014297

CONTENTS

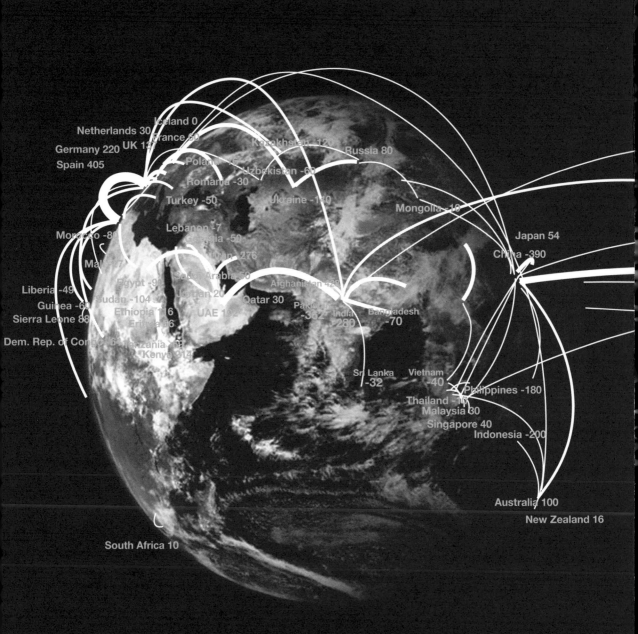

Iceland 0
Netherlands 30
France 50
Germany 220 UK 13
Spain 405
Poland
Romania -30
Turkey -50
Kazakhstan -120
Russia 80
Uzbekistan -60
Ukraine -140
Mongolia -10
Japan 54
Morocco -80
Lebanon -7
China -390
Mali 77
Tunisia -50
Algeria 276
Egypt -9
Saudi Arabia 50
Afghanistan 420
Liberia -49
Jordan 20
Qatar 30
Pakistan
Sudan -104
Guinea -60
Ethiopia 116
UAE 1
-332
India
Bangladesh
-70
Sierra Leone 88
Eritrea 6
-280
Dem. Rep. of Congo 6
Tanzania
Kenya 214
Sri Lanka
-32
Vietnam
-40
Thailand -10
Philippines -180
Malaysia 30
Singapore 40
Indonesia -200
Australia 100
New Zealand 16
South Africa 10

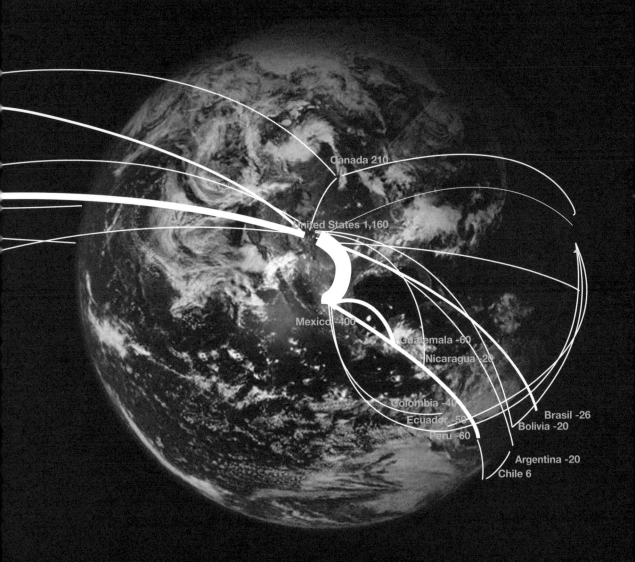

Canada 210

United States 1,160

Mexico -400

Guatemala -60

Nicaragua -20

Colombia -40

Ecuador -56

Peru -60

Brasil -26

Bolivia -20

Argentina -20

Chile 6

Average Annual Net Migration in Thousands 2000–2005

U.S.–MEXICO BORDER COMPARED TO WORLD SITES

Length of World Borders (km), top 20

6,846	1.	RUSSIA - KAZAKHSTAN
6,416	2.	U.S. - CANADA
5,150	3.	CHILE - ARGENTINA
4,677	4.	CHINA - MONGOLIA
4,053	5.	BANGLADESH - INDIA
3,605	6.	RUSSIA - CHINA
3,485	7.	RUSSIA - MONGOLIA
3,400	8.	BRAZIL - BOLIVIA
3,141	9.	U.S. - MEXICO BORDER
2,912	10.	INDIA - PAKISTAN
2,704	11.	INDIA - CHINA
2,511	12.	ANGOLA - DEM. REP. CONGO
2,477	13.	ALASKA (U.S.) - CANADA
2,430	14.	PAKISTAN - AFGHANISTAN
2,411	15.	DEM. REP. CONGO - CONGO
2,237	16.	MALI - MAURITANIA
2,203	17.	UZBEKISTAN - KAZAKHSTAN
2,200	18.	VENEZUELA - BRAZIL
2,185	19.	CHINA - MYANMAR
2,130	20.	LAOS - VIETNAM

Area of Countries (km²)

504,782	SPAIN
488,100	TURKMENISTAN
475,440	CAMEROON
462,840	PAPUA NEW GUINEA
449,964	SWEDEN
447,400	UZBEKISTAN
446,550	MOROCCO
437,072	IRAQ
408,185	U.S. - MEXICO BORDER
406,750	PARAGUAY
390,580	ZIMBABWE
377,835	JAPAN
357,021	GERMANY
342,000	REP. OF THE CONGO
337,030	FINLAND
329,750	MALAYSIA
329,560	VIETNAM
324,220	NORWAY
322,460	CÔTE D'IVOIRE
312,685	POLAND
301,230	ITALY
300,000	PHILIPPINES

Population of Countries (millions), 2006

20.6	AUSTRALIA
19.9	SRI LANKA
19.9	MOZAMBIQUE
19.7	CÔTE D'IVOIRE
19.5	SYRIA
17.8	MADAGASCAR
17.3	CAMEROON
16.4	CHILE
16.4	NETHERLANDS
15.8	ANGOLA
15.3	KAZAKHSTAN
14.4	NIGER
14.1	CAMBODIA
13.9	MALI
13.6	BURKINA FASO
13.3	U.S. - MEXICO BORDER
13.3	ECUADOR
13.1	ZIMBABWE
13.0	GUATEMALA
12.8	MALAWI
11.9	SENEGAL
11.9	ZAMBIA
11.3	CUBA
11.1	GREECE
10.6	PORTUGAL
10.5	BELGIUM
10.3	CZECH REPUBLIC
10.1	HUNGARY
10.0	CHAD

Hyperborder, the U.S.–Mexico border, is the busiest and among the most contrasting international borders in the world, with over one million crossings daily. It is the ninth longest in the world and fourth longest in the Americas, with an area bigger than Spain or Sweden and a population larger than Guatemala or Portugal. It is a dynamic site that encompasses modern global issues that range from migration to trade to international relations to national sovereignty.

The United States is the world's leading immigration country and Mexico is the leading emigration country. Today, 12 million Mexican-born people live on the northern side of their nation's border. By 2050, Hispanics will represent 25% of the U.S. population, and 11% of all Mexicans will be living in the United States. These demographic shifts affect the politics, economies, and cultures of the neighboring nations, forcing them to evaluate the future of their binational relations.

Top 10 Immigration Countries	
UNITED STATES	16.7
RUSSIAN FEDERATION	4.1
SAUDI ARABIA	3.4
INDIA	3.3
CANADA	3.3
GERMANY	2.7
FRANCE	1.4
AUSTRALIA	1.4
TURKEY	1.3
UNITED ARAB EMIRATES	1.3

Top 10 Emigration Countries	
MEXICO	-6.0
BANGLADESH	-4.1
AFGHANISTAN	-4.1
PHILIPPINES	-2.9
KAZAKHSTAN	-2.6
VIETNAM	-2.0
RWANDA	-1.7
SRI LANKA	-1.5
COLOMBIA	-1.3
BOSNIA AND HERZEGOVINA	-1.2

Cars headed toward the Otay Mesa border crossing point in Tijuana.

Often guided by a *coyote*, nearly half a million undocumented Mexicans head north attempting to cross the U.S.–Mexico border every year. In this photo, taken on June 14, 2006, migrants swim through the New River between the border cities of Mexicali and Calexico, California. The river is considered the most polluted in the U.S.

Acknowledgments

Thanks to all the people who contributed in some ways to the making of this publication. Alejandro Quinto, project director, Brittany Tobar and Devon McLorg, researchers and writers, Bárbara Miranda and Jorge Espinosa, researchers, Peter Ty, designer, and Mauricio Daniel Serna Murias, illustrator. In Mexico City: Soumaya Slim de Romero, Jorge Castañeda, Senator Jeffrey Jones, Aldo Chaparro and Vanesa Fernández at Celeste; David Shields, Carlos Monsivais, Luis Manuel Guerra, Sergio Aguayo, Guillermo Pulido, José Luis Ugalde Valdés, Pedro Reyes, Deborah Holtz, Veronica Riquelme, Claudia Arias Garcia; Iris Jiménez, Patricia Ramirez, and Emilio Cedrún of SEMARNAT; Enrique Peters Dussel, Luis Astorga of UNAM, Ricardo Salas, Rossana Fuentes Berain, Jorge Gamboa, Daniel Hajj, Alinka Echevarria, José Apolinar Ríos, Joana Parra, Ivonne Santoyo, Ana Paola, Eva Campos, and Arturo Quinto. In Toronto: Lorraine Gauthier, Vannesa Ahuactzin, and Bjarke Hjorth Madsen at Work Worth Doing; Tobias Lau, Tyler Millard, Gonzalo Cárdenas, Todd Falkowsky, Britt Welter-Nolan, Nadia Hernandez, Laura Fuentes, Manuel Saldaña, and Bruce Mau. In Tijuana: Jorge Santibáñez, MariCarmen, Erika, Nora Bringas, Paulina Yurén, Gudelia Rangel, Rodolfo Cruz, and Maria Eugenia Anguiano of COLEF. In San Diego: David Shirk, University of San Diego; Dr. David Heer, Jim Gerber, San Diego State University; Louis Hock, University of California, San Diego. In Los Angeles: Jeffrey Inaba. In El Paso: Cecilia Levine, Paola Ramos, and all the organizers and attendees of the Hyperborder conference in 2005. In Ciudad Juárez: Gonzalo Bravo; In Phoenix, AZ: Marissa Walker of CANAMEX. In Washington, D.C.: Robert A. Pastor and David Stemper, American University; Richard Jackson, CSIS; Carlos de la Parra, SEMARNAT. In New York City: Ethan Nadelmann, Drug Policy Alliance. Thanks to all who made the project financially feasible: Grupo Bimbo, Samuel Lezoreck, Carlos Menvielle, Ing. Alfonso Salem, Luis Coppel, Grupo Financiero Inbursa, Andrés Vázquez del Mercado, la Colección Júmex, Tom di Santo, Baltazar Hinojosa, Gerardo Estrada, and Volaris.

This project aims to present a contemporary perspective of the U.S.–Mexico border by defining its present conditions and provoking new ideas for its future. For our purposes, the term *border* goes beyond its traditional definition as a line separating geographical and political boundaries, to one that includes other types of barriers between the United States and Mexico, such as economic and cultural divisions. *Hyperborder* wishes to emphasize that despite the contrasts and discrepancies that separate the bordering countries, the increased levels of human, cultural, and economic exchanges between them are securing an unprecedented degree of interdependence: one nation's future depends on that of the other. Due to the globalized conditions of the world today and the projections for increased integration in the decades to come, this book seeks to promote a future paradigm of the U.S.–Mexico border that as a region considers and reacts according to global conditions.

We begin by contextualizing the U.S.–Mexico border as a telling case study for the constant flows between nations in today's global arena. This phenomenon is illustrated by the exponential increase of movement and exchange the world has witnessed in recent years, and the anticipated endurance of this trend in the future. In today's age of global connectivity, free markets, and increased mobility, borders have become more flexible, more permeable, and more blurred. They are in constant transition, and the shape they take in the future will influence multiple arenas, whether political, social, economic, or cultural.

Borders have always had significant functions: protecting countries' populations from outside threats, regulating the flow in and out of geographical boundaries, and helping to define socio-cultural identities within nation-states are just a few of their multiple objectives. Such aspects of a border's purpose are still applicable, of course, and we make no claim that international boundaries are irrelevant in the present-day world. In fact, unlike hundreds of years ago, today there is a pervasive sense of urgency to control the increased flows of people, information, currency, and goods that cross borders, despite the difficulty this task entails. This issue has reached a paradoxical state: on one side, there has developed an obsessive necessity to control border flows, while on the other, despite increased security, we are witnessing the highest flows of people and goods across international boundaries in history. The traditional functions of international borders are being tested by globalization—a phenomenon whose momentum has the potential to severely alter the future state of the world.

A new framework is needed, one that embraces complexity and multilateral viewpoints yet also considers common values that connect people throughout the world. Borders play a significant role in this context, in the way they pertain to issues like sovereignty, natural resources, human rights, trade, religion, culture, and so forth. It is through this humanitarian perspective that our notions about borders can change, and where local communities can connect directly to the global community. With this in mind, *Hyperborder* will begin its analysis at the global level before narrowing down to the specific geographic area known as the U.S.–Mexico border region, so as to demonstrate the level of integration and the inherent connection of the global context to the localized issues. Our position in this project is not pro-Mexican or pro-U.S., but pro-development, pro-cooperation. By choosing a stance that goes beyond national interests and takes a global approach, we can focus on universal needs, such as quality of life for all—a value that should be unrestricted by geographic, ethnic, or economic boundaries.

This brings us to another of *Hyperborder*'s goals, which is to contemplate and assess the benefits and drawbacks borders could have in the future toward the improvement of social welfare worldwide. As you will see in chapter one, because of its especially dynamic and active nature, the U.S.–Mexico border has the potential to provide useful insight for how to manage borders elsewhere in the world. Similarities can be found, for example, in migratory patterns and circumstances in the U.S.–Mexico border region and the Mediterranean Sea, the barrier between Northern Africa and Europe. Tactics piloted along the U.S.–Mexico border that prove to positively influence the region's conditions could therefore potentially be utilized as models for the rest of the world.

The remaining chapters of this book explore the forces that have shaped the U.S.–Mexico border, as it exists in its current state, as well as the actors who wish to improve it according to their own agendas. Furthermore, Part II of the book will introduce future scenarios that could potentially be the key to the border's development—or demise—in the decades to come. They aspire to redirect the way one conceptualizes the border, binational relations, and conditions affecting the planet in the years to come. In order to illuminate the potential future consequences that may come if progressive action is not taken now, these scenarios are not always positive; many shed light on the adverse impacts today's decisions could have in the decades to come, and thus in the interest of development and prosperity are important to consider and discuss. These scenarios are set in the context of twelve themes that relate to the state of the border, the United States, and Mexico, and will shape their future in the globalized world:

1) Security	7) Transportation
2) Narcotraffic and corruption	8) Energy
3) Informal sector	9) Environment
4) Migration and demographics	10) Health
5) Education	11) Urbanization
6) Economic development and trade	

Some of these qualitative scenarios are positive, some negative, but all provide new ways of considering future possibilities and outcomes. We are hopeful that our study and vision will catalyze relations between two countries that share a problematic border, and that it will promote solidarity and equity among people rather than division and inequality. Through investigating the complex issues that surround the U.S.–Mexico border and its global implications today, we seek to exemplify the need for change and improvement in the future. In the interest of helping the generations of the future confront imminent challenges, it is our opinion that the development of these types of visions and alternatives are necessary. We hope this book will empower people into collective action for the creation of a more desirable common future.

The U.S.–Mexico border

1. CONTEXT: THE HYPERBORDER IN A GLOBALIZED WORLD

In order to demonstrate the diverse circumstances along the U.S.–Mexico border and the various approaches to managing regional and binational relations in the current global context, this chapter explores a variety of borders from around the world. These case studies provide examples of border relations ranging from hostile to cooperative and illustrate the types of issues—including political and ethnic tension, labor and immigration, and cooperation in the realms of environmentalism, transportation, health, and trade—that can either plague a region or make it prosper.

"No country, no matter how big, can solve its own internal problems before solving the problems threatening the global system."

—Donella and Dennis Meadows, Jørgen Randers, and William Behrens, *The Limits to Growth*, 1972

The spreading concern for national security has galvanized a renewed focus on border issues around the world, further sharpening autonomous and protective tendencies. Territorial disputes, contentious borders, and terrorist activities play considerable roles in the effort to secure (and oftentimes seal) international borders. Fortresslike walls are being discussed—and in some cases erected—as nations across the planet parlay with their neighbors in the post-9/11 global political climate.

Although hostility and distrust often plagues many bordering countries' relations, some international neighbors have fostered relationships characterized by cooperation and innovative approaches toward mutual development. Cross-border transportation, binational environmental accords, and regional approaches to addressing health issues are just a few examples of the ways in which some nations have worked together despite the geopolitical boundaries that divide them. Such mutually beneficial relationships can serve as models for the rest of the world in a global climate often marked by apprehension and fear.

The United Nations Millennium Development Goals Progress Report, 2006.

Change from previous time-frame
∨ Decrease
∧ Increase
— No change

ENERGY USE
Consumption of kg oil equivalent per $1,000 GDP (PPP), 2003

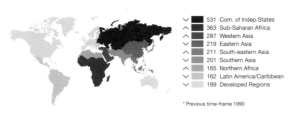

∨	531	Com. of Indep.States
∧	363	Sub-Saharan Africa
∧	287	Western Asia
∨	219	Eastern Asia
∨	211	South-eastern Asia
∨	201	Southern Asia
∨	165	Northern Africa
∨	162	Latin America/Caribbean
∨	189	Developed Regions

* Previous time-frame 1990

WOMEN IN WAGE EMPLOYMENT
Share of women in non-agricultural wage employment, 2004

∧	17.3	Southern Asia
∧	20.1	Western Asia
∧	20.3	Northern Africa
∧	35	Sub-Saharan Africa
∧	37.3	Oceania
∧	38.3	South-eastern Asia
∧	41.2	Eastern Asia
∧	43.2	Latin America/Caribbean
∧	46.4	Developed Regions
∧	51.1	Com. of Indep.States

* Previous time-frame 1990

WATER ACCESS
Proportion of population with sustainable access to an improved
water source, urban and rural, 2004

—	51	Oceania
∧	56	Sub-Saharan Africa
∧	78	Eastern Asia
∧	82	South-eastern Asia
∧	85	Southern Asia
∧	91	Latin America/Caribbean
∧	91	Northern Africa
∧	91	Western Asia
—	92	Com. of Indep. States
∨	99	Developed Regions

* Previous time-frame 1990

HOUSEHOLD TENURE
Percentage of urban population living in slums, 2001

∧	71.9	Sub-Saharan Africa
∨	59	Southern Asia
∨	36.4	Eastern Asia
∨	35.3	Western Asia
∨	31.9	Latin America/Caribbean
∨	28.2	Northern Africa
∨	28	South-eastern Asia
∨	24.1	Oceania
∨	17.7	Com. of Indep.States[1]
—	6	Developed Regions

* Previous time-frame 1990
[1] Average CIS (CIS Europe 6.0
and CIS Asia 29.4)

PROTECTED AREAS
Area protected to maintain biological diversity. Ratio of
protected area to total territorial area (terrestrial and sea), 2005

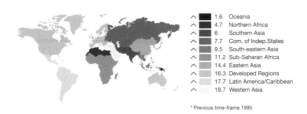

∧	1.6	Oceania
∧	4.7	Northern Africa
∧	6	Southern Asia
∧	7.7	Com. of Indep.States
∧	9.5	South-eastern Asia
∧	11.2	Sub-Saharan Africa
∧	14.4	Eastern Asia
∧	16.3	Developed Regions
∧	17.7	Latin America/Caribbean
∧	18.7	Western Asia

* Previous time-frame 1995

INTERNET USERS
Number of Internet users per 100 population, 2004

∧	1.8	Sub-Saharan Africa
∧	3.4	Southern Asia
∧	4.7	Oceania
∧	6.3	Northern Africa
∧	7.4	South-eastern Asia
∧	8.9	Com. of Indep.States
∧	10.3	Eastern Asia
∧	10.5	Western Asia
∧	11.9	Latin America/Caribbean
∧	51.4	Developed Regions

* Previous time-frame 2002

Numerous discrepancies divide our world: from hunger to AIDS to poverty, borders extend beyond their geopolitical definition.

PRIMARY EDUCATION
Primary completion rate. Percentage of students enrolled in the final grade of primary school, 2004

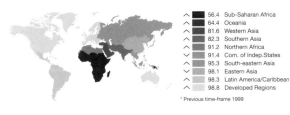

∧	56.4	Sub-Saharan Africa
∧	64.4	Oceania
∧	81.6	Western Asia
∧	82.3	Southern Asia
∧	91.2	Northern Africa
∨	91.4	Com. of Indep.States
∧	95.3	South-eastern Asia
∨	98.1	Eastern Asia
∧	98.3	Latin America/Caribbean
∧	98.8	Developed Regions

* Previous time-frame 1999

CARBON DIOXIDE EMISSIONS
Total. Millions of metric tons of CO_2, 2003

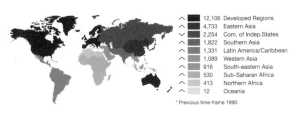

∧	12,106	Developed Regions
∨	4,733	Eastern Asia
∨	2,254	Com. of Indep.States
∧	1,822	Southern Asia
∧	1,331	Latin America/Caribbean
∧	1,089	Western Asia
∧	916	South-eastern Asia
∧	530	Sub-Saharan Africa
∧	413	Northern Africa
∧	12	Oceania

* Previous time-frame 1990

POPULATION LIVING BELOW $1 PER DAY
Percentage of population living below $1 purchasing power parity (PPP), 2002

∨	44.0	Sub-Saharan Africa
∨	31.2	Southern Asia
∨	14.1	Eastern Asia
∨	8.9	Latin America/Caribbean
∨	7.3	South-eastern Asia
∨	7.3	Oceania
∧	2.5	Com. of Indep.States
∨	2.4	Northern Africa
∨	2.4	Western Asia

* Previous time-frame 1990

HUNGER
Percentage of undernourished in total population (2001–2003)

∨	31	Sub-Saharan Africa
∨	21	Southern Asia
∨	12	Eastern Asia
∨	12	South-eastern Asia
∨	12	Oceania
∨	10	Latin America/Caribbean
∧	9	Western Asia
—	7	Com. of Indep.States
—	4	Northern Africa
—	<2.5	Developed Regions

* Previous time-frame 1990-92

CHILD MORTALITY
Under-five mortality rate. Deaths per 1,000 live births, 2004

∨	168	Sub-Saharan Africa
∨	90	Southern Asia
∨	80	Oceania
∨	58	Western Asia
∨	44	Com. of Indep.States
∨	43	South-eastern Asia
∨	37	Northern Africa
∨	31	Eastern Asia
∨	31	Latin America/Caribbean
∨	7	Developed Regions

* Previous time-frame 1990

HIV/AIDS PREVALENCE
Estimated adult (15-49) HIV prevalence, 2005

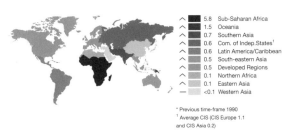

∧	5.8	Sub-Saharan Africa
∧	1.5	Oceania
∧	0.7	Southern Asia
∧	0.6	Com. of Indep.States[1]
∧	0.6	Latin America/Caribbean
∧	0.5	South-eastern Asia
∧	0.5	Developed Regions
∧	0.1	Northern Africa
∧	0.1	Eastern Asia
—	<0.1	Western Asia

* Previous time-frame 1990
[1] Average CIS (CIS Europe 1.1 and CIS Asia 0.2)

International Comparisons Among G-20 Countries

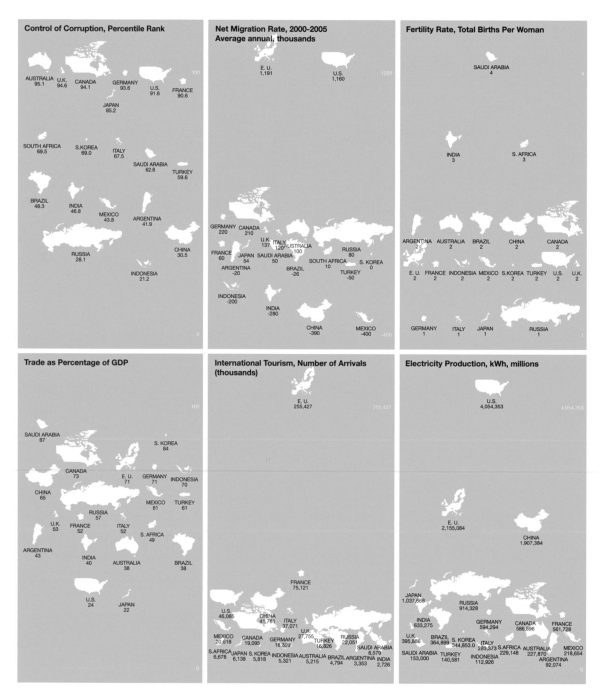

Control of Corruption, Percentile Rank

AUSTRALIA 95.1 · U.K. 94.6 · CANADA 94.1 · GERMANY 93.6 · U.S. 91.6 · FRANCE 90.6 · JAPAN 85.2 · SOUTH AFRICA 69.5 · S.KOREA 69.0 · ITALY 67.5 · SAUDI ARABIA 62.6 · TURKEY 59.6 · BRAZIL 48.3 · INDIA 46.8 · MEXICO 43.8 · ARGENTINA 41.9 · CHINA 30.5 · RUSSIA 28.1 · INDONESIA 21.2

Net Migration Rate, 2000-2005 Average annual, thousands

E. U. 1,191 · U.S. 1,160 · GERMANY 220 · CANADA 210 · U.K. 137 · ITALY 120 · AUSTRALIA 100 · RUSSIA 80 · FRANCE 60 · JAPAN 54 · SAUDI ARABIA 50 · SOUTH AFRICA 10 · S. KOREA 0 · ARGENTINA -20 · BRAZIL -26 · TURKEY -50 · INDONESIA -200 · INDIA -280 · CHINA -390 · MEXICO -400

Fertility Rate, Total Births Per Woman

SAUDI ARABIA 4 · INDIA 3 · S. AFRICA 3 · ARGENTINA 2 · AUSTRALIA 2 · BRAZIL 2 · CHINA 2 · CANADA 2 · E. U. 2 · FRANCE 2 · INDONESIA 2 · MEXICO 2 · S.KOREA 2 · TURKEY 2 · U.S. 2 · U.K. 2 · GERMANY 1 · ITALY 1 · JAPAN 1 · RUSSIA 1

Trade as Percentage of GDP

SAUDI ARABIA 87 · S. KOREA 84 · CANADA 73 · E. U. 71 · GERMANY 71 · INDONESIA 70 · CHINA 65 · MEXICO 61 · TURKEY 61 · RUSSIA 57 · U.K. 53 · FRANCE 52 · ITALY 52 · S. AFRICA 49 · ARGENTINA 43 · INDIA 40 · AUSTRALIA 38 · BRAZIL 38 · U.S. 24 · JAPAN 22

International Tourism, Number of Arrivals (thousands)

E. U. 255,427 · FRANCE 75,121 · U.S. 46,085 · CHINA 41,761 · ITALY 37,071 · U.K. 27,755 · TURKEY 22,051 · RUSSIA 16,826 · MEXICO 20,618 · CANADA 19,095 · GERMANY 18,399 · SAUDI ARABIA 8,579 · S.AFRICA 6,678 · JAPAN 6,138 · S. KOREA 5,818 · INDONESIA 5,321 · AUSTRALIA 5,215 · BRAZIL 4,794 · ARGENTINA 3,353 · INDIA 2,726

Electricity Production, kWh, millions

U.S. 4,054,353 · E. U. 2,155,084 · CHINA 1,907,384 · JAPAN 1,037,658 · RUSSIA 914,328 · INDIA 633,275 · GERMANY 594,294 · CANADA 586,896 · FRANCE 561,728 · U.K. 395,886 · BRAZIL 364,899 · S. KOREA 344,853.0 · ITALY 283,373 · S.AFRICA 229,148 · AUSTRALIA 227,870 · MEXICO 218,654 · SAUDI ARABIA 153,000 · TURKEY 140,581 · INDONESIA 112,926 · ARGENTINA 92,074

Although the United States and Mexico are next-door neighbors, other countries come between them in terms of development, education, and infrastructure.

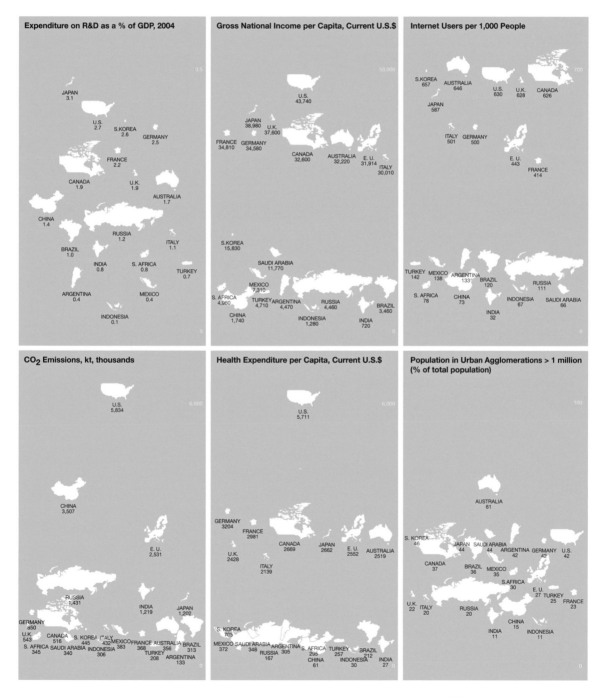

Expenditure on R&D as a % of GDP, 2004

3.5

JAPAN 3.1
U.S. 2.7
S.KOREA 2.6
GERMANY 2.5
FRANCE 2.2
CANADA 1.9
U.K. 1.9
AUSTRALIA 1.7
CHINA 1.4
RUSSIA 1.2
ITALY 1.1
BRAZIL 1.0
INDIA 0.8
S. AFRICA 0.8
TURKEY 0.7
ARGENTINA 0.4
MEXICO 0.4
INDONESIA 0.1

0

Gross National Income per Capita, Current U.S.$

50,000

U.S. 43,740
JAPAN 38,980
U.K. 37,600
FRANCE 34,810
GERMANY 34,580
CANADA 32,600
AUSTRALIA 32,220
E. U. 31,914
ITALY 30,010
S.KOREA 15,830
SAUDI ARABIA 11,770
MEXICO 7,310
S. AFRICA 4,960
TURKEY 4,710
ARGENTINA 4,470
RUSSIA 4,460
BRAZIL 3,460
CHINA 1,740
INDONESIA 1,280
INDIA 720

0

Internet Users per 1,000 People

700

S.KOREA 657
AUSTRALIA 646
U.S. 630
U.K. 628
CANADA 626
JAPAN 587
ITALY 501
GERMANY 500
E. U. 443
FRANCE 414
TURKEY 142
MEXICO 138
ARGENTINA 133
BRAZIL 120
RUSSIA 111
S. AFRICA 78
CHINA 73
INDONESIA 67
SAUDI ARABIA 66
INDIA 32

0

CO$_2$ Emissions, kt, thousands

6,000

U.S. 5,834
CHINA 3,507
E. U. 2,531
RUSSIA 1,431
INDIA 1,219
JAPAN 1,202
GERMANY 850
U.K. 543
CANADA 516
S. KOREA 445
ITALY 432
MEXICO 383
FRANCE 368
AUSTRALIA 356
BRAZIL 313
S. AFRICA 345
SAUDI ARABIA 340
INDONESIA 306
TURKEY 208
ARGENTINA 133

0

Health Expenditure per Capita, Current U.S.$

6,000

U.S. 5,711
GERMANY 3204
FRANCE 2981
CANADA 2669
JAPAN 2662
E. U. 2552
AUSTRALIA 2519
U.K. 2428
ITALY 2139
S. KOREA 705
MEXICO 372
SAUDI ARABIA 348
ARGENTINA 305
S. AFRICA 295
TURKEY 257
BRAZIL 212
RUSSIA 167
CHINA 61
INDONESIA 30
INDIA 27

0

Population in Urban Agglomerations > 1 million (% of total population)

100

AUSTRALIA 61
S. KOREA 46
JAPAN 44
SAUDI ARABIA 44
ARGENTINA 42
GERMANY 42
U.S. 42
CANADA 37
BRAZIL 36
MEXICO 35
S.AFRICA 30
E. U. 27
TURKEY 25
FRANCE 23
U.K. 22
ITALY 20
RUSSIA 20
CHINA 15
INDIA 11
INDONESIA 11

0

NORTH KOREA AND SOUTH KOREA: THE WORLD'S MOST FORTIFIED BORDER

ISRAEL AND PALESTINIAN TERRITORIES: AN ETHNIC DIVIDE

The most fortified border in the world is that which divides North Korea, one of the last communist states, from the democratic Republic of South Korea. After World War II, when Japan ceased to rule over the unified nation of Korea, the country was divided at the 38th parallel by the Cold War enemies and world superpowers of that time, the U.S.S.R. and the United States. North and South Korea have technically been at war since 1950, the fighting ended in a cease-fire in 1953, which also marked the closing of the border and the establishment of the Demilitarized Zone (DMZ)—a 2.5-mile-wide (4 km) buffer zone peppered with land mines, dividing the two countries—which former President Clinton described in 2003 as "the scariest place on earth."[1] The DMZ is split along the middle by the Military Demarcation Line, an ultimate barrier that if crossed would revive the war. Today some two million troops continue to patrol both sides of the 151-mile (248 km) DMZ on the perpetual brink of war, as North Korea continues its much contested nuclear weapons program while South Korean and U.S. armed forces remain alert little more than two miles away.

Palestine and Israel share a history plagued with hostility and conflict. During the nineteenth century, many European Jews emigrated to Palestine under the influence of a Zionist movement that called for a homeland for Jews in Israel. This exodus continued in full force during the first half of the twentieth century in the face of World War II and the Holocaust. From the start, the arrival of the Jewish people in Palestine caused strife. The native Palestinians were often displaced due to land purchases made by the immigrants, and tensions increased because Islam and Judaism historically share the same Holy Land. In 1948, after World War II ended, the United Nations General Assembly voted to partition Palestine into separate Arab and Jewish states, thus establishing the State of Israel. The partition also demarcated Jerusalem as an international zone, where neither Jewish nor Arab authority would exist, in an attempt to avoid further religious conflicts. The plan failed, however, as Israel's Arab neighbors were vehemently opposed to surrendering the land. After a period of ever-increasing tension the Six Day War broke out in 1967, resulting in Israel's seizing control of the West Bank, the Gaza Strip, the Sinai Peninsula, and the Golan Heights—areas heavily populated with Palestinians. The resulting "occupation," as it is perceived by the Palestinians, has been a continuing source of contention and bitter hostility. The decades since the war have been punctuated by suicide bombings committed by radical Palestinians, and the Israeli government's subsequent retaliations.

Map of disputed territories and settlements in the West Bank.

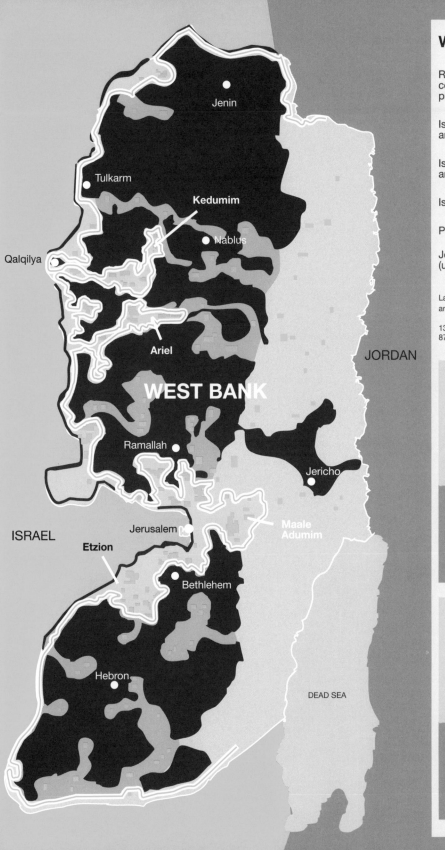

ISRAEL

Qalqilya

Tulkarm

Jenin

Kedumim

Nablus

Ariel

WEST BANK

Ramallah

Jericho

**Maale
Adumim**

Jerusalem

Etzion

Bethlehem

JORDAN

DEAD SEA

Hebron

West Bank 2006

Route of wall,
completed and
projected

Israeli settlement
areas inside wall

Israeli settlement
areas outside wall

Israeli settlements

Palestinian areas

Jordan Valley
(under Israeli control)

Land occupation in Israel, the West Bank,
and Gaza Strip, 2006.

13% Palestinian
87% Israeli

1967

LEBANON

SYRIA

WEST
BANK

GAZA
STRIP

ISRAEL

JORDAN

EGYPT

22%
Palestinian

78%
Israeli

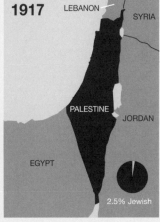

1917

LEBANON

SYRIA

PALESTINE

JORDAN

EGYPT

2.5% Jewish

One such retaliation is the extremely controversial "security fence" that Israel began erecting in 2002 to separate it from the predominantly Palestinian West Bank. The stated purpose of the security fence is to keep Palestinian terrorists and suicide bombers out of Israel, although critics say the fence unfairly annexes Palestinian territories into Israel, further exacerbating the land dispute in the West Bank.[2] The security barrier, which is already 170 miles long and is planned to stretch to 440 miles when finished, is a prisonlike fence complete with sensors, watchtowers, sniper posts, and barbed wire. Palestinians who wish to cross it must obtain permits from the Israeli government. Many of the permit solicitors—including some who have homes, jobs, or family within the fence's boundaries—have been rejected, resulting in further unrest. The wall was deemed a violation of international law by the International Court of Justice in an advisory opinion in 2004, but the opinion was rejected by the Israeli government in September of 2005.[3] Today the construction of the controversial barrier continues.

Israeli security officers in the process of removing residents from an illegal West Bank settlement east of Ramallah. An Israeli Supreme Court ruling allowed for the destruction of the settlers' homes.

MOROCCO AND SPAIN: CONTRASTING DEMOGRAPHICS AT THE DOOR BETWEEN AFRICA AND EUROPE

The case of Morocco and Spain as bordering nations is unique. Despite the obstacle the Strait of Gibraltar presents as a dividing mass of water between the two countries—and subsequently the two continents of Europe and Africa—illegal immigration has risen exponentially in the last twenty years. Today, Morocco is often described as being to Europe what Mexico is to the United States. As less-developed countries, Morocco and Mexico both lack viable opportunities for their citizens but geographically have relatively easy access to the wealthier, cheap labor–hungry nations of the European Union and the United States, respectively. Perhaps more so than Mexico, Morocco also serves as a "transit migration country": in recent decades it has become one of the primary staging areas for North African and increasingly sub-Saharan African immigrants en route to Europe.[4] It is no surprise that Spain currently has the highest immigration rate in the European Union.

In the midst of the heated debate surrounding soaring illegal immigration rates in Spain and throughout Western Europe, the region is currently facing drastic shifts in demographics due to low fertility rates and longer life expectancy. Europe's population is expected to age dramatically in the coming decades: by the year 2030 there will be one elderly person (over the age of 65) for every two people of productive, working age.[5] Today the median age in the continent is 37.7 years; by 2050 it will rise to 52.3.[6] At the end of the twentieth century,

Spain's fertility rate ranked among the lowest in the EU at 1.2 children per woman.[7] What these demographic shifts imply are a shrinking labor force, eventual economic stagnation, and a steadily growing elderly population in need of government aid, which will become increasingly unavailable if gaps in the labor force are not filled. In contrast, Morocco and the rest of the African nations have populations that are much younger. This demographic distinction, paired with the willingness (or necessity) of many Africans to migrate north in search of opportunity, could serve to fill the vacancies expected to surface in the European labor forces.

Opposite: African migrants arrive in the Santa Cruz port in Tenerife. It is estimated that over 20,000 migrants ventured in similar boats from west Africa in 2006 in hopes of reaching European territory. Above: Forty-six migrants arrive on August 3 to La Tejita Beach on this popular tourist destination. The previous month, 2,245 migrants were intercepted on the island.

THE U.S. AND CANADA: TRANSBOUNDARY ENVIRONMENTAL COOPERATION

The United States and Canada—partners in the world's largest trading relationship—work to maintain a secure and efficient border that is conducive to mutual economic growth and prosperity.[8] More than $1.2 billion in goods and services cross the border on a daily basis, and while this activity is beneficial to both economies, it has been historically taxing on the regional environment. Both countries have been committed to cooperating on environmental policies since the 1980s, and in response to increased degradation the two governments signed the Air Quality Agreement (AQA) in 1991, which required both the U.S. and Canada to reduce sulfur dioxide and nitrogen oxide emissions—contributing toxins to acid rain. In 2000, after the noticeable reduction of acid rain over the previous decade, the nations amended the AQA to include an Ozone Annex, the aim of which was to address ground-level ozone, a significant component of smog. The most recent biennial report of the AQA's progress shows that transboundary smog emissions have decreased since the implementation of the Ozone Annex, a success that encouraged the neighbors to sign the Border Air Quality Strategy in 2003, which builds further upon previous pacts made under the AQA, with a primary focus on pilot projects along the border that have launched coordinated efforts for air quality management and examinations of air pollution's effects on human health.

Along the western edge of the U.S.–Canadian border many communities have gone beyond the

Map of Canadian and American bioregions defining Cascadia.

environmental commitments made by the two federal governments in a unique relationship of cooperation uniting a cross-border bioregion. The recently dubbed "Cascadia"—a territory composed of several northwestern states in the U.S. and British Columbia and Alberta in Canada—has developed regional environmental protection programs, tourism campaigns, cross-border transportation, and economic integration of the Pacific Northwest.[9] Cascadia is considered a bioregion because of the common geological, ecological, and climatic patterns found in the area. Certain scholars also assert that a similar political ideology and social consciousness link the inhabitants of the region together, despite international and state boundaries.[10] In the recent past, cross-border coalitions in this region have proved to be more efficient than the two countries' respective governments when confronting regional environmental issues and disasters. A 1988 oil spill off the Pacific coast provides the perfect example of a cross-border response initiative, where representatives from the West Coast Border States assembled the International Oil Spill Task Force due to dissatisfaction with the federal authorities' reaction to the problem.[11] Its success has produced a snowball effect of increased cross-border collaboration among the local governments, and today the bioregion serves as a model of coalition-building and progressive cross-border environmental initiatives for the rest of the world.

FRANCE, SWITZERLAND, AND GERMANY: TRI-NATIONAL TRANSPORTATION

The EuroAirport Basel-Mulhouse-Freiburg is the only completely trinational airport in the world, and it provides transportation to its surrounding tri-national region. Located in France close to the borders of Switzerland and Germany, the airport is jointly operated by the Swiss and the French, with German representatives serving as advisors. The airport, which is administered under international law, is equipped with both French and Swiss customs sectors, as well as an international zone that all passengers enter before boarding the plane. Residents of the entire tri-national region consider it their "home" airport, through which they have access to more than a hundred international destinations.[12] The French and the Swiss each comprise about 38% of local passengers, with Germans constituting the remaining 24%—figures that demonstrate how comprehensively the airport works to serve its patrons from all three countries. The tri-border area, called Regio TriRhena, is also complemented by a public ground-transportation system equipped with trains and buses connecting the same communities that utilize the airport, further emphasizing the harmonious nature of the tri-national region.

The EuroAirport and Regio TriRhena present a unique model for the rest of the world for functional cross-border transportation and collaborative human and economic relations. In recent years, committees from the Middle East and Eastern Europe have visited the EuroAirport seeking guidance on potential application of the

The tri-national airport (EuroAirport) and highways.

European Union Formation

1952	West Germany Belgium France Netherlands Italy Luxembourg
1973	Denmark Ireland United Kingdom
1981	Greece
1986	Spain Portugal
1990	East Germany
1995	Austria Finland Sweden

2004	Cyprus Czech Republic Estonia Hungary Latvia Lithuania Malta Poland Slovakia Slovenia
2007	Bulgaria Romania
Candidate Countries	Croatia Macedonia Turkey

successful cooperative strategies to their own border regions.[13] The example of the tri-border transport systems shows that international relations around the world would be well served to implement efficient cross-border transportation programs as they demonstrate an ability to cooperate, reach agreements, and provide beneficial services to populations residing in border regions.

SOUTHERN AFRICA: CROSS-BORDER REGIONAL HEALTH INITIATIVE TO COMBAT HIV/AIDS

According to the Joint United Nations Programme on HIV and AIDS (UNAIDS) and World Health Organization's December 2005 AIDS Epidemic Update, approximately 40.3 million people are living with HIV across the globe[14]—65% of whom live in Sub-Saharan Africa, the pandemic's most afflicted region. In 2005, the region's HIV prevalence among adults was 7.2%, and 2.4 million people died as a result of the disease—a sum that accounts for 77% of the worldwide AIDS death toll. Within Sub-Saharan Africa, southern Africa is the region most severely affected by HIV/AIDS. According to U.S. Agency for International Development (USAID), it is estimated that more than one-fifth of the respective adult populations in Botswana, Lesotho, Namibia, South Africa, Swaziland, and Zimbabwe are living with the disease.[15] Prevalence of HIV among pregnant women in the region is particularly high, demonstrating that rather than being concentrated in specific sub-groups (which tends to be the case in other parts of the world) the disease has grown to severely impact the general population. At the same time certain sub-populations, particularly in border regions, maintain a greater level of risk. Statistics show that in southern Africa mobile groups like migrant workers, truck drivers, and sex workers are three to six times more likely than the rest of the population to contract the virus.[16] These groups' tendency toward mobility across borders and throughout the region makes them both difficult to diagnose and more likely to spread the disease—reasons for which they are the principal targets for new prevention and treatment programs.

In 2000, USAID introduced the Regional HIV/AIDS Program for Southern Africa (RHAP/SA), designed to complement existing programs and to coordinate prevention and treatment efforts across borders.[17] The advantage of collaboration and cohesive action between countries throughout the region was recognized by the Southern African Development Community (SADC) as the most effective way to confront the epidemic's spread across the nations' porous borders. Knowing this, the primary focus of RHAP/SA is to reduce the levels of transmission among populations—particularly those that are mobile—found along critical cross-border points, in an initiative called Corridors of Hope. This program has significantly increased access to HIV/AIDS prevention methods by providing education and risk-reduction counseling as well as distributing condoms at forty-one different cross-border sites in southern Africa. According to USAID, during the fiscal year of 2004 more than two million people at different border sites were informed about preventative measures as a direct result of the RHAP/SA and Corridors of Hope activities. Emphasizing the success and value of this type of regional development, the World Health Organization reports that a thorough program encompassing both prevention and treatment throughout Sub-Saharan Africa could avert

55% of potential infections by 2020.[18] Although the HIV/AIDS pandemic continues to be rampant throughout southern Africa, organizers involved in the cross-border health and prevention initiatives are optimistic that regional approaches and strategies will produce positive results and prove that prevention is an issue that requires cooperation rather than isolation.

THE GOLDEN TRIANGLE: A REGIONAL

APPROACH TO OPIUM ERADICATION AND NARCOTRAFFIC CONTROL

The "Golden Triangle"—a term used to refer to the border region where Myanmar (formerly Burma), Thailand, and Laos meet in Southeast Asia—has historically been a hotbed for the cultivation of opium poppies, the key component in heroin production. For decades drug traffickers were in control of the region, where borders were fuzzy and narcotics were easily smuggled into the hands of local users and the lucrative international drug market. In recent years, however, this pattern has begun to change due to international pressure and an increased concern for rural communities plagued by addiction and illicit crop-dependence. The Golden Triangle region has confronted the problem by significantly cutting back on cultivation, so much so that Laos, formerly the world's third largest opium producer after Afghanistan and Myanmar, declared itself poppy-free in February 2006.[19] This monumental eradication effort has been successful for several reasons. According to Niklas Swanstrom, director of Silk Road Studies at Sweden's Uppsala University and expert on drugs

and regional cooperation, the most effective way to tackle drug smuggling is to close down borders.[20] When China realized that the Golden Triangle's illicit industry was infiltrating its territories, the government responded by sealing its border with Myanmar, a strategy that significantly reduced opium smuggling in the region. Another approach that is increasingly being accepted and encouraged by the UN and the region's national governments is alternative development, preferably implemented on a cross-border, regional basis. According to the terms outlined by the United Nations Office on Drugs and Crime (UNODC), this is a process that provides legal alternatives to communities dependent on income from unlawful activities.[21] In the absence of initiatives that offer drug-cultivators (who are primarily impoverished farmers) alternatives for survival, narcotic crop eradication has the potential to devastate the livelihoods of entire communities. Recognizing this, the Association of Southeast Asian Nations (ASEAN) and China ratified the ACCORD Plan of Action in 2000 for a "drug-free ASEAN 2015," with the objective of introducing new alternatives to opium cultivation in the Golden Triangle area.[22] The plan requires participating nations to practice regional cooperation by sharing information, techniques, and practices of sustainable opium eradication and alternative crop cultivation in order to more effectively create change and spark development throughout the region. The positive results of the program, which has been exemplified in the case of Laos and previously in Thailand, is evidence that alternative development is successful and should be applied to other parts of the world.

In these June 21, 2005 photographs in Kunming, in the southern Yunnan province of China, recovering male drug addicts take part in a marching drill, while female drug addicts make small dolls as part of their drug rehabilitation program. Kunning borders the "Golden Triangle" region, where opium poppy cultivation dropped 85% to 24,160 hectares in 2006, down from 157,900 in 1998.

NAFTA
North American Free Trade Agreement
CACM
Central American Common Market
CARICOM
Caribbean Community and Common Market
CEMAC
Economic and Monetary Community of Central Africa
SACU
Southern Africa Customs Union
FTAA (proposed)
Free Trade Agreement of the Americas

EU
European Union
ECOWAS
Economic Community of West African States
CEMAC
Economic and Monetary Community of Central Africa
SACU
Southern Africa Customs Union

EAC
East African Community
COMESA
Common Market for Eastern and Southern Africa
GCC
Gulf Cooperation Council
SAARC
South Asian Association for Regional Cooperation

ASEAN
Association of Southeast Asian Nations
PARTA
Pacific Regional Trade Agreement
EurAsEC
Eurasian Economic Community
WTO non-members
(every other country has a certain degree of membership in the WTO)

ECONOMIC DEVELOPMENT AND TRADE ACROSS BORDERS: FREE TRADE AGREEMENTS IN SOUTH AMERICA

According to the neoliberal policies of the world's wealthier nations and global financial institutions such as the International Monetary Fund (IMF), the World Trade Organization (WTO) and the World Bank, a fundamental step toward fostering economic development in poorer countries is encouraging their participation in international trade. Through the adoption of Free Trade Agreements (FTAs), developing nations around the world have opened their markets in an effort to become more efficient, competitive, and integrated in the global economy. International boundaries are ignored to allow trade, investment, and money to flow easily, but borders remain tightly secured to prevent people and labor from crossing as freely. Yet despite the increased mobility of capital and the introduction of Multi-National Corporations (MNCs) in poorer countries, the positive results of free trade in the developing world are controversial.

The Free Trade Area of the Americas (FTAA) is an initiative that has been in negotiation between thirty-four countries since the implementation of the North American Free Trade Agreement (NAFTA) in 1994. Promoters of the FTAA seek to open the entire western hemisphere to trade and foreign investment with the establishment of the world's largest free trade bloc. Unfortunately, like its predecessor NAFTA, the agreement largely disregards the discrepancies between the economies of the countries to which it applies, leaving little hope for an equal dispersal of free trade benefits among the different nations. Recognizing this, several Latin American nations—Argentina, Bolivia, Brazil, and Venezuela in particular—have spoken out against this model and instead are working toward improved and efficient regional integration. The Southern Cone Common Market (Mercosur), which was formally established in 1991 between Argentina, Brazil, Paraguay, and Uruguay, is an example of this type of regional accord. Although the trading zone was hit hard by Brazil's currency devaluation in 1999 and the 2002 collapse of Argentina's economy, Mercosur may have the capability to balance out other global economic blocs like NAFTA and the European Union, if its members continue to deepen integration through policies such as synchronizing macroeconomic policies and market regulations, adopting a common currency, reducing barriers to trade, and liberalizing migratory flows.[23] In December 2004, the trade bloc signaled a shift toward increased regionalism when it entered talks with the Andean Community of Nations (CAN—comprised of Bolivia, Colombia, Ecuador, Peru, and Venezuela), culminating in a letter of intent calling for the establishment of the South American Community of Nations (CSN). CSN intends to apply the model of the European Union to their community by first lifting trade barriers throughout the continent, and proceeding to establish a common currency, passport, and parliament by the year 2019, thus opening borders in the region and establishing cohesive, universal economic development.

ENERGY WARS: THE RUSSIA–UKRAINE GAS DISPUTE AND RUSSIA'S RISE TO THE GLOBAL ENERGY ELITE

The present day's global economy is dependent on limited energy resources, specifically on fossil fuels. The peak oil phenomenon—the point at which half of the planet's oil reserves are expended and subsequently go into immediate decline—is looming, and soon will no longer be able to meet the ever-growing demand. Absent the rapid development of alternative fuel sources, the consequences of this imminent event will lead to price increases with an ensuing economic recession, and more ominously wars over control of the precious commodity. Experts in the field are not only unnerved by the dwindling amount of the global economy's fundamental fuel; the fact that the reserves are concentrated in the hands of countries whose political stability is in doubt and/or whose agenda is not pro-West is of deep concern.[24]

The recent emergence of a new "global energy elite" will likely put the Western nations of the world in an unprecedented position of vulnerability, as the industrialized, energy-consuming nature of their economies rely on consistent access to oil and natural gas, resources that are predominantly controlled by political actors who are not the West's unconditional allies. The case of Russia provides an apt example of this unfolding shift of power. In the advent of its largely unanticipated comeback from years in economic and political struggle in the aftermath of the fall of the Soviet Union, the Kremlin has made concerted and successful efforts to create a strategic position of power for itself in the global economy as the planet's chief source of natural gas. With 28% of the world's gas reserves located within Russia's boundaries, and estimates projecting that within two decades the country will be the provider of 50% of Western Europe's gas needs, the global political arena should be

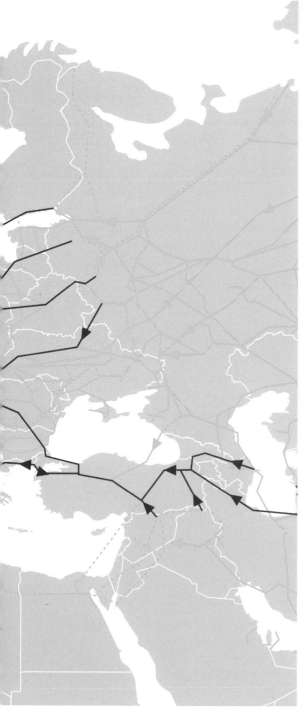

prepared for the potential ascendancy of Russia to its former superpower status.[25] That is the acknowledged intention of the country's current president, Vladimir Putin, who prior to entering the presidency wrote that the key to Russia's rehabilitation of its "former might" was to capitalize on its role as provider of natural resources.[26] The recent dispute with the government of Ukraine—which contrary to Russia's wishes is turning toward the West and may seek to join the European Union—exposed Russia's potential to use its gas reserves as leverage for enhancing geopolitical power and maintaining its traditional sphere of influence. On January 1, 2006, Russia's state-controlled Gazprom—which is the world's commanding gas extractor and the third largest corporation on the planet—cut off the gas supply to Ukraine, and effectively to that of Western Europe, which receives a majority of the energy source via Ukraine's pipeline system. The move—meant to pressure Ukraine into paying world market prices for the commodity and end a barter system where Russia exchanged gas for use of its neighbor's pipes—sent the European Union into a near panic and confirmed the region's dependency on Gazprom's product delivery, as it discovered that alternatives in the immediate and medium future are essentially not economical.[27]

Gas pipelines leading from Russia to other parts of the world

THE U.S.–MEXICO HYPERBORDER:
THE BOUNDARY BETWEEN A SUPERPOWER
AND A DEVELOPING NATION

The border between the United States and Mexico is the world's longest contiguous international divide between a superpower and a developing nation. Long-standing differences between the standards of living and economies of the neighboring nations—as well as their geographical proximity—have provided the framework for a border shaped by numerous complexities and unique levels of hyperactivity. Crime, corruption, free trade, urbanization, resource scarcity, migration, border control, death, and environmental degradation are just some of the influences that have come to define the nature of the hyperborder, making the boundary unique in the contemporary world for the breadth of issues confronting it.

With the intention of fostering economic stability and regional development, NAFTA, which established a free trade bloc between the United States, Canada, and Mexico, went into effect on January 1, 1994. As neoliberal free trade agreements advocate, regulations pertaining to labor, the environment, and trade were all liberalized to facilitate an efficient market system, and the free flow of goods and capital across borders began immediately. The positive effects of NAFTA are considered controversial. Although foreign investment in Mexico has swelled, exports to the United States have surged, and employment in the export-oriented manufacturing companies—known as *maquiladoras*—has doubled, many would claim that the overall effects of the trade agreement on Mexico, the U.S., and the border region have been largely detrimental and have not brought widespread prosperity and development.[28] Arguably the most significant impact of NAFTA has been the increase of immigration flows between Mexico and the U.S. since its implementation. When NAFTA was up for debate in the early

1990s, many academic and political advocates claimed that the quintessentially neoliberal economic policy would decrease migration between the neighboring nations. It was argued that MNCs would create jobs for the Mexican people and thus eliminate the need to migrate for survival's sake. However, since NAFTA's introduction, contrary to the arguments made by its supporters, the U.S. has been witness to an increase of migration from Mexico. Real wages in Mexico are lower since NAFTA came into effect,[29] and between 1994 and 2003 9.3 million people entered the Mexican job market while only 3 million jobs were created.[30] These harsh realities have fanned the fire of both the informal sector in Mexico and immigration rates to the United States.

In Mexico, farmworkers exemplify a sector of society that has been especially affected by the free trade agreement. As trade barriers on agricultural goods were lifted, U.S. exports have made their way into the Mexican market and have effectively saturated it. Currently, U.S. wheat products represent 75% of the Mexican wheat market, up from 56% before NAFTA's inception.[31] In 2001, statistics showed that approximately 6.2 million tons of U.S.-grown corn were exported to Mexico annually—a particularly low blow for the southern nation, considering the crop's sacred value for the country where corn originated an estimated 4,000 years ago.[32] Furthermore, crops grown in the U.S. are often genetically modified, and thus appear to be of better value due to their size, an issue that angers many Mexican farmers and activists who prefer their crops—particularly corn—in their most natural form.[33] U.S. government–subsidized crops allow American farmers to keep prices low,

Cars headed north in the Otay Mesa border crossing in Tijuana.

"If it had actually been free trade between these countries, tariffs would have been eliminated. The U.S.'s access to Mexico is real but it is not reciprocal. The U.S. wanted Mexico to have economic growth to eliminate migration. Those hopes didn't materialize."

—Joseph Stiglitz, 2001 Nobel prize recipient in economics. In interview with Victor Manuel Torres. *Excelsior*, November 29, 2006.

crippling Mexican farmers' ability to compete with the imported goods. At a loss for alternatives, farmers must opt for survival, leading them to migrate, join the informal sector, or increasingly to enter into partnerships with Mexican drug cartels as cultivators of illegal narcotics heading to the U.S. market.

Farmers and other Mexicans that choose to migrate in search of economic opportunities contribute to the urbanization of the border region. Currently the border population (90% of which lives in the fourteen sister cities) stands at around 12 million, yet by the year 2020 that statistic is expected to nearly double to 24 million.[34] Since NAFTA's implementation, border cities have become destinations for rural-to-urban migrants seeking employment or staging areas before crossing, a pattern that has created expansive slums around city limits throughout the border region. The rapid population growth in border cities has made it difficult for infrastructure to keep up and has led to water scarcity, a lack of funding, increased vehicle and factory pollution, a degrading environment, health issues such as tuberculosis and a shortage of health-care workers, and higher crime rates. All of these challenges and issues contribute to the hyper state of the region.

Due to economic disparities between the two nations, the U.S.–Mexico border has become a breeding ground for illegal activity. The trafficking of illegal drugs has become a multibillion dollar industry for the Mexican drug cartels, who utilize

their geographical proximity to cater to the lucrative U.S. market. Most illegal substances come from Mexico, which has recently displaced Colombia as the U.S.'s key supplier of narcotics. This change of power has been dubbed by many as the "Colombianization of Mexico," partly because the newfound market control has brought an upsurge in violence that is currently plaguing the nation, particularly the border region. Crimes connected to the drug cartels have reached unprecedented levels: between January and October of 2005 145 people, including 21 police officers and government officials, were killed in drug-related incidents in the border city of Nuevo Laredo alone.[35] Despite heightened border control, narcotraffickers have successfully increased the drug trade in recent years, exposing a dangerously intricate and perceivably impenetrable web of corruption. Due to the thriving nature of the business, money abounds for bribery and coercion. In order to complete and sustain illegal transactions, payoffs are made at every level, from politicians to police officers to border control officials, thus from the perspective of numerous players, incentives to dissipate the Mexican narcotrafficking industry are absent.

President Bush signing NAFTA. Canadian ambassador Derek Burney, U.S. Trade Representative Carla Hills, and Mexican ambassador Jesús Silva-Herzog stand in the back. Graph below shows the tripling in U.S.–Mexico trade since NAFTA was signed.

Tri-lateral Trade in North America
1993–2006 (Billions of Dollars)

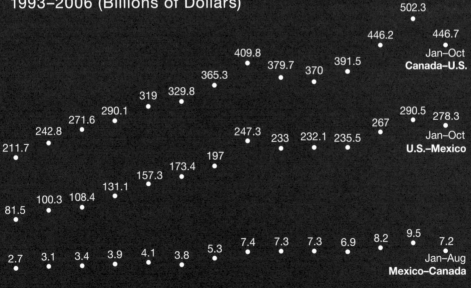

502.3

446.2   446.7

Jan–Oct
Canada–U.S.

409.8   379.7   370   391.5

365.3

319   329.8

290.1

271.6   290.5   278.3

242.8   267

247.3   233   232.1   235.5   Jan–Oct
211.7   **U.S.–Mexico**

197

173.4
157.3
131.1
100.3   108.4
81.5

7.4   7.3   7.3   6.9   8.2   9.5   7.2

2.7   3.1   3.4   3.9   4.1   3.8   5.3   Jan–Aug
Mexico–Canada

1993 1994 1995 1996 1997 1998 1999 2000 2001 2002 2003 2004 2005 2006

In 2005, deaths on the U.S. side of the border reached unparalleled numbers: at least 464 immigrants perished by the end of the fiscal year, which was a 43% increase from 2004.[36] This is largely due to the strengthening of the border control, which in the wake of September 11th has received increased funds from the U.S. government. The funding has been allocated to improve technology and to hire more border personnel, making it more challenging to cross into the U.S. illegally. Traditional crossing points have shifted from more urban, safer routes to rural, hazardous areas, requiring migrants to maneuver unknown, perilous territory and creating a boom in the human smuggling industry.

THE HYPERBORDER IN THE GLOBAL CONTEXT

The hyperborder is a distinct international boundary for the extensive array of influences that shape its current reality. Although examples of contentious issues or cooperative accords abound at other borders around the world, the U.S.–Mexico border has been set apart as a site within one localized geographic region that is exposed to daily political tensions, economic disparity, hyper flows, interdependence, and more. However, through examining other border relations around the world, questions arise about the direction the hyperborder will take in the future. Could security issues make it the next North–South Korean border? Or will binational accords shape it into an integrated, fluid region like that of the borders between France, Switzerland, and Germany? Could the drug trade be demolished and replaced by alternative crop development, as the governments of Laos, Thailand, and Myanmar have achieved? Or will racism and a fear of migrants result in the erection of high-tech border fences, like those between Israel and Palestine?

The border dividing the U.S. from Mexico is subject to a wide variety of future possibilities. Increasing the unique nature of its circumstances are the varying studies that assert the region's potential for prosperity, development, and environmental entrepreneurship—proof that the U.S.–Mexico border could serve as a global model for positive change in the future.

The Most Contrasting Border in the World

1. U.S. Congressman Silvestre Reyes of Texas; 2. Rick Perry, Texas Governor; 3. Bill Richardon, New Mexico governor and presidential candidate ; 4. César Chávez, late migrant activist; 5. Carlos Gutiérrez, U.S. Secretary of Commerce; 6. Janet Napolitano, Arizona governor; 7. José Natividad, Nuevo León governor; 8. Arnold Schwarzenegger, California governor; 9. Border patrol agent; 10. Cardinal Roger M. Mahony, activist against unfair immigration reform; 11. Antonio Villaraigosa, Los Angeles City Mayor; 12. Chris Simcox, founder of the Minutemen group; 13. David V. Aguilar, Chief, Border Patrol; 14. Felipe Calderón, president of Mexico; 15. Alberto R. Gonzales, U.S. Attorney General; 16. Vicente Fox, former president of Mexico; 17. George W. Bush, U.S. president; 18. Michael Chertoff, U.S. Secretary of Homeland Security; 19. Members of the U.S. National Guard; 20. Activists and protestors.

The U.S.–Mexico border

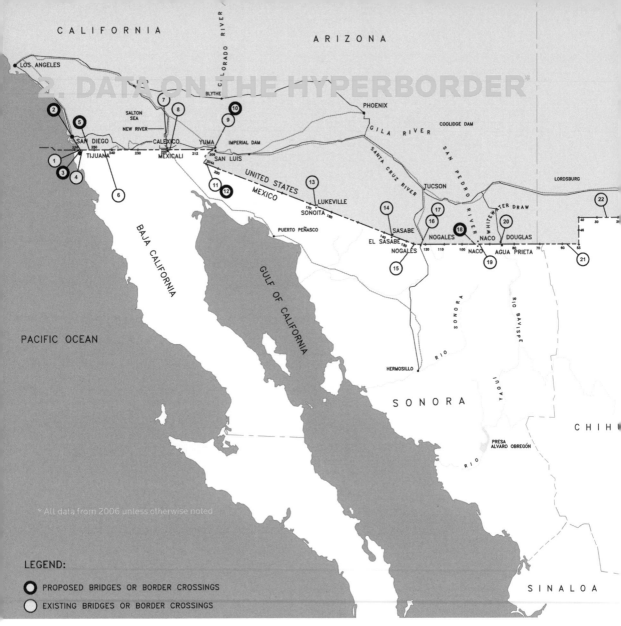

* All data from 2006 unless otherwise noted

LEGEND:

⬤ PROPOSED BRIDGES OR BORDER CROSSINGS

◯ EXISTING BRIDGES OR BORDER CROSSINGS

Border crossings

1. San Ysidro
2. **Intl. Gateway of the Americas**
3. **Virginia Avenue (San Ysidro)**
4. Otay Mesa
5. **Otay Mesa II**
6. Tecate
7. Calexico
8. Calexico East
9. Andrade
10. **Andrade II**
11. San Luis
12. **San Luis II**
13. Lukeville
14. Sasabe
15. Nogales–Mariposa
16. Nogales–Dennis DeConcini
17. Nogales II (pedestrian)
18. **Naco Railroad**
19. Naco
20. Douglas
21. Antelope Wells
22. Columbus
23. Santa Teresa
24. **Anapra**
25. Burlington Northern–Santa Fe Railroad
26. Paso del Norte (Santa Fe Bridge)
27. Union Pacific Railroad
28. Good Neighbor (Stanton Bridge)
29. Cordova Bridge of the Americas
30. Ysleta/Zaragosa (Hwy. 659)
31. **Fabens Bridge**
32. Tornillo–Guadalupe (Fabens/Hwy. 1109)
33. Fort Hancock–Porvenir (Hwy. 1088)
34. Presidio–Ojinaga (Hwy. 67)
35. Presidio–Ojinaga Railroad
36. La Linda–Boquillas del Carmen

	United States	Mexico
COMMUNICATIONS		
Telephone general assessment[1]	A large technologically advanced, multipurpose communications system; a large system of fiber-optic cable, microwave radio delay, coaxial cable, and domestic satellites carries every form of telephone traffic.	Low telephone density. Adequate telephone service for business and government. General population remains poorly served.
Telephone subscribers per 100 inhabitants (2005)[2]	130.23	62.28
Telephone lines per 100 inhabitants (2005)[3]	58.80	18.23
Mobile Phone subscribers per 100 inhabitants (2005)[4]	71.43	44.04
Average cost of local call[5]	$0.09 USD	$0.16
Satellite Earth stations[6]	61 Intelsat, 5 Intersputnik, 4 Inmarsat	32 Intelsat, 2 Solidaridad, numerous Inmarsat mobile search stations
AM radio broadcast stations[7]	4,789	850
FM radio broadcast stations[8]	8,961	545
Television broadcast stations[9]	2,218	236
Televisions per 1000 inhabitants[10]	740.53	241.048
Internet hosts (2005)[11]	195,138,696	1,523,277
Internet users per 100 inhabitants (2005)[12]	66.33	16.90
Personal computers per 100 inhabitants (2005)[13]	76.22	13.08
GEOGRAPHY		
Area[14]	9,826,630 sq km	1,972,550 sq km
Land boundaries[15]	9,557 km	4,353 km 3,141 km (U.S.–MX border)
Land boundaries with other countries[16]	8,893 km	1,212 km (U.S.–Mexico, Mexico–Belize, and Mexico–Guatemala)
Coastline[17]	19,924 km	9,330 km
Climate[18]	A wide range of climates	Varies from tropical to desert
Topography[19]	Mountains in west, vast central plain, hills and low mountains in the east	High rugged mountains; low coastal plains; high plateaus; desert
Permanent crops[20]	0.21%	1.28%
Arable land[21]	18.01%	12.66%
Irrigated land[22]	223,850 sq km	63,200 sq km
Water abstraction per capita[23]	1,730 cu mt	730 cu mt

	United States	Mexico

POPULATION

	United States	Mexico
Population[24]	301,458,841	103,263,388
Population density (2000)[25]	31 per sq. km.	50 per sq. km.
Population growth rate[26]	0.91%	1.16%
Net annual migration rate (2000–2005)[27]	1,160,000	-400,000
Children born per woman[28]	2.09	2.42
Deaths per 1,000 population[29]	8.26	4.74
Life expectancy[30]	77.9	74.5
Ethnic groups[31]	white 67%, hispanic 14.9%, black 12.9%, Asian and Pacific Islander 4.7%, other 0.5%	mestizo (Amerindian-Spanish) 60%, Amerindian or predominantly Amerindian 30%, white 9%, other 1%

EDUCATION

	United States	Mexico
Expenditure per student in primary education, % of GDP per capita (2005)[32]	21.6%	16%
Total expenditure on educational institutions for all levels of education[33]	7.2% of GDP	6.3% of GDP
Literacy rate for ages 15 and above (2003)[34]	99%	92.2%
Percentage of 15-year-old students using computers frequently (2003)[35]	43% (at school) 83% (at home)	54% (at school) 48% (at home)
Tertiary attainment for age group 25-64 (2003)[36]	38.4%	15.4%

ECONOMY 2005 unless otherwise noted.

	United States	Mexico
GDP composition by sector (2006)[37]	services: 78.6%, industry: 20.4%, agriculture: 0.9%	services: 70.5%, industry: 25.7%, agriculture: 3.9%
GDP per capita, purchasing power parity[38]	$41,854	$10,209
GDP, millions[39]	$12,455,068	$768,438
GDP growth, annual[40]	3.5%	3%
Foreign direct investment as % of GDP[41]	0.9%	2.5%
Inflation, GDP deflator, annual[42]	2.7%	5.4%
Trade as % of GDP[43]	23.7%	61.4%

	United States	Mexico
ECONOMY (continued)		
Exports of goods and services (% of GDP)[44]	9.6%	29.9%
Current account balance[45]	-6.5%	-0.7%
Real interest rate[46]	3.3%	4.2%
Labor force, millions[47]	156	43
Unemployment, % of total labor force[48]	5.5%	3%
INDUSTRY (2005)		
Industry, value added, millions[49]	$2,271,300	$178,530
Industry, value added, annual % growth[50]	3.3%	1.6%
Industry, value added, % of GDP[51]	22.3%	25.9%
Employment in industry[52]	21.6%	25%
ENERGY		
Total oil production, millions barrels per day (2005)[53]	8.2	3.8
Oil proved reserves, billion barrels[54]	22.45	12.49
Natural gas gross production, billions cubic feet (2003)[55]	24,119	1,509
Natural gas proved reserves, billions cubic meters[56]	5,451	420.5
Total output of refined petroleum products, thousand barrels per day (2003)[57]	17,794	1,409
Coal production, million short tons (2004)[58]	1,112	12.46
Electricity production, kWh, millions(2005)[59]	4,054,352.9	218,654
Electricity imports, billion kWh (2004)[60]	34.21	0.416
Electricity exports, billion kWh (2004)[61]	22.898	1.203
Carbon dioxide emissions from the consumption and flaring of fossil fuels, million metric tons of carbon dioxide (2004)[62]	5,912.21	385.46

	United States	Mexico
TRADE		
Trade, % of GDP[63]	24%	61%
Trade balance, millions of dollars[64]	-817,976	-7,559
Total imports, millions of dollars[65]	1,855,119	221,270
Imports from Mexico, millions of dollars (2006)[66]	198,259	..
Total exports, millions of dollars[67]	1,037,143	213,711
Exports to Mexico, millions of dollars (2006)[68]	134,167	..
Import partners (2005)[69]	Canada 16.9%, China 15%, Mexico 10%, Japan 8.2%, Germany 5%	U.S. 53.4%, China 8%, Japan 5.9%
Export partners (2005)[70]	Canada 23.4%, Mexico 13.3%, Japan 6.1%, China 4.6%, UK 4.3%	U.S. 85.7%, Canada 2%, Spain 1.4%

	United States	Mexico
TOURISM (2005)		
International tourism receipts, current dollars[71]	112,780,001,280	11,566,000,128
International tourism, number of departures[72]	61,776,000	12,494,000
International tourism, number of arrivals[73]	46,085,000	20,618,000

	United States	Mexico
URBAN DEVELOPMENT (2005)		
Urban population[74]	239,569,296	78,347,744
Urban population, % of total[75]	81%	76%
Urban population growth, annual %[76]	1.4%	1.4%
Population in the largest city as percentage of total[77]	8%	24%
Population in urban agglomerations > 1 million, % of total population[78]	42%	35%
Poverty headcount ration at urban poverty line, % of urban populationl[79]	No data available	11%

United States

GOVERNMENT

Proportion of women in national parliament (2005)[80]	15.2%

Congress structure

SENATE

100 members
2 per state

6-year term

HOUSE OF REPRESENTATIVES

435 members
based on population
in congressional district

2-year term

20th century presidential elections

REPUBLICAN   DEMOCRAT

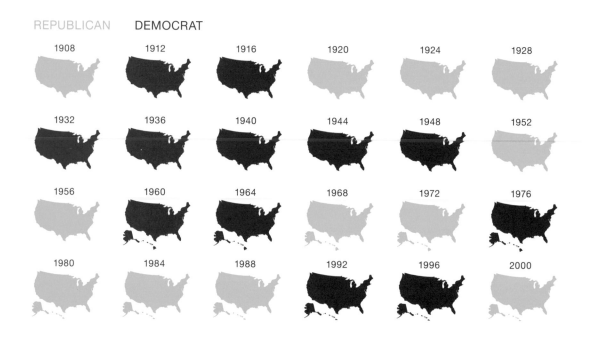

Mexico

24.2%

SENATE

128 members
2 majority per state = 64 +
1 minority per state = 32 +
proportional representation = 32

6-year term

CHAMBER OF DEPUTIES

500 members
majority vote/"uninominal" election = 300 +
majority vote/proportional representation = 200

3-year term

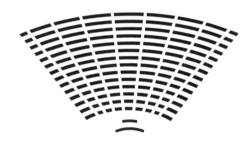

PRI Party   PAN Party   Other

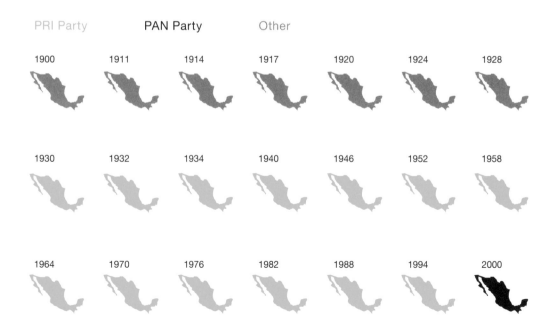

1900   1911   1914   1917   1920   1924   1928

1930   1932   1934   1940   1946   1952   1958

1964   1970   1976   1982   1988   1994   2000

TRANSPORTATION[81]

Binational railroads

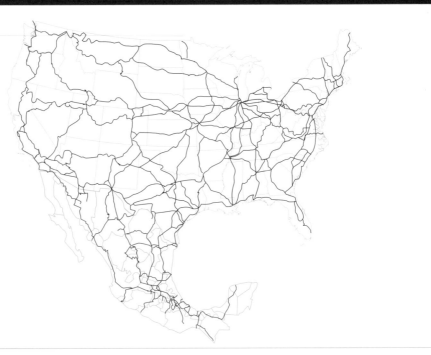

Airports serving the border region

Highways serving binational trade

Major binational trade ports

SISTER CITIES[82]

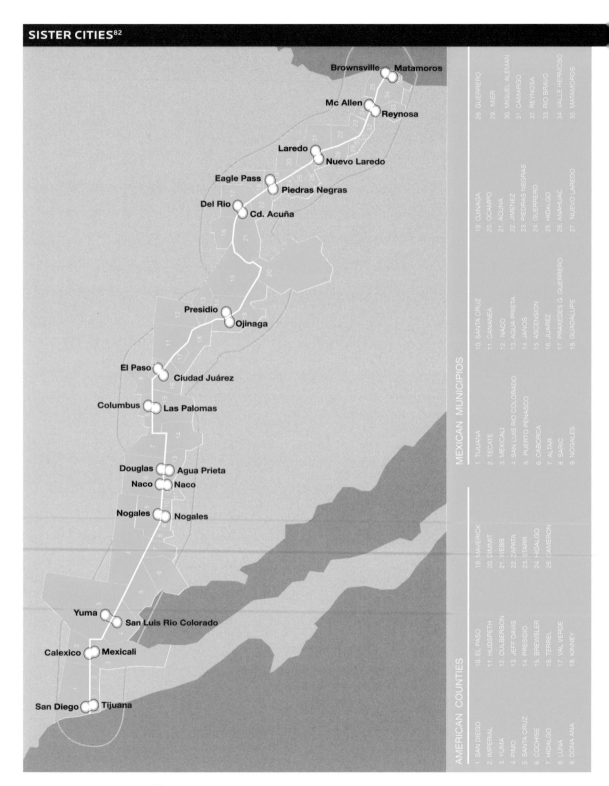

Brownsville — Matamoros
Mc Allen — Reynosa
Laredo — Nuevo Laredo
Eagle Pass — Piedras Negras
Del Rio — Cd. Acuña
Presidio — Ojinaga
El Paso — Ciudad Juárez
Columbus — Las Palomas
Douglas — Agua Prieta
Naco — Naco
Nogales — Nogales
Yuma — San Luis Rio Colorado
Calexico — Mexicali
San Diego — Tijuana

MEXICAN MUNICIPIOS

1. TIJUANA	10. SANTA CRUZ	19. OJINAGA
2. TECATE	11. CANANEA	20. OCAMPO
3. MEXICALI	12. NACO	21. ACUÑA
4. SAN LUIS RIO COLORADO	13. AGUA PRIETA	22. JIMENEZ
5. PUERTO PEÑASCO	14. JANOS	23. PIEDRAS NEGRAS
6. CABORCA	15. ASCENSION	24. GUERRERO
7. ALTAR	16. JUAREZ	25. HIDALGO
8. SARIC	17. PRAXEDES G. GUERRERO	26. ANAHUAC
9. NOGALES	18. GUADALUPE	27. NUEVO LAREDO

28. GUERRERO	
29. MIER	
30. MIGUEL ALEMAN	
31. CAMARGO	
32. REYNOSA	
33. RIO BRAVO	
34. VALLE HERMOSO	
35. MATAMOROS	

AMERICAN COUNTIES

1. SAN DIEGO	10. EL PASO	19. MAVERICK
2. IMPERIAL	11. HUDSPETH	20. DIMMIT
3. YUMA	12. CULBERSON	21. WEBB
4. PIMO	13. JEFF DAVIS	22. ZAPATA
5. SANTA CRUZ	14. PRESIDIO	23. STARR
6. COCHISE	15. BREWSTER	24. HIDALGO
7. HIDALGO	16. TERREL	25. CAMERON
8. LUNA	17. VAL VERDE	
9. DONA ANA	18. KINNEY	

Hispanic Population as a Percent
of Total Population, 2000

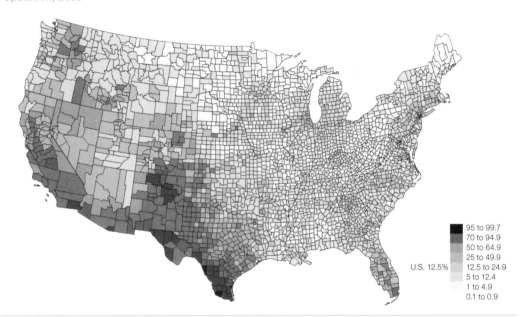

95 to 99.7
70 to 94.9
50 to 64.9
25 to 49.9
12.5 to 24.9
5 to 12.4
1 to 4.9
0.1 to 0.9

U.S. 12.5%

Hispanic Population as a Number,
2000

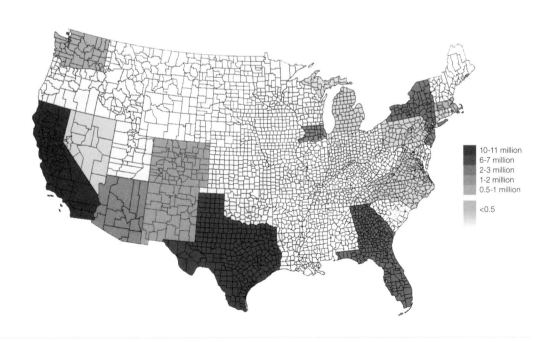

10-11 million
6-7 million
2-3 million
1-2 million
0.5-1 million

<0.5

MINORITY GROUPS IN THE U.S., 2000[84]

American Indian, Eskimo, and Aleut people

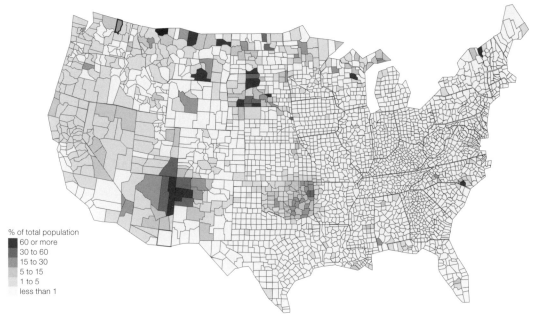

% of total population
- 60 or more
- 30 to 60
- 15 to 30
- 5 to 15
- 1 to 5
- less than 1

Asian and Pacific Islander people

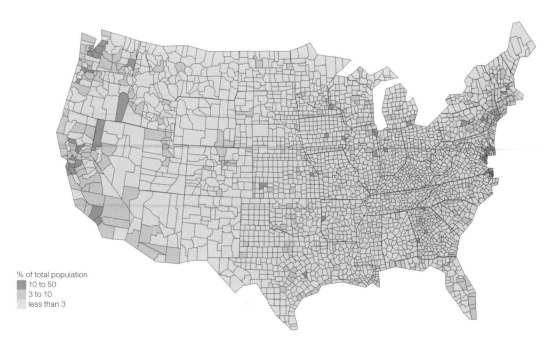

% of total population
- 10 to 50
- 3 to 10
- less than 3

African Amerian people

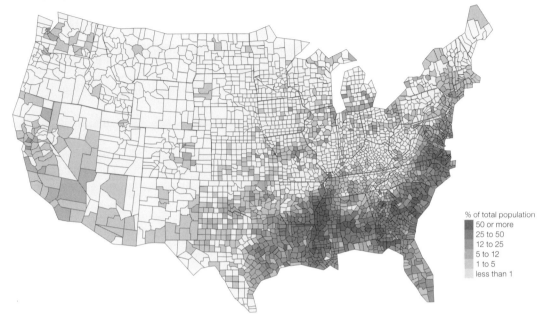

% of total population
50 or more
25 to 50
12 to 25
5 to 12
1 to 5
less than 1

Hispanic-origin people

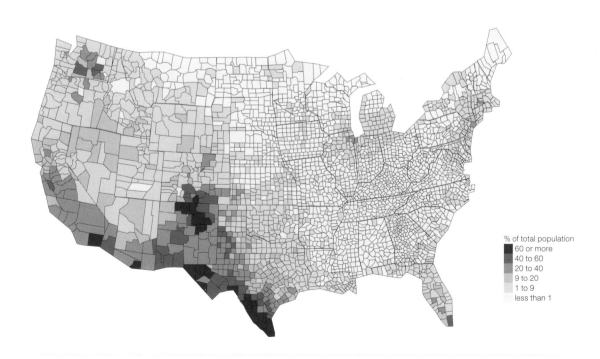

% of total population
60 or more
40 to 60
20 to 40
9 to 20
1 to 9
less than 1

BORDER CROSSINGS AND CROSS-BORDER TRADE [85]

	U.S. PORT OF ENTRY	PERSONAL VEHICLES PASSENGERS IN PERSONAL VEHICLES: 105,857,740	PEDESTRIANS
1	San Ysidro, CA	9,880,509	4,194,627
2	Otay Mesa, CA	3,452,561	757,430
3	Otay Mesa/San Ysidro, CA	NO DATA AVAILABLE	NO DATA AVAILABLE
4	Tecate, CA	582,024	285,453
5	Calexico, CA	3,504,074	1,833,501
6	Calexico East, CA	2,192,828	5,976
7	Andrade, CA	399,503	1,183,849
8	San Luis, AZ	1,705,413	1,446,600
9	Lukeville, AZ	262,424	49,560
10	Sasabe, AZ	20,854	908
11	Nogales, AZ	1,917,596	4,327,212
12	Naco, AZ	180,342	52,108
13	Douglas, AZ	1,136,562	386,137
14	Columbus, NM	218,648	127,194
15	Santa Teresa, NM	160,933	8,473
16	El Paso, TX	9,318,273	4,139,292
17	Fabens, TX	343,575	8,760
18	Presidio, TX	436,897	10,878
19	Del Rio, TX	1,032,906	45,169
20	Eagle Pass, TX	2,164,329	376,084
21	Laredo, TX	3,567,337	2,483,838
22	Roma, TX	701,095	164,052
23	Rio Grande City, TX	372,746	32,253
24	Hidalgo, TX	3,801,924	1,179,898
25	Progreso, TX	605,764	892,723
26	Brownsville, TX	4,127,944	1,692,058
	Total	**52,087,061**	**25,684,033**

TRUCKS	TRAINS	TOTAL TRADE BY ALL SURFACE MODES (dollars)	
LOADED TRUCK CONTAINERS: 1,825,590 EMPTY TRUCK CONTAINERS: 955,386	LOADED RAIL CONTAINERS: 220,559 EMPTY RAIL CONTAINERS: 237,414	To Mexico	From Mexico
NO DATA AVAILABLE	NO DATA AVAILABLE	175,489,616	368,834
NO DATA AVAILABLE	NO DATA AVAILABLE	9,941,471,540	18,661,106,058
427,994	110	NO DATA AVAILABLE	NO DATA AVAILABLE
42,772	77	586,765,447	620,858,585
NO DATA AVAILABLE	NO DATA AVAILABLE	30,988,330	0
180,887	260	4,981,973,915	6,660,908,532
974	NO DATA AVAILABLE	1,795,682	0
27,718	NO DATA AVAILABLE	381,018,734	627,004,757
383	NO DATA AVAILABLE	9,109,252	250,606
197	NO DATA AVAILABLE	622,862	0
190,293	371	6,345,594,874	12,514,661,069
2,297	NO DATA AVAILABLE	92,354,777	40,537,743
16,548	NO DATA AVAILABLE	447,557,340	708,507,573
1,423	NO DATA AVAILABLE	13,491,923	35,668,921
21,777	NO DATA AVAILABLE	425,980,316	739,987,014
448,552	1,424	20,990,793,740	25,733,217,551
NO DATA AVAILABLE	NO DATA AVAILABLE	1,172,061	0
3,508	7	314,643,917	146,430,640
39,175	NO DATA AVAILABLE	1,477,396,218	1,637,534,302
56,594	828	3,768,717,683	7,477,458,570
876,051	2,113	45,803,689,358	58,186,102,413
5,000	NO DATA AVAILABLE	130,871,969	11,208,049
27,187	NO DATA AVAILABLE	157,656,992	215,056,557
276,754	NO DATA AVAILABLE	8,257,223,800	11,770,522,759
17,804	NO DATA AVAILABLE	168,139,009	50,741,015
145,064	622	6,820,908,058	5,600,129,735
2,808,952	**5,812**	**$116,749,182,452**	**$155,205,147,481**

DEFINITION OF U.S. AND MEXICO BORDERS

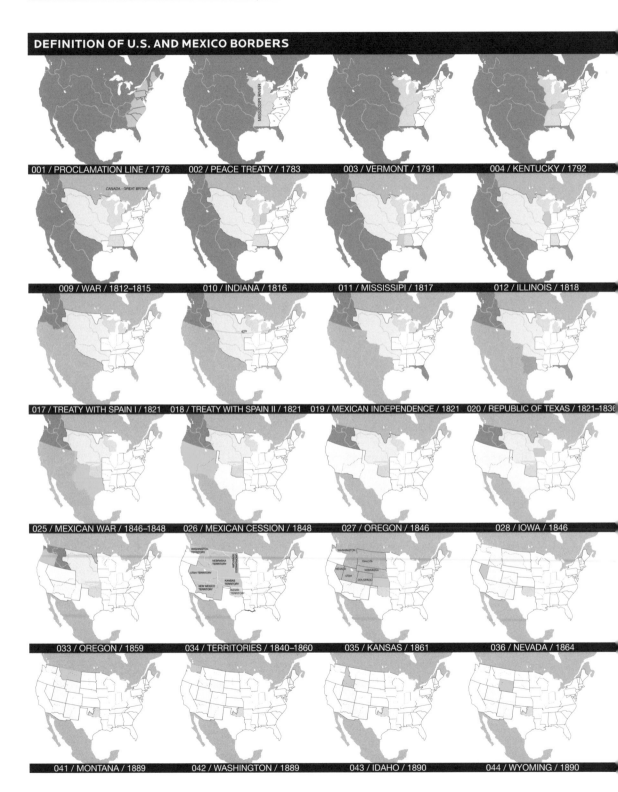

001 / PROCLAMATION LINE / 1776   002 / PEACE TREATY / 1783   003 / VERMONT / 1791   004 / KENTUCKY / 1792

009 / WAR / 1812–1815   010 / INDIANA / 1816   011 / MISSISSIPI / 1817   012 / ILLINOIS / 1818

017 / TREATY WITH SPAIN I / 1821   018 / TREATY WITH SPAIN II / 1821   019 / MEXICAN INDEPENDENCE / 1821   020 / REPUBLIC OF TEXAS / 1821–1836

025 / MEXICAN WAR / 1846–1848   026 / MEXICAN CESSION / 1848   027 / OREGON / 1846   028 / IOWA / 1846

033 / OREGON / 1859   034 / TERRITORIES / 1840–1860   035 / KANSAS / 1861   036 / NEVADA / 1864

041 / MONTANA / 1889   042 / WASHINGTON / 1889   043 / IDAHO / 1890   044 / WYOMING / 1890

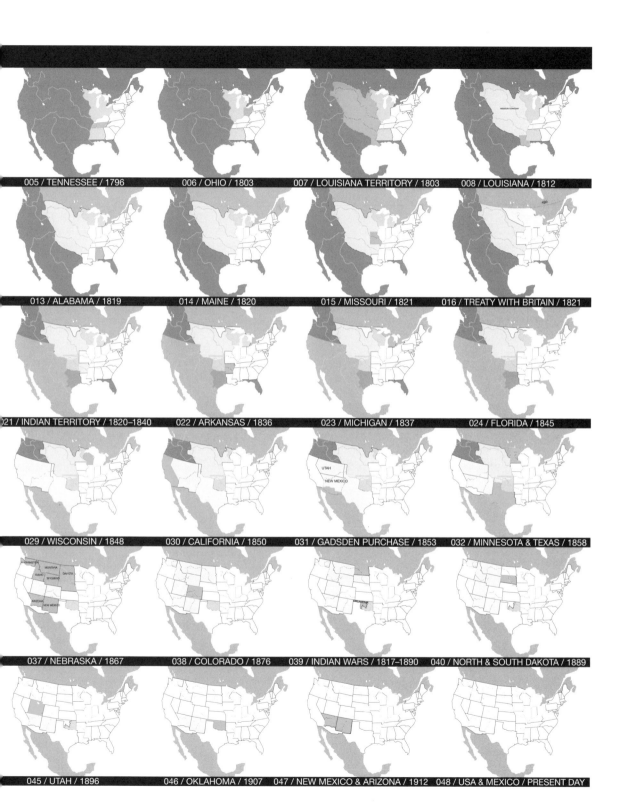

005 / TENNESSEE / 1796   006 / OHIO / 1803   007 / LOUISIANA TERRITORY / 1803   008 / LOUISIANA / 1812

013 / ALABAMA / 1819   014 / MAINE / 1820   015 / MISSOURI / 1821   016 / TREATY WITH BRITAIN / 1821

021 / INDIAN TERRITORY / 1820–1840   022 / ARKANSAS / 1836   023 / MICHIGAN / 1837   024 / FLORIDA / 1845

029 / WISCONSIN / 1848   030 / CALIFORNIA / 1850   031 / GADSDEN PURCHASE / 1853   032 / MINNESOTA & TEXAS / 1858

037 / NEBRASKA / 1867   038 / COLORADO / 1876   039 / INDIAN WARS / 1817–1890   040 / NORTH & SOUTH DAKOTA / 1889

045 / UTAH / 1896   046 / OKLAHOMA / 1907   047 / NEW MEXICO & ARIZONA / 1912   048 / USA & MEXICO / PRESENT DAY

Key Events in U.S.–Mexico Relations

The Changing Border and Independence from England and Spain

1700–1763	1776	1803	1819	1821
North America = Spain + France + England	The 13 English colonies declare independence from Great Britain on July 4th, 1776.	The U.S. buys Louisiana from the French in what becomes known as "the Louisiana Purchase."	"Adam-Onís treaty" establishes the U.S.–Mexico boundary between Spain and the United States.	Mexico wins independence from Spain. Mexico permits Stephen F. Austin to start the colonization of Texas.

Migration and the World Wars

1900–1929	1909	1914	1917
First World War Period 1900–1929 Copper mines active in Arizona, 1900 Border Patrol established, 1904 Mexican Revolution, 1910 Peak immigration to the U.S., 1924	Meeting between president Porfirio Diaz and William H. Taft marks the first official meeting between U.S. and Mexican presidents. It is also the first time an American president officially visited a foreign country.	President Wilson orders U.S. troops to invade Mexico to prevent a large arms convoy from reaching Mexican General Victoriano Huerta's army.	The Zimmerman telegram, a document petitioning Mexico to join Germany in World War I, is intercepted by the United States. In the telegram Germany offers to orchestrate the return of Texas, New Mexico, and Arizona to Mexico, but the telegram never arrives in Mexico.

Political Control of Immigration

1945–1964	1964	1965	1967	1971–1981
Postwar era and the "Baby Boom." Soldiers return from the war and there is less demand for Mexican workers.	The Bracero Program ends and "Operation Wetback" is introduced, resulting in the deportation of 3.8 million people of Mexican heritage.	Border industrialization program. U.S. companies appear along the Mexican border Maquiladora program Cheap Mexican labor available	President Johnson and President Díaz Ordaz meet and resolve a long-standing issue when the U.S. agrees to forfeit El Chamizal to Mexico. The Chamizal dispute was a boundary conflict over 600 acres of land near El Paso, Texas, between the bed of the Rio Grande (as it was surveyed in 1952) and the present channel of the river.	The Mexican economy grows at an average annual rate of 6.7% in real terms, which is its highest growth rate in history. Jimmy Carter is the last president to visit Mexico until Bill Clinton moves to the White House.

The Age of NAFTA

1989	1992	1994	1996	1997
The Canada-United States Free Trade Agreement (CUSFTA) goes into effect.	Mexico and the U.S. establish border commissions, called Border Liaison Mechanisms (BLM), to manage routine daily relations across the border. Chaired by Mexican and U.S. consul generals, BLM meetings draw in officials from federal, state, and local agencies.	NAFTA begins and the Mexican peso collapses. The border sees a massive increase in its population. President Bill Clinton uses a strict approach to limit illegal immigration in his re-election campaign in order to sway large electoral states, such as California and Texas. Under Clinton's direction the Border Patrol is bolstered. U.S. Operation Gatekeeper is introduced and a corrugated steel fence is erected.	The U.S. Illegal Immigration Reform and Immigration Responsibility Act authorizes the construction of a triple fence along the border between San Diego, California and Tijuana, Mexico, as well as other migration-related initiatives.	Clinton becomes the first president to visit Mexico since Jimmy Carter in 1979. He promises Mexican President Ernesto Zedillo to avoid "mass deportations" under U.S. immigration policy.

1846–1848	1853	1861–1865	1883	1890
Mexican War By 1848 the war had ended and most of the Mexican state had been ceded to the United States under the Treaty of Guadalupe Hidalgo.	Gadsden Purchase: 29,000 square miles of land is sold by Mexico to the U.S. for the price of $10 million.	American Civil War	Chinese Exclusion Act implemented in the U.S. leading railroad companies to search for alternative sources of cheap labor. Mexicans are increasingly recruited.	Mexican Americans work for the railroads. Copper mining continues to lure people to Arizona, driving more Mexican Americans from their lands.

1929	1934	1938	1939–1945	1942
During the U.S. economic crisis of the Great Depression, 400,000 Mexicans are deported.	President Roosevelt introduces the Good Neighboor Policy which holds that there should be "no armed intervention by any foreign power in the Western hemisphere."	Mexican President Lázaro Cárdenas expropriates 16 foreign-owned oil companies in a move to nationalize Mexico's oil reserves.	World War II 1942 Bracero Program allows Mexicans to work temporarily in the U.S.	The German submarine U-160 sinks Mexico's petroleum ship, the Faja de Oro, off the coast of Key West in Florida on its voyage from Philadelphia to Tampico. Two more ships are also targeted and Mexico decides to enter World War II as a U.S. ally.

1980	1983	1985	1986	1987
The classification "Hispanic" shows up for the first time on the U.S. census.	The La Paz Agreement is signed. It is the first environmental treaty between the two nations.	Mexico and the U.S. sign an agreement on bilateral subsidies and countervailing duties.	Mexico joins the General Agreement on Tariffs and Trade (GATT). U.S. immigration policy turns restrictionist with the Immigration Reform and Control Act (IRCA). However, the Act also includes an act of amnesty. Undocumented immigrants who entered before 1982 benefit from amnesty.	The two governments sign a bilateral framework agreement for trade and investment.

1998	2001	2002	2004	2006
Bill Clinton signs a declaration with Mexican President Ernesto Zedillo committing their nations for the first time to devise a joint strategy for combating the trafficking of drugs.	At a meeting on September 6 between President Vicente Fox and President George W. Bush, Fox pledges to help improve security along the U.S.–Mexico border. Bush states that U.S.–Mexico relations would remain a priority during his administration. Five days later the terrorist attacks of September 11 made the war on terrorism the greatest priority of Bush's administration.	Canadian Prime Minister Jean Chrétien, President Bush, and President Fox meet in Monterrey and launch the Security and Prosperity Partnership in order to help focus private investment on less developed regions of Mexico. A "Smart Border" initiative to improve border security and speed up the two-way flow of people and goods across the border is implemented.	Both Bush and Fox discuss issues ranging from free trade to border control, noting close cooperation between their countries. Bush praises the Border Partnership Agreement in which Mexico and the U.S. are using technology to create safer and more effective borders. The new North American Free Trade Agreement (NAFTA) visa for professionals is introduced.	Immigration reform becomes a hot topic in the United States. Major objectives include: securing borders, creating a temporary worker program, dealing with the undocumented immigrants in the U.S., making it easier for employers to verify legal status of employees, and honoring the American tradition of being an immigrant nation. On May 15, 2006, Bush sends the National Guard to the border.

Volunteers line up to register for the Minuteman Project on April 1, 2005, in Tombstone, Arizona, the hometown of this anti-migrant organization. Minuteman vigilantes are expected to look out for illegal aliens coming from Mexico and report them to the Border Patrol.

3. REACTIONS TO THE HYPERBORDER

The conditions and discrepancies that surround and contribute to the hyperactivity of the U.S.–Mexico border have sparked numerous reactions from varying groups and institutions. From government officials to policymakers to vigilant U.S. citizens to immigrants' rights activists to the press, the state of the border and the methods for resolving its problems have become the interests of everyone.

POST-9/11 LEGISLATION

In the wake of 9/11, politicians and policymakers in the U.S. have rallied around national security and immigration reform as central issues for today's political arena. Since the terrorist attacks, numerous bills pertaining to these themes have been proposed and many passed into law, effectively changing the way the United States, a country often referred to as a nation of immigrants, receives foreign visitors and migrants. September 11, 2001, marked a major turning point for the U.S.–Mexico border, because now in addition to illegal immigration, drug trafficking, organized crime, and the many other issues surrounding the border region, it has become an important element of the U.S. war on terrorism.[1] The following segments highlight the most aggressive legislation to come forward since the attacks of 9/11, many of which will have a profound impact on the U.S.'s common border with Mexico and immigrants residing in the U.S.

USA-PATRIOT ACT (OCTOBER 2001)

On October 26, 2001, less than two months after the tragic events of 9/11, President George W. Bush signed into law the "Uniting and Strengthening of America by Promoting Appropriate Tools Required to Intercept and Obstruct Terrorism Act"—more popularly known as the USA-PATRIOT Act. The highly controversial law dramatically changed the parameters of the government's investigative and surveillance powers by authorizing unprecedented license to conduct secret searches, tap into telephones and internet usage, obtain personal information, and exchange intelligence between different agencies. The PATRIOT Act also expanded the definition of terrorist activity and granted the Attorney General authority to order detentions of "aliens" without showing that the person poses a threat. According to the American Civil Liberties Union (ACLU), this new legislation has resulted in the deportation and detention of more than one thousand immigrants, often without due process.[2]

CHANGE OF ADDRESS REQUIREMENT (2001)

In the months following September 11, in an effort to track non-citizens residing in the U.S., the Department of Justice announced renewed enforcement of Section 265(a) of the Immigration and Nationality Act of 1952, which requires non-citizens to submit change-of-address forms to the government within ten days of moving residences.[3] For immigrants in the United States—many of whom are unaware of the law—this piece of legislation is critical as the penalty for its violation can be as grave as deportation, even if the person is a Legal Permanent Resident (LPR). The first high-profile case of the law's application, against a Palestinian man, brought something of an administrative nightmare to Immigration and Naturalization Services (INS) offices around the country, as personnel scrambled to process tens of thousands of forms that began arriving daily. As the majority of these documents—now outdated—have yet to be processed, thousands of immigrants have been put at risk of "deportation for allegedly failing to comply with the law,"[4] as Michele Waslin points out, and the INS and its successor agency, the Department of Homeland Security, have been swamped with more information than can be managed.

ENHANCED BORDER SECURITY AND VISA ENTRY REFORM ACT (NOVEMBER 2001)

In the immediate investigations that followed September 11, it was discovered that several of the hijackers had entered the U.S. on student visas, which provoked Congress to pass the Enhanced Border Security and Visa Entry Reform Act in November 2001. The bill, which was signed into law on May 14, 2002, allows for the enhanced tracking of foreign students by requiring schools they attend to provide INS with their personal information and to certify that they have enrolled within thirty days of arrival to the United States.

EXECUTIVE ORDER BY PRESIDENT BUSH: CITIZENSHIP ELIGIBILITY FOR FOREIGN-BORN SOLDIERS (JULY 2002)

In July 2002, President Bush signed an executive order stating that any foreign-born soldier serving active duty in the wake of September 11, 2001, was eligible for U.S. citizenship. The president claimed that these soldiers were willing to put their lives at risk to defend the freedom of others and should therefore be accepted as full members of the society they represent and protect.[5] At a recent citizenship ceremony, Bush stated that there are currently more than 33,000 foreign-born, non-U.S. citizens serving in the U.S. armed forces.

HOMELAND SECURITY ACT (NOVEMBER 2002)

The Homeland Security Act (HSA) of 2002 is an anti-terrorism bill that further increased federal law enforcement agencies' citizen surveillance powers and created the Department of Homeland Security (DHS), resulting in the largest government reorganization in contemporary history. In a public statement, the DHS reported that one of the principal points of its six-point agenda was to "strengthen border security and interior enforcement and reform immigration processes."[6] Incidentally, one of the numerous institutions that the DHS replaced after its implementation in March 2003 was the INS, whose immigration-related responsibilities were transferred to the U.S. Citizenship and Immigration Services (USCIS), a bureau of Homeland Security. The implication of this change is that the U.S.–Mexico border, immigration, and consequently migrants themselves are now viewed as national security issues and threats since the DHS—an institution designed to protect the nation from terrorism—is now responsible for border control and immigration services.

THE AVIATION TRANSPORTATION AND SECURITY ACT (NOVEMBER 2002)

In November 2002 Congress passed the Aviation Transportation and Security Act (ATSA), a law that requires all airport baggage screeners to be U.S. citizens, thus uniting the concept of security with citizenship. According to the legislation's critics, ATSA implicitly criminalizes and provokes fear of foreign-born persons by prohibiting their occupation of jobs in airport security. Passage of the law resulted in the immediate dismissal of thousands of legal immigrant workers who had previously composed at least 20% of baggage screeners in airports across the country.[7]

PROPOSITION 200: ARIZONA (NOVEMBER 2004)

The 2004 elections in the border state of Arizona brought a revival of anti-immigrant legislation to its voters. Proposition 200—considered very similar to California's notorious Proposition 187, which was later deemed unconstitutional—was passed by 56% of the state's vote. The law requires employees of the local and state governments to verify the immigration status of people seeking government benefits, and to report any violations that are encountered or suspected to federal officials. Failure to report is considered a criminal offense, which effectively puts local police officers, health workers, public school teachers, and all other government employees in the position to break the law if they do not enforce the new legislation. The law also requires proof of citizenship in order to register to vote. The constitutionality of the new legislation is being challenged by the Mexican American Legal Defense and Education Fund (MALDEF) with the argument that Proposition 200 violates federal law because states do not have the authority to establish their own immigration enforcement system and because the law would "jeopardize the health and well-being of families and children who depend on public benefits for their basic necessities."[8] The proposition also trespasses upon the United Nations Universal Declaration of Human Rights, which holds that no individual may be denied health services and a basic education.[9]

INTELLIGENCE REFORM AND TERRORISM PREVENTION ACT (DECEMBER 2004)

Considered the greatest intelligence reform since the National Security Act of 1947, this act creates the position of Director of National Intelligence, currently served by Michael McConnell, who acts as the principal adviser on national security issues. He oversees the National Counterterrorism Center (created with this act) and promotes intelligence sharing among all intelligence agencies such as the CIA and

FBI. The bill establishes a National Intelligence Council to produce national intelligence reports to the federal government and creates the National Counterterrorism Center as a gathering point for all terrorism intelligence. It also calls for the increase of border patrol agents by at least 2,000 per year between FY 2006 and 2010, increases penalties for human smuggling, and provides extraterritorial federal jurisdiction over offenses related to nuclear weapons and other weapons of mass destruction.[10]

REAL ID ACT (MAY 2005)

In May 2005, President Bush signed the Real ID Act—an attachment to a military spending bill—into law. Real ID requires states to follow new federal driver's license standards, including fraud and tamper-resistant features; biometric identifiers; and information about each person's name, age, Social Security number, and proof of identity, residency, and legal presence in the United States.[11] The Congressional Budget Office estimates the new system will cost each state $100 million over five years, though critics claim it will be closer to $500–$700 million. The federal government, the entity mandating the new standards, will not cover these expenses.[12] The driver's license provisions take effect in 2008; any person from a state that has not adjusted its standards will be unable to obtain federal benefits, access federal buildings, or board airplanes.[13] Temporary-visa immigrants will have a different license from U.S. citizens, legal permanent residents, asylum seekers, and refugees, which would expire on the same date of that visa or after one year if the visa holds no expiration date. Real ID also includes new provisions for asylum, requiring applicants to prove "race, religion, nationality, membership in a particular social group, or political opinion was one 'central reason' for their persecution"—something widely considered difficult to prove.[14] The law further impedes non-citizens' access to due process by limiting the federal courts' ability to review detention and deportation cases and most "discretionary actions" taken by the DHS. All provisions, aside from the national driver's license standards, went into effect immediately after being signed into law.

BORDER PROTECTION, ANTITERRORISM, AND ILLEGAL IMMIGRATION CONTROL ACT: THE SENSENBRENNER BILL, H.R. 4437 (DECEMBER 2005, NOT ENACTED)

In December 2005, the House of Representatives passed the Border Protection, Anti-terrorism, and Illegal Immigration Control Act of 2005 (H.R. 4437)—also known as the Sensenbrenner Bill for its sponsor, Representative James Sensenbrenner (R-WI), the chief proponent of the Real ID Act. The bill—which was not passed by the Senate in 2006—sparked controversy in the international community and animosity on the part of the Mexican government for its authorization of seven hundred miles of new walls and fences along the border. The endeavor—which critics called reminiscent of the Berlin Wall—would have cost U.S. taxpayers an estimated $2 billion. A noteworthy clause was the expanded definition of "smuggling" to include anyone who aids or transports an undocumented person, thus putting migrant-friendly churches, legal services, refugee agencies, and social service organizations in the same criminal category as human smuggling organizations.[15] H.R. 4437 also moved to make "unlawful presence" in the United States a felony and called for the involvement of local law officers in immigration enforcement, something opponents said would have both deteriorated trust between immigrant communities and their police force, as well as distracted officers from more pressing issues of crime and security.[16] Although the bill was referred to the Senate committee in January 2006 and was not likely to be approved, President Bush signed a measure the following October, granting the DHS $1.2 billion for border security enforcement. Days later, he approved the construction of seven hundred miles of fencing along the border with Mexico, despite a call from Mexico's President Fox to veto the bill, and a request signed by twenty-seven other Organization of American States countries.[17]

OPERATION JUMP START: NATIONAL GUARD DEPLOYED TO THE BORDER (MAY 2006)

In the midst of the heated immigration debate gripping the United States in the spring of 2006, President Bush announced plans for the implementation of Operation Jump Start, a maneuver placing 6,000 National Guard troops along the border. Then-president of Mexico Vicente Fox immediately objected to the operation, concerned about the prospect of an explicitly militarized border. Yet Bush claimed the deployment of the guard would only be temporary: by 2008, when the Border Control doubles its ranks to 18,000 agents, the National Guard's participation in Operation Jump Start will be terminated.[18] The troops are not meant to detain the migrants, but instead to operate surveillance and report what they see to the Border Patrol, who still holds the sole responsibility for capturing illegal crossers. Reports indicate that migrants are now more fearful of entering the country illegally because of the military uniforms they see on the other side. In July 2006, Border Patrol Chief David Aguilar claimed apprehensions on the southern border had fallen by 45% from the previous two months—a sign that fewer people are crossing—as a direct result of the National Guard's presence.[19]

HEIGHTENED BORDER SECURITY

A new level of anxiety surrounding terrorism and the country's national security has shaped the post-9/11 climate of the United States. The well-funded Department of Homeland Security undoubtedly represents the Bush Administration's most concerted effort to address the heightened angst found in the government, media, and population. As a result of the monumental administrative restructuring attending the creation of the DHS, the U.S. Customs and Border Protection (CBP) has become the agency within the DHS that now encompasses the offices of U.S. Customs, U.S. Immigration, Animal and Plant Inspection Service, and the U.S. Border Patrol.[20] Robert C. Bonner, the former Commissioner of CBP, outlined the changing nature of his agency:

> On the morning of 9/11, I realized that my agency's mission had been dramatically altered. It was clear to me that the priority mission of U.S. Customs had changed from the interdiction of illegal drugs and regulation of trade, to a national security mission—preventing terrorists and terrorist weapons from getting into the United States.[21]

According to Bonner, because CBP works at the border, its officers have the broadest law enforcement authority of any agency in the United States, bar none.[22] CBP is composed of more than 41,000 agents who work to manage, control, and protect all official U.S. ports of entry and the border terrain between.

Since its inception, the DHS has annually received increased funding from the U.S. government. The institution's budget for 2006 was $34.2 billion, a 7% increase from 2005. In 2006 the Border Control received $37 million for the hiring of 210

At present there are more American border patrol agents than soldiers in Afghanistan.

additional Border Patrol agents, and $20 million for new Border Control vehicles and aircrafts. Since September 11, 2001, the Border Patrol workforce has grown by nearly 1,200 agents, an 11% increase. The 2006 federal budget also enhanced the America's Shield Initiative, which calls for the application of surveillance, video, and detection systems, among other new technologies along the border,[23] which some critics point to as evidence of "the militarization" of the U.S.–Mexico border.[24]

One of the Department of Homeland Security's principal concerns for its effective enforcement of U.S. immigration laws is the detention and removal of illegal aliens from United States soil. The 2006 federal budget provided a hefty sum in order to achieve this goal: funding for "enforcement" was increased by $176 million, $90 million of which was designated to detention beds and additional detention and removal officers. Other areas set to receive funding included: repatriation costs (directed toward desert crossings, $39 million); apprehension of alien fugitives ($8 million); direct deportation of aliens convicted of crimes back to their countries ($5.4 million); and DHS attorneys working to prosecute immigration cases ($3.5 million).[25]

PUSHING THE BORDER AWAY FROM THE UNITED STATES

Part of the Department of Homeland Security's vision for the nation's protection involves expanding surveillance beyond the border and U.S. ports of entry. According to Bonner, CBP has "twin goals" in its agenda—security and facilitation:

We are achieving these Twin Goals by employing better technologies, managing risk, and through a layered, defense-in-depth strategy that pushes our borders—our zone of security—out beyond our physical borders, so that we know who and what is headed our way before they arrive.[26]

US-VISIT (United States Visitor and Immigrant Status Indicator Technology), a program that has adjusted the procedures for obtaining visas and crossing into the United States, is an example of the "pushing-the-border-away" strategy. As stated on its website:

In many cases, US-VISIT begins overseas, at the U.S. consular offices issuing visas, where visitors' biometrics (digital finger-scans and photographs) are collected and checked against a database of known criminals and suspected terrorists. When the visitor arrives at the port of entry, we use the same biometrics to verify the person at our port is the same person who received the visa.[27]

US-VISIT also claims to help protect the identity of visitors entering the United States, as one's biometric information cannot be stolen or used by another person. According to P. T. Wright, Director of Mission Operations Management for US-VISIT, "the program separates the needles from the haystack"; in other words, undesirable visitors can be stopped from entering the U.S. before they depart from their country of origin.[28] In the summer of 2005 the second phase of US-VISIT began its implementation, as radio frequency identification (RFID) tags were

RAIL VACIS

Detector

Radiation Source

Operator Station

Exclusion Zone

MOBILE VACIS

Exclusion Zone

Detector

Truck Mounted Boom

Radiation Source

Mobile VACIS

Cargo

Vehicle and Cargo Inspection Systems (VACIS) are used in U.S. ports and the U.S.–Mexico border. These gamma-ray imaging systems allow for fast inspection of containers, trucks, and personal vehicles to detect contraband items, weapons, and people. Other border inspection methods include canine scrutiny and surveillance cameras for remote areas along the border.

JUL 5 2001

JUL 5 2001

Opposite, above: Video monitors in a Border Patrol station in Nogales, Arizona. April 26, 2006. Below: Border Patrol agent Tony McAuliffe photographed in a monitoring station in Southern California on February 17, 2005.

This page, top: Border Patrol agent monitors suspicious activitiy. The station is equipped with surveillance cameras and sensors that detect illegal crossings day and night. That summer, President Bush signed an emergency $1.9 billion bill to increase border security. Below: This car was dismantled and reassembled in order to fit a woman behind the dashboard so that she could be smuggled into the United States. People often tolerate similar conditions for days when attempting to cross the border.

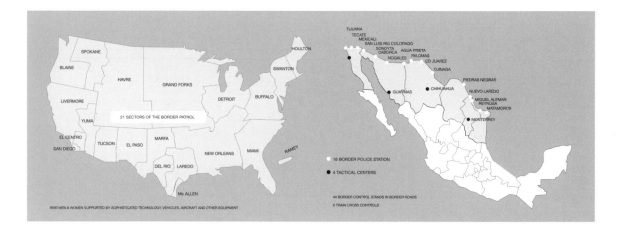

distributed to visa holders entering the U.S. The RFID tag is part of a document that visitors must present each time they enter the country. When a visa carrier reaches a crossing point, an antenna positioned up to thirty feet away recognizes their tag. Immediately the traveler's biometric information will register, notifying the guard of their identity before they arrive at the checkpoint. Over 41 million people have already gone through the first phase of the program, 900 of whom were criminals detected through this process, and 12,000 visas have been turned down based on the applicants' biometrics. As of the summer of 2005, only five crossing points between the U.S. borders with Canada and Mexico were testing the RFID tags for the second phase of US-VISIT.

Within the new DHS/CBP "Security and Facilitation" strategy, the United States has also introduced the Container Security Initiative (CSI), a program that seeks to protect the global trading system and trade lanes between ports around the world. About 90% of the world's cargo moves in containers, and nearly 7 million cargo containers enter U.S. seaports each year. The purpose of CSI is to change trade regulation processes by screening the cargo entering the United States before it departs from its point of origin. This is meant to ensure that international supply chains will not be used for the smuggling of weapons of mass destruction and other illegal or dangerous commodities. At present, eighteen countries have agreed to participate in the initiative, thus connecting thirty-eight CSI ports. With the introduction of programs such as this, the U.S. is essentially pushing its borders away by conducting U.S. immigration and customs processes abroad instead of at its own ports of entry.

PUSHING THE BORDER AWAY FROM MEXICO

The U.S. government is not the only actor interested in pushing border activities away from the physical international divide; for both convenience and security, Mexican government officials have agreed to open the first foreign and Mexican customs facility in the United States in 2006. It will be stationed in Kansas City, Kansas, the geographic center of the NAFTA region, located almost 1,000 miles from the border.[29] The new facility is expected to induce cost savings and to make the transportation of goods between Canada, the United States, and Mexico more efficient, as it will cut back on delays suffered by truckers at the border. Upon arrival at Mexican entry ports, cargo will be free to move across without further inspection as long as the electronically sealed containers have not been tampered with.

IMPROVING THE BORDER: THE INTEREST OF EVERYONE

The present circumstances of the U.S.–Mexico border have sparked action from a variety of groups at both the grassroots and institutional levels in the name of "improvement." From migrants' rights activists to the Minutemen, improving the border has clearly become the interest of everyone. The following segments feature some of today's most prominent figures and groups working toward the reshaping of the international divide that separates the United States from Mexico.

THE ROLE OF THE NGO: HUMANE BORDERS

The dramatic increase of border deaths in recent years has brought humanitarian groups to the forefront of migrant relief efforts. Humane Borders, a faith-based agency located in Tucson, has constructed more than eighty emergency water stations throughout Arizona's Sonoran Desert border region since the organization's founding in 2000. The stations are typically supplied with up to six 65-gallon barrels of safe drinking water, food rations, first aid kits, and warm clothes, and are regularly maintained by a volunteer force that is eight thousand strong.[30] In the fall of 2005 Humane Borders gained the financial support of Pima County, which covers about one third of the Arizona border with Mexico, when the organization demonstrated the cost benefits of supporting the humanitarian program instead of being forced to deal with corpses found within the county limits. According to Pima County's Administrator, local taxpayers spend $300,000 annually—none of which is reimbursed by the federal or state governments—on the recovery and storage of undocumented immigrants' bodies who die within the county's geographic

Opposite: U.S. Border Patrol sectors and Mexican security sectors.
Above: Humane Borders agent installing a water station to prevent migrants from dying from dehydration in the desert.

Migrant Deaths, Water Stations, and Rescue Beacons, FY 2000-2004

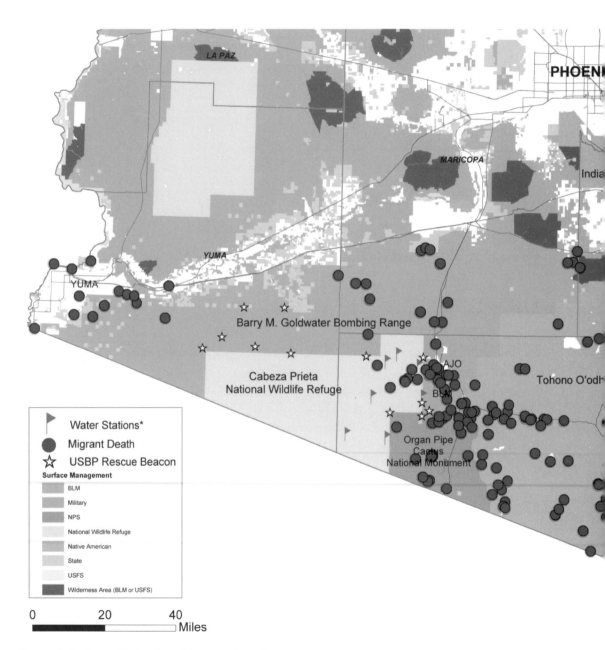

Maps created by Humane Borders. Some dots represent more than one death. Between October 1, 1999, and September 30, 2004, more than 650 migrants died while attempting to cross the deserts of southern Arizona.

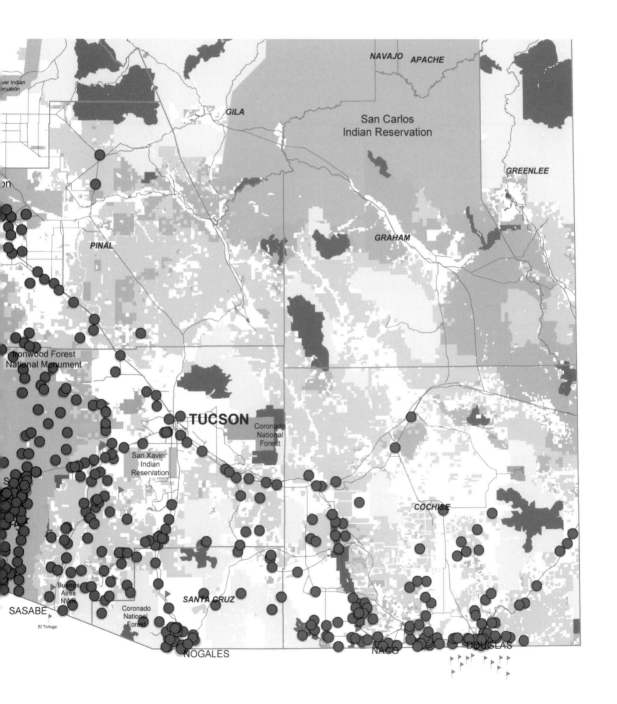

SASABE

NOGALES

NACO

DOUGLAS

TUCSON

NAVAJO · APACHE

GILA

San Carlos
Indian Reservation

GREENLEE

GRAHAM

PINAL

Ironwood Forest
National Monument

Coronado
National
Forest

San Xavier
Indian
Reservation

COCHISE

Buenos
Aires
NWR

SANTA CRUZ

Coronado
National
Forest

El Tortugo

boundaries. That sum is significantly higher than the $25,000 contribution county supervisors granted the relief agency for their rescue efforts in 2005.[31] Humane Borders has also developed a detailed map of the border region; it uses red dots to mark the sites of migrant deaths and blue flags to show where emergency water stations are located (see page 82–83). The mapped information helps the organization develop new strategies of death prevention and also strengthens the group's lobbying efforts with local authorities and private landowners by offering physical evidence of the problem's existence. In January of 2006, Humane Borders and Mexico's National Human Rights Commission (NHRC) announced plans to distribute these maps to migrants along the Mexican side of the border to inform them of the dangerous conditions in the desert and to promote responsible decision-making. The U.S. government immediately denounced the idea, claiming that the maps—which provide information about cell phone coverage as well as emergency water stations—encouraged illegal immigration and the violation of U.S. laws. The Mexican NHRC eventually decided to retract the plan, although the organization maintained their decision had not been influenced by U.S. pressure. According to NHRC spokesman Miguel Angel Paredes, the organization concluded that the maps could potentially work against the migrants because it would make them easy targets for anti-immigrant activists such as the Minutemen.[32]

THE ROLE OF THE ANTI-IMMIGRANT GROUP: THE RISE OF THE MINUTEMAN PROJECT

Worldwide, few subjects spark as much controversy as immigration. The United States has had a long, cyclical history with the issue: economic booms in the country tend to encourage immigration, while recession has led to severe backlash. In today's post-9/11 environment, however, homeland security and the war on terrorism have conquered the national psyche and have become major driving forces—and excuses—behind anti-immigrant sentiment.

Due to the continued presence of immigrants in the U.S., and their recent arrival in parts of the country that were not previously immigrant destinations, many U.S. citizens perceive the government's latest efforts to strengthen border

Above: Crosses installed by activist Claudia Smith in Tijuana along the international boundary. Each cross represents a dead migrant.

In Arizona alone, within six months of the Minutemen's founding in 2005, at least eighteen anti-immigrant bills were introduced to the state legislature.

control as insufficient. The terrorist attacks of September 11 aside, recent census reports showing that Latinos are now the largest minority in the country have encouraged new focus, fear, and debate surrounding the U.S.–Mexico border. From these sentiments have stemmed protest groups such as the Minuteman Project (MMP), an organization of armed civilian volunteers who patrol parts of the U.S.–Mexico border. The MMP, which was founded in Tombstone, Arizona, in 2005, claims its primary goal is to draw attention to the border and undocumented immigration. Since its emergence, the group's influence and activities have spread to California, Texas, New Mexico, Illinois, Washington, Oregon, and beyond.

Initially, Border Control officials reported a sharp drop in undocumented migrant apprehension, which corresponded with the appearance of the Minutemen along the border of Arizona and Mexico. However, officials made it clear that the fall in detentions most likely had more to do with military patrols on the Mexican side of the border than with the Minutemen's presence.[33] Out of concern for his fellow citizens, Eduardo Bours Castelo, the governor of the Mexican border state of Sonora, instructed the Preventative Police Force to patrol the area in Mexico opposite the Minutemen's stomping ground in order to intercept migrants unaware of the activities and consequences on the other side of the border. The chaotic atmosphere of protesters, counter-protesters, and news reporters in the normally vacant and desolate region was also a likely deterrent of migrants who otherwise would have crossed via the Sonoran Desert in Arizona.

Criticism of the MMP abounds, and much controversy surrounding the movement has arisen since the patrols of the border began in 2005. On April 6 of that year, the project was subjected to negative press when three Minutemen volunteers, one of whom was a University of California at San Diego student named Bryan Barton, apprehended a 26-year-old male migrant and convinced him to pose for a photo while holding a T-shirt that read "Bryan Barton caught me crossing the border and all I got was this lousy T-shirt." The incident put into question the MMP's motives and led to increased press coverage around the nation. President Bush has described the group members as vigilantes, and Mexico's former President Fox has dubbed them "immigrant hunters." Counter-groups and other critics claim the Minutemen are connected to white supremacy groups and that their actions stem from racism and fear. Numerous watchdog groups of legal observers have come forth from organizations such as the Human Rights Coalition of California and the ACLU in an effort to document Minutemen actions and to deter any potential violence against people crossing the border.

Many of the organization's protesters are not only concerned with the patrolling activities of the Minutemen along the border; according to some, it is the group's ideology and mentality that they find most threatening to the future of immigrants' rights in the U.S. When asked to describe the reasons behind his organization's participation in the Minutemen-countermovement, Ed Herrera, president of the Human Rights Coalition of California, said:

Opposite: Chris Simcox, executive director of the Minuteman Civil Defense Corps (MCDC). Dubbed as a "celebrity extremist" by the Southern Poverty Law Center, he founded the group in 2004.

Above: Saturday, May 27, 2006. Minutemen volunteers start building a 10-mile fence on one of their ranches in Palominas, Arizona, with the hope of deterring illegal immigration from Mexico. Below: Volunteers from human rights organizations form a human line on April 2, 2005, to observe the Minutemen activities. The protesters hold crosses representing migrants who have died in their attempt to move to the U.S.

We do not believe that we must put human rights and human worth aside simply because they are undocumented immigrants; first and foremost they are human beings....The Minuteman Project is not simply about national security and terrorism; it is about a deep-rooted concern for an ever-changing ethno-cultural shift in the American population.[34]

According to Scott Campbell, an organizer with the San Francisco Bay Area Coalition to Fight the Minutemen, the group's ideology has infiltrated the political arena: in Arizona alone, since the Minutemen's presence was first established in April 2005, at least eighteen anti-immigrant bills have been introduced to the state legislature; in California, signatures are being collected to support the California Border Police Initiative, which would increase the force by 2,000–3,000 officers and include the construction of another prison on the state's border with Mexico.[35] Arnold Schwarzeneg-

ger, the Republican governor of California, has also demonstrated support for the ideology. The former actor sparked both outrage and approval in the spring of 2005 when he publicly praised the Minutemen for their actions and invited them to begin their efforts in California as well.[36]

THE ROLE OF THE PRESS: JOURNALISTS ON THE BORDER

The Latin American Journalist Federation recently announced that between 2000 and the beginning of 2006, twenty journalists have been assassinated in Mexico, over half of whom died while working in

Above: Casa del Migrante, an NGO in Piedras Negras, Mexico, provides temporary shelter and food for deported migrants. Opposite above: Jesus Blancornelas, co-founder of *Zeta* newspaper, receiving the Daniel Pearl Award for Courage and Integrity on June 11, 2005. Editors of this Tijuana newspaper have been victims of assassination attempts for their reports on corruption in the Mexican government. Opposite below: a March 2007 issue of *Zeta*.

the Mexican border states.[37] The effects of narco-trafficking and the corruption that pervades multiple levels of public authority have been crippling for the investigative reporting community: Almost every crime against journalists in the region has gone unpunished, and few have been thoroughly investigated. This atmosphere of impunity has forced many journalists into self-censorship, as they are offered no protection, and have thus been silenced for fear of losing their lives.[38]

Despite the dangers involved with the profession, there are several voices that have spoken out against the injustices experienced by the press in Mexico. Jesús Blancornelas, cofounder and editor of the Tijuana-based magazine *Zeta* and vice president of the Mexican Society of Journalists, was one such figure. Described as the "spiritual godfather of modern Mexican journalism" by the Committee to Protect Journalists (CPJ),[39] Blancornelas devoted his career at *Zeta* to the exposure of the Tijuana drug-trafficking industry and its extensive influence over local judges, police, and politicians in the state of Baja California—issues typically avoided by the mainstream Mexican media. His work was rewarded by internationally prestigious awards in journalism, such as the UNESCO/Guillermo Cano World Press Freedom Prize in 1999 and the Daniel Pearl Award in 2005. However, his work to fight for freedom of the press and to cover corruption and the drug mafia in Mexico did not come without extreme risks. Blancornelas was critically injured in an assassination attempt in 1997, and his bodyguard, Luis Valero, died while protecting him; Blancornelas also bore witness to the murders of Héctor Félix Miranda, his cofounder of *Zeta*, in 1988, and Francisco Ortiz Franco, his editor, in 2004.[41] According to CPJ, the nature of his work required Blancornelas to remain under self-imposed house arrest, only traveling between his home and office, and always protected by

The Mexican side of the U.S.–Mexico border is currently the most dangerous place in Latin America to work as a journalist.[40]

multiple bodyguards from an army Special Forces unit. Nevertheless, he remained dedicated to the cause and what he started until his death in 2006. Approaching the age of seventy, Blancornelas once stated, "If my colleagues hadn't been killed, I would have retired a long time ago. But I can't now. I need to fight and to clarify what's happened. That's my purpose."[42]

The Center for Journalism and Public Ethics/Centro de Periodismo y Ética Pública (CEPET) has also made strides toward achieving justice for the journalism community in Mexico, particularly in the border states. Originally created in order to provide an online forum for Mexican journalists to discuss issues within their profession, the increased violence has encouraged CEPET to become something of an activist group. Through the organization of cross-border events—such as Border Conference: Both Sides of the Story, in 2004—CEPET has successfully developed a platform for protest and action against the atrocities being experienced by journalists in Mexico.[43] With the cooperation of other organizations, it established an Accountability Commission to investigate the murders of reporters in Mexico and began to actively lobby the Mexican government to prioritize the issue by putting an end to impunity.

The Mexican government has a difficult task ahead of it; untangling the deeply embedded institutional web of corruption along the border will take considerable action. However, recent advancements suggest that the federal government is gearing up to confront the challenge. Under the increased pressure of journalist advocate groups such as CEPET, CPJ, and Reporters Without

Borders (RWB), in February of 2006 President Fox announced the appointment of David Vega Vera, a lawyer and human rights defender, as special prosecutor to investigate crimes against journalists, a position that is unique in the world. According to CPJ, federal authorities have more resources and visibility and therefore are better suited to conduct investigations of murders, which have reached an overwhelming scale for local officials whom are more often prone to corruption.[44] However, Vega's position has a decidedly peculiar catch: "cases involving drugs and organized crime, the major components of attacks on the media, will be turned over to [the deputy prosecutor for the organized crime division of the attorney general's office] José Luis Vasconcelos."[45] The Mexican Attorney General, Daniel Cabeza de Vaca, states that Vasconcelos has the necessary resources and experience to tackle the country's drug kingpins, but groups like RWB lament the limitations of the new prosecutor's scope of authority. In a letter to Vega, RWB writes: "Reporters Without Borders is surprised that cases linked to drug-trafficking do not come under the competence of the special prosecutor's office that you are about to take charge of. How can one understand this when drug-traffickers, and more widely criminality in general, are the chief causes of violence towards the Mexican media?"[46] The dynamics of the new federal system for investigating crimes against journalists have yet to pan out, but the recent steps send a message that Mexico is confronting the challenge.

THE ROLE OF THE GOVERNMENT: MEXICO'S ID PROGRAM

The impact of migrant deaths on the border reaches far beyond the overburdened taxpayers of U.S. border counties. As the migrants who do not survive are often found without documents or emergency contact information, family members in Mexico rarely receive news of their loved one's death. Since 1995, more than 3,000 migrants have died trying to enter the United States.[47] Of these, more than one-third remain unidentified and have since been buried in "pauper" graves in cemeteries along the U.S–Mexico border.[48] In response to this issue, the Mexican government has developed a new program that is designed to help identify the migrants who die crossing the border. The program, which is called the System for Identifying Remains and Locating Individuals, is an internet database linking the offices of Mexico's Foreign Relations Department with the Mexican Consulates in the United States. The database will be utilized to store anything that might help identify the dead, such as passports, ID cards, and photos of distinctive tattoos and birthmarks. The program has also contracted forensic anthropologists in Texas to collect DNA samples from migrants' remains, which will be entered into the ID database.[49] If evidence is found connecting remains to a missing person report, authorities will obtain blood samples from family members to be tested by the forensic anthropologists. Although the database's success will more often than not translate into the delivery of bad news, the program's intent is to provide closure for the family members of those who died in their attempt to cross the border.

THE ROLE OF THE BINATIONAL ACCORD: PARTNERSHIP FOR PROSPERITY

When George W. Bush and Vicente Fox first met as presidents in early 2001, both acknowledged the importance of bilateral migration talks, and they publicly agreed to pursue the "narrowing of economic gaps between and within [the two] societies."[50] Later that year—less than a week before the terrorist attacks of September 11—their first sizable binational effort toward fulfilling that mission was launched. The Partnership for Prosperity (PfP) is "a private–public alliance to harness the power of the private sector to foster an environment in which no Mexican feels compelled to leave his home for a lack of jobs or opportunity," and is meant to promote development in those regions of Mexico that have high emigration rates.[51] Although the changes in the post-9/11 environment significantly slowed the progress of migration talks between the two countries, PfP can be credited with several accomplishments. In November of 2004, Secretary of State Colin Powell helped establish the first Peace Corps program in Mexico, and created the Overseas Private Investment Corporation (OPIC), which is anticipated to provide some $600 million in financing and insurance to U.S. businesses in Mexico.[52] Other notable long-term goals for PfP include investments in housing and commerce infrastructure; financing of U.S. franchise opportunities for Mexican entrepreneurs; the establishment of small-business development centers in Mexico to promote competitiveness; and the reduction of fees that accompany sending money (remittances) from the United States to Mexico to as low as two dollars per transfer.[53]

A migrant in Brandenton, Florida, where a great portion of the agricultural labor is dependent on migrants. Recent surveys demonstrate a shift among Mexican migrants away from agriculture as the main industry of employment. In 1990, 23% and 13% of Mexican male and female migrants worked in agriculture. By 2000, that figure dropped to 15% and 7% respectively.

4. A STATE OF INTERDEPENDENCE

Due to Mexico's reliance on remittances, the United States' dependence on Mexican undocumented labor, the reciprocal nature of sister cities, and the constant exchanges of goods and people across the hyperborder, the two nations have arrived at an unforeseen and unprecedented state of interdependence.

> "The only way the cities in this region can make it, is to forget that a line and a river exist here."

—Former Ciudad Juárez mayor Gustavo Elizondo, on the interdependence between Ciudad Juárez and El Paso.[1]

SISTER CITIES

The border region between the United States and Mexico has often been defined as a "third space," a zone afflicted with problems that are entirely distinct from those experienced in the rest of the two nations. Unfortunately, the national capitals—Mexico City and Washington, D.C.—are physically removed from the region, and are thus regarded by some borderlanders as "distant and dysfunctional,"[2] who claim that many of the issues confronting the border on a daily basis go unnoticed by the federal governments. Today, it is largely up to the local governments and organizations located along the border to resolve the issues that plague the cities in the region.

The majority of the border's population resides in the fourteen sister cities that straddle the international divide.[3] This concentration of people along the world's most frequented international border has resulted in unique circumstances of interdependence at the local level: firemen in Brownsville, Texas, routinely respond to emergency calls from Matamoros on the other side of the border;[4] Tijuana hospitals and clinics send shuttle buses to California to transport patients to Mexico; and McAllen, Texas, sold nearly 40% of its retail goods to Reynosa residents and other Mexicans in 2001.[5] California and Baja California, which currently make up the fifth largest economic region in the world,[6] are deepening their cross-border integration through investments in shared infrastructure and facilities such as electrical generators near Mexicali, wastewater treatment plants in Tijuana,

and proposed liquefied natural gas (LNG) receiving stations in Baja California.[7] All of these initiatives represent an unprecedented consolidation of the region and suggest a future of further integration and continued interdependence as these neighboring cities increase their linkage in the age of globalization.

In the U.S., border cities differ from other cities because their geographic location and deep economic ties with Mexico make them subject to more factors that can affect their stability and growth.[8] The state of Mexico's economy and the dollar–peso exchange rate can significantly impact cities on the U.S. side, because the large retail business that has developed in the region (particularly in south and east Texas) has come to rely on Mexican consumers. When the peso is devalued—or collapses, as it did in 1994—the U.S. side of the border suffers because their Mexican clientele can no longer afford American prices. When the peso is stronger, U.S. border cities experience economic growth as a direct result of increased spending by Mexican nationals. Depending on the industries present, and the degree of economic integration with their Mexican counterparts, some U.S. border cities are considered more aligned with the Mexican economy than with their own.[9] In Laredo, Texas, after transportation and warehousing, retail is the city's second-most important industry, and both of these are intricately related to Mexico's economic cycles.

The sister cities of Ciudad Juárez and El Paso (as well as the growing city of Santa Teresa, NM) are often referred to as the border's "metroplex."

This urbanized zone is at the junction of three states (Chihuahua, Texas, and New Mexico) and two nations, thus acting as a microcosm for the high degree of interdependence between the United States and Mexico. The region's population of two million plus makes it the largest border community in the world, a characteristic that is likely to stick if the metroplex grows at the predicted annual rate of 5% in the coming decades.[10]

The sister cities of the metroplex are linked by forces that transcend the international boundary that divides them. Problems with pollution, disease, and a faltering water supply—issues that easily escape the attention of Washington and Mexico City—are some of the primary concerns shared by El Paso and Ciudad Juárez. In response to these circumstances, the local governments in both cities have had to increase local action by

passing regional treaties and agreements in order to resolve the problems specific to their dynamic. As the former mayor of Ciudad Juárez Gustavo Elizondo put it:

"Our [federal] governments treat us like a third country, so we might as well act like one."[11]

Possibly the most immediate threat for Ciudad Juárez and El Paso is their dwindling water reserve. The sister cities lie on a common underground aquifer that is projected to run dry by the year 2025, if not sooner, for Juárez, whose city limits lie on a smaller share of the supply but continues to experience rapid population growth and urban sprawl.[12] This threat has sparked conflict between the two cities due to complications that

accompany the sharing of vital resources under distinct governments and management. Growing concern has prompted El Paso water authorities to criticize Ciudad Juárez for its limited plans of diversification in water sources.[13] Yet the metroplex's Mexican half has significantly fewer resources at its disposal, a problem that is compounded by the ever-increasing urban growth throughout the city and spreading beyond its limits. The most likely solution will be to create a transboundary taskforce responsible for the allocation and measurement of water in order to avoid an aggravated dispute.

THE MAQUILADORA INDUSTRY AND NAFTA

Although the maquiladora program along the border began in the 1960s, the implementation of the NAFTA in 1994 was the driving force behind the booming nature of the present day's multibillion dollar industry. Maquiladora companies, taking advantage of lower operation costs in Mexico, manufacture and assemble products in Mexico using American components to later export their final products duty-free into the U.S. When NAFTA lifted most trade barriers between Canada, the United States, and Mexico, the flow of goods across borders surged between the three countries, and foreign investment—particularly in Mexico— greatly increased. The U.S.–Mexico border became

Opposite: A Mexican Army Aid convoy of forty-five vehicles on its way to provide humanitarian aid to the displaced victims of hurricane Katrina temporarily located in San Antonio, Texas in September, 2005. This was the first entry of the Mexican Army in U.S. territory since 1846. Below: Maquiladora workers in Tijuana, Baja California. The maquiladora industry employs over a million Mexicans and generates nearly half of all the country's exports. Nearly half of all maquiladora companies are located in the border states of Baja California and Chihuahua.

Understanding the Border's Conditions

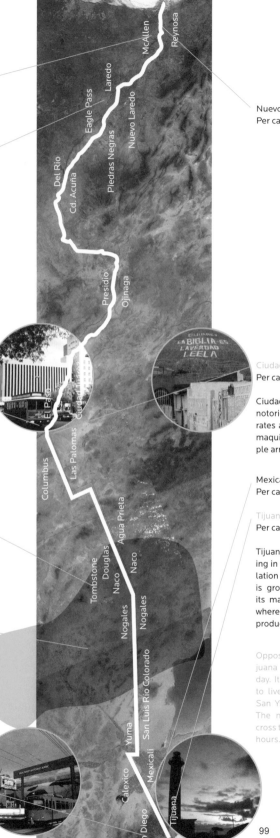

McAllen
McAllen is one of the fastest growing metro areas in the U.S. and it is also the poorest city in the country with an average income of $13,339 ($9,899 in 1999).

Laredo
Per capita GRP=14,112

The majority of goods that travel through the U.S.–Mexico border cross between the sister cities of Laredo and Nuevo Laredo. However, the region sees little of the monetary trade benefits: 29.6% of Laredo's population lives below poverty.

El Paso
Per capita GRP=17,216

El Paso and Ciudad Juárez is the largest bi-national urban area in the world. It is estimated that potable water in this region will run out by 2025.

Tombstone, AZ
Tombstone, AZ, the founding city of the Minutemen, an anti-immigrant group of civilians who are taking border security in their own hands. Critics have labeled them as "vigilantes" and promoters of a racist agenda.

Sonoran Desert, AZ
Known as the "corridor of death," due to harsh weather conditions and high migrant death rates. The total number of deaths in the 2004–05 fiscal year reached a historical record of 464. Of those deaths, 257 happened in Arizona.

Imperial
Per capita GRP=17,550

San Diego
Per capita GRP=29,488

Nuevo Laredo
Per capita GRP=5,678

Ciudad Juárez
Per capita GRP=7,074

Ciudad Juárez has recently become notorious for the increasing death rates and disappearances of female maquiladora workers. 50,000 people arrive in this city every year.

Mexicali
Per capita GRP=6,366

Tijuana
Per capita GRP=6,800

Tijuana is the busiest border crossing in the world. Tijuana has a population of more than a million, and is growing rapidly. It is known for its maquiladora industry. It is here where most TVs, and electronics are produced in North America.

Opposite: Border crossings from Tijuana into San Ysidro, on any given day. It is very common for Mexicans to live in Tijuana and commute to San Ysidro or San Diego every day. The north-bound waiting times to cross the border may take up to three hours.

the ideal factory location for corporations wishing to take advantage of access to lower-waged workers in Mexico while remaining in close proximity to the U.S. in order to maintain smooth trade processes. Under the Maquila Decree, which was first established in 1989, foreign companies are allowed to operate factories in Mexico and to import goods and equipment used for production duty-free, as long as the finished products are exported out of Mexico.[14] That decree, with the added advantage of NAFTA's relaxed trade regulations, made the Mexican side of the border a very attractive environment for foreign investment in manufacturing.

As the maquiladora industry offers thousands of low-skill jobs, the border has been a magnet to Mexican workers seeking economic opportunity for decades. The foreign capital from Maquilas also provides the Mexican government with a source of income through taxes, as big business and Pemex (the state-owned oil company) are the most heavily taxed sectors in the country. Therefore Mexico depends on the industry as a source of employment and income. These pressures have made the government eager to preserve its grip on foreign enterprises, which it does by deregulating labor and environmental laws that keep manufacturing expenses at a minimum. These ideal investment circumstances have gotten foreign entrepreneurs— and subsequently their consumers—hooked. Mexico is host to most U.S. assembly activities abroad,[15] and today electronics, textile, transport, and furniture companies owned by American corporations depend on factories from Tijuana to Matamoros to keep their production costs low and businesses successful. Essentially, the establishment of the maquiladora industry has created a partnership along both sides of the border committed to its success, as stakeholders in both countries depend on each other to maintain the benefits gained from their close trade relationship.

U.S. DEPENDENCY ON UNDOCUMENTED LABOR

A significant (although sometimes overlooked) aspect of the immigration debate is the United States' dependency on cheap labor, a large bulk of which stems directly from the undocumented immigrant community. Thriving economies in states such as California and Illinois, both hosts to large immigrant populations, has been credited in part to the vital contributions made by this workforce, and according to many economists, undocumented migrants are fundamental to Americans' access to inexpensive goods. Without them, many industries—particularly in the agricultural sector—would likely lose their business to companies south of the border,[16] as U.S. consumers have become accustomed to cheap products, which require access to low-cost labor. Affluent lifestyles in many American communities have become more attainable due to the consistent willingness of immigrant workers to accept low wages as gardeners, busboys, maids, babysitters, and more.[17] Undocumented workers have also been described as the backbone of California's agricultural sector—the nation's largest, worth $28 billion[18] and provider of much of America's food demands—as they often accept work conditions most U.S. citizens will not. Knowing this, for decades the U.S. government has practiced the "politics of tolerance" in regards to the undocumented presence throughout the country.[19] Although border control has tightened off and on in recent history, it has failed to deter the increased flow of people. The U.S. also lacks efficient methods for tracking and deporting undocumented immigrants. In 2003, across the country only ninety immigration investigators were sent to inspect day labor and work centers—known haunts of immigrant workers seeking employment—at a time when upwards of 10 million undocumented immigrants were suspected to reside in the United States.[20] Such facts reflect an implicit decision on

As of March, 2005, unauthorized Mexicans in the U.S. represented:

18% of all insulation workers

15% of all miscellaneous agricultural workers

15% of all roofers

14% of all drywall installers, ceiling tile installers, and tapers

13.5% of all helpers in construction trades

13.5% of all butchers and other meat-, poultry-, and fish-processing workers

13% of pressers, textile, garment, and related materials

12.5% of all grounds maintenance workers

12.5% of all construction laborers

12.5% of all brickmasons, blockmasons, and stonemasons

11.5% of all dishwashers

11.5% of all helpers of production workers

11% of all maids and housekeeping cleaners

11% of all graders and sorters of agricultural products

11% of all painters, construction, and maintenance

10.5% of all cement masons, concrete finishers, and terrazzo workers

10% of all computer hardware engineers

10% of all packaging and filing machine operators and tenders

10% of all packers and packagers by hand

10% of all cleaners of vehicles and equipment

10% of all carpet, floor, and tile installers and finishers

10% of all cooks

9.5% of all parking lot attendants

9% of all upholsterers

9% of all sewing machine operators

8.5% of all food preparation workers

7% of all laundry and dry-cleaning workers

2.5% of the U.S. total civilian labor force (with an occupation)

the part of the government to permit the presence of this shadow workforce in order to retain the economic benefits it generates.

In 1950, there were sixteen working adults in the United States for every retiree. That ratio dropped to just over three workers for every retired person in 2005. If the country stops or drastically decreases the amount of foreign labor permitted to enter, by the year 2050 the predicted worker-to-retiree ratio will be 1.3 to 1.[21] This presents a potential threat to the U.S. economy and suggests that in order to avoid a labor shortage, the United States could very well become more dependent on undocumented labor in the future than it is today.

THE ESCAPE VALVE

Just as the U.S. economy has an implicit dependency on the consistent access to undocumented and legal immigrant labor, Mexico's economy relies on the continued exodus of its people to the United States. The Mexican government has consistently been unable to meet the labor needs of its citizens, and in response hundreds of thousands are leaving each year. Migration has become the social norm for many communities and states throughout Mexico; around 500,000 Zacatecans, about half the Zacatecas population of 1.3 million, are either living in the U.S. or are in a back-and-forth migratory process at any given time. Thirty-one percent of the nation's municipalities are shrinking as a direct result of immigration.[22] Just as the U.S. economy has an implicit dependency on the consistent access to undocumented and legal immigrant labor, Mexico's economy relies on the continued exodus of its people to the United States. The Mexican government has consistently been unable to meet the labor needs of its citizens, and in response hundreds of thousands are leaving each year. Migration has become the social norm for many communities and states throughout

Unidentified immigrant.

Farmworkers in the U.S.

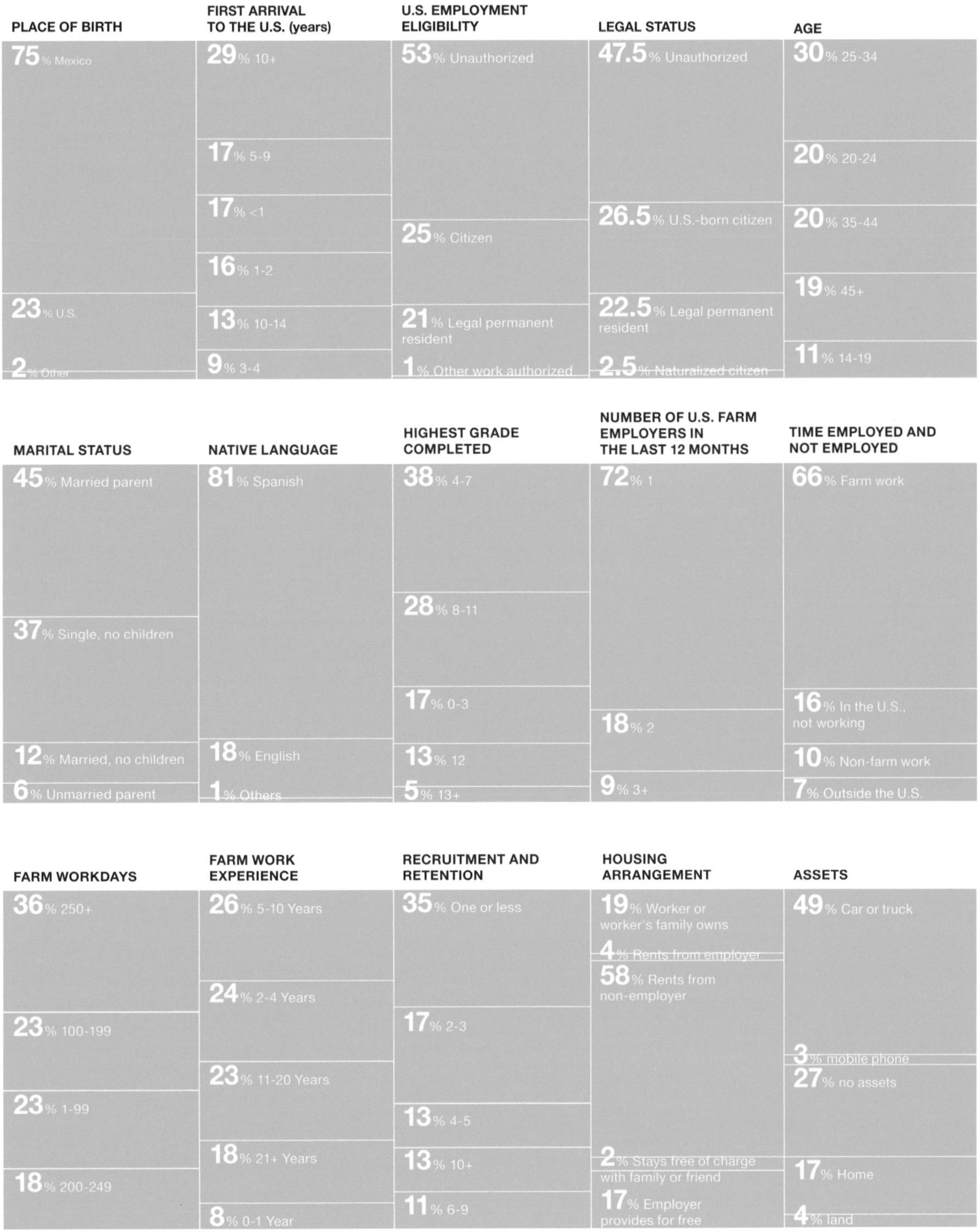

PLACE OF BIRTH

75% Mexico
23% U.S.
2% Other

FIRST ARRIVAL TO THE U.S. (years)

29% 10+
17% 5-9
17% <1
16% 1-2
13% 10-14
9% 3-4

U.S. EMPLOYMENT ELIGIBILITY

53% Unauthorized
25% Citizen
21% Legal permanent resident
1% Other work authorized

LEGAL STATUS

47.5% Unauthorized
26.5% U.S.-born citizen
22.5% Legal permanent resident
2.5% Naturalized citizen

AGE

30% 25-34
20% 20-24
20% 35-44
19% 45+
11% 14-19

MARITAL STATUS

45% Married parent
37% Single, no children
12% Married, no children
6% Unmarried parent

NATIVE LANGUAGE

81% Spanish
18% English
1% Others

HIGHEST GRADE COMPLETED

38% 4-7
28% 8-11
17% 0-3
13% 12
5% 13+

NUMBER OF U.S. FARM EMPLOYERS IN THE LAST 12 MONTHS

72% 1
18% 2
9% 3+

TIME EMPLOYED AND NOT EMPLOYED

66% Farm work
16% In the U.S., not working
10% Non-farm work
7% Outside the U.S.

FARM WORKDAYS

36% 250+
23% 100-199
23% 1-99
18% 200-249

FARM WORK EXPERIENCE

26% 5-10 Years
24% 2-4 Years
23% 11-20 Years
18% 21+ Years
8% 0-1 Year

RECRUITMENT AND RETENTION

35% One or less
17% 2-3
13% 4-5
13% 10+
11% 6-9

HOUSING ARRANGEMENT

19% Worker or worker's family owns
4% Rents from employer
58% Rents from non-employer
2% Stays free of charge with family or friend
17% Employer provides for free

ASSETS

49% Car or truck
3% mobile phone
27% no assets
17% Home
4% land

Mexico; around 500,000 Zacatecans, about half the Zacatecas population of 1.3 million, are either living in the U.S. or are in a back-and-forth migratory process at any given time. Thirty-one percent of the nation's municipalities are shrinking as a direct result of immigration.

REMITTANCES AND TRANSNATIONALISM

In 2005 migrants in the United States sent $52 billion in remittances to Latin America—a sum that exceeds what the region annually receives in foreign direct investment (FDI) and foreign aid combined.[23] Mexico was the world's leading recipient of remittances that year, and after a 25% increase from the previous year the nation gained over $20 billion, an amount that surpassed the country's revenues from tourism and equaled 71% of crude oil exports[24]—two of Mexico's largest business sectors. The fact that remittances rival these key contributors to Mexico's economy clearly carries with it significant implications.

Remittances are a critical aspect of many household incomes in Mexico; some states in the nation have become dependent on them, as families, communities, and customs have been reshaped by access to the external funds. According to the International Organization of Labor, remittances in some cases have led to weakened production in the countryside because people stop working when they find the money they receive from abroad is enough to support them.[25] Not only does this stifle Mexico's advancement in certain sectors (particularly in agriculture), but this relatively new development could prove to be precarious in the future: if remittances were to stop, what would become of the hundreds of thousands of Mexicans who depend on them?

Due to the nature of remittance exchange (typically sent by one individual to be received by another) this money is typically not utilized for the collective good of communities. Instead remittances are widely used to pay for basic needs such as food, clothing, and health care for the family members of the sender. However, hundreds of Hometown Associations (HTAs) have developed across the United States, drawing migrants together around their mutual interests.[26] These organizations and networks between migrant communities in the United States and their communities of origin in Mexico ensures a high level of communication across the border as well as a system of support in both the sending and receiving nations. Migrants have come to utilize HTAs as a means of organizing themselves and putting their economic clout to collective use, compiling resources and fundraising in the United States in order to develop public works projects in their hometowns in Mexico. Typically their efforts render between $20,000 and $100,000 for community elected projects that vary from soccer stadiums to new schools. The works have caught the eye of the Mexican government, prompting it to establish programs that match funds contributed by HTAs with as much as $3 for every $1 sent from abroad, thereby encouraging collective remittance spending.[27]

HTAs reflect an emerging movement of transnational civic action that is reshaping communities in both the U.S. and Mexico. They provide a space of comfort and support to migrants who face the challenge of living in a foreign country and adapting to their new environment. HTAs have also established heightened connectivity across the border, achieved through increased access to modern forms of communication like the internet, and the results of these exchanges can be seen throughout the Mexican countryside in the form of development and community organizing. The contributions made by migrants are not taken lightly by their hometown communities, as reflected in new legislation passed by several states (first in

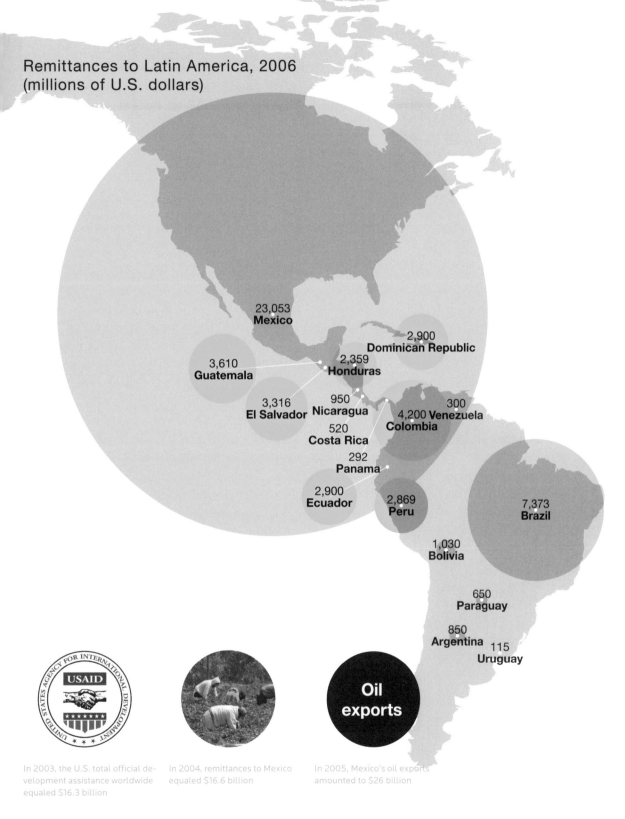

Remittances to Latin America, 2006 (millions of U.S. dollars)

23,053
Mexico

2,900
Dominican Republic

3,610
Guatemala

2,359
Honduras

3,316
El Salvador

950
Nicaragua

4,200
Colombia

300
Venezuela

520
Costa Rica

292
Panama

2,900
Ecuador

2,869
Peru

7,373
Brazil

1,030
Bolivia

650
Paraguay

850
Argentina

115
Uruguay

USAID
UNITED STATES AGENCY FOR INTERNATIONAL DEVELOPMENT

Oil exports

In 2003, the U.S. total official development assistance worldwide equaled $16.3 billion

In 2004, remittances to Mexico equaled $16.6 billion

In 2005, Mexico's oil exports amounted to $26 billion

In 2004, remittances to Mexico equaled $16.6 billion, in 2005 they reached $20 billion and in 2006 they rose higher, to $24 billion, becoming the second source of U.S. dollars after oil exports.

Zacatecas, and later in Michoacán) allowing people living outside of the country to serve in local and state governments.[28] The federal government, recognizing the benefactions made by migrants as well as the sheer number of them living abroad, also moved to open the 2006 Mexican elections to absentee ballots for the first time. Hometown Associations and binational organizing have essentially paved the way for a new age of transnational development and transnational political participation in Mexico and the United States.

THE HISPANIC/LATINO INFLUENCE IN THE UNITED STATES

Latinos are currently the largest minority group in the United States and, due to immigration and other trends, this community is expected to represent 25% of the U.S. population by the year 2050.[29] These demographic shifts are already influencing the society, economy, and political arena of the United States in unprecedented ways, and as Hispanics increase in numbers, their clout will continue to grow. The following segments reflect several examples of the ways in which Latinos—nearly 65% of whom are of Mexican descent[30]—are reshaping U.S. social, political, and economic processes. [Although the terms Latino and Hispanic do not have the same definition (see glossary), they will be used interchangeably in this section of the book as preference of term varies between different groups and individuals.]

MAY 1, 2006, A DAY WITHOUT AN IMMIGRANT

On May 1, 2006, in response to the mounting debate surrounding immigration reform in the U.S. House of Representatives, the Senate, and the general public, immigrants' rights activists around the country organized a grassroots, nationwide protest. The date was set to coincide with May Day, the international labor movement holiday, in order to honor immigrants' contributions to U.S. society and to prove the extent to which they influence the economy. It was widely referred to as a "Day Without an Immigrant" (a reference to the satirical film, *A Day Without a Mexican*) and in some circles was dubbed the Great American Boycott. May Day 2006 followed several prior protests, some among the largest in U.S. history, sparked in response to the Sensenbrenner Bill passed by the House of Representatives in December 2005 (see page 74–75). A coalition of organizers formed in Los Angeles, where months of protests preceded the May Day march. The coalition grew from the grassroots level and spread across the country via the internet and mass media catering to immigrants and Latinos in order to prompt protest participation at the national level. The movement called for immigrants to boycott work, school, buying, and selling in order to demonstrate their collective clout. San Jose, California, saw one of the biggest demonstrations in the city's history,[31] and Chicago and Los Angeles were hosts to May Day's largest marches, with police estimates of 400,000 and 500,000 protestors in their respective cities.[32] These estimates exceeded the number of protesters at the marches on Washington, D.C., for civil rights in 1963 and the

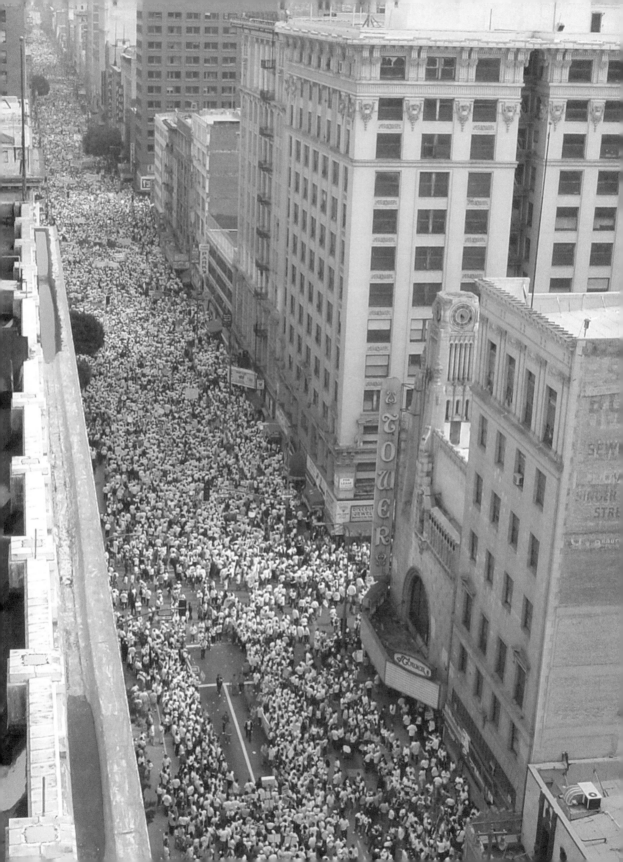

major opposition protests to the Vietnam War in the late 1960s.[33] Academics point out that if labeled as *workers* instead of *migrants*, the 2006 marches could be viewed as the United States' largest mobilization of workers in history.[34] Protesters called for amnesty for undocumented workers living in the United States, family reunification, and rallied against the criminalization of immigrants, border fences, increased enforcement along the border, and racism.

Although it was generally agreed that the U.S. economy did not receive a significant blow from the activity, several sectors—the meatpacking industry in particular—were affected. Tyson Foods and Cargill Meat Solutions closed many of their meatpacking plants due to a shortage of workers and the immigration rallies. Many restaurants, farms, factories, and markets were also shut down due to the May Day protests.[35] Goya Foods, the largest Hispanic-owned food chain in the U.S., abstained from almost all distribution for the day as an expression of solidarity with the movement and with Latinos, who are the company's primary patrons.

According to Dr. Jorge Santibáñez, Director of Tijuana's Colegio de la Frontera del Norte (COLEF), a leading research institute on border issues, the most significant impact the protests will likely have will be on Latino voter turnout.[36] In the months prior to the protest, many church and community groups sponsoring citizenship classes across the United States reported a marked increase in enrollment of students interested in learning more about becoming a U.S. citizen.[37] When considering this, it is important to realize that immigration reform will have a ripple effect on the Latino community given that within any family, legal status of family members could range from U.S. citizens to Legal Permanent Residents to undocumented immigrants, and this issue will likely provoke more political participation and

an elevated political consciousness. Santibáñez also notes that U.S. migrants' self-perceptions are changing drastically as a direct result of the political mobilization. There is a stronger sense of pride and solidarity—conditions that will likely influence the group's future actions and political involvement, which would effectively change the political arena of the United States as Latinos wield their collective power and prove their force to politicians and U.S. society.

THE HISPANIC MARKET

Recent decades have seen the emergence of a U.S. "Hispanic market" as a viable advertising demographic. Although a community of Latin American origin has existed in the United States for centuries, the concept of Hispanic marketing did not take hold until the 1980s, when the U.S. census confirmed that the Hispanic population was large and proved a mighty purchasing power.[38] Currently the Latino community in the United States is growing at a rate almost five times that of the general population, a demographic explosion that is further increasing the group's economic clout. In 2004, Hispanics in the United States earned about $686 billion,[39] some $10 billion more than the gross domestic product (GDP) of Mexico.[40] By 2009, it is estimated that Hispanics, as the largest minority group in the country, will have a buying power of between $992 billion and $1 trillion.[41]

As consumers, Latinos are understood to have specific tendencies and characteristics, which accordingly influence how they are marketed to. Hispanics in the United States are inclined to spend nearly 25% more than other groups on food products consumed at home, a characteristic that is related to the relatively large size of the average household and a tendency toward maintaining family values through shared meals.[42] The group has become an extremely important target for food

Americans spend a billion dollars a year on tortilla chips, and salsa now sells more at supermarkets than ketchup.

and beverage industries, because cultural customs and cuisine are likely to encourage Hispanics to spend more money on fresh produce, meats, dairy products, and other ingredients allowing for recipes that often require cooking from scratch.[43]

Another important market trend among Latinos is their internet use. According to a 2004 *Newsweek* report, Hispanics in the United States spend more time online per week than any other U.S. group and are also more likely to shop via the internet.[44] The Travel Industry Association of America also reported in 2004 that Hispanics were an important target market. The group increased travel by 20% between 2000 and 2002, whereas the general population's rate rose by just 2% during the same period.[45] This new trend is attributed to several factors, which include but are not limited to the group's swelling population; an upsurge of interest in traveling to or visiting countries of origin; immigrant communities and family members spreading out more within the United States; and an overall increase in economic clout among Latinos in the country.

Marketing strategies for Hispanics are generally geared toward the distinctions in culture, language, and traditions, but this is complicated by the heterogeneous nature of this sector of society. Because Latinos are so diverse—due to varying nationalities, cultural backgrounds, histories, language preferences, race, and so on—how to reach the greater Hispanic population is decidedly one of the market's most challenging issues. In order to meet the challenge, Hispanic advertising agencies are showing up everywhere: in 2001 there were more than eighty companies oriented toward Latino populations in cities across the United States.[46] The boom in Hispanic advertising has also led to the enhanced incorporation of Hispanic people in positions of authority and as sources of information within the industry—an important step in the advancement and social mobility of the minority group.

People of Mexican origin represent approximately 60% of Latinos, a circumstance that has categorically led to a larger presence of Mexican images and cultural references in Hispanic-oriented marketing.[47] It has also sparked a desire among Mexican enterprises to tap into the U.S. Hispanic market because as consumers Mexicans are characterized as being the most interested in preserving tradition and are therefore more likely to demand products from their country of origin.[48]

The affirmation of Latinos as a "market" is an important indicator that the community is gaining ground within the greater U.S. society. According to Arlene Davila, author of Latinos Inc., by recasting individuals as consumers and populations as markets—as in the case of Hispanics in the United States—a cultural recognition transpires, which resonates in the general population and alters the way the group is viewed and understood as part of society.[49] In sum, marketing to specific subgroups within a society effectively legitimizes their presence and creates space for them in the public mentality. What's more, Latinos, as the United States' largest minority group, generate a great deal of economic activity, and the U.S. economy benefits immensely from their participation as consumers.

The Growing Hispanic Influence in U.S. Markets

Business and Economy

1. From 1999 to 2004, Hispanic-owned businesses in the United States grew by 30% while other U.S. businesses grew by just 7% during the same period of time.
2. Jeff Bezos, CEO Amazon.com.
3. Marlene Coulis, vice-president of Brand Management, Anheuser-Busch
4. Mimi Valdés, Editor in Chief, *VIBE* magazine
5. Nina Tassler, President, CBS Entertainment
6. Ralph de la Vega, CEO Cingular
7. Ray Rodriguez, President of Univision
8. Emilio Azcárraga Jean, CEO, Grupo Televisa, Mexico's leading media company, provider of much of Univision's TV content.
9. Ralph Alvarez, President, McDonald's North America
10. Eduardo Castro-Wright, CEO of Wal-Mart Stores USA
11. Alvaro de Molina, chief financial officer of Bank of America Corporation
12. George Feldenkreis, chairman and CEO, Perry Ellis International
13. Antonio M. Perez, president and CEO, Eastman Kodak.
14. Remittances from the U.S. to Mexico increased by more than 300% between 2000 and 2005, jumping from $6.5 billion to over $20 billion in just five years.
15. In the United States, tortilla sales increased by almost 120% between 2001 and 2004, while white bread sales went down by 12%.
16. Wal-Mart in Mexico. Wal-Mart is the largest private employer in both Mexico and the United States; Mexico is home to more Wal-Mart locations than any other country in the world.
17. In five Mexican states, remittances exceed or match the local state incomes. In Michoacán, money sent from abroad represents 182% of the state's income.
18. The fast food market in Mexico—heavily dominated by McDonald's and Burger King—was valued at $10 billion in 2003.
19. According to The Economist's Big Mac index, a Big Mac in the U.S costs $3.15 while in Mexico it costs $2.66. The index is based on the theory of purchasing-power-parity, under which exchange rates should adjust to equalize the cost of a basket of goods and services, wherever it is around the world. The difference in Big Mac prices between the two countries suggests that the peso is undervalued by about 15.5%.
20. More Coca-Cola products are consumed in Mexico than in any other county.
21. The #1 imported beer in the U.S. is Corona.
22. Starting in 2006, the U.S. imports Mexican tequila by the bulk.
23. Most TVs in the U.S. are manufactured in Mexico along the border.
24. Foreign Direct Investment dropped significantly—by nearly half in Mexico and almost two-thirds in the U.S.—between 2001 and 2002, a reflection of investors' diminished confidence in the post-9/11 era.
25. In June, 2006, the U.S. Federal Reserve Bank announced an increase of interest rates of up to 50 points to 5.25% by the end of the month. This announcement made the Mexican market (Bolsa Mexicana de Valores, BMV) drop 2%, its highest drop in 5 months. Other markets around the world echoed in response. The Nikkei dropped 4.1%, Paris 2.24%, Colombia 8%, and Russia 9.4%.
26. The U.S. contributes more Foreign Direct Investment (FDI) in Mexico than any other nation.
27. In 2005, about 400,000 Mexicans crossed illegally into the United States. Ninety percent of these migrants had jobs in Mexico, but were still inclined to leave the country due to higher wages in the U.S.
28. Andrés Bermudez invented a tomato-planting machine that earned him the nickname "El Rey del Tomate." He went from field hand in California's Central Valley to millionaire and uses his money to help Mexican migrants, especially those from Zacatecas. He has dual American and Mexican citizenship.

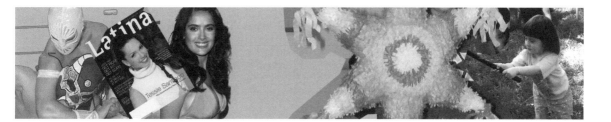

Culture and Media

29. Ricardo R. Fernández, chair of the American Council on Education
30. Sandra Cisneros, writer
31. Magazines geared toward a Latino population can be found across the United States, such as *Hispanic*, *Latina*, *HispanicBusiness*, etc.
32. Roberto Suro. president of the Pew Hispanic Center.
33. Thalía: Mexican singer, actress, record producer, composer and businesswoman. In 2003 she released her first English language album. Her clothing line, the Thalía Sodi Collection, is sold in the U.S. department store chain Kmart.
34. Wilmer Valderrama: Venezuelan American actor most famous for the role of "Fez" in the sitcom That '70s Show.
35. Salma Hayek: Born in Mexico, Hayek is the most successful Latin American actress in Hollywood since Carmen Miranda.
36. Andy Garcia, Academy Award-nominated American actor.
37. Mexican influenced cuisine in the United States can be found everywhere.
38. Salsa now sells more than ketchup in U.S. supermarkets.
39. Wrestling matches in the U.S. and "Luchas Libres" in Mexico have heavily influenced one another over the years. Mexican wrestlers have taken on the American way of inventing personalities and American wrestlers have begun to wear masks.
40. *¡Mucha Lucha!* is an animated television series that premiered on Kids WB in the United States and eventually became a phenomenon in Mexico as well.
41. *Rebelde* is a Mexican series produced by Televisa. The actors are also in a real band, written RBD to distinguish it from the series. The show and group have reached heights of great success in the U.S. and in Mexico. Their 2006 CD "Live in Hollywood" reached #3 in Mexico and was certified platinum in the United States.
42. Eva Longoria: Golden Globe Award-nominated actress best known for her role as Gabrielle on the ABC hit television series "Desperate Housewives"
43. The Mexican tradition of breaking piñatas at celebrations is now also a tradition at children's birthday parties in the United States.
44. *La Madrastra*, a 2005 Mexican telenovela. Aside from its popularity in Mexico, the soap opera was a phenomenon in cities such as Los Angeles and New York.
45. Los Tigres del Norte: All band members were born in Mexico and now live in California. The band is well-known for writing and performing "corridos," songs about the experience of migrating from Mexico to the United States.
46. *Dora the Exploradora*
47. In 2003, Hispanics' Internet-spending reached $8.1 billion.
48. In 2004 Latin American-born workers in the United States earned $450 billion, 93% of which was spent in the United States.
49. Freddy Rodriguez, actor
50. Alfonso Cuaron, movie director
51. Frankie Muniz, actor
52. Gael Garcia Bernal, actor
53. Edward J. Olmos, Academy Award-nominated Mexican-American actor
54. Shakira, singer
55. Alejandro González Iñárritu, movie director
56. Robert Rodriguez, film director
57. Carlos Santana. Mexican Grammy award-winning Latin-rock musician and guitarist.
58. Of Mexican descent, Jaime Luis "Taboo" Gómez is a musician who joined the Black Eyed Peas in 1995.
59. Oscar de la Hoya, boxer
60. Lorena Ochoa, LGPA best golf player of 2006.
61. In 2004, the Hispanic population in the U.S. was estimated to be 41.3 million, 31 million of which (or about 75%) spoke Spanish in the home. This number represents about 1 in every 10 U.S. residents.

Politics and military

62. There are 622,000 military veterans who are Mexican-Americans in the U.S. There are 1.1 million Latino veterans in total and in 2003, 53,000 people of Hispanic origin were actively serving in the armed forces.
63. In 2004, 7.6 million Hispanic citizens voted in the elections, up from 5.9 million in 2000.

The Increasing Political Influence of Hispanics in the U.S.

1. Alberto R. Gonzáles, U.S. Attorney General. Son of Mexican migrants, a personal friend of president George W. Bush since he was governor of Texas. On February 3rd, 2005, he became the first Attorney General of the United States, the first Hispanic to occupy that position.
2. César Chávez, Mexican American activist (1927–1993) who defended farm worker rights. He was the founder of the United Farm Workers. His birthday on March 31st is celebrated in Texas, Arizona, and Colorado. It is the only holiday dedicated to a Mexican American.
3. U.S. Congressman Silvestre Reyes. A Vietnam War veteran, he is the only Congressman to have served in the U.S. Border Patrol. In 1996, he was elected a Democrat to the U.S. House of Representatives.
4. Senator Richard Alarcón, member of the California State Senate.
5. Antonio Villaraigosa, Los Angeles mayor.
6. Ernesto Zedillo, former president of Mexico became the director of Yale University's Center for the Study of Globalization in 2002.
7. Carlos Gutiérrez. Born in Cuba, he became the president of Kellogg's in 1999. In 2004, president George W. Bush assigned him the position of U.S. Secretary of Commerce.
8. Rosario Marín. 41st. Treasurer of the United States. She was born in Mexico City; the first foreign-born to serve as Treasurer of the United States. Her signature was used in U.S. dollar bills.
9. Roger Noriega. He is the grandson of Mexican migrants and was part of the White House staff in the 80s. He was the U.S. ambassador to the Organization of American States. On March 24, 2003, he was assigned by George W. Bush as United States Assistant Secretary of State for Western Hemisphere Affairs.

10. Mel Martinez, born in Cuba. In 2000, he became the Secretary of Housing and Urban Development and is currently a U.S. Senator for the state of Florida.
11. Bill Richardson. Born of Mexican and Nicaraguan parents. He is the first Hispanic to run for president during the 2008 presidential elections. In 1997, during the Clinton administration he was the U.S. ambassador to the United Nations. In 1998, he became the Secretary of Energy. He is currently the governor of New Mexico.
12. David Aguilar, the highest ranking Border Patrol officer.
13. Robert Menendez, Democratic Senator from New Jersey.
14. Hilda Solis, Democratic member of the U.S. House of Representatives, representing the 32nd district of California.
15. Federico F. Peña. Son of Mexican parents, he was the first Hispanic mayor of Denver, Colorado. In 1993, he was the Secretary of Transportation and later Secretary of Energy during the Clinton presidency.
16. Henry Cisneros. Son of Mexican parents, he was the first Hispanic mayor in a major U.S. city. As mayor of San Antonio, Texas, he was reelected three consecutive times. He was the secretary of the U.S. Department of Housing and Urban Development during the Clinton administration.
17. Lauro F. Cavazos. He is the son of Mexican parents and the first Hispanic to serve in the United States Cabinet, where he served during the Reagan administration. He was named Secretary of Education in 1988.
18. Manuel Lujan Jr. Son of Mexican parents. He served as the United States Secretary of the Interior from 1989 to 1993. He was a Republican Congressman from 1969 to 1989.

OIL

Mexico is still a world leader in oil production. The country is home to Cantarell, the world's second-largest oil field,[50] and after Canada Mexico is the most important source of petroleum for the United States, the globe's biggest oil consumer and importer.[51]

In 1938 the Mexican government nationalized its oil reserves by expropriating sixteen foreign-owned petroleum companies and establishing Petróleos Mexicanos (Pemex), a state-owned company, in their place. Today Pemex's revenues (which reached $55.9 billion in 2004) provide the Mexican government with one-third of its budget, making the company one of the single most important pillars of the nation's economy.[52] If oil prices were to drop, or if the country fails to discover more oil supplies—which is a challenge, as the constitution bars Pemex from inviting foreign investors and oil companies to participate in oil exploration and production—the finances of Pemex (and thus Mexico) would be in danger. Problems in Mexico's oil sector could also have a ripple effect on the United States, who would be forced to shift their oil dependence even more on the volatile Middle Eastern and African oil-producing nations.

Unfortunately, recent events indicate that Mexico's peak oil production may have already passed, as the Cantarell oil field—which supplies 60% of Mexico's annual crude oil production—is in decline after the field peaked at 2.13 million barrels per day (mb/d) in 2004.[53] To further compound the problem, at present Pemex has little hope of replacing Cantarell, as the company lacks the capital to explore more regions in search of new fields. Although exporting crude oil in mass quantities is an indisputably lucrative business—especially when market prices are high—Pemex is in debt, largely because the state absorbs most of its revenues, leaving the company unable to invest in the diversification of its capacities and forcing it to remain oriented toward little more than crude-oil exports. In 2004 Pemex had or shared control of just seven refineries between Mexico and Texas, whereas other major oil companies such as Exxon-Mobil and Shell were running forty-two and fifty-five, respectively, all around the world.[54] This means that Pemex must export huge quantities of its crude oil (42% in 2004)[55] to be refined in the U.S., only to import it back to Mexico in the form of gasoline, natural gas, and petrochemicals. In 2005 Mexico exported $28 billion of crude oil (80% of which went to the United States), yet it imported half of that amount in refined oil products, leaving the petroleum-producing nation's energy balance at $15.6 billion.[56] Thus Pemex—and consequently Mexico—not only relies on the United States to purchase its petroleum exports, which float government spending, it also depends on U.S. refining capacities for its own access to finished energy products.

TOURISM

The United States shares a reciprocal tourism dependency with Mexico. The two countries are the third and eighth tourism destinations in the world, respectively[57]—and Mexico is the country most visited by Americans, while the U.S. is the primary destination for Mexican tourists.[58] Mexico's tourism industry is vital to the country's economy and employment. In 2005 this sector represented 8% of the GDP, was the direct provider of 1.87 million jobs, and was the target of more than $2.7 billion in private investment.[59]

As Mexico's single most important source of tourists, the U.S. essentially drives the tourism economy. Between 2000 and 2004, nearly 46.5 million Americans (88.5% of foreign tourists visiting Mexico) went south of the border, primarily for the purpose of pleasure (60%) or family visits (30%). Texas and California—the two U.S. states with the

By 2050, racial and ethnic minorities in the U.S. will outnumber non-Hispanic Whites, one out of every four will be Hispanic.

largest Mexican and Mexican-American populations—send more residents to Mexico than any other states, with 29% and 15% of tourists, respectively.[60] Similarly, of all U.S. states, half of Mexican visitors arriving by plane visit the border states of California and Texas.[61]

Canada and Mexico are the two largest sources of tourist visits to the U.S. each year[62]—yet most Mexican tourists don't go beyond the U.S. border region. In 2003, of the 10.5 million arrivals from Mexico, only 3.7 million were to the interior of the United States, beyond the 40km border region.[63] That same year, out of the 18.6 million international visitors to Mexico, 8.3 million remained in the border region.[64] Although half of tourists in Mexico are border tourists, most of their money is spent in Mexico's interior. Of the $9 billion spent by international tourists in Mexico in 2005, only $640 million was spent in the border zone.[65] Due to these circumstances, Mexico has heavily invested in its interior tourism development, with particular emphasis on beach destinations that appeal to American tourists with resorts serving American-style food served by English-speaking staff. Of the total investments made in 2005, just over 69% were directed toward beach destinations, while nearly 19% went to tourism development on the Mexican side of the U.S.–Mexico border.[66]

Most of the visits between the two countries, however, are daytrips north and south of the border via land transportation. Nine out of every ten visitors from Mexico to the United States return to their homes the same day, and about four in every five U.S. visitors to Mexico travel just for the day.[67] These daytrips bring about $2 billion every year to the Mexican frontier economy, while the U.S. side of the border receives about $4 billion from Mexican visitors, again highlighting the interdependence between sister cities along the hyperborder.[68] Although the population size on either side of the divide is roughly the same,[69] northbound trips are more frequent as security issues prevent American visitors from entering Mexico. On various occasions throughout his term as U.S. ambassador to Mexico, Tony Garza declared the border zone as being in a state of emergency. In September of 2006 he warned Americans planning visits to Mexico to stick to well-known tourist areas, claiming that 1,500 Mexicans had been murdered in the country due to drug-related violence that year.[70] Although both federal governments encourage U.S. visitors to stick to sun-and-sand tourist destinations, daytrips across the frontier are irresistible, especially for borderlanders.

Pharmacies on the Mexican side of the border provide lower priced drugs than their U.S. counterparts.

DENTAL OFFICE
DDS. DRA.
MINERVA NAVARRO NOGAMI
VISTA OPT
OPEN
DENTIST
DENTIST
DRA.
MINERVA

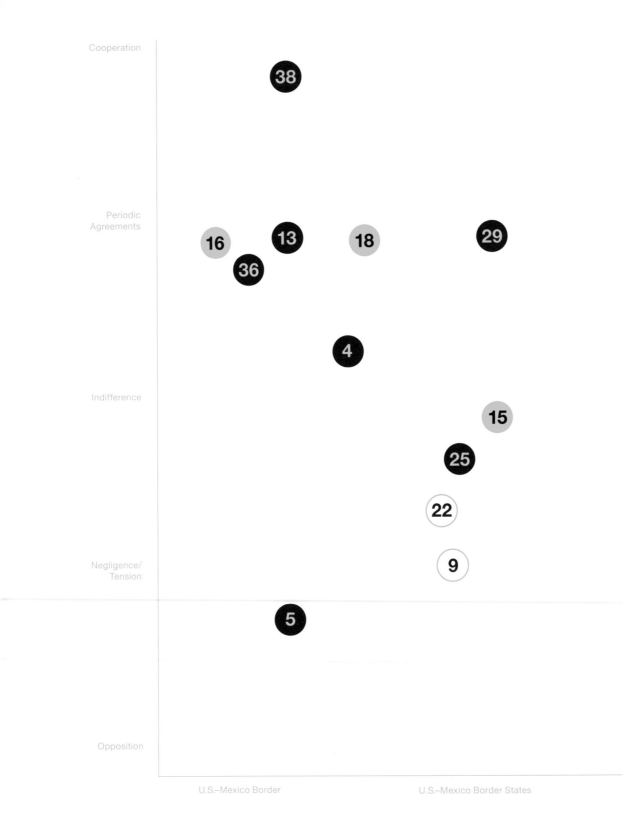

Cooperation

Periodic
Agreements

Indifference

Negligence/
Tension

Opposition

U.S.–Mexico Border

U.S.–Mexico Border States

FUTURE SCENARIOS

● PRESENT–2020
● 2021–2035
○ 2036–

5. SECURITY

The post-9/11 climate created the largest security reorganization in U.S. history with the establishment of the Department of Homeland Security. Its reach embraces policies related to migration, terrorism, the environment, and trade, both at home and abroad. Everything entering the country is now subject to inspection, interrogation, and regulation.

THE BORDERING NATIONS' DIFFERENT APPROACHES TO THE MEANING OF NATIONAL SECURITY

During the 1990s the binational security topic for the United States and Mexico revolved around narcotrafficking. But in the aftermath of September 11, 2001, security has leapt to the forefront of U.S.–Mexico relations. Today, the U.S.'s primary focus is on external threats, specifically terrorism, while Mexico's most pressing concern is domestic security against threats stemming from organized crime, gangs, and street violence.

Mexico's interest in the fight against terrorism is relatively minimal, except in regard to proximity with its northern neighbor, while the United States has little interest in Mexico's domestic insecurity, with the exceptions of the drug trade and violence in border cities. Yet the infrastructure for programs and plans needed to fight threats in one country are essentially the same that are needed for the other. The two nations share grave concerns with narcotrafficking and violence in the border region, and would do well to cooperate and synchronize their security programs to effectively solve their binational problems.

Despite the differences in their approaches to national security, in recent years both countries have implemented important internal security reforms. In 2004, Mexico passed the Ley de la Seguridad Nacional (National Security Law), which created a new Consejo de Seguridad Nacional (National Security Council). This law regulates the funding of the agencies involved in the collection of information and the fight against crime. In the United States, Homeland Security (introduced in 2002) and the National Intelligence Office (implemented in 2005) seek to unify the flow of intelligence obtained by the multiple agencies involved in protecting the country and its borders against terrorism. The programs in both countries work toward establishing more efficient channels of processing and exchanging information and intelligence, underscoring similarities in each other's security agendas.

The United States' Approach to National Security

The United States' national security strategy is based on two basic ideas: first, that the nation will be more secure if there is democracy and prosperity everywhere in the world; and second, the assumption that the United States can successfully confront the new challenges of the globalized world if it works in cooperation with other countries.[1] The ideals behind these two tenets support the notion that binational cooperation between the U.S. and Mexico regarding security issues along the border are fundamental. However, the methodologies used by the U.S. government and the DHS suggest otherwise. Considering that the principal challenges cited for U.S. national security are pandemic diseases, proliferation of weapons of mass destruction, the international drug trade, human trafficking, natural disasters, and terrorism—all of which are global issues and thus have international implications—the DHS has done little to incorporate external actors in its endeavor to protect the United States. Instead it has opted to increase border control and national security forces as the optimal ways of curbing the entrance of dangerous materials and people into the country, rather than applying its own national security strategies that encourage international cooperation.

Mexico's Approach to National Security

On the other hand, Mexico's national security strategy is based on several principles: democracy, sovereignty, national unity promoting a plural community, the rule of law, development, social peace, and integrity of the national patrimony through the protection of natural resources and

"We will disrupt and destroy terrorist organizations by…defending the United States, the American people, and our interests at home and abroad by identifying and destroying the threat before it reaches our borders. While the United States will constantly strive to enlist the support of the international community, we will not hesitate to act alone, if necessary, to exercise our right of self-defense by acting preemptively against such terrorists, to prevent them from doing harm against our people and our country."[2]

—President Bush discussing the nation's national security strategy in 2003

territory.[3] Among these, the two most important principles are the preservation of the country's sovereignty and independence, and social peace that prioritizes the protection of the community from gangs and crime.

After 9/11, however, Mexico's national security agenda was adjusted. The new policy still includes the preservation of sovereignty and the maintenance of the nation's constitutional order, but new threats have been included. Of these, terrorist activities, weapons of mass destruction, and hindering intelligence actions stand out the most.[4]

In the years since the attacks of 9/11, the Mexican government has taken several actions to combat terrorism.[5] The Agencia Federal de Investigación (AFI, the Federal Investigation Agency) was established in November of 2001 to replace the Federal Judicial Police, and was modeled after the United States' FBI. AFI is operated by ex-members of Mexico's Interpol and maintains contact with over 177 countries in order to exchange intelligence information. The government also created an elite anti-terrorist group, which answers to the Procuraduría General de la República (PGR, the Mexican Federal Prosecutor's Office) and works with the FBI. In compliance with the United States, Mexico has developed a list of more than sixty countries from which citizens will need special permission to visit the country. They are all countries that require visas to enter the United States, and among them are: Cuba, Colombia, Congo, North Korea, China, Russia, Mongolia, Taiwan, Afghanistan, Azerbaijan, Bosnia, India, Macedonia, Pakistan, Sri Lanka, Turkmenistan, Uzbekistan, and Turkey.

In order to advance Mexico's U.S.-influenced national security efforts, the country also established strategic zones of vigilance located throughout the country. These zones consist of airports, seaports, major highways, electric plants, petroleum ducts, chemical complexes, communication headquarters, refineries, and government buildings, among others.[6] Several regions within the country are also considered strategic zones, with extensive national guards stationed throughout the areas. They are located in the Yucatán Canal, the Gulf of Mexico at the Sonda of Campeche, Istmo, and the Gulf of Tehuantepec, as well as along the U.S. and Guatemalan borders.

U.S. National Security Programs

As part of the U.S. national security agenda, new screening programs have been implemented for travelers, visitors, students, and immigrants entering the country while others focus on identifying and deterring all potential threats arriving at U.S. borders.[8]

Traveling Data for the Twenty-first Century

This program requires an electronic passport equipped with a chip containing biometric and biographical data of the person entering the United States. It also promotes study abroad and exchange for foreigners in American universities through the adjustment of policies and time parameters related to issuing student visas. Whereas today a student visa is granted no sooner than ninety days before school starts, and students are not allowed to enter the country until thirty days before classes begin, the new adjustments would allow for student visas to be issued 120 days before the school year and will permit students to enter 45 days in advance. These policy changes were introduced at the end 2006.

Terror Strikes Again: State of General Emergency in Maricopa County, Arizona

Yesterday, on the tenth anniversary of 9/11, terrorists infiltrated the nuclear power generating station in Palo Verde, Arizona, and released radioactive material that can travel to an area of about fifty miles in radius. Immediate evacuations were ordered in the county, the fourth most populous in the nation. Two coyotes have been detained for aiding seventeen terrorists across the U.S.–Mexico border illegally. They claim that the perpetrators looked and spoke like Mexicans. The Mexican government has begun investigations into a sleeper cell that could have been planning the attack for the last decade while in Mexican territory.[7]

Surveillance cameras capture terrorists as they prepare to jump over the U.S.–Mexico border fence.

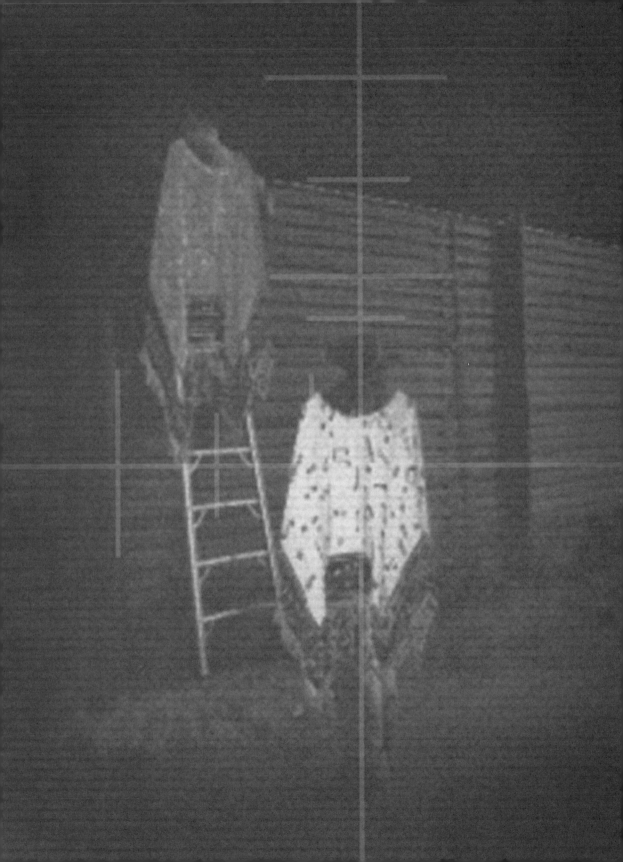

US-VISIT

This program aims to improve intelligence cooperation with allied countries in order to avoid possible terrorist attacks. Its entry-exit system uses biometric technology to identify visitors from the moment they apply for a visa at a U.S. embassy to the time they leave the country. It uses intelligence systems to distinguish real and legitimate threats from low-risk activities. See pages 76 and 80.

Secure Border Initiative

This DHS program has two goals: to secure the northern and southern borders and increase immigration enforcement efforts in the country's interior by 2010. The former effort calls for doubling border security agents to over 18,000

by 2008 and increasing technology through a virtual fence system known as SBInet, consisting of more sensors, cameras, infrastructure, and communications technology. The latter streamlines and shortens the detention-and-removal processing of illegal migrants. All of this is done through a "system of systems" approach that promotes collaboration between different DHS agencies, so they better understand each agency's role in the border enforcement process and can make more informed decisions without depending on a command-and-control layered system.[9]

A Brazilian passenger is screened at the airport in Atlanta, Georgia using the US-VISIT biometric system, a typical procedure in U.S. airports since 2004.

MEXICO'S NATIONAL SECURITY PROGRAMS

Several cooperation agreements have been signed pertaining to border protection, some on the part of Mexico while others have been bilateral with the United States.[10] Among the former are:

Operation Secure Mexico (JUNE 2005)

This measure aims to confront organized crime and guarantee the security of communities that have suffered violence from disputes between criminal organizations. It was first introduced in the cities of Tijuana and Mexicali in Baja California; Nuevo Laredo, Reynosa, and Matamoros in Tamaulipas; and Mazatlán, Culiacán, and Novolato in Sinaloa. It is comprised of a set of actions that combat large-scale operations involving drug dealing and smuggling, human trafficking, possession of illegal arms, and car theft.

Successes of Operation Secure Mexico between June and October 2005:

Criminal detentions	4,965
Arrest warrants	1,675
Weapons seized	485
Arms cartridges seized	20,053
Marijuana seized	30,638 pounds
Cocaine seized	287 pounds
Heroin seized	164 pounds
Psychotropic pills seized	299,252
Other illegal goods seized	102,978
Vehicles recovered	1,489
Money seized (U.S. dollars)	2,004,504

Operation Centinela (2006)

This national operation, directed by Mexico's army (SEDENA), is the equivalent of an orange terrorist alert in the U.S. It focuses on the detention of undocumented immigrants who are of restricted nationalities, the fight against organized crime and human trafficking groups, and the deterrence of potential terrorist threats in strategic entry points and infrastructure facilities. In Mexico, Operation Centinela has been implemented various times by the army and other security agencies in 124 embassies and consulates, fifty-nine airports, forty-three maritime ports, thirty-one entry points along the northern border and eighteen on the southern border, thirteen Pemex facilities, thirteen dams, and in twelve destinations for U.S. residents and tourists. For instance, when the 2005 London terrorist attacks occurred, 18,000 soldiers were sent to patrol various sectors of the country.[11]

BILATERAL NATIONAL SECURITY PROGRAMS

In order to secure both nations from new and old threats, the United States and Mexico have signed several bilateral agreements. Some of the main goals are the detention of undocumented migrants, criminals, and potential terrorists, as well as the establishment of a secure border infrastructure.

The Smart Border Agreement (MARCH 2002)

This agreement is a plan of action signed by Presidents Bush and Fox to build a "smart" border. It is composed of twenty-two points ranging from relief of border bottlenecks to pre-screening travelers to the electronic exchange of information between the two governments and their agencies. The different points aim to achieve the supreme goals of establishing secure infrastructure and secure flows of people and goods.

Operation Against Smugglers (and Traffickers) Initiative on Safety and Security (OASISS) (AUGUST 2005)

This is a standardized prosecution program between Mexico and the United States, which seeks to identify and prosecute human smugglers and save migrants from the risk of becoming involved with criminal organizations.

Security and Prosperity Partnership of North America, SPP (MARCH 2005)

President Fox, President Bush, and Prime Minister Martin launched this agreement in March of 2005, with the aim of enhancing security while also promoting the economic and social development of the region. SPP seeks to implement a border facilitation strategy that builds capacity, improves the legitimate flow of cargo at the shared borders, and maintains a common response to threats. It also works to strengthen North American protection by inspecting subjects both before they exit their foreign port and at their first port of entry on the continent.[12]

Action Plan to Combat Border Violence and Improve Public Safety (MARCH 2006)

The objective of this plan is to better coordinate efforts against criminal organizations and to facilitate solutions to border crime. It was developed in response to cross-border issues at the local level and currently operates in each of the sister cities.[13] The agencies involved will work under the framework of the Border Liaison Mechanisms (BLM) between U.S. authorities and Mexican consulates located in border cities.

SECURITY IN THE GLOBAL ARENA

The concept of cooperation between countries for strengthened national security is not new. An international balance of power was a dominant topic during the nineteenth century, and the twentieth century witnessed the establishment of collective security and unified international organizations like the League of Nations, the United Nations, and NATO. After the Cold War, however, as globalization and increased access to communication greatly enhanced interdependency and information exchange between people, communities, and nations around the world, terrorism became a more dominant subject of international headlines. Threats to national security in one country can easily spread and destabilize an entire region—or potentially world peace. This reality has invigorated the efforts and agreements pertaining to international cooperation on security issues.

There are three principal types of agreements or treaties relating to international security: collective defense, collective security, and cooperative security. Collective defense is a treaty that guarantees assistance in the case of an external attack if a nation has membership status in one or more international defense organizations, such as NATO or the OAS. Collective security is an agreement made by the international community to resort to the use of force in order to come to the aid of a nation that is wrongfully under the attack of another. In the case of violations of international peace, this system allows for the use of force by the entire community against the offender. The UN is a good example of an organization that applies the use of collective security. Cooperative security applies multidimensional approaches to security. This approach does not limit admission to members, favors multilateralism, eschews military solutions, emphasizes trust more than dissuasion, maintains that states are the primary actors in the security system, and does not demand the creation of formal security institutions.

INCREASING SECURITY: WILL THE BORDERS BE "SEALED"?

The unregulated nature of the border with Mexico has been the focus of public unease in recent years, and as a response immigration reform in the U.S. has been primarily enforcement-based. In October of 2006, a few weeks before the mid-term elections, President Bush approved the Secure Fence Act, a bill that involves the construction of a seven-hundred-mile security fence along its border with

Today's North American borders = 13,264 km

If a joint border patrol was created, a single 1,212 km North American border with Guatemala and Belize would allow easier flows between Canada, the U.S., and Mexico.

2

JANUARY 15, 2008

Uneasy Collaboration between the U.S. and Mexico's Border Patrols

The Mexican Government is in talks with the U.S. Border Patrol regarding the establishment of a mutual fund to enforce security in the Mexico–Guatemala border. Given the joint patrolling of the U.S. and Mexico's Border Patrols in Mexican territory, top Mexican immigration officials claim that their nation lacks the financial resources to both teach English to its task force and to cover the deportation expenses of the rising number of immigrants from South America, the Middle East, and Southeast Asia trying to get into the U.S. through Mexico. The possibility of a joint border patrol fund has met resistance in the U.S., especially in the border region where members of civil defense corps argue that Mexican citizens should take vigilance matters in their own hands.[14]

"Good fences make good neighbors."
—Robert Frost

Mexico. Some critics claim not enough funds have been allocated to border security initiatives, both for building more fencing and for increasing the number of border patrol agents,[15] however, the goal of recent legislation changes (see page 73), including those of the Department of Homeland Security, is to ensure that everyone crossing U.S. borders is identified and that the rule of law is enforced whenever a border crossing is made. DHS and CBP are due to install a state-of-the-art border security system in the twenty-eight–mile Tucson sector in 2007; this system will later be implemented along the entire Canadian and Mexican borders as part of the Secure Border Initiative.[16] The fence is expected to be twelve feet tall and equipped with an anti-vehicle trench, surveillance cameras, night lighting, and buried motion detectors.[17] The sealing of the borders has been partly defined in legislation and reflects previous state initiatives such as Operation Hold the Line in the border city of El Paso (1993), Operation Gatekeeper in San Diego (1994), and Operation Safeguard in Nogales, Arizona (1994), all of which sealed local sectors of the border to illegal migrants. Similar initiatives are expected in coming years. The border will likely be sealed to products and people representing a security threat, but will remain open for the majority of legal visitors and trade.

Opposite: California governor, Arnold Schwarzenegger, is briefed by Lt. Col. Jay Brookman on the potential deployment of National Guard troops along the hyperborder. Two months later, in July, 2006, a National Guard battalion from Kentucky (below) gets deployed along the Arizona sector of the border as part of President Bush's Operation Jump Start.

Above: Since 2004, unmanned aerial vehicles along the hyperborder have contributed to over 3,000 arrests and the seizure of over 10,000 pounds of marijuana. The latest addition, the MQ-9 Predator B, started being used along the Arizona sector of the hyperborder in 2006.

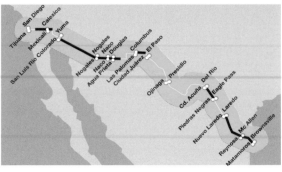

Left: Homeland Security Secretary Michael Chertoff takes border security into his own hands and welds a piece of fencing in Arizona as part of Operation Jump Start on Feb. 20, 2007. Between 2001 and 2006, funds for Border Security increased over 60%. Above: Members of the Utah National Guard build part of the extended fence in San Luis, Arizona. Diagram below shows the areas where fencing has been installed or proposed to be installed.

Ringleader of Nationwide Fake ID Network Detained in Las Vegas

A former employee of the Department of Homeland Security was arrested at Caesar's Palace yesterday for running a billion dollar fake ID operation. Federal agents seized computer equipment used for creating national ID cards containing forged biometric information. A decade ago one could purchase simple "identity kits"—a driver's license, green card, and social security card—for only $100, but since the United States sealed its borders undocumented residents are willing to pay up to $5,000 for the mandatory national ID cards implemented by the DHS last year and hailed as a breakthrough in surveillance technology.

MORALES, OSCAR
MEXICAN
STATUS: EXPIRED VISA

A12714GP96LAM-087Z

NOVEMBER 5, 2016

Study Assesses The Effect of the 700-mile Fence Along The U.S.– Mexico Border

Since the nation sealed its borders four years ago, following the second largest terrorist attack on U.S. soil in history, both legal and illegal immigration has decreased dramatically. A decade ago, 157,992 Mexicans were allowed to enter the United States on immigration visas, but that number has dropped to a meager 1,000, largely limited to diplomats, individuals with skills deemed exceptional, and Mexico's top students. Also in 2006, on average 14,000 illegal crossings were halted each day along Arizona's border with Mexico; thus far in 2016, less than one hundred such arrests have been made along the entire U.S.–Mexico border—thanks in large part to the President's decision to position the National Guard as a military presence. Guardsmen staff surveillance posts along every five hundred yards of the border, and survey the area with cameras, radar, and ground censors as well as unmanned aircraft.

In addition to severely hampering immigration flows to the U.S., sealing the borders has also had a significant impact on the tourism industry, as the U.S.'s steps against immigration have been seen by many in the international community as isolationist at best, and xenophobic and racist at worst. Many international tourists have been discouraged from visiting the country, and consequently the tourism industry reported this week that it risks bankruptcy within the next decade if the current immigration policies continue.

An undercover U.S. police officer, with equipment to identify the legal status of pedestrians, detects an illegal visitor from Mexico based on the status of his radio frequency I.D. His scanner, disguised as a digital camera, provides background information on pedestrians' criminal and migratory records. Since 2012, police have arrested 5,000 illegal aliens whose U.S. visas have expired.

Military and police officers from Mexico and FBI agents search for mass graves at a ranch near Ciudad Juarez on December 4, 1999. Nearly 400 murders have been documented since 1993, a high portion of whom have been women, often referring to this case as femicide. There is still no resolution to this criminal investigation due to corruption in the judicial and law enforcement agencies, coupled with the violence related to drug cartels in the area.

6. NARCOTRAFFIC AND CORRUPTION

The drug trade between the U.S. and Mexico—and its rippling effects on society—is made possible by corruption that infiltrates multiple levels of authority. Addressing these issues will require moving away from the criminalization and militarization of drug traffic and toward new policies related to drug rehabilitation and increasing transparency in government and corporate operations.

Mexico has the world's highest incidence of kidnappings. In 2004 there were an estimated 3,000 kidnappings, many of which had alleged police involvement.[1]

CORRUPTION RUNS RAMPANT IN THE ORGANIZATIONS LEADING THE WAR ON DRUGS

In Mexico, drug traffickers have enjoyed pervasive levels of corruption in the police force as well as in the agencies charged with fighting the drug trade. This is not a recent problem. In 1996, the commanding officer of Mexico's national police force was arrested with $2.4 million in his car, and was later convicted for accepting $20 million to protect a major drug kingpin. Also in the mid-1990s the Mexican Army General José de Jesús Gutiérrez Rebollo was named the country's drug czar—the leading authority in national counter-drug operations—yet within months he was imprisoned for accepting bribes from the traffickers against whom he was fighting. Such corruption has not tempered in the new century: in October 2004, six hundred soldiers of the 65th infantry battalion were investigated for having connections with the Sinaloa Drug Cartel.

Mexican law places the police and military under state control, with 400,000 police officers employed nationwide, plus 5,000 personnel supplied by the military for the Federal Preventive Police (PFP) for counter-narcotics activities. Despite advances made toward eradicating corruption and impunity within the government, reports of human rights abuses and police involvement in kidnappings and extortion abound. The intertwined relations between narcotraffic and corruption shape a circular feedback system, as corrupt law enforcement agencies protecting drug dealers incite a dysfunctional justice system, allowing drug cartels' influence to grow, perpetuating corrupt judicial practices and keeping law enforcement at bay.

Corruption related to drug traffic is not only present in Mexican agencies; it has infiltrated institutions in the United States as well. In August and September of 2005 the FBI, the U.S. Internal Security Department, and the Attorney General's office arrested four Border Patrol agents who allowed the entrance of large quantities of cocaine and 750 undocumented immigrants into the United States. Responding to the incident, Manuel Mora, the FBI chief at the U.S.–Mexico border, has said that the American security corps has become menaced by corruption, which is especially problematic because of its integral relationship with narco-trafficking.[2] Mexican drug cartels are known to be operating in the United States; they are major distributors of cocaine in cities such as Chicago, Dallas, Denver, Houston, Los Angeles, Phoenix, San Diego, San Francisco, and Seattle. Their leaders are perpetually at the top of the FBI and DEA's Most Wanted lists.[3]

TRANSPARENCY INTERNATIONAL'S GLOBAL CORRUPTION PERCEPTION

Transparency International (TI) is an international organization dedicated to combating political corruption. Each year, after evaluating the governmental corruption levels of countries around the world, TI presents the Corruption Perception Index, which ranks governments from 0 to 10, with 10 being the least corrupt and 0 the most. In 2006, the United States ranked twentieth, with a grade of 7.3, while Mexico was placed seventieth, tied with Ghana, Brazil, India, and China, all of whom earned a grade of 3.3.[4] In another 2005 report gauging the public's perception of corruption in both countries,

In Mexico the average amount paid in bribes per household per year is $111.[6]

TI found that 51–70% of people in Mexico and 31–50% in the United States believe corruption affects political life to a large extent. Asked which sectors in their respective countries were most corrupt, and ranking that corruption on a scale of 1 to 5 (1 being not corrupt and 5 being extremely corrupt), the public in Mexico put political parties and the police corps at the top of their list, ranking them at 4.7; in the United States political parties were viewed as the most corrupt sector, ranked at 3.9, with the media and the business sectors also perceived as somewhat corrupt, earning 3.5 and 3.2, respectively. TI's "Global Corruption Barometer" also investigated incidences of bribery, and in 2005 found that 31–45% of people in Mexico and fewer than 5% of people in the United States had paid a bribe in the past twelve months.[5]

COUNTER-DRUG TRADE OPERATIONS IN BOTH COUNTRIES: INTERDICTION, ERADICATION, AND COOPERATION

The U.S. government's drug enforcement activities focus on interdiction and eradication efforts in both drug transit zones and drug-source countries, as well as encouraging other countries to adopt similar policies. Approaches to bilateral counter-drug programs between the United States and Mexico center around improved cooperation between organizations responsible for law observance and the war on drugs. This involves the pursuit of all elements of organized crime, the seizure of drugs, arms, explosives, and other illegally smuggled items that could harm society, and the strengthening of judicial institutions.

The U.S. has also successfully encouraged Mexico to apply many of its tactics and policies in the war on drugs. Mexico has invested in government training programs, technical assistance, equipment and infrastructure for the eradication of illegal crop production, and activities to strengthen the control of money laundering.[7] The government has also introduced a program called *Cultura de la Legalidad*, or "culture of legality," a school initiative promoting respect for the law.

Despite these efforts, the UN estimates that only 10–15% of heroin and 30% of cocaine is intercepted worldwide, and that in order to substantially impact the illegal narcotics industry, at least 70% of international drug shipments need to be intercepted.[8] Changes in drug policy are necessary. In the U.S., the street value of illegal narcotics is extremely high, making their production and sale more profitable and therefore more attractive to traffickers who can earn as much as 90% in profits.[9] Economists refer to this as a balloon effect—the "squeezing" by law enforcement in one area leading to a rise in criminal activity and market profitability in another.[10] U.S. policies have contributed to the consolidation of North America as the world's largest cannabis market, worth somewhere between $10 billion to $60 billion, and home to about one third of global cannabis production.[11]

AS DRUG CARTELS' POWER GROWS, SO TOO DOES VIOLENCE IN BORDER CITIES

Drug cartels tend to be highly advanced and influential organizations, capable of handling the complex logistics of drug transport, money laundering, and the coercion of authorities. Contrary

Candidates in Mexico's Next Presidential Election Tied to Rival Drug Cartels

Violence will surely escalate due to a recent investigation revealing ties between Mexico's political parties and the main drug cartels operating in the nation. At least two of the candidates running in Mexico's presidential election have received more than 50% of their campaign funding from rival drug cartels. A video has surfaced showing a close aid to Óscar Bárcenas, the PAN candidate, in two separate meetings with a representative of Osiel Cárdenas, the imprisoned leader of the powerful Cartel del Golfo. The links between Leonel Tirado, the PRD candidate, and Juan Parada Gómez, the cousin and successor of the late Pedro Parada Díaz, former drug lord of the El Cacique Oaxaqueño Cartel, are overt. Both men appear in campaign pictures together, and pundits suspect that the candidate wants to benefit from Mr. Parada Gómez's popularity among the populations of Oaxaca and other southern states. In the last five years Mr. Parada Gómez has laundered vast sums of money sponsoring education and social welfare initiatives in the region. He is also the subject of a very popular narcocorrido, a Mexican drug ballad that praises his slyness at making the law work his way.

Over the past fifteen years, the U.S. has spent more than $25 billion on drug crop eradication and interdiction.[12]

to popular belief, eliminating cartel leaders is not enough to dismantle a drug organization. Between December 2000 and March 2006, fifteen drug cartel leaders, fifty-three financial heads, seventy-three landlords, 190 public officials, and 63,361 distributors were captured. Much like corporations and the mafia, drug cartels are prepared to replace leaders if necessary, making them extremely difficult to break down and explaining the spikes in violence that erupt when a leader is captured, as the remaining cartel members vie for ascension to the leadership role. Furthermore, cartels are often equipped with extremely high-tech armaments and other technologies, sometimes more advanced than those possessed by the police forces working against them. In the same five-year period, 32,000 long- and short-range weapons were seized by Mexico's Federal Prosecutor's Office (PGR)—more than double the number of weapons owned by the federal agency.[13]

Currently there are approximately one dozen significant drug trade organizations in Mexico, seven of which are especially powerful: the Gulf Cartel, headed by Osiel Cárdenas Guillén; the Guzmán Loera-Palma Salazar Cartel, under Joaquín "El Chapo" Guzmán; the Tijuana Cartel, led by the Arellano Félix family; the Juárez Cartel, under the Carrillo Fuentes family; the Amezcua Contreras cartel under Jesús Amezcua; the Cacique Oaxaqueño Cartel, under Pedro Díaz Parada; and the Milenio Cartel, headed by Luis Valencia Valencia.[14] All of these criminal organizations have major operations along the northern Mexican border with the United States: the Tijuana Cartel has used Baja California and Tijuana as their center of operations for

decades; the Guzmán Loera-Palma Salazar Cartel is based mainly in the state of Nayarit, though its influence extends into most of the northern border states; the Juárez Cartel works in the border state of Chihuahua; the Milenio Cartel is headquartered in Michoacán, though they have strong connections in the border states of Nuevo León and Tamaulipas; and the Gulf Cartel primarily works in the border state of Tamaulipas.

These Mexican drug cartels, along with the Colombian cartel known as Del Valle del Norte, are fighting to control Mexico City's lucrative drug market. The turf war has brought dangerous gangs from throughout the country to the streets of the nation's capital, fighting for power and control. In 2005 alone, there were more than 1,500 murders caused by the turf war between the Gulf Cartel and the alliance of the Sinaloa-Juárez-Milenio Cartels.[15]

The cartels use threats of violence or murder by example as a means of remaining competitive and keeping the authorities and media at bay. It is commonly understood that disloyalty or divulging information to authorities or to the press will result in threats, violent acts, and often murder. In 2004, these tactics were employed in several cases that won the attention of the press. Roberto Javier Mora García, editorial director of the Nuevo Laredo-based daily *El Mañana*, and Francisco Javier Ortiz Franco, lawyer and co-editor of the

Right: Joaquín Guamán Loera "el Chapo" Guzmán, in a 1993 file photograph in Mexico's highest security prison known as the Almoloya de Juárez in central Mexico. On January 20, 2001, "el Chapo" escaped and has not been captured since. He is considered one of the most powerful drug cartel leaders by U.S. and Mexican authorities.

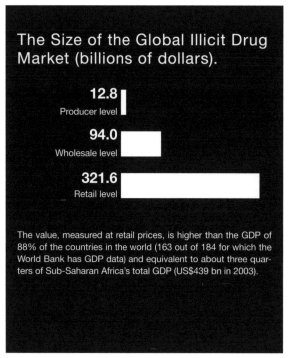

The Size of the Global Illicit Drug Market (billions of dollars).

12.8
Producer level

94.0
Wholesale level

321.6
Retail level

The value, measured at retail prices, is higher than the GDP of 88% of the countries in the world (163 out of 184 for which the World Bank has GDP data) and equivalent to about three quarters of Sub-Saharan Africa's total GDP (US$439 bn in 2003).

Tijuana-based weekly newspaper *Zeta* were both murdered by gunmen for having exposed key drug-lords and cartels. Ortiz Franco was apparently killed in retaliation for an article he had written revealing details and identities behind a scheme to obtain fake police credentials for members of the Arellano Felix-Tijuana cartel.[16]

Drug-related Homicides by Border City

Nuevo Laredo, Tamaulipas: According to the Mexican newspaper *El Universal*, Nuevo Laredo witnessed at least 1,537 drug-related killings between February and December of 2005. Drug-related homicides continued at high rates in 2006, with more than 860 drug-related murders between January and mid-June in Nuevo Laredo alone.

Tijuana, Baja California: There were a record-breaking 396 drug-related homicides in Tijuana in 2005, up from 355 in the previous year.

Ciudad Juárez, Chihuahua: Between January and mid-June of 2005, 108 people were killed, many of whom showed signs of torture.

Culiacán, Sinaloa: Over the past decade there have been approximately 500 violent murders annually, most of them drug-related. From February to May 2006, Sinaloa saw 142 drug-related homicides, with nearly half of those occurring in Culiacán.[17]

THE DEMAND FOR DRUGS IN BOTH COUNTRIES

Herbal cannabis, the plant from which marijuana derives, is by far the most widely used drug in the U.S., Mexico, and the rest of the world. In 2004, of the 200 million people in the world who consumed drugs, 162 million used some form of cannabis. The latest statistics suggest the demand for the world's most popular drug is almost ten times higher in the U.S. than in Mexico.[18]

Annual prevalence of abuse as percentage of the population aged 15–64 (unless otherwise noted).

	U.S.	Mexico
Opiates	0.6% 2000	0.1% 2002
Cocaine	2.8% 2004	0.4% (12-65), 2002
Cannabis	12.5% (15-64), 2004	1.3% (15-65), 2002
Amphetamines	1.5% 2004	0.1% 2002

THE MILITARIZATION OF THE WAR ON DRUGS AND ZERO TOLERANCE LAWS

For both countries, the drug trade is seen as a threat to security. The United States' controversial "War on Drugs" has been handled to a great extent by the Departments of Justice and Homeland Security at the federal level. Under the philosophy of "low-intensity wars," counter-drug operations use military resources to stop narcotics' entrance into the country, with particular focus on the southern border—the entry point for 65% of all cocaine and virtually all marijuana.[19] U.S. drug policies tend to take a hard line, focusing primarily on the criminality

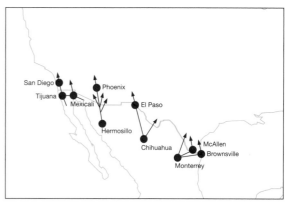

Main drug entry points into the U.S.

Main drug cartels in Mexico

U.S. Immigration and Customs Enforcement agents and a television cameraman at the U.S. exit point of a drug-smuggling tunnel that connected two warehouses in Tijuana and San Ysidro, California. The half-mile tunnel, found on January 30, 2006, was the longest cross-border tunnel ever discovered. Dozens of tunnels have been found in border regions of California and Arizona since security regulations toughened after 9/11.

In recent years, most of global cannabis herb seizures have occurred in North America (with Mexico, United States, and Canada accounting for 54% in 2004, up from 32% in 1990.)

of drug possession and use. Zero tolerance laws in many states criminalize both the possession and distribution of sterile syringes as part of their effort to eradicate drug use and distribution. Critics charge that one of the greatest failures of current U.S. drug policy is the emphasis placed on investigation, prosecution, and incarceration of people convicted of drug possession, rather than funding drug treatment and preventative drug education.[20]

It costs the U.S. roughly $40 billion per year to fight the war on drugs. Each year, the average American pays nearly $300 in state taxes to deal with drug abuse and addiction, and only $10 on prevention and treatment.[21] This is reflected in the growing number of individuals arrested for drug-related crimes each year: 21% of state, and 55% of federal inmates are held for drug law violations.[22] Furthermore, various state and federal laws deny former drug offenders access to public housing, loans for college, federal benefits, and the right to vote, emphasizing the punitive nature of drug policy in the U.S.[23]

U.S. drug policies have resulted in many consequences for the greater society: prison populations are rising; drugs bought on the street are often impure, making them even more hazardous; and incidences of diseases such as HIV/AIDS and hepatitis have increased because users are unable to access sterile syringes due to zero tolerance laws. Furthermore, because they are illegal, drugs are expensive, which contributes to buyers resorting to criminal activity in order to feed their addictions. This same phenomenon helps consolidate the power of criminal organizations that profit from the illegality of the market.[24]

ALTERNATIVE DRUG POLICIES

Harm reduction began in the 1980s as a public health strategy to stem the spread of HIV/AIDS among people who inject drugs with needles. According to the Drug Policy Alliance, an organization working to end the war on drugs through alternative, compassionate policies, "Harm reduction is grounded in the conviction that people should not be punished for what they put into their bodies, but only for crimes committed against others. It acknowledges that no society will ever be free of drugs. It holds that drug policies should seek to reduce the negative consequences of drugs, principally death, disease, crime and suffering of both drug abuse and the policies themselves."[25] Harm reduction policies favor the treatment of drug addiction by health care professionals over incarceration in the penal system; maximizing the potential benefits of drugs; emphasizing that intervention should be based on the relative harmfulness of a drug to society; and reducing the hazards of drug use through education, prevention, and treatment. It is important to consider such preventive measures, since the costs of drug abuse have grown in previous years with the current war on drug policies. In 2002, the costs of drug abuse to society were estimated at $180.8 billion, of which $15.8 billion were direct health care costs and the rest derived from productivity losses.[26]

Considering half of all U.S. high-school students have tried at least one illicit drug by the time they are in 12th grade,[27] the Drug Policy Alliance launched the "Just Say 'Know'—Safety First" campaign, which aims to inform teens about the harmful effects of using drugs. By providing teens with the necessary information and knowledge, they can make informed decisions about their own drug use and prevent themselves from being exposed to harmful side effects.

Various studies and pilot programs in other countries show that the key to combating drug use is to treat consumption as a health problem rather than as a criminal offense. Drug addicts are people dealing with a disease, and according to the developers of alternative policies addicts need treatment just as any other sick person does. Some treatment policies outlined by the Drug Policy Alliance include:[28]

Drug Substitution and Maintenance

This approach provides addicts with legal access to drugs, or the pharmaceutical equivalent of the drug they are addicted to. Access helps reduce risks of overdose and crime, as addicts will no longer have to break the law in order to support their habit.

Access to Sterile Syringes

Increasing access to sterile syringes through needle exchange programs, pharmacy sales, and physician prescriptions will reduce needle sharing among drug users, which will help decrease the transmission of HIV/AIDS and hepatitis.

Proposition 36: Substance Abuse Reduction and Crime Prevention Act of 2000

This legislation, passed in California in November 2000, allows for the use of medical marijuana for treatment, and instead of incarceration promotes treatment by diverting low-level, nonviolent drug offenders convicted of possession for personal use into community-based treatment programs instead of prison.

Legalizing drugs

There are two principal options for handling the legalization of drugs: the market could either be regulated by the state, or a competitive market involving private entrepreneurs could be developed. Legalization could also be partial, meaning access to and consumption of certain drugs would be allowed, while buying and selling others would remain illegal.

In 2006, the Mexican government nearly passed legislation that would have decriminalized the possession of small amounts of drugs that were clearly for personal use. However, President Fox vetoed the law due to alleged pressures from the U.S. Drug Enforcement Administration (DEA). The law would have allowed addicts and consumers to possess up to 25mg of heroin, 5g of marijuana, and 0.5g of cocaine; it also permitted small quantities of LSD, MDA, and MDMA (ecstasy).[29]

The issue of drug legalization generates debate around the world, often surrounding the use of certain drugs for therapeutic treatment. Marijuana has been proven to be effective in reducing nausea induced by cancer chemotherapy, stimulating appetite in AIDS patients, and reducing intraocular pressure in people with glaucoma. There is also appreciable evidence that marijuana reduces muscle spasticity in patients with neurological disorders. A synthetic capsule is available by prescription, but for many patients it is not as effective as marijuana that has been inhaled through smoking. Pure THC that is used in the capsule form can also potentially produce more unpleasant psychoactive side effects than marijuana that has been smoked. Many people in the United States, Mexico, and other nations use marijuana medicinally today, despite its illegality. In doing so, they risk arrest and imprisonment.

An open debate must be fostered around the world in order to realistically consider drug legalization. Ethan Nadelman, director of the Drug Policy Alliance, asserts that a change in rhetoric

6

Twenty-year-old NYU Student Sentenced to Life in Prison without Parole

Classmates describe Dylan Grant as "a friendly music geek" who is very smart, if a little shy around members of the opposite sex. But in June of last year he was busted for selling marijuana at a music club in Manhattan's Lower East Side. Felix Hayes, a close friend of Grant, claims he was not a drug dealer, although Grant was found guilty as charged. "If he happened to sell some marijuana to an under-cover cop, it might have been because someone gave him a joint he didn't want," Hayes said. "He probably was low on cash and wanted to be able to buy himself a couple of beers." His outraged parents, along with family, friends, and a host of other protesters, rallied in front of City Hall in downtown Manhattan last Saturday, arguing that the sentence is unfair and disproportionate to the crime their son committed and asking representatives to advocate for a change in the "zero tolerance" legislation criminalizing possession and sale of drugs. They say that if such legislation is to continue, it should also penalize the abuse of the psychiatric drugs that are consumed by more than 40% of the population on a daily basis and regulate the purchase of over-the-counter cold remedies, with which potent illegal drugs can be made.

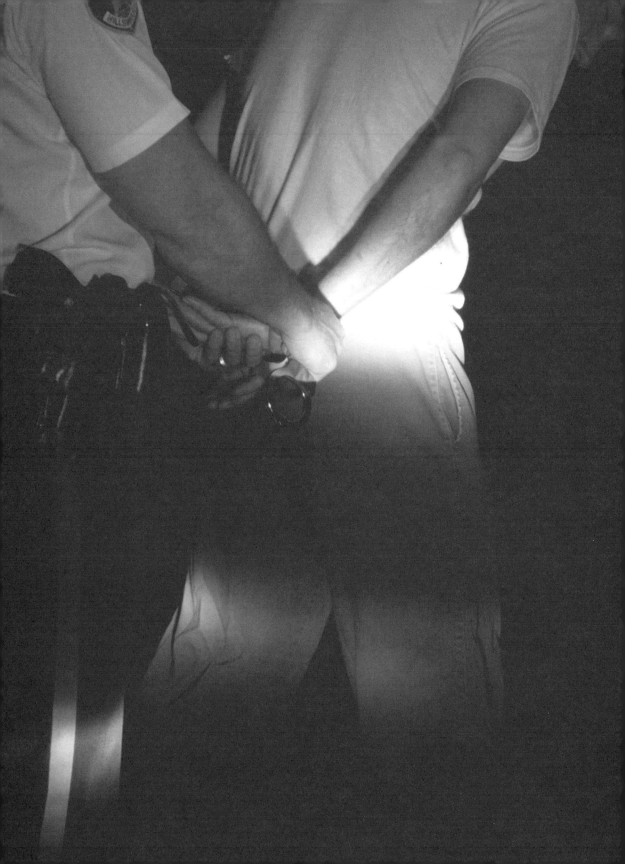

is needed to distinguish between the harms of drugs and the harms of prohibition—the latter of which represents a greater danger to Latin American societies than the former. In his own words, "it is Latin America that possesses both the moral standing and the critical mass of political leadership needed to force a fundamental re-thinking of global drug policy in the 21st century."[30]

What Is an Addiction? Binational Agreements on Preliminary Legalization of Drugs Under Discussion

Having acknowledged that the trade and consumption of illegal drugs is a binational problem and that criminalizing it only creates incentives for illegal drug-dealing, officials of Mexico and the U.S. gathered in Tijuana to discuss initiatives to gradually legalize the possession and sale of drugs. Similar initiatives have been introduced by Mexico in the past, but were blocked by the U.S. Drug Enforcement Administration. Areas of drug legalization up for discussion include legalizing marijuana for medicinal use and allowing addicts to possess regulated quantities of the more dangerous drugs they depend on while enrolling them in programs to fight their addictions. Officials fear they might reach a standstill when trying to establish guidelines to determine what will qualify as an addiction and which medical purposes will be sanctioned by the new legislation. Some argue marijuana, in addition to treating cancer, AIDS, and glaucoma, could cure common eating disorders such as anorexia and should be made available to teenagers afflicted by those illnesses. Others foresee the development of new drug-dealing networks if all types of consumption are not legalized at once.[31]

Marinin, a marijuana start-up, gets ready to make its first shipment of marijuana pills. Its drugs have been in storage for six months as the company awaits legislative approval to sell the drug.

A series of informal settlements on the outskirts of Mexico City. As the cost of housing is out of reach for many Mexicans, informal housing has remained a viable option for many communities in Mexico. Similar settlements can be found in border communities in Texas.

7. THE INFORMAL SECTOR

The lack of formal employment opportunities in Mexico has fostered a flourishing informal sector and contributes to increasing migration flows to the United States. In the future, Mexico will need to incentivize participation in the formal economy, increase access to loans, generate jobs, and reduce piracy, while the United States will need to deflate the number of employers who hire workers through informal means. Integrating the millions of informal workers is vital for the future of both countries' citizens and economies.

Mexico has the world's highest incidence of kidnappings. In 2004 there were an estimated 3,000 kidnappings, many of which had alleged police involvement.

THE INFORMAL SECTOR'S IMPACT ON THE ECONOMY

The struggle between the formal and informal economy (which we will define as the economy that is absent of formal labor relations and legal permission to operate) has been ongoing in Mexico. The illegal economy (that which includes the sale of everything outside of the legal market including contraband, pirated goods, stolen merchandise, and illegal transactions) has become standard in Mexico. In a country where around half of the population suffers from poverty, the informal sector is a means to survival for an estimated 12 million workers, representing a quarter of the economically active population.[1] Informal jobs are often the only alternative for many workers in a depleted job market, but they are also a substantial drag on the economy. Operating outside of government taxation, the informal sector prolongs poverty by allowing the economy to go unfed. A study done by the Center for Strategic and International Studies (CSIS) and the Instituto Tecnológico Autónomo de México (ITAM) shows that only 40% of the Mexican workforce pays taxes;[2] and whereas developed countries collect 25% of their GDPs in sales and property taxes, only 10% of Mexico's GDP is collected through such means.[3] According to a 2004 report prepared for the Consejo Nacional Fomento a la Vivienda (CONAFOVI, or the National Commission of Housing Promotion) and Centro de Investigación y Documentacion de la Casa S.C. (CIDOC) by the Joint Center for Housing Studies at Harvard University, "50 percent or more of all new homes are self-built by low-income households and large shares of these are built on land without clear title and often without basic infrastructure and services."[4] That is to say, the legality of many homes in Mexico is questionable or absent.

Remittances

Remittances sent from the United States play an important role in the economies of many countries. With an estimated 12 million Mexicans living in the United States,[5] many of whom work informally, remittances were the biggest source of foreign income for Mexico in 2005, accounting for approximately $20 billion (see pages 104–106 for more on remittances).[6] But as untaxed dollars are sent out of the U.S. and into Mexico, animosity between the two countries grows.

In 2005, the state of Texas proposed a law that would make remittance dollars taxable, placing a .5% levy on all money sent out of the state—which would earn the state about $26.9 million.[7] Sponsored by legislators Royce West of Dallas and Vilma Luna of Corpus Christi, the law, HB 2345, would invest these earnings in public sectors that are supposedly drained by immigrants. In Arizona, a similar resolution was approved to impose an 8% state tax on all money leaving the country electronically. Ironically, the tax will be used to support the construction of a fence between Arizona and Mexico.[8]

Chinese Contraband Entering Mexico Compromises Economic Growth

High levels of Chinese contraband illegally entering Mexico from the United States heavily impact the Mexican economy. According to the Cámara

Nacional de la Industria del Vestido (CNIV, or The National Chamber of the Clothing Industry), close to 60% of clothing sold in Mexico passes through illegal channels.[9] Clothing, toys, and even products traditionally associated with Mexican nationalism such as the country's flag, *zarapes* (ponchos), chilies, and the Virgin of Guadalupe are only a handful of goods now made in China and illegally imported into Mexico. From industrial cities such as Shanghai, Tianjin, Beijing, or the municipality of Chongqing, exports are packed on trains carrying them to any of the 350 ports within China, from which they are shipped to the Americas where it is presumed that corrupt customs agents allow the contraband to pass.[10] Another method for moving Chinese products into Mexico takes flagrant advantage of NAFTA. Because the trade agreement allows U.S. exports to enter Mexico tariff-free, the infamous "made in China" tags are switched for those that read "made in the U.S.A." before entering Mexico, allowing Chinese products to arrive on the streets of Mexico tax free, with such low prices that it is nearly impossible for similar Mexican products to compete.[11] The Mexican business community continues to be startled by the increasing number of Chinese products, claiming that their illegal importation is putting the livelihood of thirty different industries at risk.[12]

Dumping

Despite China's entry to the World Trade Organization (WTO) in 2001, the saturation of Chinese products in the Mexican market has persisted. With wages as low as 13.5 cents an hour, Chinese products are made at costs significantly lower than Mexico, where the average wage at a Tijuana factory is $1.80 an hour.[13] The process of "dumping"—substituting domestic goods with foreign goods at a lower price—was expected to be WTO-regulated when China became a member.

In the wake of China's entrance into the WTO, President Hu Jintao of China and President Fox signed several trade agreements in response to the influx of illegal Chinese goods entering Mexico and because trade is approaching $15 billion annually.[14] The pacts made between the two governments included Mexican grape and pear exports to China, and during the talks, President Hu stated he was open to discuss cooperation with Mexico in areas of agriculture, fishing, mining, and light industry.[15] Fair prices as well as balancing the existing trade deficit of the illegal and legal entry of goods is pivotal to the economic standing of Mexico.

Children Raised in the Informal Sector are Sacrificing Their Education

According to UNICEF, 4 million of the 37 million Mexican children under the age of fourteen (the country's minimum working age) are working.[16] As children are born into poor families that are part of Mexico's informal economy, skipping school to vend in the street or on the subway has become a common way of life. The International Labor Organization reports that "Children with no access to quality education have little alternative but to enter the labor market where they are often forced to work in dangerous and exploitative conditions."[17]

PIRACY: A MAJOR CONTRIBUTOR TO MEXICO'S INFORMAL SECTOR

Piracy is a growing phenomenon in cities across Mexico. Copies of original CDs and DVDs can be found virtually anywhere. Pornography, video games, movies, music albums, and mp3 compilations containing entire artist catalogues are sold in the street before their official release. Although the quality of the products is often poor, it does not stop the annual sale of millions of pirated products.

In a country where half of the population lives in poverty, and where a movie ticket costs about five

8

Recent Trade Accords with China are Predicted to Boost the Mexican Economy and Have Significant Social Impact in Mexico

With 45% of its population under the poverty line and up to thirty local industries, including textiles and agriculture, in shambles, Mexico has invited China to invest in the country and develop its natural resources. Foreseeing an influx of Chinese businesspeople into the country and aiming at a larger Mexican presence in China, bilingual Chinese-Spanish education programs are being devised with great difficulty in certain high schools and universities, although ways of optimizing the similarities between the Chinese language and some tonal indigenous languages such as Yucatec Maya and Mazatec are being developed by the Ministry of Education. The looming presence of some pioneering Chinese-American businesses, such as Fresco Tortilla, a fast-food chain specializing in Mexican food described as "ridiculously cheap and acceptable," has a segment of the restaurant industry—mainly small taquerías and fondas specializing in home-style cuisine—on edge.

dollars—more than the minimum daily wage—a family outing to the movie theater is not always feasible. At around twenty pesos, or less than half the cost of one movie ticket, piracy gives the majority of the population the opportunity to participate in mainstream entertainment. But all of this comes at a cost—to the entertainment industry, and to the Mexican economy.

Although piracy rates in 2005 were highest in China, Russia, and Thailand, the greatest damage to the Motion Picture Association was done by Mexico. According to a report put out by the Motion Picture Association of America, Mexico accounted for Hollywood's biggest losses in 2005 at an estimated $483 million dollars.[18]

In respect to the music industry, Mexico experiences a 60% piracy rate, according to the International Record Organization and the International Federation of Phonographic Industry (IFPI).[19] This especially high level of piracy has grave consequences for Mexico. Jobs are lost, investment plunges, and organized crime can be funded all due to piracy.

Opposite, clockwise from top left:

Jonathan, 11 (left) takes a break from selling *churros* to pose with his friend who works selling tacos for his father. Neither of them go to school and they work at least eight hours per day six days a week.

Knock-off Barbie dolls imported from China are sold in Tepito for 18 pesos or about US$1.50. At the U.S. chain store "Toys 'R Us", an average Mattel Barbie sells for US$22.

The price of knock-off running shoes in a Tepito vending stall sell at a fraction of the originals.

Figurine of the Virgin of Guadalupe, a Mexican cultural icon manufactured in China.

Chinese chilies, symbols of Mexican identity, are increasingly being imported into Mexico.

Food vendors in the streets of the Tepito, the zone with the highest density of informal vendors in Mexico City.

Black Market Culture Permeates the Borders

The burgeoning informal economy that was once specific to developing countries has now entered first-world nations. In many areas of the United States, the growing influence of the informal economy can be found. In Los Angeles the Fashion District is home to the illegal trade and sale of the same pirated commodities that exist in Mexico. What's more, the informal deeds and services once particular to Mexico have now become integrated into the informal economy of the U.S. as well. In Latino-influenced cities, street vendors with carts patrol the streets selling homemade Mexican specialties such as tamales, quesadillas, chicharrones, elotes, aguas frescas, raspados, and fresh cut fruits seasoned with salt, lime, and chili. Once only found in highly concentrated immigrant communities, informal vendors have now exported the methods to create an informal economy abroad. Middle- to upper-class suburbs are also witnessing this infiltration. In suburbs just outside of Los Angeles, amidst soccer mom–driven SUVs and flashy sports cars, Latino men selling boxes and bags of fresh fruit on corners have become common.

Today, the informal sector represents a large part of the U.S. economy. The National Center for Policy Analysis reports that as many as 25 million Americans profit from "underground activities," which includes the buying and selling of merchandise and services unlawfully.[20] According to the International Monetary Fund, the shadow economy has experienced growth of 4–9% GDP from 1970 to 2000, and the IRS reports that the federal government loses $195 billion annually because of the country's underground market.[21]

Using the Informal or Illegal Sector as a Means to Enter the Formal Sector

In the past couple of decades, using illegal methods to incorporate oneself into the formal economy has become a de facto procedure. False documents proclaiming U.S. citizenship, birth, social security status, permission to work and live, and permission to operate a motor vehicle can all be purchased for low prices on Mexican and U.S. streets. Areas like MacArthur Park in Los Angeles have garnered fame for the authenticity of the counterfeit documents vendors sell to people hoping to pass for legal status in the U.S.

In cities around the U.S., people are being caught more and more frequently for the production of false documents. Furthermore, the Identity and Benefits Fraud unit (IBF), a sector of the U.S. Immigration and Customs Enforcement (ICE), has developed the National Fraud Strategy in order to combat immigration fraud.[22] In the fiscal year of 2003 the IBF unit opened around 3,700 cases of immigration fraud in addition to existing cases.[23]

Although false documentation allows many of the estimated 5.3 million undocumented Mexican immigrants[24] to work in the United States, it does not allow them to claim the benefits that they ought to be granted. Around three-fourths of the U.S. undocumented population pays into the Social Security system—amounting to $7 billion in 2005—although they never receive these benefits.[25] At the same time, complaints persist from Americans about the cost of undocumented immigrants. Permitting this population to work legally in the United States is essential for both nations.

False Social Security cards can be easily purchased in various flea markets throughout the U.S.

FORMALIZING THE INFORMAL ECONOMY

Incorporating the informal sector into the formal remains a challenge. Previous overtures have been made toward one segment of the informal economy, for instance, as local governments have attempted to get illegal street vendors into organized areas. Many of these efforts have failed so far. According to anthropologist Joana Parra, one major reason for failed marketplaces is that their locations have not been ideal. Parra explains that in Mexico City's Historic Center, for instance, having your stall located in the middle of the street is optimal because of the large amount of tourist and pedestrian traffic that passes through the area; being in a market does not attract as many customers. Only one government market has yielded successful results in the Historic Center, as it was located in a place that obligated pedestrians to pass through on their way between principal destinations.[26] Other effective strategies for formalizing the informal include government incentives such as taxes proportional to earnings and granting benefits such as health care and pensions currently being tested in Mexico City.

Formalizing the Informal through Property Rights

Peruvian-born economist Hernando de Soto has become famous for his controversial ideas about the informal economy. In his works *The Other Path* and *The Mystery of Capital*, de Soto presents his theory, which holds that poverty is a result of lacking formal property rights in poor countries.[28] Because many citizens do not legally own their property, they cannot use it to apply for loans, expand businesses, or improve the conditions of their property.[29] Essentially, de Soto asserts that poverty will exist as long as informal property remains in its current state. His Institute for Liberty and Democracy calculates that half of the estimated 26.4 million urban estates in Mexico and

70% of the 197 million hectares of the country's territory, are outside any legal property. Adding to this the 8.2 million companies operating extra-legally, ILD concludes Mexico has about $600 billion worth of dead capital in informal land property. This is not surprising, as the process for registering a business and getting a mortgage loan is typically long and costly.[30]

Ending Piracy in Mexico

The internet has enabled what just over a decade ago was considered impossible: today we can communicate with someone continents away in a matter of seconds, shop without leaving our homes, and even date someone we may never actually meet. Services such as Apple's iTunes, Musicmatch, and Napster are just a few examples of the ways in which one can access and download music legally. Consumers can buy full albums or individual songs for less money via the internet than buying the hard copy at a store. Major movie studios are already making movies legally available for download for as little as $9.99.[31]

As new technology allows for cheaper and more streamlined channels of distribution, entertainment becomes accessible to larger segments of the population. As long as the cost of legitimate modes of entertainment remains low, pirated merchandise will have a diminished impact on the formal economy.

Suburban sprawl outside of Mexico City; many of the settlements are informal.

GO HOME

9

FEBRUARY 13, 2050

Recent Study Estimates that Only 35% of the Mexican Workforce Is Legal. Informal Sector Represents 65% of the Country's Workforce

Specialists are assessing the effects of the United States' massive deportation of undocumented workers of Mexican origin in 2010. Upon the return of approximately 3 million workers, the formal sector proved unable to incorporate them, yet underground networks gradually allowed for a majority to engage in piracy, street vending, peddling, working as house staff, gardening and construction, and providing a wide array of services that now have become essential to city-dwellers, such as traffic and parking control, car washing, and private protection. It is estimated that someone in the informal economy has a 5% chance of being incorporated into the formal sector. If no jobs are developed within the next thirty years, by 2080 the informal sector is expected to represent 60% of the work force. Researchers recommend a nationwide system to collect taxes from informal workers in order to generate employment, yet warn officials of the political unrest that such a policy might provoke. Although some of these measures were implemented at the beginning of the twenty-first century at a small scale, some of the most powerful networks in Mexico City, such as the one in Tepito, proved resilient to governmental control.

DECEMBER 12, 2009

Guest Worker Program to Begin in May of 2010

As both the Senate and the House of Representatives approve a bill granting ten-year work permits to undocumented workers already in the U.S. and temporary work visas to foreign workers, another bill is being discussed involving how to penalize those employers who despite the new legislation continue to hire illegal workers. If the bill proposed by the House passes, businesses might face suspensions of up to two years, and the operations of vigilante groups trying to keep immigrants out of U.S. territory will be criminalized. Southeast Asian nations discuss welcoming corporations that rely on cheap labor and wish to reallocate.[27]

Miguel shows his work permit. He arrived in the U.S. five years ago illegally. He can now travel back and forth between Mexico and Kentucky without having to pay a coyote.

Opposite: Street vendors in the city of Querétaro where the government has made great efforts to formalize irregular businesses.

11

APRIL 28, 2018

Officials at the Mexican Ministry of Labor Try to Devise a System by which a Worker in the Informal Sector Can Qualify for Retirement with a Pension Plan

The Ministry of Labor announced today that a retirement package would be made available to workers in the underground economy, which make up more than a quarter of the Mexican workforce. Given the demographics of the country, specialists predict many complications to arise as a great number of workers in the informal sector reach retiring age. Some propose that given the expenses of the bureaucratic process involved in registering the workers, it might be more cost-effective to simply offer a pension plan to citizens over 65 who are not formally employed, regardless of their employment history. This could be made possible through tougher tax-collection measures. Critics in the private sector oppose the initiative, arguing that it will reward the criminal activities that informal workers tend to engage in, such as piracy and selling contraband merchandise.

Both legal and undocumented migrants march during the 2006 Day without an Immigrant in Washington D.C. Demanding immigration reforms and a path to legalization for the millions of undocumented migrants in the U.S., protestors from across the country joined on April 10, 2006 in the largest synchronized sets of protests in the history of the U.S.

8. MIGRATION AND DEMOGRAPHICS

The growing presence of Mexican and other Latin American migrants in the United States will continue to influence and shape politics and society in both the U.S. and Mexico. By 2050, 20% of each country's population will be elderly, presenting a demographic challenge that will strain the social security programs of the U.S. and Mexico if the two nations do not develop methods of retaining competitive workforces for the maintenance of economic prosperity.

The number of legal Mexicans living in the U.S. greatly exceeds that of illegal migrants. Nevertheless, in recent years, most U.S.-bound migration from Mexico has been illegal.

WHY ARE MEXICANS MIGRATING TO THE UNITED STATES?

Mexico is the only developing country that shares a common border with a major world power, and this condition has significant migratory implications. The constant and increasing demand for cheap labor in the United States, the relatively higher U.S. wages for unskilled work, the lagging regional development in the Mexican countryside, and limited opportunities throughout Mexico help explain the magnitude and driving forces behind today's Mexican migratory current.[1] The current U.S. border control policies will need to be enhanced with further employment regulations in the country's interior, while it is essential for Mexico to increase employment opportunities for marginalized communities and prevent illegal migrants, bound for the U.S., to enter its southern border.

IMMIGRANTS IN THE UNITED STATES: DEMOGRAPHIC IMPLICATIONS FOR THE NATION

As the world's primary immigrant-receiving country, the United States is host to more than 37 million foreign-born migrants from across the world.[2] According to a recent study conducted by the Pew Hispanic Center, Latin America and Asia represent the largest immigrant groups in the U.S., with foreign-born Mexicans composing the biggest immigrant population from a single nation. The same report reveals that the Mexican population residing in the U.S. has experienced and maintained rapid growth in recent decades, increasing 15-fold from 760,000 Mexican-born people in the U.S. in 1970

to the current population of over 12 million. This population expansion represents an average annual growth rate of 8%, or the addition of some 500,000 Mexican-born immigrants to the U.S. population every year. In recent years this migratory phenomenon has largely been driven by unauthorized means, whereby 80–85% of Mexican immigrants find ways to dodge the legal system in order to live, work, and be educated in the United States.[3]

Foreign-born workers account for a large segment of the U.S. labor force. In 2004 immigrants were one in every nine U.S. residents, one in every seven U.S. workers, one in every five low-wage workers, and one in every two new workers.[4] This is primarily due to the tremendous growth in recent decades of the Latino population—largely composed of immigrants from Latin America. Between 1990 and 2000, the Latino population rose from 22.4 million to 35.3 million, which at a growth rate of 58% far exceeded that of other minority groups and the white, U.S.-born majority.[5] In 2005, one in every seven U.S. residents (nearly 42 million) was a Latino,[6] and current demographic indicators suggest that within fifty years this ratio will dramatically change to one in every four.[7]

UNDOCUMENTED IMMIGRATION ON THE RISE

In 2006 researchers estimated that the undocumented population living in the United States stood at around 12 million, more than half of whom were from Mexico.[8] According to the Pew Hispanic Center, nearly half of the unauthorized immigrants currently residing in the country initially arrived through legal means. Overstaying

Nation

Carolinas: Par
skies and unu
will persist. H
along the coas
mountains. We

SCIENT
CLIM
POL

EFFEC

Woe
Mo

po
m
be
b
i
t

Evelyn Hockstein for The New York Times

Roy Martinez gives a speech at the National Mall to a crowd of supporters in Washington DC.

Latin America Reshapes American Politics: Roy Martinez

By CELIA W. DUGGER

WASHINGTON — Thousands of supporters of Roy Marinez gathered at the National Mall in Washington DC. The controversial Hispanic Democrat called for a shift in policy towards Latin America. "U.S. relations with these countries have become quite dormant in the current and previous administration," mentioned Lindsey Jacoby, leader of the largest Hispanic think tank. "The proportion of Hispanics in government is a dismal figure nationally This is due to the fact that Latin American migrants are three times less likely to enter public service. In a press conference delivered partly in Spanish, the charismatic Jacoby remarked the strong economic

marking the seventh year of protests nationwide. Walkouts have become more of a collective tradition in recent years. Even though their power to change marking the seventh year of protests nationwide. Walkouts have become more of a collective tradition in recent years. Even though their power to change policy is questionable, they have functioned to bring together migrants from Latin America and jointly express their political views. This year's marches witnessed the presence of political leaders from across Central and South America.

Joaquín Segura, a nationalist leader in El Salvador participated in this year's May Day events in Dallas, Texas. He has been accused of interfering in human rights and immigration affairs in the U.S.

whose tough stance on immigration defined last year's presidential elections in the states with the largest Latino population. Hughes addressed the nation several times in Spanish, a move considered unpatriotic by his critics. "Embracing bilingualism in our country should not be considered a crime," the first lady said in a recent interview. Our country is at cross-roads. We should capitalize on the cultural diversity of our nation."

The border states, where about half of t population can read Spanish news, according to recent survey by Omnitec, are dealing with the sa issues. Conservative opponents in New Mexico prodding the state's Congress to introduce new that will not favor Spanish-speaking candidates

Polls Predict that Winner of 2020 Presidential Election must be pro-Latino and Speak Spanish Fluently

Based on demographic patterns and the accelerated rate at which the Latino population is expanding (58% per decade), Latinos will play a decisive role in the 2020 presidential election. It is rumored that former Colorado governor Steve Michael, who lived in Monterrey until he was thirteen, might try to run for office a second time. Others mention Democrat Antonio Saldaña, who in 2011 was the first Latino to be elected mayor of Denver, and Democrat Roy Martinez, member of the U.S. House of Representatives and former Chief Patrol Agent of the Tucson Border Patrol sector.

U.S. TOTAL POPULATION, 2005
289 million

100%

Hispanic and Mexican population in the U.S. as percentage of total population, 2005.

NATIVE
252 million

FOREIGN-BORN
37 million

87.62%

17.38%

HISPANIC
41.8 million

NOT HISPANIC
247.2 million

Native
23 million

Foreign-born
18.8 million

85.3%

NATURALIZED
U.S. CITIZENS
11.5 million

NON-U.S.
CITIZENS
25.5 million

4%   9%

MEXICAN
AMERICAN
15.9 million

LEGAL NON-CITIZENS
14.4 million /
UNAUTHORIZED
11.1 million

5% 4%

71% of the 11.1 million undocumented population live in just 10 states

Illinois
400,000

New York
600,000

New Jersey
387,500

Virginia
275,000

California
2.6 million

North Carolina
350,000

Georgia
400,000

Arizona
475,000

Texas
1.5 million

Florida
875,000

NATURALIZED
U.S. CITIZENS
FROM MEXICO
1.8 million

LEGAL NON-CITIZENS
FROM MEXICO
4.2 million

0.6%   1.5%   2.1%

UNAUTHORIZED
FROM MEXICO
6.2 million

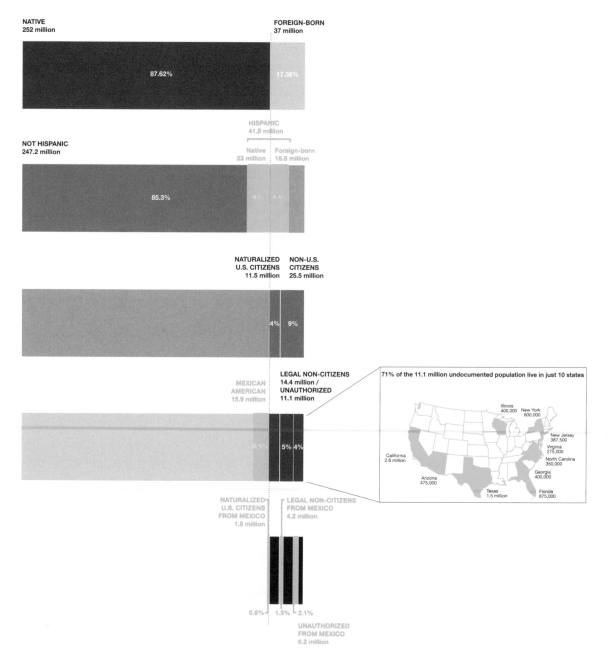

visas or violating the conditions of border-crossing cards, however, have folded many of these visitors into the fabric of the undocumented immigrant community.[9] The rest of the unauthorized, foreign-born residents (slightly over half) entered the U.S. through a myriad of illegal channels, mostly via land borders and ports. Some hiked for days across the Sonoran desert, while others, for a high price, were smuggled into the country by coyotes—human smugglers. Many simply evaded inspection officers at ports of entry.[10]

In 2005, more than two-thirds of the undocumented population was distributed throughout just eight states: California (24%), Texas (14%), Florida (9%), New York (7%), Arizona (5%), Illinois (4%), New Jersey (4%), and North Carolina (3%).[11] Although it appears that this community is concentrated in a relatively small portion of the United States, its settlement patterns have actually changed over the last decade. Due to a variety of factors—including networking trends among recent immigrants and newfound job opportunities in growing sectors in rural areas—the regions in the U.S. experiencing the most growth in undocumented communities are those that previously had comparatively small foreign-born populations.[12] As a result, states such as Arizona and North Carolina may be among those currently hosting the largest immigrant groups in the country,[13] while cities like Denver, Chicago, and Salt Lake City are now home to Mexican populations making up 22%, 18%, and 13% of their total populations, respectively.[14] In the heart of the plains states, the small town of Lexington, Nebraska, home to an IBP meatpacking plant, has a population of 10,000, more than 37% of which is Mexican, thus earning itself the nick name "Mexington."[15] The increased migrant presence in these areas has added fuel to the immigration debate in the U.S., with congressmen from cities like Madison

and Denver sponsoring anti-immigration bills and leading the counter-immigration debate.

Undocumented migrants represent about 4.9% of the U.S. labor force, and as a group is characterized by several tendencies. Almost one-third of undocumented workers occupy jobs in the service sector, whereas only one-sixth of native workers do the same. The undocumented also make up 24% of employees in the farming industry, 14% of construction workers, and 21% of workers in private household positions.[16]

A recent report by the Chicago Council on Foreign Relations cited three major failings in the current state of undocumented immigration that must be addressed as a condition to any long-term solution. First, the current system undermines the rule of law and the immigration system established for documented immigrants; second, the present system exposes workers to exploitation, limits economic growth, and may adversely affect the wages of legal workers; and third, the process—which promotes deportation of unauthorized immigrants—separates families and ignores social realities.[17] These are all issues that have contributed to the fiery nature of both sides of the immigration debate in the U.S., and help illustrate the fundamental challenges that come with being an undocumented immigrant in the country.

In 2006 the debate surrounding this issue polarized Americans over what they wish to see in immigration reform. Restrictionists view undocumented immigration as a drain on the economy, citing taxes, welfare, and social security consumed by the unauthorized community. Many also argue that immigrants take jobs away from U.S. citizens, particularly during times of economic recession and increased job competition. This argument has been challenged by Stephen H. Legomsky, law professor at Washington University School of Law and expert in U.S. immigration issues, who states

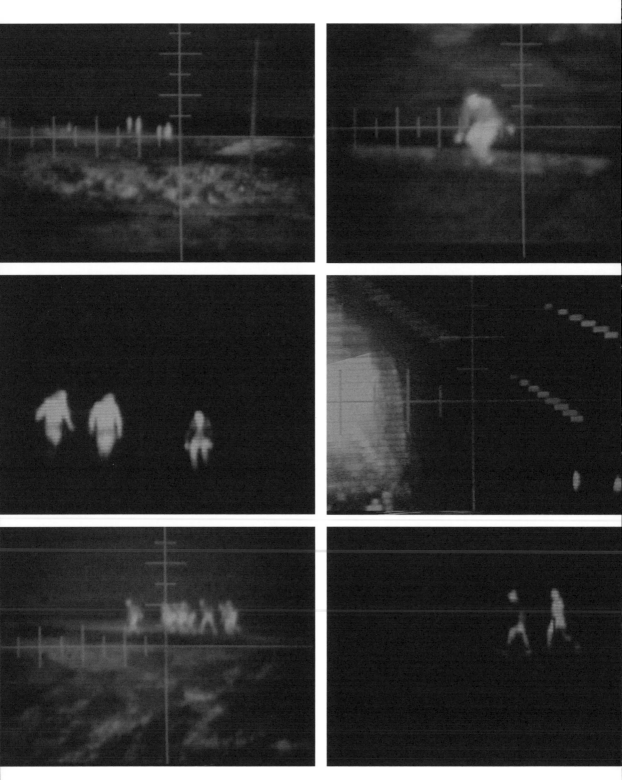

that although immigrants—both documented and undocumented—do take jobs, they also create jobs by consuming products and services in the U.S., and by establishing businesses that employ U.S. citizens and non-citizens alike.[18] Legomsky goes on to point out that immigrants have played an important role in the revitalization of many communities and neighborhoods formerly in decay, through their entrepreneurial activities.[19] Immigrants' tendencies toward community-building and social participation have also helped invigorate many urban spaces.

Whether or not undocumented immigrants utilize more public services and social programs than they contribute to is subject to debate, as the answer can vary from state to state or community to community. However, most economists argue that immigrants actually represent a net positive for the economy, meaning that overall, at the federal level, they pay more in taxes than they acquire in services.[20] Whether they are sales, gasoline, property, or social security taxes, as people residing in the United States, undocumented immigrants contribute to the tax system just as legal workers do.

As far back as 1997, the National Research Council concluded that migration (both legal and illegal) produced a domestic gain in the order of $1 billion to $10 billion a year to the U.S. economy.[21] And although the undocumented often use government medical and emergency services, enroll their children in public school, and sometimes receive welfare, most will never be able to collect Social Security. Stephen C. Goss, Chief Actuary of the Social Security Administration, estimated that 75% of undocumented immigrants pay Social Security tax.[22] This phenomenon is chiefly a result of the 1986 Immigration Reform and Control Act (IRCA), which formally placed penalties on employers of undocumented immigrants, leading to a thriving black market in the sales of fake Social Security

cards and green cards. Employers continue to hire unauthorized workers, thereby semi-integrating them into the formal economy by deducting payroll taxes feeding government programs like Social Security and Medicare.[23] The outcome has been the "earnings suspense file"—where all mismatched or fabricated earnings reports have been stored since the mid-1980s—which has grown by billions of dollars per annum and has generated 10% of Social Security's current surplus.[24] Although this situation may prove to be positive for the U.S.'s struggle with Social Security, full integration of the

Above: *Brinco* sneakers come with a compass, map of illegal migration routes of the San Diego/Tijuana region, painkillers, and flashlight. Brinco shoes were designed by artist Judi Werthein to create discussion on issues of migration for the occassion of inSite_05, a binational arts festival that took place in November, 2005, in San Diego and Tijuana. Opposite: Migrants crossing into the U.S.

MAY 4, 2015

American Employers to Offer High Incentives for Mexican Guest Workers to Migrate to the United States instead of Canada and Spain

Large agri-business corporations that had benefited from illegal labor until guest worker programs in Canada and Spain were initiated in 2012 are now trying to lure Mexican workers into returning to work for them. Desperate for employees, they have devised packages that include subsidized housing, pension plans, health care, and schooling for their children, which in the long run will cost them less than having no workers pick their crops.

undocumented will not occur until a reform is introduced allowing this shadow labor force to receive benefits from the programs they have contributed to and supported with their taxes.

CONSEQUENCES OF MIGRATION FOR MEXICO

For many communities and states throughout Mexico, migration has become part of the collective social psyche. For decades, male community members have left their families and homes behind in search of opportunity in the United States, after watching generations of men do the same before them. The results have been broken families, regions lacking the contributions of productive male workers, and an increasingly heavy dependence on remittances.[25] The current difficulty of obtaining legal status in the U.S. further exacerbates many of these issues, as undocumented migrants are forced to remain in the country for longer periods of time because the risk of getting caught crossing the border again is too high.

BORDER DEATHS INCREASE AS SECURITY AND REGULATIONS TIGHTEN

Today, undocumented migrants frequently attempt to enter the United States through the dangerous Sonoran desert in Arizona, also known as the "corridor of death." Studies show that more than half of 2005's migrant deaths occurred in this region, most likely because temperatures rose to 120°F (49°C) during the summer months. The leading causes of migrant deaths are heat stroke, dehydration, and hypothermia in the desert regions, although deaths by vehicle accident and homicide have also become prevalent. In recent years, as immigration between the two nations has continued to surge, Human Rights Watch and Amnesty International have made several reports citing violations of human rights and migrants' deaths along the hyperborder at the hands of the U.S. Border Patrol.[26]

Despite the increases in migrant deaths over the last decade, the issue has received relatively minimal attention, resulting in a grave lack of action on the part of the U.S. and Mexican governments. The counties along the U.S. side of the border—which are relatively poor by national comparison—have expressed outrage at the government's inaction, as the burden of the migrants' deaths has been left to them. In most cases, instead of the federal government taking responsibility for the fatalities and corpses, local tax dollars are spent on post-mortem necessities such as autopsies, caskets, and burials. This financial burden has only heightened frustration with undocumented immigration and other border issues, adding fuel to various causes ranging from increased border control to anti-immigrant rallies to NGO and faith-based groups working toward migrant relief (see pages 81–84).

MEXICAN MIGRATION DEMOGRAPHICS ARE CHANGING

The demographics of the Mexican migrant population in the United States—particularly those of the undocumented group—are changing. Patterns that existed in previous decades allow for the stereotype of the Mexican migrant to be a young adult male, however women, children, and middle-aged to elderly adults have become an increasing presence within this group. In a 2005 report on the characteristics of the unauthorized population in the U.S., the Pew Hispanic Center reported that one in six undocumented migrants was a child, and about 29% of the group were women, meaning adult men represent just over half of all undocumented immigrants.[27] The report went on to point out that a fast-growing group emerging as a result of immigration are the U.S.-born children of undocumented immigrants. This phenomenon carries significant implications for many because legal status can vary greatly between immediate family members, making policy issues and immigration reform integral influences over family life. According to the research center, determining the population size of U.S.-born children of unauthorized migrants is difficult, although the organization estimates that in 2004 more than 3 million children were part of this group.[28]

THE INCREASING POLITICAL INFLUENCE OF MIGRANT ORGANIZATIONS IN THE UNITED STATES

Mexican migrants in the United States have registered over six hundred hometown associations throughout the country, a testimony to this community's desire to remain connected to its origins and to provoke change through civic action abroad.[29] Initially established to collectively improve and develop hometowns, many of these migrant organizations and networks are now being used as tools to gain political clout in the U.S.[30] This emerging phenomenon is largely due to current conditions in the U.S.'s social and political climate, as well as common circumstances inherent to the immigrant experience that naturally forge connections between the foreign-born living in the country. The 2006 debate over immigration reform in the U.S. signaled a turning point for Mexican migrant participation in U.S. politics. Formerly focused on issues affecting their communities of origin, Mexican migrants in the U.S. became mobilized by significant advancements in the anti-immigration movement. Migrant associations assumed positions of leadership within the counter-movement, fighting for the legalization of the undocumented community and migrants' rights. Through the utilization of the Spanish-language mass-media, Mexican migrant associations and other leading Latino groups became the principal organizers of a grassroots social movement that swept the nation with peaceful marches, rallies, and

Mexican-born population in U.S.
Projection toward 2050 in millions

● Mexican-Born Population in the U.S. (millions)
● Percentage of Mexico's Population in the U.S.

22.2 (2050) | 15%
21.2
19.1
16.2
12.8
10.6 (2004)
9.2
6.7
4.5
2.2
760

1840 1860 1880 1900 1920 1940 1960 1980 2000 2020 2040 2050

In 2005, Antonio Villaraigosa became the first Latino mayor of Los Angeles since 1872. Los Angeles, the biggest city in California hosts 3.1 million Mexicans, more than any other city in the United States. If California were an independent country, it would be the ninth biggest economy in the world, with a GDP of 1.5 trillion dollars, bigger than Mexico's 1 trillion dollar GDP.

protests. Their principal demands entailed amnesty for the unauthorized and rights for all migrants, who like their U.S.-born counterparts represent contributing community members and workers who deserve to exercise their full membership in U.S. society.[31] This ideal was expressed by the slogan "Today we march, tomorrow we vote," a popular chant at the nationwide rallies and protests that came into effect during the 2006 mid-term elections. About 70% of Hispanics favored Democrats nationwide and only 30% voted Republican, a drop from two years earlier when President Bush received 44% of the Latino vote.[32] The participation of Mexican migrant associations in the U.S. political arena represents an important step in the United States' history of worker and migrant mobilizations. Like countless communities and ethnic groups before them, Mexican migrants are confronting the U.S. political system by demanding rights, respect, enfranchisement, and social membership, and if history repeats itself, they will likely find success.

AGING SOCIETIES: WILL MEXICO GROW OLD BEFORE IT GETS RICH?

Latin America, the Caribbean, and Asia are the fastest-aging regions in the world.[33] Their elderly populations are expected to double by 2030, carrying harsh implications for the future of their societies, economies, and governments.[34] As developing countries are lacking in sufficient health care and support programs for the elderly, these nations will face significant challenges in the accommodation of their growing elderly populations. This issue will be compounded by the gradual decline of the traditional informal support systems historically enjoyed by these regions, as family dynamics are changing and are no longer conducive to caring for the elderly—the result of dropping fertility rates, increased life expectancy, and new social developments involving increased rural-to-urban migration, education, and independence among the younger generations who previously dedicated more direct moral and material support to their parents.[35] Swelling elderly populations will also strain the governments of developing nations, as the demand for pensions will grow while productivity in the labor force and economy will decrease when elders leave the workplace.[36]

The case of Mexico reflects this looming aging challenge. Currently the nation is considered "young," as compared to Europe and Japan, with an elderly population that makes up only 5% of its total.[37] In 2005, Mexico's median age was 25, whereas that of the United States was 36.1.[38] Yet for Mexico these demographic conditions are expected to drastically change between now and 2050. By mid-century, the median age in Mexico is expected to jump 14.5 years to 39.5,[39] and the elderly (defined as 65 or older) will increase from 5% to 20% of the population.[40] It is anticipated that the median age in the United States, which traditionally experiences more consistent and even population growth, will rise by less than 5 years, to 40.7,[41] and according to the U.S. census the nation's elderly population will also comprise 20% of the total. However, this shift is not nearly as drastic as that of Mexico, since the elderly made up 12.5% of the U.S. population in 1990, representing an increase of just 7.5 percentage points over the course of sixty years.[42]

North America to start recruiting young workers from India, China and Pakistan to fuel its economy

With approximately one out of ten of the region's inhabitants aged 65 or older, Canada, Mexico, and the United States are starting to develop a program that will provide incentives for workers between the ages of 18 and 35 to migrate to North America and settle there with their families. The program will initially focus on recruiting young Indian migrants, given the competition for jobs and opportunities in that country, by far the most populous nation in the world. If it yields positive results, the program will expand gradually to China and Pakistan, which are also severely overpopulated. The three North American countries will determine the ratios of young workers they need to sustain their aging populations, and will allow migrant workers to decide to which country they prefer to migrate. Each country is expected to come up with attractive packages to lure workers to their territory.[43]

More than 3,000 registered deaths are estimated to have occured in the ten-year time frame beginning in late 1994 when Operation Gatekeeper began.

CALIFORNIA Víctor Nicolás Sánchez · Adolfo Pérez Hernández · Daniel Barrientos · Santos Orozco Aguilar · Raúl Hernández Soria · Sandra Edna Durán · Jesús Medina Contreras · Edgar Venegas Brambila · José Gutiérrez · Melquíades Gómez Baca · Martha Rivera García · Benito González Cruz · Benito González Serrano · Javier Rojas Bracamonte · Juan José Romo Zetina · José Luis Garza · Roberto Acegueda López · Román Robles Rojas · Reynaldo González Corona · Juan Lara Mentado · José Santos López Fonseca · Luis Ramírez Escobar · Felipe Aragón Anzaldo · Salvador Sánchez Sánchez · Reyes Jiménez Zamora · Javier Zataraín Gamboa · José Guadalupe Martínez · Celerino Alvarado · Benito Pacheco López · Marcelino Ramírez · Lorenzo Gaytán Ramírez · Cipriano Orozco · Pedro Calixto Maganda López · Eliseo Santos Carmona · José Luis Centeno · Zenaido García de Los Santos · José Manuel de La Luna · Martín Leonardo Hernández · Modesta López · Olivia Cruz Juárez · Carlos Bejar Vázquez · Alejandro Cornejo Reséndiz · Felipe de los Santos · Enedina Beatriz Enciso Palma · Juan Guillén Domínguez · Benito Ávalos Romero · Juan Carlos Córdova · Sergio Jiménez Villanueva · Antonio Zacarías González · Gregorio Ortiz · Pedro Morales Ramírez · Félix Zavala Ramírez · José Manuel Moreno · Guillermo Ayala Méndez · Daniel Loera Salinas · Carlos Loera Salinas · Gustavo Barajas · Oscar Alcalá Gopar · Práxedis Salinas Palma · Juan Pablo Córdova · Ramiro Castorena Martínez· Álvaro Padilla Herrera · Virginia Murillo Díaz · Nicolás Méndez · Alfonso Villalobos Rodríguez · Gustavo Bañuelos · Onésimo Ledezma Hernández · Enrique López Maciel · Héctor Daniel Torres · Luis Oswaldo García Bando · Raúl Castro Ortiz · Abrahán Tomás Cortés· Roberto Valdez Valencia · Roberto González · Rafael Valenzuela Zúñiga · Teresa Urbano García · Lorenzo Barrera Cortez · Benjamín Zaragoza Arias · Jorge Ramírez Amarillas · Pablo Meraz Rosales · Eloise Maya Rodríguez · Roberto Vázquez · Joel Godoy Juárez · José Herrera Martínez · Juan José Pérez González · Raúl Santana Nájera · Raúl Anzures Galarza · Osvelia Tepek · Trinidad Santiago Martínez · Catalina Enríquez Néstor · Gustavo Muñoz Cázares · Gerardo Gaspar Chompa · Alejandro Ramos Zavala · Juan Magaña Hernández · Emigdio Vera Pérez · José González Chacoya · Alejandro Mendoza Pacheco · Rosario Torres Pérez · Osvaldo Serrano Reyes · Enrique Santos Nieto · Aristeo López García · Isaías López Alvarado · Joaquín Mendoza Chávez · Francisco Ramón Segura Saldaña · Alfonso Guillén Guillén · Ismael García Vásquez · Herminio Martínez Altamirano · Alfredo Barriga Ruiz · Roberto Sánchez · Mario Alfredo Clemente Díaz · Antonio Rocha Trejo · Rafael Arias Sotero · Agustín Chaparro Huitrón · Héctor Jesús Méndez Brown · Verónica Manzanares Cárdenas · Fredi Barrera Sánchez · Pastor Raya Zamora · Yuridia Rodríguez Sánchez · José Luis Rey Lugo Vidal · José Froylán Morales Camacho · Gregorio López Otero · Daniel Martínez Osvaldo · Isabel Gabiño Díaz · Gil Aroche Ayala · Armando Gilberto Quiroz Jiménez · Guillermo Rodríguez Barajas · Fernando González Gallegos · Rodolfo García Campuzano · Rafael Espinoza Espinoza · Guadalupe Romero González · Ramón Arenas Olmedo · José Alfredo Godoy Chávez · María González Flores · Ana Gabriela González López · Víctor Manuel Ramírez Ochoa · Jorge Chaparro Garduño · César Pineda Vizcaíno · Clara Zaldívar García · Juan Ochoa Valencia · Germán Santos Cruz · Maximino Rojas Cordero · Valentín Monge Cárdenas · María Torres Contreras · José Carmen Herrera Orea · Domingo Estrada Pérez · Roberto Ramírez González · Pablo Ramírez González · Marco Antonio Bustamante · Apolinaria Santiago Hernández · Evedo Osorio López · Guillermo Osorio López · Gerardo Escobar Luévano · Juan Manuel Rodríguez Vásquez · Rodolfo Gómez López · Oswaldo Zamorano González · Juan Carlos Purata Purata · Gil Félix Medina · Serafín Andrade · José Carmen Raya Hernández · Remigio Salomón Barrientos · Bertha Carrillo Topete · José Ramírez Tirado · Cruz Piña Reyes · Noé Beltrán Mendoza · Ulises Ortiz Cruz · Florencio Mendoza Luciano · Roberto Xoyatla Orzuna · Arturo Mercado Arriaga · Victorino López Santiago · Moisés Díaz García · Mario Carrillo Ruiz · Juan Gabriel Gregorio Granados · Cristina González Ramírez · Pedro Ismael Orozco Gómez · Adán Mosqueda García · Emeterio Castañeda Aguirre · José Espinoza · Longinos Benítez Barrera · Raúl González Cruz · Julio Manuel Flores Salazar · Margarita Campos Romero · Roberto Bailón Camacho · Bellanira Ramos González · Juan Domínguez Morales · Guadalupe Ramírez · Francisco Morales Olvera · Francisco Paredes · Miguel Ángel García Navarrete · María del Carmen Dorantes Durán · Marcelino Valdivia Montes · Raúl Mendoza Díaz · Manuel Carrillo Rivera · Osvaldo González Guzmán · José Refugio Valle Gamiño · Roberto Saavedra Carrazco · Daniel Hernández González · Aureliano Cabrera Morales · Justino Rugerio Rodríguez · Felipe López Rodríguez · Antonio Morales Morales · Irma Estrada Gutiérrez · Wilfrido Santiago Alvarado · Fernando Salguero Lachino · Noel Guzmán González · Julio César Gallegos Durán · Evaristo Carrasco Luna · Eduardo Díaz Hernández · Cayetano Robles de la Torre · Luis Illescas González · William Benítez Cervera · Guillermo Cedillo Balderas · Margarita Melchor Rangel · Natalio Teodoro Solís · Pedro Felipe Juárez · Luis Manuel Ramírez Melgoza · Raúl Figueroa Cortés · Marcos Sánchez Sarabia · Adán Figueroa Ortiz · Homero Meza Fernández · Álvaro Rueda Hernández · Antonio Rentería Martínez · Óscar Cardoso Varón · Uriel Asunción Hernández · Celia Flora González Reyes · Víctor Aguilar Fernández · Efraín Barragán · Óscar Abel Córdova Vélez · Leonel Huicaza Valenzuela · Antonio Galván Carrillo · Fernando Mejía Alamilla · Epifanio Cárdenas Silva · Adrián Rogel Jaime · Olegario Márquez Morales · Isidro Zavala Lerma · Jesús Zavala Lerma · Andrés Valerde Hernández · José González Betan · Abel Uribe Mercado · Edithtrudis Agatón Flores · Juan Eduardo Chávez Ceballos · Jesús Nolasco

García · Ambrosio Ramírez Olvera · Carlos Segura Rosales · Jorge Alvarado Hernández · Felipe de Jesús Cervantes Hernández · Joel León
Montenegro · Armando Hernández López · Jaime Suárez Cázares · Daniel Toro López · José Ángel Leobardo Márquez García · Gonzalo
Cardeña Solorza · Andrés Artemio Ríos Canseco · Filemón Bañuelos Herrera · José Ricardo Ríos Aguilar · Alejandro Rodríguez Cazorla
Samuel Yépez Cervantes · Martín Mendoza Blaz · Rogelio Rodríguez Cobarrubias · Javier Martínez Fuentes · Antonio Ventura Torres · José
René Benítez Tadillo · Jaime Rocha Franco · Sebastián Díaz Ávila · Juan Martín Picasso Vega · José Ricardo Ríos Aguilar · Jaime Martínez
Martínez · Pedro Pérez Pedroza · Moisés Pérez Pedroza · Amado Morales Herrera · José Luciano Pérez Madrid · Rodrigo Olmos Esparza
Ildegardo Esteban Miranda · Óscar Vicencio Reyes · Irineo Aguilar Soto · Everardo García Estrada · José García Proaño · Alfredo Rodríguez
Ramos · María del Socorro Duarte Negrete · Enrique Luna Alaniz · Miguel Ángel Pérez Salazar · Timoteo Roblero Morales · José Jiménez Toala
Fabián Gutiérrez Rico · Oliver Mosqueda del Castillo · Mauricio Gutiérrez Lozano · Julio Millán Ávila · Loreto González Molina · Adelaida
Hernández Luna · Arturo Magallón Galarza · María Félix Tepal González · Silvia Barrera Tapia · Romualdo López Fuentes · Teresa Inés Vera
Navarrete · María Cruz Rosas · Marlene Tapia Gutiérrez · Evaristo González Mendoza · José Jorge Rivera Zúñiga · Ana María Padilla Echeverría
Miguel Zaragoza Santiago · Juan Manuel Rodríguez Ramírez · Leticia Hernández Sánchez · Ismael Apolinar · Osvaldo Martínez García ·Iraida
Medina Aguirre · Margarita Villa Rodríguez · Raymundo Sánchez Gómez · Onésimo García Ramírez · Melitón Juárez Cruz · Noé Juárez Cruz
Rubén Barragán Larios · Jesús Manuel González Aguilera · Sergio Figueroa Ceja · Javier López · Gustavo Uribe Durón · David Hernández Zúñiga
José Encarnación García Valle · Pablo Alberto Álvarez García · Carlos Adrián Corona Jiménez · Pedro López López · Luis Alejandro Bautista
Guadalupe Zacarías Hernández · Héctor Manuel Osaki Carreras ·Hugo Serrano Ángeles · Mario Orozco Zurita · Macario Vázquez Zurita
Manuel Moranchel Quintero · Roberto Montiel · Serafín Rivera López · Marcelo Figueroa Vázquez · Cupertino Retama Solís · Fernando Dimas
Bernal · Margarita Jarquín Pérez · Jorge Lemus Contreras · Emeterio Flores Sotelo · Inocente Bueno Eriza · José Ediberto Rodríguez Ruiz
Gerardo Torres Ramírez · Arcadio Rodríguez Pérez · Guillermo Valdovinos García · Rafael Silva Romero · Arturo Suástegui Altamirano · Juan
Luis Romero Garnica · Alejandro Jiménez Ruiz · Luis Ortiz Murillo · José Manuel López Guzmán · Felipe de Jesús Díaz · José Antonio Flores
Pérez · Belzar Haro Rodríguez · José Julián Gómez Ponce · Roberto Ávila Rodríguez · José Luis Uriostegui · Roberto García Hernández · Miguel
Estanislao Vicente · Antonio Gutiérrez Sánchez · José Arnulfo Estrada Pérez · Antonio Figueroa Velásquez · Nicolás Pablo Sánchez Martínez
Nemesio Castañeda Vargas · Manuel López Sánchez · Gabriel Vargas Méndez · José González de Santos · José Roberto Haros Avitia · Trinidad
Orozco Hernández · Marcelino Diego Castro · Jesús Plascencia Peinado · Leonardo Plascencia Morales · Roberto Castell Guzmán · Manuel
Hernández Solís · Jorge García Rivera · Jorge Lua Landín · Efigenia Chávez Solorio · José Antonio Araujo Álvarez · Efrén Ruiz Reynoso · Enrique
Belman Díaz · Carmen Albarrán Romero · Irma Castillo Hernández · José Trinidad Ruiz Lozano · Fidel Ramírez López · Vicente Coto Muñoz
Rubén Mendoza Sánchez · Horacio García Vásquez · María Mota López · Alma Rosa Pérez García · Amelia Calvo Asunción · Luisa Olivera
Santos · Gerardo Martínez Castro · José Luis Pantoja Arteaga · Feliciano Canseco Aguilar · Luis Morales Acosta · Jesús Herrera Romero
Prócoro Monterrosas Serrano · José Arturo Gutiérrez Salinas · Arturo Domínguez Moreno · Plutarco Ambriz Ambriz · Efraín Morales Cervantes
Raúl Hernández Echeverría · Aarón Vega Cruz · Johnathan Zaldívar Mimila · Juana Francisca Castellanos García · Miguel Castellanos García
Salvador Castellanos García · Juan Marcial Albino · Agustín Romero Luna · Jesús Márquez Pacheco · Santos Velásquez Villegas · Héctor Rubén
Moreno Valle · Antonio Ramírez Vargas · José Trinidad Hernández Atilano · Salvador Gerardo Sánchez Hernández · Maricarmen Risas Ponce
Luis Campa Molina · Cliserio Cristóbal Castañeda · Bernardino Valdez Huendo · Raúl Alfonso Campos Favila · Héctor Uriza Garzón · Margarita
Hernández Rodríguez · Roberto González Pantoja · Nilson López Vallinas · Luis Manuel Aguilar García · Leticia Torres Solís · Hugo Barajas Pérez
Bertha de la Merced Tapia · Cristina Castro Lucas · Arnulfo Flores Badillo · Edgar Adrián Martínez · Mario Castillo Fernández · Julián Ambros
Málaga · Enrique Landero García · Reyno Bartolo Fernández · Raymundo Barreda Maruri · Raymundo Barreda Landa · Alejandro Marín Caludio
Lorenzo Hernández Ortiz · Heriberto Badillo Tapia · Sergio Ruíz Marín · Marina Juárez Herrera · Efraín González Manzano · Jesús Ulloa González
Irene Islas Morales · Alberto Vigueras Alejandre · Luis Urzua Delgadillo · Anselmo Catalán Nava · Carlota de la Cruz Flores · Sergio Hernández
Jiménez · Wilfrido Valdez San Agustín · Agustín Torres García · Javier Hernández Hernández · Rosa Espino Jacobo · Arturo López Cevallos
Heraclio de Jesús Morales · Pedro Zaya Vergara · Miguel Ángel García Torres · Humberto Díaz Hernández · Ignacio de Loya Carmona Carmona
José René Labastida Cortez · Natalia Pérez Hernández · Víctor Ever Murillo Arzate · Margarita Miranda Martínez · Manuel de Jesús Espinoza
Gallegos · Rogelio Meléndez Sánchez · Marcelino González Aquino · María del Carmen León Camacho · Salvador Botello Cortés · María Isabel
Pacheco Madera · Quirino Lara Primo · Gonzalo Mora Carrillo · Socorro Arroyo Hernández · David Barrios Pérez · Samuel Núñez Cruz · Refugio
Belisario Jiménez · David de Jesús Flores Villarreal · Esteban Eleazar Alcántara · Alberto Aparicio Hernández · Arturo Arriaga Villa · Luz María
Centeno Zárate · Humberto Abad Carpio · Alejandro Acuña Isaías · Oseas Díaz Montejo · Austreberto Pérez López · Zacarías Hernández Díaz
Esperanza Vallejo Hernández · Rafael Carrillo Méndez · Sósimo Miguel Rodríguez · Juan Antonio Gómez Díaz · José Carmen Pamatz Molinero
Luis Ernesto Gil Cota · Julio César Hernández Morales · José Luis Vásquez Gutiérrez · Joel Aguilar Pérez · Ramón Díaz García · Raúl Lule
Hernández · Daniel Castro Bayón · Rogelio Contreras Navarrete · Gustavo Chávez Muñoz · Rubén Salcido Mesa · José I. Márquez Cervantes
Marcelino Luna Cabrales · María Pinita Ramírez Marques · Luis Francisco Hernández López · Martín Gómez Horte ·José Antonio Alcaraz?
David Girón López? · Rubén Pérez Sánchez? · Guadalupe Fragoso Dávalos? · Manuel López López? · Cresencio García Estrada? · Néstor
García Aburto · José Luis Pérez Cruz? · Romualdo Quintero Gutiérrez? · Adolfo Ríos López? · Justino Hernández Barrios? ·Pedro Jiménez
Briones? · Jorge A. Salas García · Cristóforo Meza García? · Orlando Eric Altamirano Jiménez? · Martín Aguilar Meza? · Zeferino Pérez Padilla?
Florina Pérez Padilla · Martha Olivia Cevallos García? · Ismael Bravo Vargas? · Alejandro Gomes Farías · José Guadalupe Carcamo Ortigaza?
Ana María Vargas Mendoza? · Isaac González Cevallos? · Juan Hernández Gamino · Victoria Sánchez Gasca · Elvia Rumbo Leyva · Moisés Fitz
Flores · Esteban Nieto Caballo · Rodolfo Jáuregui Quiñónez · Mario Alberto Bastidas Jiménez · Juval Martínez Jiménez · Juan José Escalera
Valdez · Juan Santiago Ocampo · Claudia Morales Salinas · Juan Carlos Quero Quero · Marcos César Moreno Solano · Arturo Martínez Olmos
Edgar Valdez García · Paulino Solís Verduzco · Eduardo Díaz Estrada · Gildardo Díaz Guerra · Luis Alonso Ceja González · Juventino Bravo
Curiel · Jesús Eduardo Cervantes Camacho · Mario Ortega Pérez · Leonardo Sánchez Placido · Severiano Miguel López · Gustavo Sánchez
Delgado · Javier Margarito Cortez · Gerardo Bailón Martínez · Eréndira Jiménez García · Santos Jiménez Pagle · Alma Rosa Cárdenas Moreno
José Luis Baltasar Santiago · Leonides Ortega Melo · J. Guadalupe Damián Govea · Esteban Vargas Lemos · Salomón Vega Guerrero · Maribel
Solís Blas · Juan Piña Soto · Julio César Villegas Gómez · Ana María Morales · Verónica García Álvarez · Fernando López Coria · Francisco
Gómez Anaya · Héctor Chavarín Zárate · Adri   Patricia Zavala Negrete · Raúl Sánchez Chávez · Rosa Lilia Parada Bermúdez · Juan Armand

…e León Pérez · Jaime Zúñiga Barragán · Reynaldo Velenzuela Camacho · José Refugio Ortega Nieves · Rosalba Maldonado Romero · Carlos
Echeverría Bribiezca · Iván Escalante Maldonado · Rufino Cordero Castillo · Martín Vilchis Ángeles · Francisco Juárez Ozuna · Gabriel Álvarez
López Herrera · Pedro Ramírez · Marcos Gildardo Montes · Rosa Valencia Torres · Rafael Mata García · Jesús Saénz Mendoza · Felipe M.
Ramírez · José Jesús Santana · María del Consuelo Morales Ávalos · Luisa Zagal García · Lorena García Temozihui · Estanislao Torres Coria ·
Emilio Ramírez Morato · María Oralia Varela Padilla · Pedro Contreras González · Noé Carreón Rojas · Gustavo Vallejo Delgadillo · Elvia Huerta
Gocobachi · José Luis Nicolás González · Miguel Ángel Duarte Meza · Víctor Arzola Méndez · Raúl Garibay Alvarado · Gabriel Mercado Cota ·
Víctor Carrillo Medina · Tomasa Ochoa Zamora · José Antonio Bautista Herrera · Bernardino López Gabriel · María del Carmen Rodríguez
Martínez · María del Pilar González Hernández · Gumercindo Reyes Loxada Hipal · Onésimo Salazar Cruz · Manuel Pérez Chávez · Eliseo
Benítez Santos · Rubén Salcido Meza · José I. Márquez Cervantes · Dionisio Alvarado Gutiérrez · Alejandro Gómez Farías · José Guadalupe
Carcamo Ortigoza · Felipe de Jesús Aviña Jiménez · Carlos Manuel Rivera Chávez · Leandro Leyva Luna · Miguel Mejía Amarillas · Miguel
Castro Rodríguez · María Oralia Varela Padilla · María Isabel de la Cruz Medina · Rubén Vargas Bernal · Erick José Antonio Noriega Patiño · Iván
Fontes López (Alejandro) · Alvino López Bautista · Angélica Echiveste Limón · Gerardo Rodríguez Zaranda · Alejandra García Álvarez · Lorena
García Temozihui · Estanislao Torres Coria · Emilio Ramírez Morato · María Oralia Varela Padilla · Pedro Contreras González · Noé Carreón Rojas ·
Gustavo Vallejo Delgadillo · Elvia Huerta Gocobachi · José Luis Nicolás González · Miguel Angel Duarte Meza · Víctor Arzola Méndez · Raúl
Garibay Alvarado · Gabriel Mercado Cota · Víctor Carrillo Medina · Tomasa Ochoa Zamora · José Antonio Bautista Herrera · Bernardino López
Gabriel · María del Carmen Rodríguez Martínez · María del Pilar González Hernández · Gumercindo Reyes Loxada Hipal · Onésimo Salazar Cruz ·
María Isabel de la Cruz Medina · Rubén Vargas Bernal · Erick José Antonio Noriega Patiño · Iván Fontes López (Alejandro) · Alvino López
Bautista · Angélica Echiveste Limón · Gerardo Rodríguez Zaranda · Alejandra García Álvarez · Víctor Mondragón de Jesús · Aurelio Ramírez
Barraza · José Ciriaco Monroy Chávez · René Salvador Ramírez · Guillermo Feria Morales · Isidro López Navarrete · José Luis Salazar Chairez ·
Ignacio Solís Montiel

ARIZONA Juan Ezequiel Gutiérrez Andrade · Evelio López Laines · Rosa Palomino Pérez · Raúl Mendoza · Everardo Amaya · Jiménez · Ana
Claudia Villa Herrera · Miguel Ángel Vázquez Godínez Elidia Martínez Macario · Rolando Morales Solano · Arturo Acosta Soto · José Martín
Molina Panuco · Efraín Molina Ruiz · Abel Acero Díaz · Jorge Ayala Trujillo · Francisco Hernández Morales · Roberto Plascencia González ·
Pedro Velázquez Quintero · Telésforo Franco Hernández · César Ramos Fernández · Héctor Carrizosa López · Juan Mejía Álvarez · Martín
Ortega Campos · Marco Antonio Cortez Iriqui · Marco Antonio Castillo Puga · José Ramón González Salazar · Cuauhtémoc Lavín Valentín ·
Héctor Lavín Martínez · Martín Martínez Zaragoza · Roberto Ramírez Ramírez · José Guadalupe Llanitos Villalobos · Manuel de Jesús Flores
Hartalejo · José Antonio Rodríguez Hernández · Aarón Moisés Delgado López · Alejandro Félix Barraza · Carmen Margarita Rodríguez Martínez ·
Guillermo Barrera · Ana María Pacheco Mejía · Manuel de Jesús García Coronado · Gerardo García Cota · Teófilo Camacho Salinas · José
Macías Fernández · Verónica Nadia López Muñoz · María Eugenia Aguillón Díaz · Olivio Velázquez Pérez · Modesto Santos Flores · Francisco
Chima Mil · Cirilo Larios Guzmán · Ramón Figueroa Chávez · Abelino Armenta Martínez · Antelma Graciela Castelán Gutiérrez · Cándido
Rodríguez Pacheco · Roberto Baltazar de Jesús Zamora · María del Rocío Bravo Candia · Nátali Hipólito Enríquez · Luis Roberto Morales
Avendaño · Emma Monteclaro Castillo · Rodolfo Lagunes Beltrones · Rafael Ortega Ramírez · Jesús Vidal Ramírez · María Inés González Álvarez ·
Jesús Magaña Otero · Alfredo Ubieta Domínguez · José Inés Díaz González · Delia Moreno Pérez · Gerardo Nevares Gallegos · Carlos Miguel
González Corona · Edmundo Ángel Selvas Ruiz · Zenón Reséndiz Nieto · Teresa Cabrera Baltasar · Herlindo Martínez de Jesús · Eusebio García
Pérez · Julio Alfredo Lagunas Castillo · Enrique Soto Pacheco · Juana Medina Butanda · Marina Montaño Mercado · Héctor Guadalupe Sánchez
Murrieta · José César Mendoza Mendoza · Fermín Aguilar Rabadán · Maura Zacarías Sánchez · María Cruz Ruiz · Yolanda González Galindo ·
Juan Manuel Acosta Rojas · Alberto Márquez Castelán · Víctor Talavera Figueroa · María E. Morales Sierra · Jesús Rodríguez Coronel · Omar
Sánchez Guevara · Justino Vidal Bautista · Janet Mata Méndez · Juan Manuel Ruiz Dávalos · Gerardo Rosas Martínez · José Luis Vergara Flores ·
Juan Rodríguez Sánchez · Víctor H. Dávila Ehuan · José Carlos Wicab Chable · Adán Martínez Faustino · Salvador Mendoza Guizar · Abel
Martínez Faustino · Hugo Sánchez Acevedo · Manuel Gómez Hernández · Óscar Cervantes Melquíades · Froylán Flores Hernández · José
Guadalupe Rico Sánchez · Ramón Gámez Mesa · Guillermina Herrera Guzmán · Enedina Torralba Martínez · Laura Vargas Ortiz · Pedro Basulto
Neri · Antonia Méndez Méndez · Eutiquio Dorantes Marín · Modesta Pacheco Pérez · Mario Calderón Jiménez · Roberto Arturo Olvera Morales ·
Julio Yáñez Hernández · Rosalía Bazán Miranda · Juan José Ontiveros Lizarraga · Raúl López Sánchez · Demetrio Vélez García · Cazares
Sánchez · Miguel Ángel Chigüil Arres · Paula Isela Romero Palacios · Yolanda Novoa Ponce de León · Isaura Viviana Medina Paredes · Pedro
Mejía Palacios · Leticia Herrera Navarro · Ángel González Hernández · Elizabeth Esther Gómez Balbuena · Luis Cáseres Cabrera · Juan Pedro
Patiño Rojas · Felipe Sánchez Nájera · Fernando Mendoza Cruz · Alicia Adela Sotelo Mendoza · María del Rosario González Ortiz · Víctor Juárez
González · Sergio Pérez Pescador · Abelardo Pérez Hernández · Armando Rosales Pacheco · Buenaventura Ayala Zamora · Iván Centeno
González · Tiburcio Agudo Martínez · Adela Salas Pérez · Guadalupe Nieto Octaviano · Lauro Barrios Domínguez · María Dolores Espinoza
Rosario Sánchez Roguel · Roberto Bautista López · Anastasio López Guerrero · Martín Espinoza Cruz · José Aldegundo Romero · Enrique
Mendoza Castillo · Jorge Alonso Mireles · Andrea Alcántar Cruz · Álvaro Segovia García · Alberto Maldonado Viveros · Irasema Martínez
Jiménez · Carlos Armando Gracián Bustamante · Petra Verónica Tenerio Soto · Juana Martínez Sánchez · Abel González Domínguez · Esteban
Durán Aburto · Hermila Romero Carreño · Jorge Montes Montejano · Marco Antonio Grado Miramontes · Dalvin Eugenio Urbina Krik · Santiago
Pacheco Ramírez · Didier García Villanueva · Lidia Dimas Téllez · Catalina Ventura Mendoza · Irene González Hernández · Elizabeth Juárez Río
Frío · Graciela Hernández Alvarado · Lorena Chávez Martínez · Prócoro Flores Ortiz · Heriberto Núñez Robles · José Ángel García · Ernesto
Alonso Gutiérrez Ramírez · Casimiro Chavira Ramos · Héctor Salcedo Hernández · Gerardo Rubén Jiménez Martínez · Gerardo Román Jiménez
Martínez · Carmelo Monárrez Ramírez · Diego Enríquez Quevedo · María Dolores Martínez Vega · Samuel Fernando Arce Muñiz · Wenceslao
Torres Torres · Rafael Alberto Palma Salas · Tomás Molina Pérez · Mario Bustillos Sallet · Cástulo Salazar Ontiveros · Carlos García Aguirre ·
Miguel Fructuoso Hernández · Martín Grijalva Martínez · Miguel Ochoa González · Arturo Heras Espinoza · Esteban Bulmaro Olvera Alabarrán ·
Jesús Rojas Villa · David González Soriano · Víctor Acevedo Díaz · Alonso Hernández Hernández · Claudio Martínez Cortez · René Rodríguez

Ramírez · Francisco Trujillo Ruiz · Simeón Díaz Cruz · Miguel Ochoa González · Domitila Mondragón Alvarado? · Rogelio Cruz Cervantes?
Jaime Rodríguez Gutiérrez? · Sofía Rubio Chávez? · Paula Hernández Tapia? · María Guillermina Sánchez Salto · Raúl López de Anda? · Arturo
Gómez Castro · Antonio Vargas Torres? · José M. Raygoza Gil · Alex Sosa Coba? · Margarito Escorcia Franco? · Arturo Jiménez Gutiérrez
María E. López Gómez · Santiago Arcos Mota? · Adilene López Moreno · Rafael López Méndez? · Eva Hernández Escárcega? · Norma
Rodríguez Amado? · Margarita Ríos Rodríguez? · Eraís Quintana Martínez? · Florencio Pedroza Guadarrama? · Ángeles Contreras González?
Víctor Galindo Torres · Ricardo Pantaleón Santiago? · Felipe Hernández? · Gonzalo González Saldaña? · María Luisa Lozano de la Rosa?
Martín Moreno Montero? · Beatriz Cuautle Gutiérrez? · Alfonso Caloca Vargas? · Juana González Ramírez? · José Lara Ávila?· René Reséndiz
Rodríguez · Santos Fabián González Paredes? · Blanca Estela García Reyes? · Ramiro García Abarca · Mauro Santos Tolentino · Rogelio
Sánchez Santoyo · María de Jesús Candelario Rodríguez? · José Luis Hernández Aguirre? · Rubén González Miranda? · José Salazar Velarde?
Cristina Domínguez Librado? · Alejandro Hernández Badillo? · Jesús Torres Santiago? · Máximo Barrera Esquivel? · Domingo López? · Lucía
Agustina López? · Leonel Tuxpan Jarno · Raúl Estrada Frías ·Joel Hernández Águila? ·Eledi Sánchez Cirilo? · Manuel Escandón Morales?
Ismael Tepox Gamboa? ·Dolores Trejo Ramírez? · María Dolores Trejo? · Alberico Córdova Robledo? · Oscar Ireneo Santillán? · María de Jesús
Ruiz García? · Francisco Cueva Ochoa? · Zenaida Colmenero Dircio? · María Mancero Rojas? · Jesús Beltrán Hernández? · Dámaso Rosales
Zamudio · Emma Mercedes Quintal Parra? · Elizabeth Hahuatzi Martínez? · Maribel Muñoz Bustos? ·Roberto Rodríguez? · Maricarmen Xaltenco
Serapio · Alejandrina de la Soledad Félix Sánchez · Leandro Bautista Alba? · Juana Santacruz García? · José Alfonso Abortes ·Eugenio Reyes
González? · Alfredo Escobar López · Alma Delia Cruz López? · Pablo Espinoza Hernández ·Cecilio Cabrera Pedro? · María de la Luz Magaña?
Alfredo Campos Márquez · Oscar Borbón Mendoza · José Antonio Pérez Rubio · Jorge Cruz Becerril · Liliana Robles Enríquez · Carmen A.
Robles Enríquez · Lorna Robles Enríquez · Gonzalo Gómez Gómez · Cesario Ruiz Cortez · Albino Montes Campos · Amalia Ortiz Licona · Celso
Villa México · Antonio Mora Martínez · Mariano Durán Saucedo · María Dolores Vera Mendoza · Gabriel Torres Alcalá · Palemón González Avilés
Efraín Salinas Zagal · Noé Álvarez López · María del Carmen Infante Hernández · José Andrés Aguayo Contreras · José Luis Rodríguez Tavares
Francisco Chávez Mújica · Josefina Martínez Sánchez · José Refugio Ferral del Ángel · Rocael Hernández Gómez · Martín Gallegos Pérez
Guillermo Federico Sánchez Lomeli · Juan Matías García Zavaleta · Roberto Torres Ramírez · Teresa Vela Velásquez · Azucena Ortiz · Miguel
Ángel Rodríguez Ortiz · Miguel Ángel Rodríguez Esparza · Federico Medina Rodríguez · Avelino Andrés Cabrera González · Genaro Rosales
Martínez · René Olvera Medina · Elías Hernández Hernández · Mario González Hernández · Herminia Fuentes Sánchez · Luis Fernando Noriega
Ayala · María Cristina Hernández Pérez · Sergio Enrique Mejía Pérez · Manuel Hernández Martínez · Jorge Aburto Zamorano · Juan Tova
Hernández · José Ángel López Cárdenas · Zita Islas Uribe · Adriana Aparicio Ortega · Eliseo Vargas Luna · Adrián Díaz Dionisio · Honorio
Ramírez Martínez · Armando Valadez · Antonio Álvarez Solórzano · Keila Velásquez González · Pedro Xichicale Tlapalcoyoa · Antonio Aguirre
Bustamante · Leticia Villagrán Flores · Javier Gabriel Valdez · María Alejandra Orea Guzmán · Juan Manuel C. Mojuto · María Teresita Galván
Ávila · Nora Cecilia Huertas Hernández · Rocío Quintero Ramírez · Teodomiro Vázquez Marcos · Efrén Gutiérrez Hernández · Juan Miguel Cano
Elvira · Carlos Valentín Bahena · Patricia Cortazar Espitia · Guadalupe Cayetano Cornelio · Antonio Rolon Hernández · Ángela Contreras Rojas
María Guadalupe Vázquez Saavedra · Fortino Vázquez García · Elonina López Alfaro · Saúl Domínguez Luján · Héctor Romero Correa · Delia
Herrera Atilano · Sergio Benítez Hernández · Sergio García González · Ricardo Olivares Martínez · Juan Carlos Lopez Hernández · Marcial Pérez
Álvarez · Mauricio Sasas Guerra · Agustín Hernández Jiménez · Amado de Jesús de Jesús · Abigail Dalia Rodríguez López · Martín de Jesús
Bernabé · Irene Ayllón Velásquez · Miguel Rodríguez Marentes · Ernesto Rivelino Ramírez Blancas · Flora María Reyes Cruz · Zenaida González
Robledo · Alfredo Fabián Gudiño Ruiz · Juan Miguel Velásquez Navarro · Manuel de Jesús Sánchez Rodríguez · José Fernando Martín Fuentes
Víctor Manuel Plascencia Basilio · Hilda Roblero Roblero · Nicolás de Jesús García Ventura · José Manuel Gómez Cruz · Alma Rosa de la Torre
Hurtado · Juan Antonio Nila Valdivia · Pascual Carbajal Maya · Florencio García · Lorenzo López Díaz · Lucio Hernández Hernández · Carlos
Ramón Bejarano Cañez · Miguel Díaz García · Efraín Castro Ramírez · Jaime Monroy Gamiño · Miguel Ángel Laurel · Antonio Gómez García
Rubén García Gamiño · Ana Cruz García · Juan Carlos Rico Orihuela · Rosa María Arriaga Castillo · Rafael Martínez Ruiz · Nahum Martínez
Solano · Juan Mendoza · Martín Chaires Corral · Magdalena Antonio Pérez · Jorge Rolando Cano Yeh · José Antonio Ruiz Campos · Atanasio
Castañeda Ramos · Miguel Ángel Velázquez Hernández · Abel Alemán Cabrera · Daniel Haro Martínez · Faustino Bermeo Rayón · Agustín Rita
Santos · Nicolás Padilla Reyes · Isidro Gutiérrez Reyes · Ciro Vega Velásquez · Pedro Zárraga Ramos · Hilda Hernández Baltasar · Carlos
Francisco Casanova Estrada · Óscar Antonio Arrequidez Ortega · Adrián Gárnica Hernández · José María Martínez Espinoza · Adelfo Rosales
González · Leopoldo Alvarado Sánchez · Oscar Chávez Torres · Florencio Monroy Rocha · Sotero Gómez Viveros · María Lucía Martínez · Daniel
Alvarado Patiño · Carlos Castro Ilescas · Antonio Ávila Cortés · Margarito Aguillares Hernández · Gabriel Ortega Flores · Raúl Ramos Chávez
José Paz Arriaga Mercado · Maria del Carmen Sabino García · Concepción Anfreas García · Rolando Pérez Vázquez · Juan Leonel Lizárraga
Jaime González Pablo · Fortino Soto Armenta · Rosario Muñoz Berelleza · Francisco Javier Acosta Sandoval · Reynael Cortínez Roblero
Rodrigo Miranda Rivera · Feliciana Tadeo Hernández · Reyes Salazar Campos · Tomás Soto Granados · Norma Alicia Moreno Hernández
Fidelina Bravo de Marzan · Yecxal Alvarado Monterrosa · Mario Alberto Rodríguez Pérez · Álvaro Ramos de Castilla · Altagracia Marbella Tapia
Guillen · José Juan Pacheco Salazar · Aurelio Torres Soto · Carmen Ávila Vargas · Juan Manuel Guerrero Díaz · Federico Campos Mayor
Armando Antunez Mendoza · Socorro Ayala Beltrán · Sofía Beltrán Galicia · María Cristina Salinas Gonzales · María Fabiola Palomares Ríos
Mario Soto Trejo · Carlos Alberto Argueta Lezama · Emilio León Domínguez · Raymundo Santana Hernández · Armida Martínez Preciado
Roberto Parra Orduño · Marcelo Infante Pereira · Leopoldo Méndez Murrieta · Rosa Viviana Torres Corona · Emelia Pérez Santiago · Edgar Isidro
Díaz Estrada · Issac Melo Mejía · Adalberto Tello Encarnación · Isaias Espinoza Gonzales · Olivo Martínez de la Cruz · Manuel Luis Ramírez
Herrera · Teofilo López Manrique · Jovita Martínez Agudo · Ángel Alberto Lizárraga · Silvia Rodríguez Gómez · Víctor Machuca Quesnell · César
Andrés Moya Vargas · Blanca Estela Ferreyra Vidal · Maricruz Frías Amador · Ismael Gómez Herrera · Raquel Hernández Cruz · Ana Montes
Gámez · Óscar Valderrabano Hidago · Librado Tolentino Velazco · María de la Cruz Fores Martínez · Nancy Navarrete Hernández · Marcos de
la Cruz Sandoval · Julio César Romero Espargo · Paulina Morales Exiquio (María Adriana Alvarado Leyva) · Joséfina Useda Barajas · Mario
Alberto Díaz Ponce · Sergio Cabrera Hernández · Reyna Figueroa Espinoza · Omar Francisco Ortiz Camacho · Luciano Limón Sánchez
Verónica Dueñas Ramírez · Jesús Hernández López · Rogelio Juárez Torres · Eufracia Cuautláhuatl Cuautle · Rafael López Méndez · Eraís
Quintana Martínez · Florencia Pedroza Guadarrama · José Martín Alcaraz · Gonzalo González Saldaña · Santos Fabian González Paredes
Ramiro García Abarca · María de Jesús Candelario Rodríguez · José Luis Hernández Aguirre · Domitila López López · Saúl Segura Oliveros

lonso Caloca vargas · Salvador Macedo de la Paz · Eleuterio Guzmán Hernández · Alfredo Rosas Ramos · Isidro Domínguez Ledesma · Miriam Maldonado Peraza (Medrano Pedraza) · José Ángel Miranda Escobar · Pablo Gerardo Lázaro · Enrique Vital Aguinaga · Francisco Javier Sánchez Aguilar · José Enrique de Jesús Serrano · Eduardo Amador Munguía de la Cruz · Albertano Herrera Liborio · Aurelio Ríos Venegas Antonia de la Cruz Andrade · Karina Portillo Cortez · Madilio Luis Gutiérrez Pérez (José Luis Pérez) · Manuel Batalla González · Rosa Peña Ocampo · Jesús Román García · Gustavo Adolfo González Cruz · Eleuterio Guzmán Hernández · Adrián Gárnica Hernández · José María Martínez Espinoza · José Antonio Pérez Rubio · Adelfo Rosales González · Leopoldo Alvarado Sánchez · Oscar Chávez Torres · Florencio Monroy Rocha · Sotero Gómez Viveros · María Lucía Martínez · Daniel Alvarado Patiño · Carlos Castro Ilescas · Antonio Ávila Cortés · Margarito Aguillares Hernández · Gabriel Ortega Flores · Raúl Ramos Chávez · José Paz Arriaga Mercado · María del Carmen Sabino García · Concepción Anfreas García · Rolando Pérez Vázquez · Juan Leonel Lizarraga · Juan González Pablo · Fortino Soto Armenta · Rosario Muñoz Berelleza Francisco Javier Acosta Sandoval · Reynael Cortinez Roblero · Rodrigo Miranda Rivera · Feliciana Tadeo Hernández · Reyes Salazar Campos Tomas Soto Granados · Norma Alicia Moreno Hernández · Fidelina Bravo de Marzan · Yecxal Alvarado Monterrosa · Mario Alberto Rodríguez Pérez · Álvaro Ramos de Castilla · José Juan Pacheco Salazar · Aurelio Torres Soto · Carmen Ávila Vargas · Juan Manuel Guerrero Díaz Federico Campos Mayor · Armando Antunez Mendoza · Socorro Ayala Beltrán · Sofía Beltrán Galicia · María Cristina Salinas Gonzales · María Fabiola Palomares Ríos · Mario Soto Trejo · Carlos Alberto Argueta Lezama · Emilio León Domínguez · Marcelo Infante Pereira · Leopoldo Méndez Murrieta · Rosa Viviana Torres Corona · Emelia Pérez Santiago · Issac Melo Mejía · Adalberto Tello Encarnación · Olivo Martínez de la Cruz · Manuel Luis Ramírez Herrera · Teofilo López Manrique · Jovita Martínez Agudo · Ángel Alberto Lizárraga · Silvia Rodríguez Gómez · Victor Machuca Quesnell · César Andrés Moya Vargas · Blanca Estela Ferreyra Vidal · Maricruz Frias Amador · Ismael Gómez Herrera · Raquel Hernández Cruz · Ana Montes Gámez · Óscar Valderrabano Hidago · Librado Tolentino Velazco · María de la Cruz Flores Martínez · Nancy Navarrete Hernández · Marcos de la Cruz Sandoval · Julio César Romero Espargo · Paulina Morales Exiquio (María Adriana Alvarado Leyva) osefina Useda Barajas · Mario Alberto Díaz Ponce · Sergio Cabrera Hernández · Reyna Figueroa Espinoza · Omar Francisco Ortiz Camacho Luciano Limón Sánchez · Verónica Dueñas Ramírez · Jesús Hernández López · Alfredo Rosas Ramos · Isidro Domínguez Ledesma · Miriam Maldonado Peraza (Medrano Pedraza) · José Ángel Miranda Escobar · Pablo Gerardo Lázaro · Salvador Andrés González Leyva · Enrique Vital Aguinaga · Francisco Javier Sánchez Aguilar · José Enrique de Jesús Serrano · Eduardo Amador Munguia de la Cruz · Aurelio Ríos Venegas Albertano Herrera Liborio · Antonia de la Cruz Andrade · Karina Portillo Cortez · Madilio Luis Gutiérrez Pérez (José Luis Pérez) · Rosa Peña Ocampo · Manuel Batalla González · Jesús Román García · Gustavo Adolfo González Cruz · José Alfredo García Martínez · Aurora Cuamba Magallón · Enrique Morales Flores · Isaías Juan Gálvez Pérez · Telésforo Arroyo Santos · Leonardo Plata Escamilla · José Trinidad Alcoce Martínez · Leticia Ruiz Ruiz · Dante Roldán Flores · Abel Salinas Cortes · Humberto Hernández Hernández · José Narciso Hernández Ledezma Óscar Francisco León García · Edith Cuevas Avelar · Miguel Cano Delgado · Ana Laura Aguilar Anaya · Luis Alberto Arévalo Morales · Alberto Salmerón Merino · Miguel Santos Robles · Miguel Ángel Domínguez · David Orozco Romo · Alejandro Rangel Luna · Casildo Hernández Almaraz o Sergio García Ruiz · Diana Raquel García Velasco · Usterlin Tránsito Masariegos · Uziel Baldón Martínez · Gregorio Martín García Cárdenas · Luis Cisneros Ventura · María del Pilar Hernández Espinoza · Mauro Guadalupe Mecedal Hernández · Eric Sánchez Domínguez Felipe Nañez González · Pedro Alejandro Valencia Pinedo · Octavio Ortiz Martínez · Leobardo Contreras Rodríguez · Juan Luis Vea Ruelas Rosalba Castillo López · David Gonzalo Castillo · Fernando Rodríguez Flores · Araceli Estrada López · Emilio Solis Trinidad · José Salomón López · Jorge Ruiz Bravo (José Ruiz Bravo) · Inés Enríquez Bamfi · Miguel Hernández Hernández · Salvador Díaz López · Raúl Avelar Martínez Reyna Antonio Pérez · Leonel Trujillo Beltrán · Francisco Gerónimo Flores · Jesús Sánchez Rincón · Ramón Pérez Urrea · Oralia Soto Madrigal José Luis Zavala Morales · Marín Pérez Morales · Julio César Moreno

NEW MEXICO Víctor de Jesús Montalvo · Eunice Ávila Hernández · Remedios Rojas Fernández · María A. Montellano Jiménez · Juan Pablo Miranda García · Isidro Badillo Barrientos · Miguel Jiménez Pérez

TEXAS Espiridión Rosales · Alberto Salazar Martínez · Juan Espinoza · René Ortiz · Ofelio Linares · Francisco Chávez Hernández · José Antonio Larrazola · Apolonio Ramírez · Pablo Vilchis Bravo · Luis Alejandro Lejona Barrón · Benjamín Cabrera Velásquez · Telésforo Velásquez Mario Valdez · Alfredo Izaguirre · Menor Torres · Sixta Cruz Cruz · Miguel Saldívar Medrano · Marco Antonio Hernández Reyes · Cleto Ramírez Vite · Andrea Cortez · Luis Villanueva González · Juan Pablo González Amaya · Gerardo Muñiz · José Israel Rodríguez Lara · Amador Pasillas Sergio Vargas Calderón · Hugo Vargas Calderón · Arturo Cardona Omaya · Javier Cárdenas Hernández · Christian Escamilla Noriega · Roberto Ramírez Cubos · Rufino Lara Guevara · Rafael Mejorada Castillo · Jorge Carlos Luna Muñoz · Valentín Caballero Landeros · Rogelio Nolasco Márquez · Javier García Herrera · Miguel Ramírez Vázquez · Jesús Pérez Luna · César Arenas · Osiel Valdez González · Alejandro Hernández García · Javier Estrada Soto · Aquiles Peña Chávez · César Campos Gómez · Humberto Martínez Galindo · Ramón García Jiménez · Nemesio Vallejos · Froilán Cervantes Muñiz · Jesús Manuel Marentes Escobar · Juan Manuel Marentes Escobar · Antonio Sánchez Morales · Pedro Solorio Enríquez · Hiram Martínez Mendoza · Juana Ávila Martínez · Salvador Colín · Eliud Cardiel Rodríguez · Manuel López · Antonio Espinoza Luna · Salvador Martínez Martínez · Ricardo Salazar Juárez · Sergio Rodríguez Almaguer · José Luis Huizache Ramos · Armando Martínez Alvarado · Adrián Flores Hernández · Carlos Villalobos Sandoval · Filiberto Carrillo Ramírez · José Alonso Figueroa de la Luz · Bernardo Carbajal Pineda · Alejandro García Gasca · Gerardo González de la Rosa · Héctor de Jesús Hernández Hernández · Bernardo Carbajal Pineda · Daniel Rojas Lara · Alejandro Torres Ramírez · Enrique Miranda Colín · José de Jesús Gómez Regalado · David Serrato Mondragón · Martín Dorante Castillo · Josué Escobar Castillo · Ricardo Ortega Díaz · Juan León · Juan Manuel Flores García · José Fidencio Sierra Maldonado · Iván Arellano Zavaleta · Alicia Ponce Juárez · Gustavo Chagoya Estrada · Raúl Salas Longoria · Osvael Samayoa Calderón · Juan Hernández Hernández · Juan de la Cruz Aranda Rodríguez · Rosina Loma Ramírez · Fidel Martínez Mojica · Roberto Pérez Gaytán · Marcelo Ortiz Maldonado · Juan Fidel Segovia Martínez · Gustavo Oropeza Carrasco · Antonio Loredo Flores · Armando Río Acosta · Joel Andrés Rivera

Rogelio Castro González · Javier Aguilar de Dios · Juan Fuentes Bernos · Julio Arturo Verástegui Martínez · José Tomás Medrano Martínez · Roberto Pozos Onofre · Magdaleno Ramírez García · Raúl Martínez Delgado · Jesús Martínez Prado · José Isabel Rodríguez Martínez · Juan Valles Romero · Juan Manuel Cervantes Arriaga · Carlos Rayas Rodríguez · Álvaro Salinas Salinas · César Gutiérrez Hernández · José Carrizales Méndez · Martín de la Garza Cruz · Manuel Mendoza Ledesma · Miguel Ángel Martínez Castillo · Enrique Bustamante Córdova · Yolanda Hernández Morales · Jerónimo Mendoza Guzmán · Raúl Albarrán Ortiz · Alberto Arévalo Gutiérrez · Jorge Cabrera Tovar · Vicente López Barbosa · Pablo Salazar Puente · Eustorgio Fermín Flores Martínez · Joaquín Contreras Rabino · Leobardo Ortiz Pérez · Enrique Guzmán Jiménez · Roberto Zavala Álvarez · René García Pérez · Isaac Hernández · Rubén Alonso Segura · Fernando Fraga Ortega · Jorge Alberto Reyes Hermilo Olvera Patlán · Luis Antonio Gallardo Mendoza · Marcos Pacas Gutiérrez · Esperanza Flores de Almanza · Nelson Herrera Refinos José Eduardo Arriaga Alonso · Esthela Ruiz Torres · José Víctor Jiménez Torres · Jorge Garcés Rogel · Emilio Maqueda Villeda · Juan Carlos Juárez Cast illo · María del Carmen Martínez · José Manuel Ayala Flores · José Montero Gómez · Alfonso Villalobos Álvez · Francisco Bazares Jaime Montoya Ramírez · Edgar Villalbo Salgado · Miguel Ángel Martínez Herrera · Juan Antonio Sixto Contreras · Jorge Murillo Ríos · Gustavo García Rosales · Gildardo Sánchez · Luisa Hernández Cruz · José Vélez Leos · Luis Augusto Juárez Castellano · Guillermo Castilla Islas Romualdo Martínez Estévez · Eduardo Rea Ramírez · Eugenio Saucedo Valdez · Adolfo Sánchez Salgado · Marcial Rodríguez Niño · Enrique Mancera Ortiz · Ramiro Ramírez Martínez · Eutimio García Ibarra · Leonarda Rodríguez Castillo · Gustavo Miranda Granados · Guillermo Solís Ramírez · Norma Ramos Becerra · Félix García Domínguez · Andrés García Esquivel · Juan Maldonado Silva · Sergio Alberto Llanas López Joel Hernández Domínguez · Edgar Hernández Sánchez · Rubén Pérez Ríos · José Sánchez González · Arturo Villaseñor Vega · Agustín Vega Bastida · Verónica Ramírez Ramírez · Mateo Ledezma González · Jesús Trujillo Vallejo · Miguel Palafox Carreón · Salvador Dávalos Rico Magdalena Luna Ulloa · José Juan Prieto Soto · Roberto Vargas Domínguez · Heriberto Parra Estopellano · Rosendo Eduardo Luna Domínguez José del Carmen Rivero · María Inocencia Velásquez Fernández · Antonio García López · Osvaldo García Herrera · Eric Rojas Márquez Raimundo González Rangel · Juan Martín Alvarado Pérez · Avelino Reyes Promotor · Manuel Idanguray Puente · Juan Villanueva Martínez Sergio Armando Salinas Cisneros · Rubén Alanís · Lenin Guzmán Cuevas · Abraham González López · Guillermo Luna Rivera · Raúl Quintos Cuéllar · Humberto Espinoza Gallegos · Ernesto Zúñiga · Teresa Delgado Mercado · Juan Carlos Cuenca Valadés · Teresa Villa Dimas · Salvador Flores Torres · José Quintero Vargas · José Cruz Quintero Vargas · José Jesús Quintero Vargas · Francisco Espinoza Vázquez · Miguel Ángel Rivera Castillo · José Narmo Ramírez Mendoza · Florentino Mayerido Rico · José de Jesús Andrade Lugo · Esaúl Balderas Quiñónez · Tereso Delgado · Eusebio de Haro Espinosa · Dionisio Muñoz Pérez · Marcelino García Colunga · Manuel Romero Torres · Ricardo López Puente Marcial González Padrón · Teodolfo Rubio García · Francisco Javier Copián Rangel · Alfonso Rodríguez Rodríguez · José Gregorio Méndez Antonio González Reina · Daniel Castillo Morales · Ricardo Morales Barajas · Alfredo Garza García · Eleuterio Arteaga · Ricardo García Márquez Armando Maldonado · Walter María Sandoval · José Antonio Ramírez Martínez · Luis Hernández Guerrero · José Francisco Cabello Pichardo Miguel Hernández Ibarra · Juan José Domínguez Paredes · Gustavo Cruz · Octavio Vargas Jaimes · María Elena Gutiérrez · Martha Llanas Torres Santos Espinoza González · Juan Alberto Treviño Baez · Humberto Frabe · José Vargas · Guillermo Zamora Acosta · Hugo Antonio Solís Cruz Rubicel Solís Cruz · Concepción Prieto Bermea · Celestino Ledesma · Martha Irma Cervantes Juárez · Ismael Cerda Hernández · Ambrosia González Hernández · Fortunata Hernández Rebollar · Feliciano Flores Hernández · Enrique García Sosa · David Benítez González · Fernando Arellano Covarrubias · María del Refugio Hernández Rojas · Juan Narciso Muñoz Ruiz · Emmanuel Godínez Muñoz · Martha Herrera Buendía Santos Peña Lara · Rubén Mejía Cruz · Casimiro Morales Temich · Ebodio Martínez Muñoz · Jaime Alvarado Salazar · Geisel Rodríguez García Heriberto Mendoza Faz · María Antonia Zamudio Martínez · Tranquilino Ramírez Sotelo · Fidel González San Juan · Pascual Ramírez Huerta Efrén Gómez Morales · Rogelio Vargas Almaguer · Juan Escalante Torres · Carlos Gutiérrez Álvarez · Juan Francisco González Martínez Fernando Martínez Gallardo · Pedro Enrique Martínez Flamenco · Ariel Linares Cruz · Agustín Meléndez Soto · Isabel Aguillón Mejía · Hugo Ventura Mejía · Mario Ramírez Luna · Gustavo Martínez Loredo · Filiberto Cruz Ferrer · Pedro Hernández Mata · Víctor Pérez Hernández · Efraín Olguín Cabrera · Eusebio Herrera Ávila · Gabriel Salazar Rangel · Juan Antonio Sánchez Reyes · Salvador Zapata Castillo · María de Jesús Pérez Olvera · Fernando Camarena Reyes · Juan Jesús Quevedo González · Daniela Navarrete Rivera · Agustín Quintanilla Tamayo · César Martínez Briones · Manuel Hernández Rodríguez · Juan Campa Ortiz · Teresa Santos Baena · Ronulfo Salazar Martínez · Felipe Trejo García · Óscar Guadalupe García Mata · María Luisa Navarro Romero · Angélica Gómez Martínez · Platón Mar García · Oliverio Aguilar Ramos · Andrés Roberto Barrón García · Alfonso Yáñez García · Roberto Rodríguez González · Douglas Arturo Flores Martínez · Jorge Robledo Martínez · Luis Manuel Galeno Vásquez · Cirino Ramírez Otero · Maribel García Solano · Eleazar Ramírez Peña · José Alberto Cabrera Gómez · Ismael Carrizales Espinoza · Maximino Rubio Romero · Erick Iván Salas Reyes · Alberto García Vásquez · Leopoldo Celso Lucio Camargo · Andrés Salas · Asunción Sánchez Espinoza · Alma Delia Simón Fernández · Armando Hernández Silva · Rubén Zurita Bengas · Camilo Aguilar López Angélica García Morena · Antonio Vaca · Jaime Espinoza Torres · Cristóbal Díaz Castillo · Marco Antonio Ponce Piniero · José Guadalupe Macui Zamora · Noé Tapia Colorado · Ernesto Alonso Martínez Ibarra · Maximino Ramírez Hernández · Rafael Puerta Romero · Ricardo Hernández Cruz · José Guadalupe Carrión López · Isaac Ortiz Bello · Víctor Manuel Aragón López · Antonio Vences Morales · Angélica Ramírez Canchola José Dolores Camacho García · Pablo Morales Martínez · José Cano Carranco · Enrique Navarrete Merlos · Francisca Zárate Pérez · Arturo Barbosa Medina · Pablo García López · Enriqueta Noria Huerta · Rogelio Corrales Muñoz · Javier Alfonso Cepeda Gallegos · Francisco Torres Santiago · Vicente Ramón Moreno · Amado Franco Vidales · José Carlos Demes Contreras · Melitón Yáñez Hernández · Rosalba Martínez Francisco Huerta Medina · Antonio Solano Chávez · Antonio Vázquez Ávalos · Juan Carlos Morán · Víctor Manuel Saavedra · Ezequiel Gutiérrez Hernández · Ernesto Gómez · Óscar López Aregil · Juan Antonio Díaz Rivera · Domingo Crispín Gapi · María Antonia Trujillo · Ramón Herrera Núñez · Arturo Blancarte González · Matías Acosta Hernández · Juan Hernández Cisneros · Jusafat Rivera Miranda · Martín Daniel Vargas · Elías Salaiz · Celso Leyva Montalvo · Juan Miguel Núñez Cabada · Bernarda Torres Macedo · Luis Palma Guerrero · Horacio Alejandro Sandoval Carlos Lázaro Díaz Díaz · Rutilio Salinas Aragón · Jesús de Jesús Menchaca Martínez · Gonzalo López Castañeda · Israel López López · José de Jesús Menchaca Martínez · Gonzalo López Castañeda · Raúl Pérez Mora · Florentino Villa Medellín · José Guerra Ledesma · Job Martínez Cobos · Antonio Rico Medina · José Inez Guel Vásquez · Roberto Gasca Mancera · Florencio Antonio Gámez Gutiérrez · Saúl Flores Manzano Rigoberto López Hernández · Alejandro Martínez Banda · Orlando Losada Molina · Salvador Ramírez Barrón · Juan Gabriel González Ortiz María Mata Montiel · Alfredo Huerta Ruiz · Cecilia Martínez Pizarro · Mario A. Montellano Jiménez · Alicia Rentería Bautista · Faustino Aguirre Palma · Evaristo Narváez Cantú · Santiago Martínez Medina · Pedro Pérez Escobar · Ernesto Baltasar Sánchez · Salvador Rodríguez Palacios

Amalia Martínez Esparza · German Rivera Negrete · Anastasio Bolaños Ordóñez · José Luis Torres Reza · Rafael Ruiz Hernández · Maximo Reséndiz García · Carlos Sánchez Perdomo · Ezequiel Arceo Guerrero · Israel Molina Fuentes · Guadalupe Barrientos Padrón · Jesús Sánchez López · Antonia León Zavala · Alejandro Sánchez Santos · José Correa Aguado · Pablo Segura Salinas · Alberto García García · José Luis Pérez Reyes · José Manuel Espino · Víctor A. Márquez Salas · María Rosa Guerra Sánchez · Evelio Castro Loredo · Gloria Sonora Morán · José García Ledesma · Darío Vera Martínez · Alfredo Alfaro Gutiérrez · Amado Zúñiga Díaz · Antonio Santos Ventura · Jesús Anaya Pastor · Saúl Garza Pedroza · José L. Medina Cobarruvias · Faustino Olvera Rodríguez · Luis López Arellano · Antonio Edmundo Hernández Serrano · Pánfilo Santiago Martínez · Julián Landero Ruiz · Angélico Pérez Vásquez · Rosa Pérez Guzmán · José Mauricio Pérez Guzmán · Ángel Gabriel Pineda de la Cruz · Roberto Reyes Luna · Jesús Villa Ramírez · Galdino Morales Hernández · Francisco Mata Arias · Serafín Rivera Gámez · José Luis Ramírez Bravo · Elisendo Cabañas González · Roberto Rivera Gámez · Edgar Gabriel Hernández Zúñiga · Marco Antonio Villaseñor Acuña · José Antonio Villaseñor León · Juan Carlos Castillo Loredo · Ricardo González Mata · Óscar González Guerrero · Juan José Morales · Juan Carlos Estrada Álvarez · Juan Carlos Franco Romero · Héctor Ramírez Robles · Mateo Salgado López · David Bernabé Pérez González · Eliseo Carrillo Hidalgo · Pedro Chávez · Eduardo · Ismael González Mejía · Regino Hernández Martínez · Gerardo Dolores Paulín · Jesús Vázquez Barrera · Manuel Herrera Martínez · Alejandro Herrera Martínez · Leopoldo Romero Mandrujano · Rogelio Domínguez Benítez · Cheve Benítez Jaramillo · Catarino González Merino · Ismael Ruiz Castillo · Manuel López Sotelo · Edgardo Tavera Nava · Miguel Ángel Nuncio Urbina · María del Carmen Martínez Mendoza · Francisco Javier Aguilar Galarza · Alfonso Puentes Villegas · Mundo Salomón Zanaca · Antonio Salazar (José Antonio Pérez García) · Jorge Luis Melendrez Ruiz · Issac Ariza Ruiz · Mario Jiménez Terrazas · Marisol López Echeverría · José Armando González Cervantes · Guadalupe Martínez Martínez · David Rama Rez Mendoza · Nestor Salazar Yépez · José Martín Martínez Campos · Damián Serrato Jiménez · Eladio Hernández García · Miguel Sánchez Olvera · Ricardo Rosas Álvarez · Augusta Porfirio Arredondo Luna · Edgardo Ayala Dávila · Ramón Miranda Segovia · Guadalupe César Pérez · José Alfredo Castro Villa · Antonio Hernández Lazos · Abelardo Flores Olascuja · José de Jesús Bañuelos García · Eva Ponce Ramírez · Luis Fidencio Hinojosa Arredondo · José Manuel Gutiérrez Rodríguez · Gerardo Cobillos Ramos · Silverio Cruz Alvarado · Guadalupe Ortiz · Celestino López Espino · Juan Manuel Sandoval Vargas · Rodolfo Guerrero Ruiz · Freddy de Jesús Aban Cano · Ma. Cristina Jiménez Ponce · Pedro García Hernández · Adán López Núñez · Ernesto Aarón Rosas Sánchez · Gabriel Martínez Maya · Felipe Escobedo Gines · José Luis Alejandro Méndez · Florencio Herrera Arteaga · Liberato Aban Cano · Jesús Martínez Antunes · Rosa Isela González Garibay · Huber León Muñoz · Benita Alvarado Venegas · Catalina Juárez Pozos · José Luis Jaime Patiño · Marco Antonio Camacho Rosas · Hermilio Mayen Luna · Luis Javier González Padilla · Melitón Barrera Reséndez · Mónica Martínez Mundo (Garduño Martínez) · María Elena Martínez De Castillo · Guadalupe Balero Gardea · Gerardo Miguel Velasco Martínez · José Socorro Pineda Morales · Roberto Acosta Rodríguez · Esau Gamaliel Pérez Pérez · Miguel Ángel Sandoval Mercado · Julio César Lazcano Luna · Gabriel Delgado Parga · Ricardo Martínez Carrillo · Delfino Humberto Sifuentes Favela · José Ventura López · Refugio Desiderio Esquivel · Gabriela Cornejo · Juana Mojica Martínez · Miguel René Morales · Eduardo Sánchez Rodríguez · Ezequiel Martínez López · Antonio Maqueda Sánchez · Guillermo Guerrero Rincón Gallardo · Araceli Rodríguez Zamora · José Luis de Jesús Olivares · Juan G. Cerna Mejía · Enrique Salazar Romero · Gustavo Salazar Romero · Pablo Simón Nicolás · Miguel Torres Ascensión · Luis Enrique Rodríguez Vicencio · Leticia Almazár Carmóna · Maricela Pérez Valente · María Esther Segura Juárez · Antonio Millán Mena · René Torres Salazar · Daniel Vázquez Gutiérrez · Miguel Galicia Salinas · Antonio López Ortiz · María de los Ángeles Guerrero Rojas · Abraham Loera Alcalá · María Cruz Mata Montiel · Cecilia Martínez Pizano · Santiago Martínez Medina · Anastacio Bolaños Ordóñez · José A. Hernández Hernández · Salvador Romero Ledesma · Guillermo Murillo Barragán · Gumaro Sánchez Maqueda · María Beatriz Rodríguez Camacho · Paola Juanita Aboytes Guerrero · José Luis Hernández Rodríguez · José Jiménez Sánchez · Celestino López Espino · Juan Manuel Sandoval Vargas · Rodolfo Guerrero Ruiz · Freddy de Jesús Aban Cano · Ma. Cristina Jiménez Ponce · José Luis de Jesús Olivares · Adán López Núñez · Ernesto Aarón Rosas Sánchez · Gabriel Martínez Maya · Felipe Escobedo Gines · José Luis Alejandro Méndez · Florencio Herrera Arteaga · Liberato Aban Cano · Jesús Martínez Antunes · Rosa Isela González Garibay · Huber León Muñoz · Benita Alvarado Venegas · Catalina Juárez Pozos · José Luis Jaime Patiño · Marco Antonio Camacho Rosas · Hermilio Mayen Luna · Luis Javier González Padilla · Melitón Barrera Reséndez · Mónica Martínez Mundo (Garduño Martínez) · María Elena Martínez De Castillo · Guadalupe Balero Gardea · Gerardo Miguel Velasco Martínez · Roberto Acosta Rodríguez · Esaú Gamaliel Pérez Pérez · Miguel Ángel Sandoval Mercado · Gabriel Delgado Parga · Ricardo Martínez Carrillo · Delfino Humberto Sifuentes Favela · José Ventura López · Gabriela Cornejo · Juana Mojica Martinez · Miguel René Morales · Eduardo Sánchez Rodríguez · Ezequiel Martínez López · Antonio Maqueda Sánchez · Guillermo Guerrero Rincon Gallardo · Araceli Rodriguez Zamora · Salvador Romero Ledesma · Guillermo Murillo Barragán · Gumaro Sánchez Maqueda · María Beatriz Rodríguez Camacho · Paola Juanita Aboytes Guerrero · José Luis Hernández Rodríguez · José Jiménez Sánchez · Fernando Valdez Sánchez · Alejandro Pérez Contreras · Juan Humberto Ramos Estrada · Alberto Esquivel Grimaldo · Noe Esparza Ramos · José Ezequiel Avendaño Medina · Fernando Suárez Carreño · Susana Maya Salazar · Adriana Martínez Gómez · Eduardo Rojas Franco · Diego Alberto Guadarrama Rosas · María Guadalupe Gómez Patiño · Hector Jesús Ortiz Guevara · María Margarita Zamora Estrada · César Barrera Roa · Jesús Iván Dragustinobis Campos · Raúl Cortez Cabello · José Moisés Del Ángel García · Epigmenio Jacobo Nicanor · María Reyes Carranza Mendoza · Salvador García García · Enrique Galindo Ruiz · Juan Antonio Haro Robles · José Ángel Bravo Sosa

...and around 1,000 unidentified migrants.[44] About 1.5 times as many people have died on the border since its militarization process began in 1994 than those who perished in the 9/11 terrorist attacks.

The Mobile Transborder Archive contains materials from a diverse range of universities, libraries, and institutions from the U.S. and Mexico. Other contributors include grassroots organizations, and individuals, questioning the authorship of public archives. This moving archive juxtaposes diverse educational materials including interviews, photographs, films, video and audio materials. Pictured here, the Archive sits in front of the San Ysidro Library in its first U.S. stop, part of the inSite 05 festival.

9. EDUCATION

Both the U.S. and Mexico will need to increase opportunities for higher education among youth and respond to the realities of a knowledge-based global economy. Educational reforms are especially needed in Mexico to increase the quality of teaching and foster future planning.

> "The illiterate of the future will not be the person who cannot read.
> It will be the person who does not know how to learn."
>
> —Alvin Toffler

CIRCUMSTANCES OF BASIC EDUCATION IN BOTH COUNTRIES

In Mexico, 87% of students attend public schools, while 13% are enrolled in private institutions, and 74% of teachers hold post-graduate degrees, 22% of which are PhDs.[1] Mexico has reached 80% of the education goals set by the United Nations Millennium Development Goals scheduled for 2015, which aim to provide basic education to every child. In 2006, investment in public and private education ascended to U.S. $60 billion, representing 7.5% of Mexico's GDP. Despite such high investments, primary and secondary school attendance remains an ongoing challenge. According to the Instituto para la Evaluación de la Educación (INEE), twenty-eight out of a hundred students do not finish primary school, seventeen out of a hundred are one year behind, and twelve out of a hundred are two or more years behind. In other words, the transition from primary to secondary school is one of the biggest obstacles facing almost 50% of students, who do not continue on to middle school.[2] *Oportunidades*, Mexico's recently launched human development program, is a tri-fold effort to reduce poverty combining initiatives in health, education, and food assistance, targeting the country's most marginalized communities. Families with school-aged children receive financial support and food assistance in order for their children to remain in school. In return, the family is expected to pay frequent visits to doctors. This program, overseen by Mexico's Social Development Agency (Secretaria de Desarrollo Social, SEDESOL), is creating a "virtuous cycle" that allows children to perform better

and stay in school without the need of working to support the family, increasing their chances of achieving higher living standards in the coming decades. About one quarter of the country's population has received support from this program, which has allowed 5.1 million children and teenagers to remain in school. Enrollment rates in middle schools and high schools have increased 35% and 85%, respectively, in rural areas since the program started in 2000.[3] These efforts are expected to increase enrollment in higher education institutions, a level currently attained by fewer than one out of five young adults between the ages twenty-five and thirty-four.[4]

The Public Education Secretariat (SEP) in Mexico has made several notable efforts to improve the nation's education levels. Among those efforts include the funding of new libraries for public schools around the country and the growing bestowal of education grants.[5] In 2005, the SEP

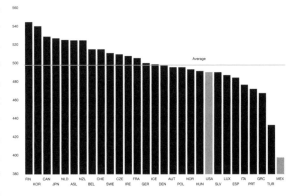

Graph showing the results of the Programme for International Student Assessment (PISA) exam in mathematics, reading, science, and problem solving. PISA is carried out by the OECD and ranks the education competencies of 15-year-olds. In 2003, both the United States and Mexico ranked below the average.

also designated money to programs proven to be successful like "Escuelas de Calidad," which are similar to magnet schools in the U.S., and "Enciclomedia," a $2 million computer literacy and interactive blackboard program (partly funded by Microsoft) used throughout Mexico.

Despite spending over 20% of its public funds on education,[6] Mexico still needs to improve the overall quality of education to reach the levels of other countries. In a 2003 OECD survey comparing different countries' fifteen-year-olds' knowledge and skills, Mexico ranked last in math performance. The United States ranked only five positions higher.[7]

On average, the annual expenditure of OECD countries per student for their primary through high school education is $7,343.[8] For the United States, however, that figure is significantly higher at nearly $12,000—an amount six times greater than Mexico's.[9] That extra spending has not necessarily led to outstanding results, however. The quality of learning for fifteen-year-olds is particularly low in math and problem solving, especially as compared to many European countries and Japan, Korea, Australia, and New Zealand.[10] With its relatively high per-student expenditure, yet its relatively low student achievement, the U.S. education system is clearly inefficient. In the face of all this, in 2006 President Bush committed over $5.9 billion over the next ten years toward education funding, promotion of entrepreneurship, and research and development as part of the American Competitiveness Initiative.[11] Other reforms under his administration include the High School Reform Initiative, calling for more accountability from high schools for test results; the National Security Language Initiative, aiding students and teachers in acquiring critically needed foreign language skills such as Arabic, Chinese, Korean, Japanese, and Russian; and the No Child Left Behind Act, giving more freedom to school districts on how they spend money and ensuring all minority groups meet minimum education standards.[12]

DEMOGRAPHIC CHANGES IN BOTH COUNTRIES' EDUCATION SYSTEMS

Many countries around the world have experienced decreased enrollment in elementary levels due to lower fertility rates—a trend that recently caught up in Mexico. Between 1995 and 2002, student population in primary, middle, and high schools increased 11%. This pattern is also present in university enrollment, which increased 42% in the same time-frame,[13] marking a peak in Mexico's student population. Yet by 2015, the elementary and middle school–aged population is expected to decrease 10%. By comparison, the U.S. is expected to increase this student population sector by 3%,[14] reflecting the increase in the number of schools in recent years. Between 1984 and 2002, 16% more public schools opened throughout the U.S., and in the ten years leading to 2002, Hispanics accounted for 64% of school enrollment increases, representing the highest addition in the student population since the baby-boomer generation enrolled in public schools.[15] The demand for higher education is also increasing, causing the system to expand in recent years as it continues to attract students from abroad. For the 2005–06 academic year, India ranked number one in sending foreign students to U.S. universities, with a total of 76,503 students, followed by China (62,582 students), the Republic of Korea (58,847 students), and Japan (38,712 students). Canada is the only non-Asian country in the top five, with 28,202 students. Mexico ranks seventh, with 13,931 students.[16]

According to Open Doors 2005, the annual report on international academic mobility published by the Institute of International Education (IIE), 2004–05 marked the sixth year in a row that

Although Mexico is the number one source of immigrants into the United States, it ranks seventh in foreign enrollment in U.S. universities.

America hosted more than half a million foreign students in higher education institutions.[17] The organization mentioned several challenges for U.S. universities to continue attracting the best students from around the world, including real and perceived difficulties in obtaining student visas (especially in scientific and technical fields), rising U.S. tuition costs, and vigorous recruitment activities by other English-speaking nations. In addition, universities in students' home countries and other regional host countries have increased their capacity to provide a high-quality education to a greater number of students at both undergraduate and graduate levels.[18]

Back in 1970, over half of all the world's science and engineering doctorates were granted in the United States; by 2010 that rate is expected to fall to just 15%.[19] China already has the most researchers after the United States, and they are the second biggest investor in research and development (R&D) in the field.[20] As global companies browse the world in search of talent and to establish their operations, a more competitive education system that adapts to a changing global worforce will be needed.

ECONOMIC AND CULTURAL GAPS RELATED TO EDUCATION IN THE UNITED STATES

Education is crucial for the economic performance of a country and its individuals. The OECD reports that for every additional year in a country's education attendance, that country's economy benefits with 3 to 6% of increased economic output.[21] At just $22,300, Mexican immigrants' average incomes are vastly lower than those of both native-born citizens ($45,400) and the average income of all immigrants combined ($37,000). This disparity is due to most Mexican immigrants' low educational levels. More than 60% of Mexican immigrants are high school dropouts, compared to fewer than 10% of native workers.[23] Although college enrollment among Hispanics has increased in recent years, an even larger increase in enrollment of white students in four-year college programs occurred in the same time-frame.[24] Latino students are half as likely as white students to finish undergraduate education in the U.S., placing them even further behind in the education gap. It is in the interest of both countries to address the missed economic opportunity of education. The current wave of Mexican migrants in the U.S. carries with it the potential for higher poverty rates in communities across the U.S. As noted by Roberto Suro, director of the Pew Hispanic Center,

Latino poverty will not be remedied by the welfare-to-work programs that are now virtually the sole focus of U.S. social policy, and it will not be fixed by trying to close the nation to further immigration. The Latino poor are here and they are not going to go away. Unless new avenues of upward mobility open up for Latino immigrants and their children, the size of America's underclass will quickly double and in the course of a generation it will double again.[25]

Addressing this education deficit in Mexico and the U.S. will be one of the greatest challenges

15

Demand for Graduates from Bicultural Universities along the U.S.–Mexico Border Boosts Development of Similar Programs Elsewhere[22]

Due to the popularity among certain sectors of the corporate world of students who graduated from bicultural universities located in border cities including El Paso, Tijuana, and Nogales, similar programs are being developed in other American cities with a significant Hispanic population. A handful of universities in Chicago, New York, and Los Angeles are discussing how to implement programs similar to the ones in the border cities that would appeal to students who want to immerse themselves in American and Mexican cultures. The success of the bicultural universities is due to their unique programs offering a wide range of subjects in both languages and, especially, in the context of U.S.–Mexico relations throughout history. Designed by faculties recruited from high-ranking universities in both countries, these programs partially eliminate the need for exchange programs. In the words of student Cindy Cisneros, "It's like getting a degree from two top universities instead of just one."

both countries will continue to share. With Hispanics poised to become 25% of the population by 2050, this demographic change could represent a great opportunity to narrow the economic and cultural gaps between both countries and cultures. Today, around 30 million Spanish-speakers live in the United States; in coming decades, the U.S. will be the second biggest country with Spanish-speakers after Mexico.[26] Already a shortage of bilingual teachers exists in states like Texas, California, and Illinois,[27] but programs like one discussed by Mexico's SEP and the Dallas school district in 2006 involving sending Mexican bilingual teachers to instruct Mexican-American students in the city, could prove fruitful in the future, and the border region could play an important role in this process as testing ground.[28]

THE BORDER AS TEST BED FOR BINATIONAL RESEARCH

The California-Baja California region is considered the fifth largest economic region in the world. Combining the knowledge-based industries of California with Baja California's manufacturing capabilities has proved a fruitful strategy for decades since the maquiladora program started. However, the Mexican state is losing competitiveness in areas like computer equipment and textile production, finding it difficult to match Asian competitors' lower production costs. In response, the state has intensified its knowledge-based industries. Currently, consumer electronics represents the most mature sector in the region but it is also beginning to carve a market in biotechnology, medical products, software, car parts, specialized electronics, and air space parts. There are about fifteen industry clusters in the state specializing in fields such as medical services, plastics, tourism, and winemaking.[29] Developing clusters in the border region combining U.S.-based industries with Mexico's

education programs holds potential to develop technical expertise, improving the science and technology know-how of the region. A forerunner in this model is the newly formed Silicon Border, a semi-conductor industry park in Mexicali that is developing curricula with local universities and technical colleges to prepare a technology savvy workforce for the complex and contribute with 100,000 jobs. In the future, Silicon Border could gain "free trade zone" status and create a North American "silicon corridor" running from San Francisco to Mexicali.[30] Other similar projects include the Binational Sustainability Laboratory in Santa Teresa, New Mexico, a network of research centers and universities from the U.S. and Mexico developing and commercializing new products in areas like energy, water, and emerging technologies, and Delphi's operations center in Ciudad Juárez, one of the few U.S. manufacturing companies with a Mexican-staffed design and engineering center.

The Binational Sustainability Laboratory in Santa Teresa, New Mexico is fostering the development of startups focused on micro electro mechanical systems (MEMS) for use in the automotive and aerospace technology industries.

16

MARCH 23, 2022

Expansion of Nano Valley in Baja California Triggers Boom of Local Wineries

The increasing scale of the nanotechnology research complexes in operation in the northern area of Baja California is radically transforming the population of the region and making a number of local businesses grow at an unprecedented rate, particularly the wineries and the tourism industry. With the increased demand for the applications developed in these complexes, more scientists and skilled workers from both Mexico and the U.S. are migrating to the Nano Valley and boosting the local economy. Consumption of Mexican wine has increased 50% in the last 10 years due to investment, more efficient production and better quality control.

California Governor Arnold Schwarzenegger meets with Mexico's president Felipe Calderón in Mexico City, on November 10, 2006. The same day, Schwarzenegger attended the Border Governors Conference. The ten governors of border states from both countries have been meeting annually for twenty-five years to promote collaboration in issues ranging from agriculture to trade.

10. ECONOMIC DEVELOPMENT AND TRADE

Economic growth and trade are key requisites to the elimination of poverty and ensuring national prosperity. As increasing competition from emerging countries challenges NAFTA's status as the biggest economic bloc in the world, the U.S. and Mexico will need to become more competitive, reduce trade deficits, diversify, and expand exports markets in order to perform in a global economy.

NEOLIBERALISM'S INFLUENCE ON ECONOMIC POLICIES IN MEXICO AND U.S.–MEXICO RELATIONS

Neoliberalism is a structural adjustment policy that, according to its supporters, helps emerging nations manage foreign debt and become reoriented toward the world market economy by engaging in trade, an activity inherently meant to spark economic development. It is a political-economic philosophy strongly promoted by the United States and global financial institutions like the International Monetary Fund (IMF) and the World Bank. Neoliberalism emphasizes fiscally responsible governments, the shrinking of the state, minimal or no government intervention in the economy, the establishment of attractive environments for foreign investment, and open markets. These policies have greatly influenced Mexico's current economy, which through NAFTA has become deeply integrated with the U.S. and is now widely considered one of the most open economies in the world.[1] Mexico's adoption of the neoliberal agenda has also strengthened its relationship with the U.S. by opening its market to increased trade, foreign investment, and development along the common border.[2]

Free trade is controversial. Critics claim it largely sidesteps the "human" side of trade by placing too much focus on numbers. Mexico currently has twelve international free trade agreements,[3] the most important of which is NAFTA. NAFTA has produced both negative and positive effects for the U.S. and Mexico alike. Since its implementation, trade between the two countries has grown from $89.5 billion in 1993 to $275.3 billion in 2004—a threefold increase, widely understood as a positive change.[4] However, during that same period, real wages for Mexican manufacturing workers have dropped 13.5%, proving that increased trade does not necessarily bring social benefits.[5] Because of Mexico's comparative deregulation of labor and environmental laws and its proximity to the U.S., it is considered a desirable location for Multi-National Corporations and maquiladoras. The foreign investment keeps the government and the IMF satisfied, but extreme working conditions and low wages perpetuate poverty. Although neoliberalism has triggered economic growth overall, the wealth and resource distribution is hardly equitable, and Mexico's popular sector continues to be impoverished. What's more, remittances sent home by Mexicans in the U.S. overwhelmingly surpass the wage increases in the maquiladora sector since NAFTA's implementation by nearly tenfold. If the likely wages of the 700,000 jobs created in the industry were combined (assuming each worker earns the average $1.47 an hour and works fifty hours a week for fifty-two weeks a year), only $2.68 billion will have been brought to the Mexican economy.[6] In 2005, by comparison, Mexico received $20 billion in remittances. Thus NAFTA and the maquiladora sector can only provide a fraction of what immigration to the U.S. offers to both the citizen and the nation, which explains its direct influence on the increase in migration since the agreement was put into effect.

One of NAFTA's most negative effects in Mexico has been on the country's small farmers. According to Laura Carlsen, the Americas Program Director at the International Relations Center (IRC), "a recent study shows two million small farmers displaced from the rural sector and rising unemployment despite huge growth in the informal sector growth and out-migration."[7] At a loss for alternatives, farmers in Mexico must opt for survival, which in this case can be provided by the production of illegal substances and partnerships with the Mexican drug cartels. NAFTA and its domino effect of negative impacts are making criminals out of the people who previously fed the nation.

The negative effects of NAFTA are not only found in Mexico: the United States experienced a

After Canada and China, Mexico is the United States' most important trade partner, and the common border between the two nations—a site of rapid development and exponential growth in trade—plays an integral role in the partnership's dynamics.[11]

loss of more than 766,000 actual and potential jobs since the agreement's enactment.[8] According to the Economic Policy Institute, every state in the country and the District of Columbia experienced a net loss of jobs as a direct result of NAFTA.[9]

TRADE ACROSS THE U.S.–MEXICO BORDER IS THE DRIVING FORCE OF THE BORDER ECONOMY

The proximity of the border to the United States' market and the cost-effective benefits of low-wage labor in Mexico have brought a myriad of U.S. companies to the border. Since 1994, when NAFTA went into effect, the U.S. has comprised 62% of all foreign direct investment in Mexico.[12] This proximity is also credited for the establishment of "just-in-time" production, whereby the NAFTA nations can import, assemble, and export with speed unparalleled in the world, as the majority of the products will stay within the region.[13] This form of integration has created a relationship that allows for mutual prosperity, and the level of investment found along the border has stakeholders on both sides committed to maintaining and advancing the immense synergy found there.

The maquiladora industry, which in 2000 represented 54.7% of Mexico's manufacturing exports,[14] is one of the most important aspects of this trade relationship. In recent years, however, the border industry has faced competition from rising Asian economies for U.S. investment and trade. In Mexico's domestic market, Chinese and Korean products compete with goods that are manufactured domes-

tically. The enormous market in Tepito, Mexico City, is a prime example of this. Asian-made products that arrive to this market—the largest informal commercial zone in the Americas—are highly competitive because they are cheaper and thus sell more quickly. This has also sparked gentrification in the area, as Korean and Chinese vendors—who tend to have more economic clout—have begun to displace many of the Mexican residents by raising the costs of rent in local residences and in businesses.[15]

In 2003, Chinese exports to the U.S. surpassed those of Mexico,[17] and in October, 2006, China displaced Mexico as the United State's second economic trade partner—a trend that will be very difficult to reverse.[18]

DISTRIBUTING WEALTH AND DEVELOPING NEW EMPLOYMENT OPPORTUNITIES THROUGHOUT MEXICAN SOCIETY

One of free trade's fundamental problems is that it does little to benefit society as a whole, and in the case of Mexico this is evident. Mexican society is afflicted by one of the largest gaps between the rich and poor in the world. The distribution of wealth currently has minimal social impact because relaxed labor laws allow capital to remain in the hands of those that control the maquiladora industry, namely the wealthy Mexican elite or foreign investors.[21] When NAFTA was signed, then-President Carlos Salinas announced the country would soon be entering the "first world." A simple comparison of the per capita income between the

17

APRIL 15, 2018

Presidents of Argentina, Brazil, Chile and Mexico Gather in Rio de Janeiro to Finalize Mexico's Becoming a Full Member of Mercosur, the South American Trading Bloc

It was more than a decade ago that left-leaning politicians and economists skeptical of the adherence of Mexican technocrats to neoliberal economic policies became wary of the negative effects of the North American Free Trade Agreement (NAFTA) on the Mexican economy. Back then they saw trading with growing Latin American democracies as a solution to the ever-increasing dependence of Mexico on the U.S. Time would prove them right. Nowadays, high officials admit that had it not been for China's preeminence as a U.S. trade partner, Mexico would be in an even worse situation. Today they see hope in fair trade models that are more sensitive to the cultural and economic needs of the Mexican population. Mercosur officials say major trade deals with the European Union are on the horizon.[10]

United States and Mexico ten years after the signing of NAFTA is proof enough that the country has not: on average Mexicans earn $6,000 a year, while their U.S. counterparts earn $40,000.[22] Mexico's average income is the highest in Latin America, but this is credited to the increase in the population of the extremely wealthy, who skew the averages with the gains they've made through privatization processes and the implementation of NAFTA. Half the Mexican population still lives below the poverty line, with many surviving on less than two dollars a day.[23] In order to allow the benefits of economic development to reach the country's masses, systemic changes would be necessary to more effectively distribute capital. Obvious answers—at

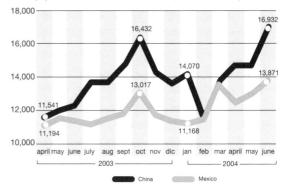

Mexican Products Status in U.S. Market
(Exports of Mexico and China to the U.S., millions of dollars)

China   Mexico

In 2003, China surpassed Mexico in exports to the United States. Below: Workers in a factory in Xiamen City, China, 2005.

During its first six years, NAFTA created 700,000 *maquiladora* jobs. However, as a result of external influences, namely a recession in the U.S. economy and the advent of Chinese competition, the sector lost 300,000 of those jobs by 2003.[16]

least from the human rights standpoint—would be to improve labor laws to offer fair pay to workers, and to increase spending on social programs that benefit the general population. Unfortunately, those are changes that would likely diminish the interest of foreign investors, the primary sources of economic development under Mexico's current neoliberal model.

As previously discussed, one of the major negative effects of NAFTA was the displacement of Mexican farmworkers who found they could not compete with the U.S.-subsidized goods that had saturated the domestic market. In the face of this crisis, and lacking other opportunities, many farmers have either turned to migration, the informal sector, or to the cultivation of illegal drugs for survival. Developing alternatives for this population is imperative for the Mexican government, which witnesses an increased emigration of its citizens with each passing year. The example of Southeast Asia's successful drug eradication and alternative crop replacement in the Golden Triangle offers evidence of the viability of government- and region-sponsored programs that create new opportunities (see page 36). Given that both the U.S. and Mexico have vested interests in the reduction of drug cultivation and drug use, the two governments could apply a similar program along the U.S.–Mexico border region.

In order to attain economic growth of 6%, which is necessary for development, the Organisation for Economic Co-operation and Development (OECD) suggests six main steps that ought be taken:

Remain committed to macroeconomic stability, put public expenditure on a more solid and predictable footing, ensure that resources for education and training are used more effectively, raise and improve the stock of infrastructure capital, pursue labor market reforms, and ease regulatory measures and other impediments, including failings of the judicial system and high perceived levels of corruption.[24]

One program already in place is the Partnership for Prosperity (PfP) initiative, which has the potential to develop new opportunities for Mexicans in the future. PfP aims to "harness the power of the private sector to foster an environment in which no Mexican feels compelled to leave his home for a lack of jobs or opportunity" and is meant to promote development in those regions of Mexico that have high out-migration rates.[25]

INCREASING MEXICO AND NORTH AMERICA'S COMPETITIVENESS

According to the World Economic Forum (WEF) there are two principal aspects of competitiveness related to growth and business climate: having a stable macroeconomic environment, and maintaining an institutional climate based on respect of the law, low instances of corruption, protected property rights, and high levels of transparency both in the government and business sector.[28] In 2006, after evaluating 117 countries, the WEF placed the United States at number six in competitiveness, down from first position the previous year, while Mexico was

JULY 16, 2027

Culinary Offers Abound in Cities of Global Commerce along the Mexican Border with the U.S.

Your best bet is to travel to any of the global commerce cities along the Mexican side of the border with the U.S. if you're ready to go on a shopping spree or crave Szechuan food, Italian wines, Venezuelan arepas, Japanese sake, Spanish chorizos, Argentine beef, Indian curry, Belgian beer and chocolate, French cheese, or the best Mexican tacos. You'll need to recharge your energy at the food courts while you shop till you drop in the duty-free malls, outlets, and wholesale stores that teem these cities, and what is better than indulging in the best foods the world has to offer? Word has it that since Chinese businesses moved their corporate headquarters to this area, some of the best Chinese food in the Americas is to be found here. Visit www.citiesofglobalcommerce.com for more information.[19]

Cities of global commerce on the coastal city of Matamoros (above) and along the border (below). Different parcels are rented to major global corporations and countries.

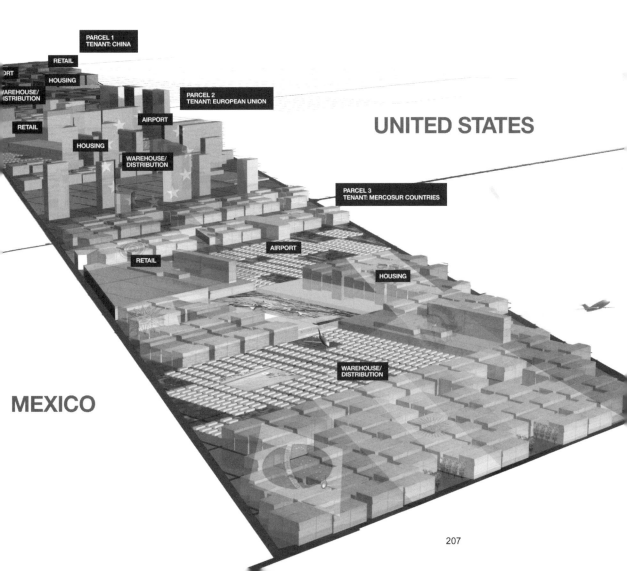

PARCEL 1
TENANT: CHINA

RETAIL

HOUSING

ORT

WAREHOUSE/
DISTRIBUTION

RETAIL

AIRPORT

PARCEL 2
TENANT: EUROPEAN UNION

HOUSING

WAREHOUSE/
DISTRIBUTION

UNITED STATES

PARCEL 3
TENANT: MERCOSUR COUNTRIES

RETAIL

AIRPORT

HOUSING

WAREHOUSE/
DISTRIBUTION

MEXICO

Speak Chinese? As More and More Countries Change Their Reserves to Yuan, the Ultra Rich Devise Ways to Open Bank Accounts in China

It's hard to believe that only forty years ago people in the globe looking to secure their wealth opened bank accounts in the U.S. Approximately 75% of these accounts have closed in the last twelve years, since the European Union changed its national reserves to yuans and Chinese banks started offering high yielding interest rates of over 4% in competition for global investment. Current trends have seen the emergence of a new type of professional: all over the world the wealthy now hire bilingual financial consultants to travel to China a couple times a year to manage their accounts.[20]

ranked number fifty-eight, one place higher than in 2005.[29] According to the organization, Mexico's relatively low level of competitiveness is due to a number of problems reaching up to the institutional level. Poor quality in public institutions, an inefficient tax system, few reforms due to a lack of political consensus, and high levels of crime all severely affect the business climate.[30] The high rates of criminality in Mexico make it the third most expensive country in the world in terms of insurance for entrepreneurs and businesses wishing to protect themselves against crime.[31] These institutional problems all work to debilitate the country's capacity for growth. According to the OECD, Mexico currently experiences an annual growth rate of 4%.[32] However, in order to successfully generate employment, growth levels need to climb to 7–9%, as they do in China and India.[33] If Mexico were to address the institutional problems that undermine its ability to compete (particularly crime and corruption), the

country would be able to generate further growth. The U.S. could play a role in this process by pressuring its neighbor to work out institutional dilemmas rather than encouraging it to undermine its social and economic issues in order to remain attractive to foreign business and investment.[34] By promoting the establishment of a more competitive and economically developed Mexico, the competitiveness of the North American continent could potentially advance, thus benefiting all three NAFTA nations.

PROMOTING COMPETITIVENESS THROUGH FAST AND SECURE TRADE

North America has developed several programs with the aim of accelerating trade processes, an important aspect of increasing the region's competitiveness in the future. The Free and Secure Trade (FAST) program is a joint initiative between Canada and the United States that allows certain pre-authorized goods to be transported across the border efficiently, thus reducing inspection time at the border and allowing products to arrive at their destination more quickly.[36] Program participants are pre-approved and pre-registered importers, carriers, and drivers. The FAST initiative improves the U.S.–Canada border exchanges by reducing the information requirements for customs/border clearance; eliminating the need for importers to transmit data for each transaction; dedicating lanes for FAST clearances; reducing the rate of border examinations; verifying trade compliance away from the border; and streamlining accounting and payment processes for all goods imported by approved importers (Canada only).[37]

The Container Security Initiative (CSI) was developed by the U.S. Customs and Border Protection in order to increase trade security. CSI allows for products destined for the United States to be inspected and sealed before arriving at U.S. ports, limiting opportunities to tamper with goods and reducing the likelihood that the international trade infrastructure will be used for the trafficking of illegal commodities.

Some other important initiatives that have been developed to advance the security and efficiency of trade have been: the CANAMEX Corridor, one of many trade corridors crossing the NAFTA region from Mexico to Canada; the SENTRI program, which allows pre-registered civilians to cross in a special lane at the U.S.–Mexico border; and C-TPAT, the U.S.–Mexico equivalent to the FAST program, which allows agri-business and manufacturing companies to apply for permits that enable them to more speedily move goods across the border.

ECONOMIC GROWTH MUST PRACTICE SUSTAINABLE DEVELOPMENT

Although sustainability principles are often associated with environmental stewardship, the social and economic aspects of sustainable development are increasingly being adopted by businesses. Trade and investment based on principles of sustainability are reaching wider consensus among global institutions and multinational companies as a way of ensuring economic prosperity in the long term while protecting the environment. Adopting a triple bottom-line approach as a way of increasing companies' profits is proving to be a fruitful strategy, since a fully implemented sustainability approach in a large company returns at least 46% more profits in only five years.[38] Using quantifiable methods companies, institutions, countries, and cities have designed systems for tracking emissions, reducing operation costs, and trading, thus following sustainability guidelines. Terms such as ISO 14000 standards, the Kyoto Protocol, green investments, the Global Compact, eco-design, cycle-to-cycle manufacturing, social inclusiveness, the Global Reporting Initiative, and the Global Environment Fund are becoming more

widely embraced by the corporate world. By adopting this array of standards, methods, and agreements, international markets are remodeling and are integrating sustainability principles into their business makeup.

Numerous institutions holding assets of more than $4 trillion are supporting the United Nations' Principles for Responsible Investment.[39] Socially and environmentally responsible investment firms frequently report comparable returns on their investments compared to similar firms that do not focus on sustainability.[40] In the same manner, many corporations are following the Global Compact principles, abiding to environmental precaution and responsibility as well as the use of environmentally benign technologies. The Global Compact model, which concerns itself with issues of human rights, labor, the environment, and anti-corruption, is being adopted in various sectors, not only by business associations but also by civil society, academia, the public sector, and as of 2003, several cities.

In regards to the industrial sector, eco-efficient manufacturing methods bring economic gains by producing more with less through the reduction or elimination of waste from manufacturing, and by increasing energy efficiency. According to the 2004 World Energy Outlook, up to 70% of carbon-emission reductions could have been offset by the implementation of renewable energy,[41] thereby increasing the percentage of GDP generated with less energy. It is expected sustainability will be part of most business practices in various sectors in the near future.

The Kyoto Protocol, designed to reduce international Greenhouse Gas (GHG) emissions to approximately 5% less than the 1990 levels by each protocol signatory country by 2012, uses a markets-based system. For instance, through the Clean Development Mechanism (CDM), designed

Mexico Develops Service-based Exports that Compete with India for American and Canadian Markets

Given that Spanish-speakers represent the second largest segment of the U.S. population after English-speakers, and that the rate at which this community is growing is higher than any other, Mexican companies specializing in services such as bilingual call-centers and customer service are determined to replace India as the main country to which American companies outsource. A survey by Consumer Reports magazine found that 80% of Spanish-speaking customers were extremely dissatisfied with the service in Spanish provided to them over the phone. 95% of those interviewed did not know how to respond to the poorly phrased question "Hola, mi llamo Yolanda García. ¿Cómo te sirvo hoy?" which in English would be equivalent to "Hello, my call Yolanda García. How do I serve you today?" Representatives of the Mexican businesses estimate than within a year Mexico can replace India, provided Mexican employees receive proper tutoring in American pop culture and English pronunciation. [26]

21

APRIL 11, 2024

Mexico City Officials Consider New Ways of Controlling the City's Expansion Toward Newly Completed Trade Corridor

New hotels, service stations, and restaurants will open within the next year along the recently completed trade corridor spanning from Manzanillo on the west coast to Coatzacoalcos on the east, and passing between Mexico City and Toluca. Once it is in full operation the trade corridor is expected to displace the Panama Canal as the most important in the region. Officials fear that in the long run the sprawl of Mexico City, which has kept expanding toward the west in the direction of Toluca, might end up causing the corridor's highways to be congested and hence obstructing the expedient shipment of domestic and foreign goods from one port city to another. The metropolitan area's officials plan to implement measures to halt such a sprawl by making the city grow southeast toward Puebla instead.[27]

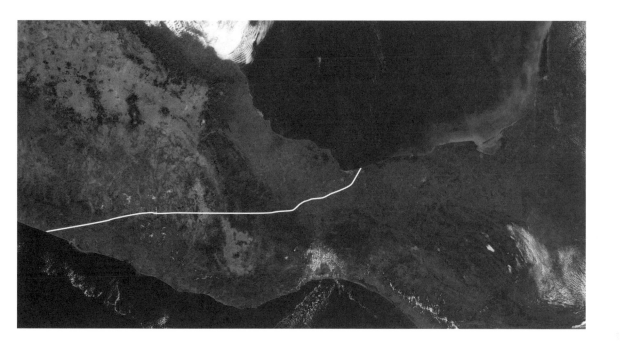

as part of the Kyoto Protocol, countries can offset their emissions by investing in renewable energy. Alternatively, if a country wishes, it can purchase carbon credits from other countries to meet its Kyoto targets. The Chicago Climate Exchange (CCX) is an example of a similar trading system through which investors buy and sell GHGs; currently over $2 billion worth of sulfur dioxide (SO2) emissions are traded annually.[42] So far, most industrialized signatory countries are behind schedule in meeting their Kyoto targets, and some opponents claim economic losses would be incurred if the protocol were fully implemented. Other economic studies suggest that less than a 1% GDP loss would be created by the year 2100 even if the Kyoto targets were toughened.[43] While the U.S. is the only industrialized country besides Australia that has not signed the Kyoto Protocol, it is committed to making an 18% reduction of GHG emissions by 2012.[44]

Mexico, a signatory of the Kyoto Protocol, has great potential to become a major exporter of GHGs to other countries, including the U.S. However, appropriate measures and legislation changes need to be made to continue opening up the energy market to private investment, as well as to promote the use of technologies that capture or mitigate GHGs. The Kyoto Protocol, which is due to expire by 2012, will need to be reevaluated if Mexico is to become a major exporter of carbon credits in the coming decades.

The U.S., a pioneer in numerous sustainable technologies and market mechanisms, holds great potential to protect the many ecosystems that are currently threatened in the country. In order to unlock its potential it will need to increase its capacity to offset GHGs, increase energy efficiency, reduce dependence on oil, and eliminate harmful pollutants in order for it to play a leading role in the global greenhouse gas reduction efforts and remain competitive in the world economy.

Trade corridor from Manzanillo to Coatzacoalcos.

22

AUGUST 5, 2037

Moving South, Unforeseen Migration Patterns Emerge Upon the Establishment of the North American Union

Ever since the U.S., Canada, and Mexico united to form the North American Union seven years ago, there has been a steady flow of residents of the northern states of the U.S. to the Mexican south. Scholars and researchers studying this puzzling phenomenon claim that since there are no longer significant discrepancies in the average incomes of the three countries, as well as standardized education and universal health care throughout the union, there is no obvious reason for these migrations. Barbara Morgan, a researcher from the University of California in San Diego, has an explanation: "Blame it on the weather. Although the union's currency is worth the same everywhere, it can be stretched further down south, where families don't have to spend their money heating their homes during long winters."[35]

View of North and South-bound lanes in Tijuana heading to Mexico from the United States. Unlike the highly scrutinized border crossings north-bound, heading into Mexico is an open process. The majority of vehicles do not stop for inspection. The open nature of Mexico's northern border allows the entrance of contraband, weapons, and law-dodging criminals.

11. TRANSPORTATION

Transport plays an important role in trade and cross-border development. Dealing with the present issues in transportation will require: untying bottlenecks in border cities; synchronizing cross-border traffic and trade; reducing dependence on the currently unsustainable energy sector; finding new ways to fund and maintain highway infrastructure; implementing inter-modal transport facilities in ports; and developing sustainable mobility systems in urban centers.

In the United States, transportation represents 11% of the nation's GDP, and 75% of all goods in the country move through 4 million miles of public highways, roads, and streets.[9]

"FUEL-AND-HIGHWAYS" TRANSPORTATION: THE MOBILITY STANDARD FOR COMMERCE AND EVERYDAY LIVING IN BOTH COUNTRIES

Throughout North America, urban and intra-state transportation have especially significant impact on the economies and quality of life of all three countries. Yet dependence on this mode of mobility carries implications that each nation must face: secure energy sources, trade and urban transportation efficiency through inter-modal facilities, cross-border congestion, and reduction of air and water pollution.

Everyday-living Mobility

Within the next twenty to thirty years, the number of vehicles in the world—a number which has already grown tenfold since 1950—is likely to double from its present total of 630 million vehicles.[1] The automobile, so embedded in Americans' desire for personal freedom, is expected to continue to be the preferred mode of transportation in urban centers throughout the United States. Even when on average American drivers spend a half hour commuting by themselves each day,[2] leaving their cars parked 90% of the time, their loyalty to the automobile has increased. In 2001, 92% of U.S. households owned one or more vehicles, up from 86% in 1983.[3] As most population growth in the country will take place in cities in the coming decades, the number of passenger miles traveled is predicted to increase even more rapidly than the population or the economy—growing from 5 trillion in 2000 to 8.4 trillion in 2025.[4]

In Mexico, by contrast, most people use public transportation—mostly by necessity, since the average income of Mexicans is almost seven times lower than that of Americans.[5] Car ownership is on the rise in affluent cities, however. Mexico City is producing more new cars than babies on a two-to-one ratio[6]—and generating major traffic jams and numerous vehicle accidents. Mexico is the number three country in the Americas with regard to traffic-related fatalities, while the U.S. is first.

Trucks Ensure Trade Flows in North America

The car-manufacturing industry in North America feeds this constant appetite for vehicles and is proof of tri-lateral coordination. Just-in-time (JIT) manufacturing, a production model from Japan, allows the car industry to process different aspects of a car lifecycle in different plants distributed among the three NAFTA countries. JIT allows suppliers to ship car parts to be assembled at distant plants as they are needed in the assembly process. This synchronization makes logistics efficient and reduces inventory necessities to a bare minimum. Mexico, for example, exports 75% of the vehicles assembled in the country, mostly to the United States.[8]

By far, trucking is the transport mode through which most trade flows in North America, followed by rail and air cargo, respectively. In 2004, over 8 million full truck containers entered the U.S., compared to less than 2 million full rail containers.[10] The main ports through which NAFTA trade flows are Detroit, Michigan, and Laredo, Texas. This route traversing the central plains is often called the NAFTA highway, extending north to Montreal and south to Mexico City. Based on this trade route, a group called North America's Super Corridor

Coalition was formed to coordinate efforts between the three countries, the state governors, academics, and industry leaders to make trade seamless along this corridor and to lobby to their respective governments for improved and increased infrastructure. A similar group exists covering the states of Montana down to Arizona. The CANAMEX Corridor, as it is known, an initiative of various U.S. state governors, involves leaders from Canada and Mexico in their meetings to jointly improve tri-national trade flows. Over forty similar corridors traverse the U.S. highway network.

SECURING ENERGY SOURCES, REDUCING POLLUTION: TWO INTER-RELATED CHALLENGES FOR THE INDUSTRY

Reducing dependence on a fluctuating energy sector and lowering greenhouse gas emissions will continue to be two major challenges for the transportation industry in the coming decades.

Reducing Dependence on a Fluctuating Energy Sector

All three North American countries are vulnerable to international oil price fluctuations since trucking, the main transportation mode for NAFTA trade, is mostly powered by diesel and gasoline. The United States, the biggest oil consumer in the world, imports about half of the crude oil it consumes.[12] Although new fuel sources and transport vehicles are already available—electric, liquid hydrogen, fuel cell, ethanol, natural gas, and bio-fuel vehicles—it is hard to predict how long it will take for them to reach the tipping point of consumer sales to compete with gasoline and diesel vehicles. Current trends seem to point to a future where oil demand—and prices—will rise, allowing alternative fuels and fuel cells to compete in the marketplace with oil-derived fuels, turning energy dependence away from fossil fuels. Lester

Brown, President of the Earth Policy Institute, suggests that raising gasoline taxes as much as three dollars per gallon over the next decades would allow to transition to alternative fuel sources.[13] John B. Heywood, director of Sloan Automotive Lab at the Massachusetts Institute of Technology, suggests the creation of a "feebate" scheme—a package that would include fiscal and regulatory policies requiring automobile makers to produce more energy-efficient vehicles as well as providing fuel tax incentives for consumers who purchase energy-efficient automobiles—could be an option to promote change toward more fuel efficiency.[14] In any case, implementing alternative fuel sources in large truck fleets remains a challenge.

Reducing Transportation-related Air Pollution

As cities are host to the three most energy-intensive industries—automobile, food, and airline[15]—new solutions will be needed for the way we travel and bring food to our tables. There are currently 226 million motor vehicles in the United States, contributing to one third of all energy-related carbon dioxide emissions in the country generated from transportation.[16] According to the International Energy Agency, 75% of the oil demand increase this century is expected to come from the transportation sector.[17]

Food in the U.S. travels long distances to reach its destination cities. As the average supermarket offers a wide variety of produce and imported food products from countries as far as South Africa and New Zealand, the average trip food makes from farm to plate now averages between 1,553 to 2,485 miles.[18] The free trade of food and agricultural products has added the "hidden cost" of air pollution to our food, stemming from its transportation plus other production costs. Estimated at $9 per gallon, the indirect costs of burning gasoline include health care costs for treating respiratory

23

FEBRUARY 28, 2025

No More Spur-of-the-moment Air Travel: Commercial Airliners Limit Flights along the West Coast of the U.S.

Airlines face a tough challenge due to the unprecedented success of the bullet train connecting British Columbia to Los Cabos, Baja California, and making stops in major cities along North America's west coast, including Vancouver, Seattle, San Francisco, Los Angeles, San Diego, and Tijuana. Fewer and fewer travelers are choosing to fly to and from destinations along the west coast, since a train ride from downtown San Francisco to downtown Los Angeles can cost as little as $25. Airliners estimate that if they don't limit the number of flights along this route to four a week they might risk bankruptcy. Ironically, airliners have a booming regional trade and tourism industry to blame, since the train was developed in order to facilitate the shipping of goods and people along this Western corridor and that is exactly what it is doing.[11]

MAY 17, 2027

Sunny California, Yes, But Windy? Residents of California Oppose Expansion of Wind Farms along the State's Coastline

There is a price for the state's near total reliance on clean renewable energy sources, and some Californians are not willing to pay. Although this state leads the nation in the use of renewable energy sources with 90% of its vehicles powered by electricity, plans to expand wind power are facing significant obstructions. As new technologies for storing the power generated by windmills thrive, the project to establish wind farms near Mendocino, San Jose, Big Sur, Carmel, Santa Monica, San Diego, and other coastal cities have met fierce opposition from residents who do not want wind turbines to block their scenic ocean views. Officials argue that in five years' time solar power alone will not provide sufficient energy for the state's 15,000 electric charging stations.

diseases.[19] This condition affects all of the NAFTA nations. In Mexico, for instance, thanks to NAFTA's lowering of trade barriers, about one quarter of corn is imported from the U.S., yet an invisible air pollution "price tag" is added to the apparently cheaper corn Mexicans purchase from their neighboring country's subsidized farmers.[20] These air pollution costs translate into a mix of greenhouse gases produced while shipping U.S.-grown corn to Mexico, plus the contamination created from the larger economies-of-scale that farmers in the U.S. are used to, such as the use of oil-derived fertilizers and fuels to run farming vehicles.

SYNCHRONIZING AND SECURING CROSS-BORDER TRAFFIC AND TRADE

Cross-border transportation has been less than optimal and poses an ongoing challenge for binational trade and human transport in the coming decades. This is partly due to truckers' unions and regulations that impede the opening of the U.S. borders to Mexican and Canadian truckers. Despite these limits placed on the flow of people between both countries, all transport modes are used to illicitly introduce migrants and drugs into the United States from south of its border. More than 2 million empty truck containers and nearly a million empty rail containers enter the U.S. annually[21]—all as potential vessels for human, drug, and

NAFTA has favored the flow of goods, but not of people. It is the biggest economic trading bloc in the world, yet truckers from one nation are not allowed to drive through their neighbor's.

weapons smuggling into the country. As mentioned earlier, since 9/11 the transportation industry in North America has had to abide by new security regulations demanded by the U.S. Department of Homeland Security, adding yet another challenge to the North America's transportation industry (see pages 73–75).

Already in existence, dedicated SENTRI (Secure Electronic Network for Travelers' Rapid Inspection) lanes for frequent travelers and C-TPAT (Customs-Trade Partnership Against Terrorism)–certified companies and agricultural producers expedite trade flows crossing north of the hyperborder. However, cross-border transport systems and road infrastructure need to be improved in the near future.

The San Diego and Arizona Eastern (SD&AE) Railway, a train that went from San Diego to Arizona—a 134-mile-long rail link, forty-four miles of which ran through Mexico—was cancelled in 1983 based on fears of being a potential drug smuggling channel into the U.S. If restored, the line would provide San Diego and Tijuana with a direct freight connection to the east via the Union Pacific's Sunset Line. The Desert Line, rechristened "the NAFTA train," has been stalled by political and legal hurdles on both sides of the border.[22] There were also talks of doing a "Twinports" binational airport shared between Tijuana and San Diego that was stalled as well. More recently, in 2004, Ciudad Juárez built 2.17 miles of a Bus Rapid Transport (BRT) system as part of its growing TransBorder network; however, the new mayor has made no commitment to the project and the system is not currently operating. This is unfortunate in that a

unique opportunity may be missed to link the system trans-nationally with a similar BRT system in El Paso.[23]

In Tijuana, the surface street system is barely adequate to meet present needs. Approximately 50% of the paved streets are in poor repair, and many newer residential and other areas lack paving, contributing significantly to regional pollution due to the high levels of dust.[24] Bottlenecks in border cities' crossing points contribute to the damage of roads and pollution created from lines of idling trucks. Funding for these sorts of infrastructure projects are already being supplied by a mix of sources, such as the North American Development Bank (NADB) and state and local municipalities.

DESIGNING FUNDING MECHANISMS TO MAINTAIN AND EXTEND HIGHWAY INFRASTRUCTURE

The improvement and expansion of Mexico's roads and highways benefit the United States. From the perspective of U.S. trade, investment in Mexico's ports and highways connecting directly to U.S. trade routes would reduce shipping costs of products shipped from Asia. Investments in infrastructure in Mexico's southeastern states could greatly boost that region's economy, which at the moment

Top: Map shows potential congestion points in U.S. roads by 2020. The orange areas are points with exceeded capacity. Black shows aproaching capacity, while gray represents roads below full capacity.

Bottom: Map shows estimated average annual daily truck traffic in 2020.

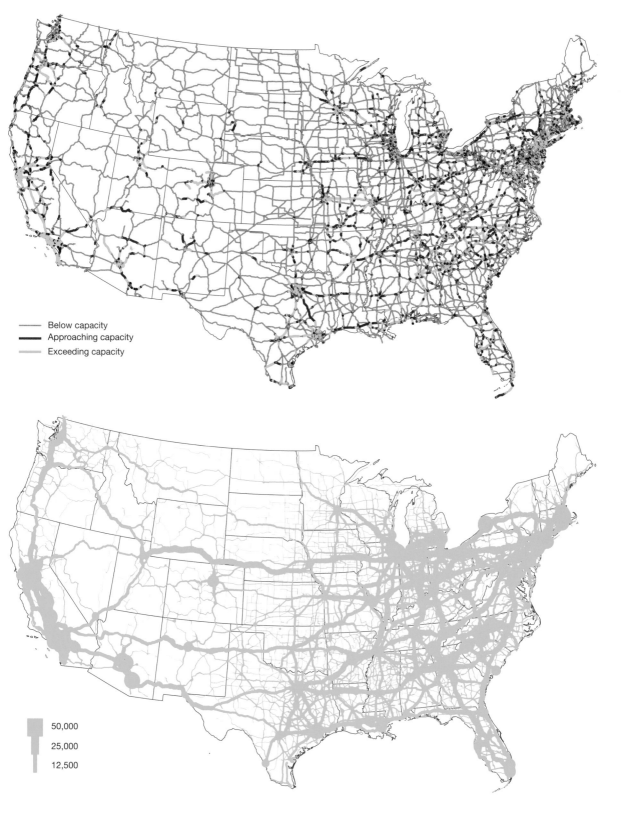

Below capacity
Approaching capacity
Exceeding capacity

50,000
25,000
12,500

225

Nearly 40,000 people who live in Tijuana commute every weekday across the border to work in San Diego and surrounding areas.

remains poor and is a point of origin of many undocumented migrants bound to the U.S. Dr. Robert A. Pastor, director of the Center for North American Studies at the American University, calculates that an investment of $200 billion over ten years in Mexico's roads and communications infrastructure could likely double Mexico's GDP growth rates to 6% or higher and reduce the income gap between both countries. The European integration model is a lesson in this regard. The EU countries invested in Greece, Portugal, Ireland, and Spain to join the European Union by financing infrastructure development in these countries. The result was a GDP increase for all four countries from 65% of the average EU member's to 82% between 1986 and 2003.

Although binational efforts to invest in highway infrastructure could unfold in the future, both countries will need to face their own internal financing challenges. In the U.S., the fuel tax system was created to provide funding for roads and highways, but as fuel efficiencies have increased, drivers travel farther with the same amount of fuel, making the fuel tax insufficient to maintain and expand highways. Between 1985 and 1999, vehicle miles of travel on U.S. roadways grew by 76%, whereas lane miles increased by only 3%.[25]

In Mexico, on the other hand, the financing of highways has a mixed source of funding coming from federal, state, and municipality budgets as well as private investors who help fund toll-highways. Mexico has one of the largest networks of toll-highways in the world and allows foreign investment in this type of infrastructure development. Today, the majority of highways in the country are un-tolled, reaching 66,200 miles, compared

to 3,724 miles of toll-highways. The density of highways—the ratio of highway kilometers per square kilometer—is very low in Mexico, with a ratio of just 0.14, versus 0.64 in the U.S., 1.61 in the UK, 1.62 in France, 1.77 in Germany, and 3.04 in Japan.[26]

DEVELOPING INTERMODAL TRANSPORT FACILITIES

"Intermodal transportation"—that involving multiple modes of transportation during a single, uninterrupted journey[27]—is an obvious "next step" to the reduction of trade barriers that free trade agreements have allowed. Dr. Paul Stephen Dempsey, Director of the National Center for Intermodal Transportation at the University of Denver, describes this eloquently:

> As the gateways to an increasingly global market, transportation corridors are the arteries through which we and everything we consume flow. Transportation networks stimulate trillions of dollars in trade, commerce, and tourism. In a global economy, they enable specialization in the production of goods and services which, under the law of comparative advantage, stimulates broader economic growth.[28]

One of the advantages of developing intermodal transport facilities in the movement of freight is to reduce transportation and energy costs by saving on logistics and reducing shipping times, creating a single flow of containers—in some cases from overseas to inland destinations; other times between two inland points of origin and destination—adding value to the final products being delivered.

In cities, intermodal transport hubs can seamlessly connect passengers to various destinations depending on distances traveled. For distances under 12 miles bikes are suitable; under 31 miles, buses and light-rails; over 62 miles, automobiles are the preferred choice; and between cities, trains and airplanes are the logical transportation mode. The advantage of intermodal facilities such as "park-and-ride" facilities in cities is the reduction of congestion and the need for more roads and highways, as these promote the use of other modes of transportation such as bicycles and public transportation.

Below: Maps showing main trade corridors in North America.

● Pacific corridor/
Rocky Mountain corridor

● Canamex
● Alaska Highway
● Camino Real

● NAFTA Corridor
● Plains/Prairies corridor

● Atlantic coast corridor
● Champlain-Hudson corridor
● Appalachian international corridor
● Gulf corridor

Architect James Corner/Field Operations' vision for the border proposes to build on existing security infrastructure to create a continuous energy harnessing strip along the entire border, augmenting the border's security functions into a productive renewable energy generator. It is, after all, one of the regions with the highest solar radiation in the world.

12. ENERGY

As supplies of the world's fossil fuels dwindle while demand increases, the development of new energy resources is crucial to the future of the planet, humanity, and the global economy. Both the United States and Mexico will be greatly affected by changes coming to the energy sector, since neither country has yet to sufficiently develop alternative sources. However, their common border holds potential solutions for the looming challenges.

THE ENERGY CRISIS IS THE GREATEST CHALLENGE FACING HUMANITY IN THE TWENTY-FIRST CENTURY

Today the world economy depends on non-renewable energy resources such as oil and natural gas, the supplies of which are rapidly depleting as demand grows, making global resource scarcity something of a reality. The "peak oil phenomenon," deriving from the geophysicist Dr. Marion King Hubbert's "Hubbert peak theory," assumes that after oil reserves are discovered, oil production will increase exponentially until a peak is reached, at which point production will exponentially dwindle to nothing.[1] According to many experts, the world is nearing the zenith of this curve. Geologists' predictions in 2005 say that 94% of available oil on Earth has already been discovered,[2] and Colin Campbell, a retired petroleum geologist who is widely considered today's leading peak oil expert, predicts that global peak oil will be reached during this decade, after which production will initially decline at 2–8% a year.[3] The International Energy Agency (IEA) predicts that oil demand will rise 37% by 2030, and importing nations will need to import 85% of their oil by that same year—a 20% increase from their current rate—posing a great diplomatic problem for countries like the U.S. and European nations.[4] As countries around the world strive to model their lifestyles after those of Americans—who on average consume their body weight a week in oil (approximately 150 pounds)[5]—the global demand will continue to threaten the ever-dwindling supply.

AS CHINA AND INDIA INDUSTRIALIZE, WORLDWIDE COMPETITION FOR ENERGY RESOURCES INCREASES

China has emerged as a major competitor for energy resources, as it is now the number two importer and consumer behind the United States.[6] India, with few energy resources of its own and a steeply climbing population, is quickly becoming a competitive concern as well: by 2010, with 16% of the world population and rapid economic growth, the country is expected to depend on foreign oil for 80% of its petroleum needs.[7] According to the IEA, developing nations in Asia, including China and India, will continue to expand their economies and GDPs more rapidly than the global average, by about 5% annually. The energy demand attending such radical economic growth is expected to double by 2025, accounting for 40% of the projected total increase in world energy consumption over the next two decades.[8] Furthermore, these nations—particularly China—are forming stronger alliances with countries rich in natural resources (like Russia), while at the same time tensions between the U.S. and several resource-exporting nations (Iran) are heightening. This is cause for great concern to the energy security of energy-importing nations, including the U.S.[9]

U.S. AND MEXICAN ECONOMIES DEPEND ON DEPLETING FOSSIL FUELS

It is a fact understood worldwide that oil and other fossil fuels are the driving force behind the global economy and economic growth. Energy resources are used to fuel transportation, produce food, manufacture goods, provide power generation and electricity, develop new sources of energy, and

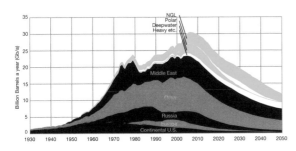

In 2004, the world pumped nearly 31 billion barrels of oil, while discovering less than 8 billion barrels of new oil.

much more. Without access to energy resources, the global economy as it is today could not exist. As of 2005, the world market consumed 82 million barrels of petroleum a day, half of which was absorbed by transportation and 25% of which was consumed by the United States alone.[10] The U.S. is the world's leading oil consumer and importer, and after Canada, Mexico is the United States' most important petroleum supplier. The Mexican government currently depends on Pemex, the state-owned oil company, for one-third of its spending, making petroleum a vital source of income for Mexico.[11]

MEXICO'S DEPLETING OIL RESERVES WILL SEVERELY IMPACT GOVERNMENT SPENDING

Recent events indicate that Mexico's peak oil production may have already passed, as the Cantarell oil field—the world's second largest oilfield, which supplies 60% of Mexico's annual crude oil production—is officially in decline after it peaked at 2.13 million barrels per day (mb/d) in 2004.[12] To further compound the problem, at present Pemex has little

hope of replacing Cantarell because the company lacks the capital to explore more regions in search of new fields. Although exporting crude oil in mass quantities is an indisputably lucrative business—especially when market prices are high, as they are in the current world market—Pemex is in debt. This is largely because the state absorbs most of its revenues, as petroleum in Mexico is a nationalized industry, leaving the company unable to invest in the diversification of its capacities and forcing it to remain oriented toward little more than crude-oil exports. In fact oil profits currently provide the government with one-third of its spending.[13] Since petroleum is one of the nation's most important exports, and is also used to provide for the country's domestic use, its decline could potentially provoke a significant economic recession if alternative sources of income are not developed.

UNCERTAIN ENERGY SECURITY

Current conditions and patterns in the global energy arena reveal distressing news for the energy security of the United States. As Mexico's petroleum resources are set to decline while demand is rising in the U.S., America's dependence will have to shift toward oil-producing nations that are considered unstable and are understood to have interests that do not "coincide" with those of the Western nations.[16]

A new global energy elite is emerging as a result of dwindling natural resources and the energy crisis. Those in control of the precious commodities—the fossil fuel–exporting nations of the world—are finding themselves in unprecedented positions of power, while the energy resource–importing countries are in a historic state of vulnerability. Several natural resource–rich countries, such as Ecuador, Iran, Venezuela, and Russia, have already proved a willingness to use their energy-producing role as a weapon in diplomatic disputes. Ecuador and Iran

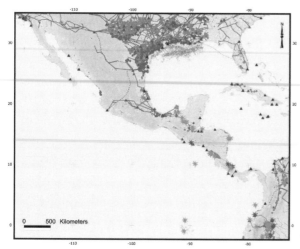

Gulf of Mexico: U.S. and Mexican urban settlements and oil fields.

25

OCTOBER 17, 2011

Protesters Block Main Roadways in Mexico City as President Announces that Oil Industry Will Be Open to Foreign Investment in 2012

Mobilized by representatives of a leading Left party, thousands of protesters blocked Reforma and Insurgentes, two of the main arteries in Mexico City's road system, in opposition to the president's announcement that the government-owned oil monopoly Pemex will soon be open to foreign capital investment. Claiming that the notion of sovereignty has become obsolete and detrimental to the financial stability of the country, the federal government is confident that only foreign investment will allow for the exploitation of oil fields that remain untapped to this day. Analysts predict protests will dwindle by the time the new policy is implemented.[14]

Panic in Mexico: The Nation Faces its Worst Economic Crisis in History as Pemex Announces its Oil Reserves are Completely Depleted

A day after the President of Mexico held a televised press conference in which he announced that the oil reserves of Pemex, the state-owned oil monopoly, had been used up, and that an austerity plan was to be implemented, people flocked to banks and currency exchange houses in fear of massive layoffs and a devaluation of the Mexican peso. Financial institutions proved incapable of handling the resulting throngs and had to close their doors early in the afternoon. Consequently, the downtown areas of Mexico City and other major cities, including Guadalajara and Monterrey, erupted in violence; the police could not prevent lootings, as enraged crowds ransacked local businesses. Officials are to meet with representatives of the World Bank and the IMF as early as tomorrow morning to discuss a rescue credit line.[15]

have terminated contracts with foreign oil companies, and both Venezuela and Iran state they will cut supplies if they receive threats from the U.S.[17] The Russia–Ukraine gas dispute of January 2006 highlighted concern for Europe's energy security, when Gazprom, Russia's state-owned natural gas company, briefly closed the gas line that crossed Ukraine and fed into the rest of Europe (see page 41). The action proved Russia's relative control over the continent and its willingness to exercise that power.

AS THE BORDER POPULATION GROWS, SO TOO DOES ENERGY DEMAND

As the U.S.–Mexico border has become a magnet for Mexican migrants seeking economic opportunity, the region has experienced massive population growth and urban sprawl. This process of "hyperurbanization"[18] has induced a high and ever-growing demand for energy resources in the region. The number of energy consumers has sharply increased in recent years—especially since the implementation of NAFTA and the expansion of the maquiladora industry—and the population continues to rise. The growth in electricity consumption in the Mexican border states reflects this phenomenon: from 1982 to 2001, the share of these states' electricity use grew from 27% to 32% of Mexico's total, a fact that is credited to increased industrialization in the region.[19]

As of 2002, the border region counties and municipalities had a population of 12.5 million, a figure that is estimated to hit 24 million by the year 2020.[20] In that same year, the metropolitan zone between Tijuana and San Diego is expected to be home to 5.8 million residents;[21] the population on the Mexican side of the border, which is growing even faster, is expected to have surpassed that of the United States' side by 2015.[22] With these population increases, the demand for energy power

in northern Mexico has seen growth by 6.5% per year, a rate that within eleven years will render a demand double that of today.[23] The Mexican state of Mexicali, located on the border with California, currently has the highest per-capita residential energy use in the country.[24] Energy needs on the U.S. side are also growing, but at a lower rate, between 1–3% a year.[25] The border is located in an arid region made up of fragile ecosystems, and with relatively few natural resources immediately available to it, the area is unable to sustain the projected population growth.[26] At the global level, energy demands are expected to double between the years 2001 and 2025, yet according to Frank Verrastro, Director of the Energy Program at the Center for Strategic and International Studies in Washington, D.C., little change is expected in the diversification of fuel sources before that time.[27]

THE DEMAND FOR WATER WILL INCREASE WITH THE DEMAND FOR ENERGY

Rapid population growth not only increases the demand for energy but for water as well. It is a well-known fact that water is a vital resource, and therefore access to it is imperative; it is less known, however, that water is an indispensable element to the production of energy resources. In the U.S., limited water supplies are projected to inhibit energy generation by the year 2038, though this reality may come even sooner for many areas.[28] Access to adequate water and energy is necessary to economic growth, and the limited supplies of both resources in the border region will likely stall or prevent development very soon. The Tijuana–San Diego binational zone, for example, has experienced phenomenal economic development in recent years, however increases in population and industrial activity strain local resources. By the year 2010, the region will require 24% more water than it consumed in 1996.[29] This demand partly stems from the generation of electricity, which requires large amounts of water for production, since it is mostly generated through a process called gas turbine combined cycle (GTCC) technology. GTCC technology utilizes a combination of a gas turbine and conventional steam generator to produce electricity and requires the use of purified water for steam generation, and less-pure water (similar to tap water) for the cooling process. When the system is applied at the industrial level, the necessary quantities are tremendous: for the cooling process alone, 1,000 acre-feet (af) of water—or 325.8 million gallons—are required to generate every 100 megawatts (MW) of power. By 2015, the region encompassing California and Baja California is expected to have an increased demand of some 25,000 MW, requiring 250,000 af of water.[30] That translates into the consumption of 81.46 billion gallons of water just to meet the increase in energy demand in a region already plagued by limited access to potable water.

FURTHER ENVIRONMENTAL DEGRADATION AND HEALTH ISSUES DEVELOPING FROM INCREASED FOSSIL-FUEL BURNING

Extraction, distribution, and consumption of energy are the greatest sources of environmental degradation and subsequent environmental health problems and diseases.[31] The border region's air and water resources are contaminated due to high rates of local pollution caused by traffic congestion in the sister cities and border-crossing points, as well as toxic wastes and other pollutants produced by the maquiladoras. Phenomena like the decaying ozone layer and global warming, both of which are consequences of the emission of chemicals produced by incessant fossil fuel–burning, are threatening global society with increasing force and have arrived at the forefront of today's environmental protection agenda. These environmental problems and climate changes (especially global warming) will certainly

worsen if oil and gas shortages provoke a return to the use of coal, a process already underway in some nations around the world. Health issues such as skin cancer, respiratory illnesses, and cardiovascular diseases that are related to smog, contamination, and ozone depletion will rise if the burning of fossil fuels follows the anticipated rates.

THE HYPERBORDER'S POTENTIAL FOR DEVELOPING ALTERNATIVE, RENEWABLE ENERGY RESOURCES

The Mojave Desert, spreading across southern California, southwestern Utah, southern Nevada, and northwestern Arizona, is home to the world's largest solar power plant, owned by the Israeli company Solel, which produces 90% of the world's commercially generated solar energy.[33] Wind power has proven to be a successful source of energy in countries like Denmark and Germany, as well as in states like California and Kansas, and is currently the most rapidly growing alternative energy source.[34] Vermont is the leading state in "cow power," which utilizes methane from cow manure as an energy source that not only powers the farms where the cows are raised but could also provide for the energy needs of hundreds of homes in the surrounding communities.[35] Studies show that the border region also has the potential to provide these energy resources, yet currently there are no established long-term plans to exploit these opportunities.

Renewable energy resources have been deemed capable of meeting all potential energy needs for the future.[36] But major obstacles to replacing nonrenewable fossil fuels with renewable alternatives must be overcome. These include implementing new forms of energy storage; dedicating land to the sites of production; making the sources more cost-effective; and convincing governments and societies that supporting a transition toward renewable energy will ultimately improve national energy security

JUNE 6, 2015

Bikes in short supply as gas reaches record high of $10 per gallon

As the market price for a barrel of oil hikes up to $150, American drivers have figured out that the easiest way to limit their car use to a strict minimum is by resorting to the reliable vehicle of yore: the bicycle. Sporting goods stores claim there are not enough bicycles to meet the new demand, which has increased 350% in the last two weeks. A new line of bicycles especially designed for overweight cyclists of all ages will hit stores by mid-July. Sales of scooters have also gone up two-fold.

"I'd put my money on the sun and solar energy. What a source of power! I hope we don't have to wait 'til oil and coal run out before we tackle that."

—Thomas Edison[32]

and self-sufficiency.[37] Over the long term, replacing fossil fuels with renewable energy resources will greatly reduce pollution and environmental health problems along the border region, and considering the U.S., Mexico, and their common border have an abundant supply of renewable energy resources, the two countries could work together to harness their capacities.

Solar Energy

The border region between the United States and Mexico is dry, arid, sunny, and for the most part vacant—making it an ideal location for solar power plants. Solar photovoltaic energy is considered to perform well and is a clean fuel source, which in itself could help pave the way to a healthier environment in the border region through the reduction of fossil-fuel burning. As the costs of fossil fuels increase, solar power will increasingly become more economical.

Biomass Fuel

Cattle ranches in northern Mexico could implement "cow power" techniques, using the methane found in cow manure as a source of energy generation. This could serve as a new source of income for the "cow power" producers, help displace reliance on depleting fossil fuels, and provide an innovative, clean biomass fuel source for a region plagued by pollutants.

Solar energy is available at a rate of 1,367 watts on every square meter facing the sun. In one day, 6.7 kilowatt hours of solar energy fall on every square meter of horizontal surface, of which .7 kilowatt hours come from all directions other than directly from the sun. Commercial solar plants have achieved leveled energy costs of about 12–15 cents/kwh, and the potential forecast reduction are expected to ultimately lead to costs as low as 5 cents/kwh.

The U.S.–Mexico border region is one with high potential for solar energy development. Approximately three quarters of Mexico's territory receive an average solar insulation of 5KWh per square meters each day. To illustrate the potential for solar energy development in Mexico, if the three border states of Sonora, Chihuahua, and Coahuila were covered with average consumer solar panels, enough electricity would be generated to feed all of Mexico's electricity demand, or about 178,510 Gwh/year.

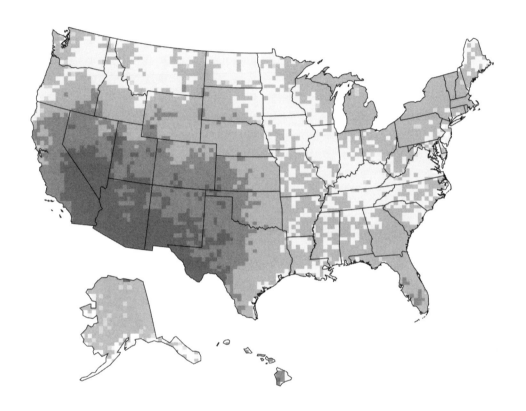

Solar radiation in U.S. southwestern states is the highest in the country.

Farming Becomes the Second Fastest-growing Profession as Biofuels Become Mandatory in North America

Small-scale farmers who were forced to find jobs in cities as the agribusiness became more corporate at the beginning of the twenty-first century now have a chance to return to the land and earn above-average wages. As corn-based ethanol and soybean biodiesel has replaced fossil fuel in Canada, Mexico, and the United States, in the last decade traditional migration patterns from the country to the city have begun to reverse. City planners in Mexico City are optimistic about the positive effects these patterns are already having on daily life in the megalopolis: the city's population has decreased by 4% in the last three years.

Fueling station offering a varied menu of fueling options at competitive prices with gasoline, such as biodiesel, ethanol, liquid hydrogen, and natural gas.

CITGO

425 ⁹⁄₁₀	REGULAR UNLEADED
447 ⁹⁄₁₀	SUPER PREMIUM
433 ⁹⁄₁₀	E55 ETHANOL
450 ⁹⁄₁₀	E25 ETHANOL
422 ⁹⁄₁₀	M65 METHANOL
585 ⁹⁄₁₀	REGULAR HYROGEN
625 ⁹⁄₁₀	PREMIUM HYDROGEN

CAR WASH

Tire dump site in the border city of Mexicali. As part of a binational effort lead by the Environmental Protection Agency and Mexico's Environment Secretariat, the site was cleaned up and 420,000 scrap tires were turned into asphalt to pave streets in the region. Used tires from the U.S. are often resold in Mexico.

13. ENVIRONMENT

Environmental degradation plagues the border region, when high levels of air and water pollution and diseases related to environmental contamination disproportionately affect its residents. Their future resolutions require binational attention and action.

LOSS OF BIODIVERSITY THREATENS BOTH COUNTRIES

Mexico is the world's fifth most biodiverse country after Brazil, Colombia, China, and Indonesia. The nation hosts 12% of all species, and over half of the flora in Mexico is unique to the country. Around the world, 15.4% of species eaten as food have their origins in Mexico. Many plants, including tomatoes, corn, avocados, vanilla, tobacco, sweet potatoes, cocoa, and peanuts, were first domesticated in the country.

Indigenous communities are host to 80% of the ecosystems found in good preservation conditions in Mexico.[1] (As of today, 291 indigenous languages are spoken in Mexico, the equivalent to 30% of those spoken in the North American continent and 4% of the world's indigenous languages.) The destruction of these ecosystems threatens not only the sustenance of these cultures but also the rest of the country's habitants, as these regions provide services that sustain Mexico's web of life.

The geographical location of the country makes it more vulnerable to droughts and hurricanes, an issue that has been compounded by the loss of agricultural land, drying-up of aquifers, erosion, and desertification. In Mexico, land use and management are two of the country's greatest challenges. While land parcels are being transformed into agricultural or grazing fields, 13 million cubic meters of logs are sold illegally every year, contributing to the desertification of forests. The U.S. ranks fourth in the world in total forest cover and Mexico ranks eleventh,[2] yet wood represents 40% of energy demand in Mexican households, and between 5 and 10% of Mexico's GDP is lost every year due to loss of biodiversity.[3] Despite all this, Mexico ranks number one in the handling of sustainable template and tropical forests in the world,[4] while the percentage of U.S. land covered by forest has risen by 1.7% in the last decade. However,

1,230 species remain endangered or threatened in the U.S.[5] Restoring threatened eco-systems in both countries should be a priority.

INCREASING WATER SHORTAGES

Access to water, considered a human right, will continue to be a challenge in the context of international relations in the future as 80% of the food needed in the world by 2030 will depend on cross-border irrigation. The hyperborder is no exception to this global trend. More than sixty years after the U.S. and Mexico signed the water distribution treaty in 1944, which established the International Boundary & Water Commission, water availability in the border region has changed due to drought, population growth, and the depletion of underground aquifers, among other factors. Although the agreement is still in effect, the binational politics around water must be revised to reflect the current reality of water availability in the region. According to Carmen Maganda, the coordinator of the Border Water Project at the University of California in San Diego, the main challenge to meet water needs is political:

> The availability and accessibility of water depends on various factors that are not just technical, but also political. The technology is certainly necessary to extract water from underground or for transporting it across long distances. However, the political power for its negotiation, along with the economic power for the development of public works, is the central element for guaranteeing water access today.[6]

Every day about 408 billion gallons of water are withdrawn in the U.S., primarily for thermoelectric power generation and irrigation. Since 1985, the national population has grown steadily, yet water withdrawals have remained stable.[7] The

AUGUST 22, 2016

New Travel Ecotourism Packages Available in Mexico, with a Twist

As a way to fund the protection and development of numerous state parks across the country, the Mexican government, in collaboration with Greenpeace International, is developing eco-reality tours to be marketed among Latin American, European, and American tourists who want to immerse themselves in the harsh Mexican reality and experience the urgency of greater environmental awareness. To fully grasp the importance of eco-friendly programs, tourists traveling to Chiapas, for instance—a state with approximately 1,300 native tree species—will be able to visit not only the Agua Azul waterfall and natural protected areas, but also the state's highlands, which have had the highest rate of deforestation in the country since 1960. Similar tours across the country include Mexico City slums and the Xochimilco Ecological Park, as well as national protected areas and border cities formerly engulfed by industrial waste.

southwest, however, is prone to water scarcity. California alone accounts for one quarter—or 3.8 trillion liters—of water withdrawals from the Colorado River.[8]

Throughout Mexico, access to water varies widely. The greatest water availability is found in the country's southern region and Gulf area, with an availability of 24,549 and 10,574 cubic meters, respectively, per person per year. In Mexico's northern region, near the Rio Grande and Baja California peninsula, only 1,350 cubic meters per person are available per year. However, this number is much higher than that of Mexico City's metropolitan region, where only 188 cubic meters are available to each resident, a quantity almost ten times lower than the official international water scarcity levels of 1,700 cubic meters per person per year. Of the 653 aquifers in the country, 104 are overexploited, and 73% of water bodies in the country are contaminated since 80% of all wastewater is returned to these bodies without any previous treatment.[9]

The water availability prospects for the border state of Texas point to an increase in demand of 27% by 2060.[10] By then, the state's population will have grown from 21 million to about 46 million, water supplies will have decreased by 18%,[11] and the state will need an additional 8.8 million acre-feet of water if no new water supplies are developed. On the Mexican side of the border, the non-renewable aquifer of Bolsón del Hueco, the main water source for El Paso and Ciudad Juárez, is expected to run dry by 2020, and so will the Bolsón de Mejilla, a secondary aquifer for these cities.

THE ENVIRONMENTAL EFFECTS OF THE BORDER'S CLOSING

In Tijuana, the construction of the Todo Americano canal, a few meters from the Mexicali border, plus the expansion of border walls and fences, could seriously affect the local watershed shared by both San Diego and Tijuana. Maganda explains:

If [the construction of a double frontier was completed], the city of Tijuana would be seriously affected by the dragging congestion of water and mud, the result of water and mud landslides that wouldn't be able to naturally exit to the San Diego estuary. The Los Laureles Canyon in Tijuana would be one of the most affected areas. In this region, hundreds of families live in fragile housing units and are already vulnerable to raining seasons. Their situation would be aggravated if the drags didn't have an exit. The natural park Estuary Tijuana–San Diego, on the American side, has as one of its objectives the cleaning and redirection of the flow of the water drags coming from Tijuana. Also in this park they work on the preservation of *humedales* ecosystems [birds and vegetation] which would also be evidently at risk if the conditions of the estuary should change.[12]

The Secure Fence Act passed by President Bush, promoting the construction of a 700-mile fence (see page 126), is extremely controversial, and not just for the expected social and political reasons. Environmental protectionists have come forward in strong opposition to the border wall due to the potential consequences for the region's ecosystems. According to a representative from the *Defensores de la vida salvaje* (defenders of the wildlife association) in Tucson, a border wall will tamper with the habitat of jaguars, wolves, and owls, among other animals, which all need large, open spaces in order to survive.[13] In California many environmental agencies have taken issue with the Department of Homeland Security for its border enforcement tactics. In the winter of 2006, under powers granted by Congress that allow the

DHS to waive any law in the name of national security,[14] the DHS announced the construction of 3.5 miles of fencing just south of the Tijuana River National Estuary Research Reserve, which is federally protected land. The California Coastal Management Program, a state agency that reviews federal activities affecting the coast, said the project—which entails the construction of three fifteen-foot-high steel fences, new roads, and stadium-style lighting—violates California's federally approved coastal management program. Yet under Congress's protection, the DHS has the right to go forward with the border enforcement project—despite the endeavor's negative effects—exposing the nature of the U.S. government's priorities under its current national security agenda.

CLIMATE CHANGE: AN ONGOING THREAT TO BOTH COUNTRIES' ECONOMIES

Climate change due to global warming originates from human-related activities, the most impacting of which are carbon dioxide emissions.[16] The effects of climate change result in loss of habitat and species, change of weather patterns, increased droughts and rainfall, a rise in ocean levels, and an increase of the Earth's temperature. Over the course of the present century, global temperatures are expected to rise between 2.5°F to 10.4°F,[17] causing ice sheets and glaciers to melt, which will eventually flood coastal cities and small nation-state islands. The United States, with only 5% of the world's population, contributes about 25% of the world's greenhouse gas emissions (GHGs), which mostly stem from fossil fuel combustion.[18] The country's GHGs increase 1% each year due to population growth and further economic growth.[19]

Between 1980 and 1999, damage caused from tropical storms and hurricanes in Mexico claimed seven hundred lives and cost the country about $4.5 billion.[20] Loss of agricultural land due to natu-

ral disasters is expected to continue. Drought is expected to raise corn prices in the U.S., and fuel prices will continue to escalate. Yet according to the U.S. Department of Agriculture, global agricultural production is expected to remain stable this century, as farmers are likely to adapt to climate changes by, for example, selecting the most profitable input and outputs on existing farmland.[21] Nevertheless, Mexico's farmers, who are less knowledgeable in cropland adaptation, are much less likely to be capable of adapting to disruptive weather patterns caused by climate change than their U.S. counterparts.

Hurricane Katrina in August 2005 put over a million people out of their residences and destroyed thousands of homes in Louisiana, and was the most economically devastating hurricane ever recorded, taking place when the Gulf of Mexico's water temperatures were at their highest.[22] Currently 35 million people live in hurricane-prone areas in the U.S.'s east and Gulf coasts, from North Carolina to Texas.[23] As higher global temperatures continue to cause floods, hurricanes, and droughts, these coastal areas are at risk of being hit by the effects of climate change.

THE IMPACT OF NAFTA'S LIFTING OF TRADE BARRIERS AND MEXICO'S UNSUSTAINABLE DEPENDENCE ON THE U.S. AGRICULTURAL SECTOR

Today, half of all agricultural products in Mexico are imported; in 2005, agricultural production fell for the first time in thirteen years.[24] Today, only 65% of basic grains in Mexico are grown in the country; the rest are imported.[25] In 2008, all trade tariffs in the agriculture sector—which includes corn, sugar, and dairy products—will be lifted under the NAFTA agreement, putting Mexican farmers at further risk since they are already not able to compete with U.S. government–subsidized farmers, agri-businesses,

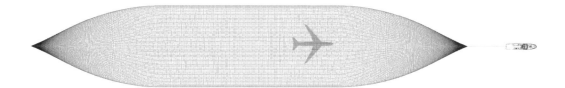

30

NOVEMBER 28, 2026

Lootings of Tugboats Shipping Drinking Water from Canada to the Juárez–El Paso Region Continue

Since the water supplies of the sister city region of Juárez–El Paso dried out two years ago, potable water has become a precious commodity. Boats used for tugging medusa bags containing 100,000 cubic meters of water every week have been subject to a new form of piracy that is feeding the black market for drinking water, where a gallon of fresh spring water can be bought for half its market value. The police have not been able to identify the looters, who could be hiding on either side of the fence along the border.[15]

JUNE 11, 2014

United Nations Announces Creation of Agency to Aid Environmental Refugees

In recognition of the overwhelming number of people around the world who have been forced to leave their places of residence due to environmental and climate-related catastrophes, including life-threatening pollution, droughts, floods, and hurricanes, the United Nations is to establish the first aid agency for environmental refugees by September of the current year. The agency's primary goal is to secure areas around the globe to which refugees can relocate. Countries such as Canada, New Zealand, and Australia are expected to allow the agency to develop refugee settlements in regions in which the population density is extremely low. The terms in which these nations might permit the refugees' entry into their territory remain to be seen.

and meatpacking companies.[26] While the U.S. has increased 55% of its agricultural exports thanks to NAFTA—making Mexico the number two recipient country of U.S. agricultural exports[27]—Mexico has not been able to compete with industrialized farming techniques. This condition is contributing to an unsustainable food dependence on the U.S. Mexico increasingly imports food products from the U.S. at low prices, diminishing Mexico's self-sustenance capacity, increasing air pollution, and deteriorating the environment. By shipping U.S. agricultural products hundreds of miles south of the border, both countries are perpetrating a highly pollutant, oil-intensive food-delivery system. Growing food in U.S. farms accounts for only one-fifth of their energy consumption—the remaining energy is used to move, process, package, sell, and store food. More than 30% of energy used in U.S. agriculture goes into fertilizer and pesticide production, and 14% is used in transportation.[28] Reducing the distance food travels from farm to table should be a policy implemented in both countries in order to support regional farmers and avoid further environmental degradation.

EMERGING BINATIONAL PROGRAMS ARE TACKLING ENVIRONMENTAL PROBLEMS

U.S.–Mexican environmental cooperation is still in its infancy. As recently as 1983, the La Paz Agreement formalized environmental transborder cooperation between the two nations. A little more than a decade later, environmental regulations were embedded in the NAFTA agreement, and in 1995, the Border Environment Cooperation Commission (BECC) and the North American Development Bank (NADB) established funding mechanisms and acted as coordinating bodies to improve infrastructure and revert some of the environmental damage in the hyperborder region. The BECC has achieved notable goals since its founding: it has certified

Binational environmental programs.

1983
The La Paz Agreement
Mexico and United States of America Agreement on Co-Operation for The Protection and Improvement of The Environment in The Border Area

1995
Creation of the Border Environment Cooperation Commission (BECC) and the North American Development Bank (NADB)

1996–2000
Border XXI Program

2002
Border 2012 Program by the EPA and SEMARNAT

more than seventy projects that as of March 2006 have benefited nearly 8 million people. In 1994, only 20% of wastewater was treated in the border region, whereas today 80% is treated locally, a much higher percentage than in Mexico as a country (25%). In the border cities of Baja California, the BECC plans on paving over 80% of all streets, an important health improvement since asthma and bronchitis are caused due to air pollution that is partly due to unpaved roads.[29] In the Mexican state of Chihuahua, the Río Conchos project is improving irrigation methods that extract water from the Rio Grande, from 35% to over 60% irrigation efficiency. Between 1994 and 2000, over two hundred photovoltaic water-pumping systems were installed in Mexico, mostly in the north, part of a ten-year Mexican Renewable Energy Program with help from the U.S. Agency for International Development (USAID), the U.S. Department of Energy, and Sandia

National Laboratories, among other Mexican institutions. The solar pumps replaced gas- and diesel-powered pumps, often adapted from automobile motors.[30] Although the results of these programs should be praised, additional support, corresponding with today's environmental realities, is still needed from both federal governments.

The Mexican side of the border is often considered the U.S.'s "backyard dumpster," but in reality a constant flow of waste products in solid, liquid, and air forms travel between the two countries on a daily basis. Lower environmental standards and enforcement in Mexico contribute to air pollution levels in the U.S. Pollutants generated in Mexican power plants and maquiladoras are tracked as far as the Big Bend National Park three hundred miles away, reducing visibility for up to a week at times. Wastewater from cities like Tijuana, Mexicali, Nogales, and Ciudad Juarez, among others, make their way to water-treatment plants in their respective sister cities north of the border. Pollutants also travel to Mexico from the U.S. Over the years 420,000 U.S. scrap tires made their way to the border city of Mexicali and were just removed in 2006 from the Innor tire dumpster to be turned into asphalt as part of the Border 2012 program. In 1997, the Environmental Protection Agency, in conjunction with its Mexican counterpart, SEMARNAT, developed the Border XXI program, defining ten areas in need of improvement for both countries. Five years later, the Border 2012 program inherited these plans and defined six goals: to reduce water contamination; reduce air pollution; reduce land contamination; improve environmental health; reduce exposure to chemicals as a result of accidental chemical releases and/or acts of terrorism; and improve environmental performance through compliance, enforcement, pollution prevention, and promotion of environmental stewardship. Considering 2% of all deaths in the U.S. are annually attributed to air

pollution,[31] ensuring American maquiladoras in Mexico pollute less should become a priority for the U.S. since pollution in many shapes and forms easily crosses borders without a passport or visa.

"Bioparque" during construction in 1988 (top) and 1993 (middle). Bottom: Aerial view of "Bioparque" in Tijuana. The park treats wastewater in a natural process that uses different varieties of plants to remove harmful pollutants. It was developed by Carlos A. de la Parra.

32

FEBRUARY 3, 2025

Mexico Becomes a Major Exporter of Carbon Credits

Ironically, the fact that Mexico did not completely industrialize in the twentieth century has aided its current status as a leading exporter of carbon credits. Since the Kyoto Protocol revised the international agreement that most countries could not meet by 2012 and set new goals for the reduction of greenhouse gas emissions for 2025, Mexico has closed inefficient businesses, shut down the most polluting foreign-owned assembly plants, and has capitalized on trading gas emissions. In the long run trading is expected to fund the country's development of renewable energy with state-of-the-art-technology.

APRIL 18, 2015

Advances in Technology Developed by Global Agri-business Corporations Give a New Meaning to the Phrase "Local Produce"

As people's food preferences become more sophisticated with globalization, it is now possible to grow avocados and pineapples in the northeastern United States and cherries and pumpkins in the desert of Sonora in Mexico, thanks to advances in genetic modification. Rich in proteins and vitamins, new species being developed are resistant to the most adverse climate conditions and will be distributed locally to curb pollution and cut transportation expenses. North American agribusiness corporations plan to hire thousands of workers within the next couple of years.

Pharmaceutical biologists process genetically designed "gen5-maguey," extracting important fibers for producing fire-resistant fabrics.

Ventanilla de Salud in the Mexican Consulate in Dallas, TX. These health stations provided basic health information to families without health insurance. This pilot program started in California in 2002 with the support of Mexico's Foreign Affairs Secretariat and the California Endowment Foundation.

14. HEALTH

Due to unsafe living spaces and poor environmental conditions, health risks are especially high at the border. At a time when pandemics are spreading across continents and longer life expectancies are changing diseases, binational health planning and research are becoming realistic options for the future.

HEALTH CARE AND DISEASES ARE CHANGING AND GLOBALIZING

Today's most deadly diseases in affluent nations are no longer communicable diseases like pneumonia, tuberculosis, and influenza. They are heart disease, lung cancer, and other illnesses that are clearly affected by individual behavior with respect to diet, exercise, alcohol, drug use, smoking, stress, sexual activity, and international travel.[1] The nature of health care is changing, and the health care sector is one of the fastest growing segments of the world economy both in developing and developed nations.

Health awareness seems to have reached unparalleled heights, yet preventable diseases continue to affect millions of Americans. According to the Department of Health and Human Services' (HHS) Centers for Disease Control and Prevention, heart disease, cancer, and diabetes are responsible for 70% of deaths in the U.S. and are also the costliest health problems.[2] The Surgeon General reports that almost 50% of nonsmoking Americans are exposed to secondhand smoke on a regular basis, increasing their chances of developing heart disease and lung cancer by 25 to 30%.[3]

As health professionals are in high demand across the globe, 56% of all migrant physicians move from developing countries to developed nations, while only 11% move in the opposite direction, according to a 1998 United Nations/World Health Organization study. At a time when pandemics spread through continents like wildfire, the response to these challenges demands speed. International travel catalyzed the SARS spread in 2003 to North America, South America, and Europe from Asia, where it originated. Meanwhile, a University of Houston study concluded that the combination of sex workers and transportation workers at the U.S.–Mexico border is a potential threat to the spread of HIV/AIDS through North and Central America.[4] New diseases and viruses contractible through casual contact are impairing our ability to protect ourselves.

MEXICO AND THE UNITED STATES SHARE MUTUAL HEALTH CONCERNS

The high levels of illegal migration flows northbound into the United States has created common health concerns for both countries. Firstly, lack of health care access for migrants throughout the country and their shared border is posing a challenge for the U.S. institutions dealing with migration and health. Secondly, both countries' growing urbanized lifestyles are increasing rates of cardiovascular diseases stemming from high overweight and obesity rates. Thirdly, both countries' populations are aging, which will increase health care costs in both nations. Already, the United States spends 15.3% of its GDP on health care, while Mexico spends only 6.5%.[5]

Both Countries Will Need to Increase Health Care Access

In both the United States and Mexico, high costs already pose hurdles for many people in receiving health care. In the U.S., 46 million Americans lack health insurance, even when the country spends more on health care than any other industrialized nation.[6] Border residents face especially difficult circumstances for medical access. Health Professions Shortage Areas (HPSAs) categorize 80% of the border's primary health care—a large jump from the U.S. national average of 63%.[7] Because the workforce is not growing consistently with population growth, the ratio of primary care physicians per 100,000 population is 25% lower than the national average. Border counties experience more than double the dental HPSA of the U.S. national average, while the mental health HPSA is 30% greater at the border than for the U.S. as a whole.[8]

Culturally sensitive physicians and dentists who can provide services for Hispanic populations in the U.S. are also an important asset to health care access. The inability to communicate or even feel culturally understood impedes many from seeking professional health care. The odds of finding such care are slim: presently 29% of Latinos don't even finish high school, let alone medical school. Yet Hispanics will be the majority in Texas in thirty years; in Brownsville, 93% of the population is Hispanic as of today.

While there are numerous health care facilities around the border region, affordable health care is still lacking as poverty bars many from acquiring the medical attention they deserve. Diseases can be avoided if preventive and primary health care were more accessible throughout the U.S. to vulnerable groups such as undocumented migrant workers, or by reducing costs for hospital treatments when diseases worsen. In Tijuana there are 133 private hospitals and only four public ones—the former offering a wide range of services including laboratories and pharmacies that cater to local middle-class residents.[9] There are a few programs that try to deal with the health workforce shortage by bringing workers from abroad: the Partnership Institute created the Fellowship of International Development (FIND) program for Mexican trained nurses to become licensed and employed in the U.S., and the San Francisco-based Welcome Back program helps immigrants who were trained in health professions abroad enter the health workforce in the U.S.[10]

The need for Spanish-speaking physicians in U.S. southern states will continue to grow. In California, 6 million people do not speak English well—3.2 million of which do not speak English at all. In Texas, it is estimated that less than 4 to 7% of nurses speak Spanish.[11] In 2001, legislation in California was introduced that sought to initiate a three-year pilot program that would have allowed thirty physicians and thirty dentists from Mexico to work in underserved populations, primarily rural and farmworker communities in the state, where most Mexican citizens with no health care access live. However, the program was not approved.[12]

Jennifer Eldridge, an expert in binational health, has enumerated why it is important to provide health care for migrants in the United States:

A. Communicable disease poses a public health threat to everyone—regardless of immigration status—and so diagnosis and treatment benefits the general public.

B. County-funded programs bear the burden of caring for undocumented immigrants in hospital emergency rooms. Providing primary and preventive care to these people would be less costly than waiting until acute conditions are presented in hospital emergency rooms.

C. All employed people, regardless of immigration status, are contributing to county-funded programs through sales and property taxes. Even people working in the "cash economy" are contributing to these programs through the sales tax.[13]

As the working and living conditions of migrant farm and factory workers in the U.S. is very unique, the community presents high numbers of diabetes, cardiovascular disease, asthma, and tuberculosis, as well as others created from repetitive motion injuries and pesticide exposure in meatpacking and farming industries. In addition to hardships that farmworkers face in terms of medical care, their offspring often share equally frustrating barriers to health care. Because migrant farmworkers are often traveling, Medicaid services that their children are entitled to often cannot be received outside of their home states.[14]

Both nations experience unique medical needs in the zones where they merge—mostly diseases of the elderly. The ten leading causes of death in the hyperborder, in consecutive order, are diseases of the heart, malignant neoplasms, diabetes mellitus, accidents, cerebrovascular diseases, chronic liver disease and cirrhosis, chronic obstructive pulmonary diseases, pneumonia and influenza, diseases originating in prenatal period, and homicide. Of particular interest are the high rates of diabetes and tuberculosis. Close to 16% of border residents suffer from Type 2 diabetes, whereas the national rate for the U.S. and Mexico is notably lower at around 7%.[15] Nearly 4,000 border residents die each year due to diabetes, most of which happen in Mexico. Tuberculosis, considered a third-world disease, is of particular concern along the U.S. side of the border. Of all communicable diseases in 2000, tuberculosis ranked at number one, with 2,124 and 653 cases reported on the Mexican and U.S. sides of the border, respectively.[16]

Obesity: A Health Concern in Both Countries

Obesity is now considered a global epidemic. Today there are more than 1 billion obese people in the world—more people than those who are considered undernourished.[17] This modern phenomenon is due to the adoption of more sedentary and urban lifestyles throughout the world. In the United States, the non-profit organization Trust for America's Health reports that 64.5% of the adult population are overweight or obese—a statistic that may rise to 73% by just 2008; Mexico, where 68.6% of the population is considered overweight, does not fare any better.[18] Obesity is just one example of the health issues that both nations face and will continue to face in the future.

Both Countries are Aging, Increasing Health Care Costs

The results of a study done by the RAND Corporation indicate that Americans are living longer, but with increased chronic diseases at the end of life. During the last century, the average lifespan of Americans nearly doubled, from just forty-nine years in 1900 to nearly eighty years in 2000.[19] Age-related illnesses such as Alzheimer's disease currently affects over 4 million Americans and is expected to affect 12 million by 2050.[20]

In Mexico, the rapid aging phenomenon is of equal concern. Life expectancy has also risen in Mexico, to seventy-four years.[21] By 2050, both the United States and Mexico will have the same percentage of their population over sixty-five years of age. According to United Nations' research, people over the age of eighty-five are the fastest-growing demographic in Mexico, increasing at a rate of 3 to 5% per year. With more people living longer, cardiovascular illnesses, diabetes, cancer, traumas, and handicaps have become the most important health problems,[22] but health care in Mexico today is either unavailable or unaffordable for many elderly people. Serving the needs of this population is already presenting many challenges, which will only become more pronounced as this demographic grows.

While the demand for more trained medical assistants continues to rise, the aging phenomenon in both countries is compounding existing problems even further. In the U.S., the statewide shortages of registered nurses is expected to increase from 126,000 in 2000 to as much as 800,000 by 2020.[23] Due in part to the low wages nurse aides receive—equivalent to that of a bakery worker, or about $8.50 per hour—fewer people are entering the nursing field. Simultaneously, demographic shifts are contributing to the shortage as aging professionals are reaching retirement age. These

DECEMBER 15, 2019

Mexico Displaces Florida and California as the Most Popular Location for Nursing Homes Catering to Elderly Americans

Where would you like to visit your elderly parents—Florida, with its constant hurricane alerts, or the beautiful colonial town of San Miguel de Allende in Guanajuato, Mexico? It's a no-brainer: healthy meals, stunning views, idyllic weather, low taxes, a bilingual staff—for about a third of the price you pay in the U.S. Developers estimate that each year there are about twenty-five new nursing homes and retirement communities geared specifically toward the American elderly operating near different tourist destinations in north and central Mexico. Third-generation Hispanics, who no longer have families in their countries of origin, were first to take advantage of these services. But slowly more and more Americans across the board are exploring the opportunity to expand their horizons at a late stage in life.

Ana Paola, a medical student from Oaxaca, is graduating today as a binational physician. Her expertise in U.S. and Mexico's health care systems will give her a job next year in 2023 when she goes to work in Dallas, Texas. This year, she is an intern at a nursing home in San Miguel de Allende, in the Mexican state of Guanajuato.

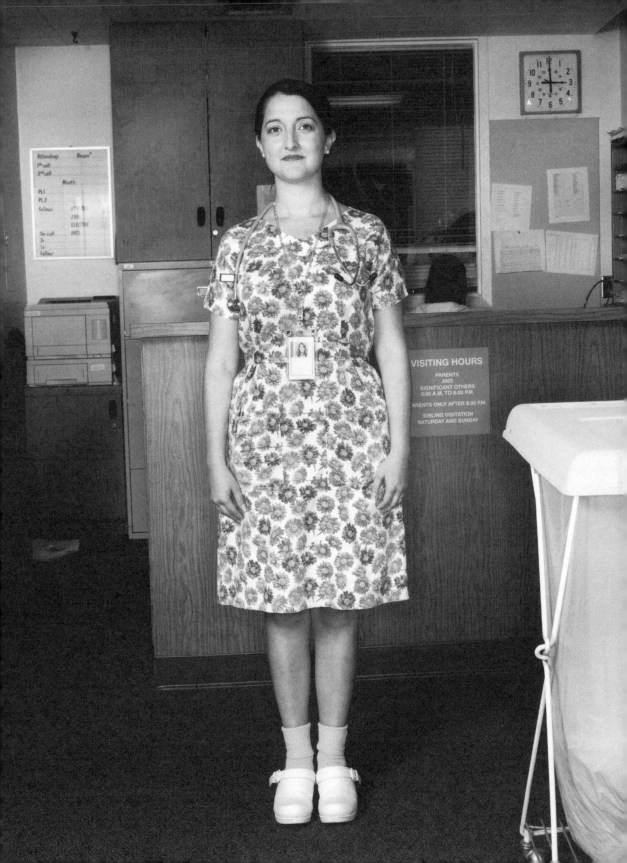

two factors are expected to affect border regions even more so than the rest of the country.[24]

Health care spending in the U.S. accounts for more than 14% of its GDP. Health care costs for those over sixty-five years are three to five times greater than for those younger than sixty-five.[25] By 2040, the costs of long-term care will reach $346 billion. The baby boomer generation will experience high rates of late-life disabilities and progressive chronic illness between 2020 and 2030. In 2030, 22% of Americans (80 million) will be over sixty-five, and 2.5% (9 million) will be over eighty-five—far exceeding the numbers for the 1960s, when only 9% (17 million) of the population was sixty-five or older, and only 0.5% (1 million) was older than eighty-five. The effects of these changing demographics will be substantial.[26]

This impending toll on the health care system is compounded by the fact that there is already a shortage of physicians and registered nurses. Enrollment in nursing schools has been declining since 1993. In Texas, nurses are an aging workforce, where the average age of a nurse is forty-six and their average age when they leave hospital nursing is fifty-three.[27]

NEW DISCOVERIES, TREATMENTS, AND TECHNOLOGIES SHOW PROMISE FOR PREVENTING AND TREATING DISEASE

Stopping many chronic diseases before they start is becoming easier today than ever before, especially with rapidly developing science and technology. Simple steps such as lifestyle education and drug-abuse prevention play an important role in avoiding illnesses caused by unhealthy habits, and thanks to the World Wide Web it is possible for patients to learn about diseases, treatments, and prevention methods—often reading up on the latest medical developments regarding their personal conditions even before their doctors. Addictions

can be prevented through programs such as the "Just Say Know" campaign sponsored by the Drug Policy Alliance that educates high school students on the effects of drugs (see pages 144–145) or the *Vete Sano. Regresa Sano* ("Go healthy. Return healthy") program that educates migrants on disease prevention in their hometowns, while in transit, and in U.S. destinations.

Modern disease detection methods such as genetic testing for disease likelihoods during childhood or genetic haplotyping (which screens defective chromosomes) are just two promising techniques for screening gene-related diseases before they occur later in life. Other advanced treatment methods, such as gene therapy and drug delivery systems—which isolate and treat specific genes and affected organs—also have the potential to be more widely adopted. Remote health care also promises to complement health care shortages. Smart cards used to track patients' current and previous health procedures, as well as at-home health treatment and monitoring devices plus a series of organ-replacement methods such as in-vitro organ cloning and organ "manufacturing" techniques, could resolve various health care needs in both countries in the future.

BINATIONAL HEALTH INITIATIVES AND THE BORDER AS A HEALTH TOURISM DESTINATION

Over the years there have been various binational health initiatives, including the recent Healthy Border 2010 program established by the U.S.–Mexico Border Health Commission, a ten-year old binational body involving all levels of government in both countries. Healthy Border 2010 establishes a set of health improvement objectives to be met by the year 2010 binationally using twenty common indicators to reach those targets. Access to health care, including immunization, injury prevention, maternal, infant, and child health, and mental health; as well as treating common diseases such as cancer, diabetes, HIV/AIDS, and respiratory diseases, are just some of the program's goals. It is the most extensive binational health agreement.

During Vicente Fox's presidency, the Seguro Popular (People's Insurance) was established, offering coverage for those who need health care services and are not already enrolled in the Instituto Mexicano del Seguro Social (IMSS) or Instituto de Seguridad y Servicios Sociales de los Trabajadores del Estado (ISSSTE) programs. In 2006, the Seguro Popular offered free health services and medicines to about 20 million people who could not otherwise afford such expenses, especially in cases of terminal or chronic diseases.[28] Already, five states in the country are considered to have full universal health coverage. One advantage of this health insurance is its coverage throughout Mexico, a benefit for those internal migrants who travel around the country. It also features a fee-based insurance for migrants living in the U.S. wishing to pledge health insurance to relatives residing in Mexico.

Other achievements in binational health coverage are the California–Mexico and Texas–Mexico health weeks. In these programs, during one week a year, free health services are provided in different rural areas of California and Texas that have a high concentration of Mexican migrants. The California Health Care Foundation has also helped sponsor binational health programs targeted to migrants such as the *Ventanillas de Salud*, or health information booths, installed in Mexican consulates in California to provide health care information such as available clinics and trans-national health insurance services.[29]

Considering that the typical older American takes an average of four prescription drugs a day,[30] and that both the Mexican and U.S. populations are becoming older, pharmacies in Mexican border cities have great potential for further growth in pharmaceutical drug sales since they provide medicines at prices significantly lower than in the U.S., where the purchase of pharmaceuticals constitutes 12.3% of health care costs.[31] Already, border residents make frequent trips to Mexico to buy necessary medications. The city of Tijuana is well known for catering to Californians seeking dental services and surgery options.

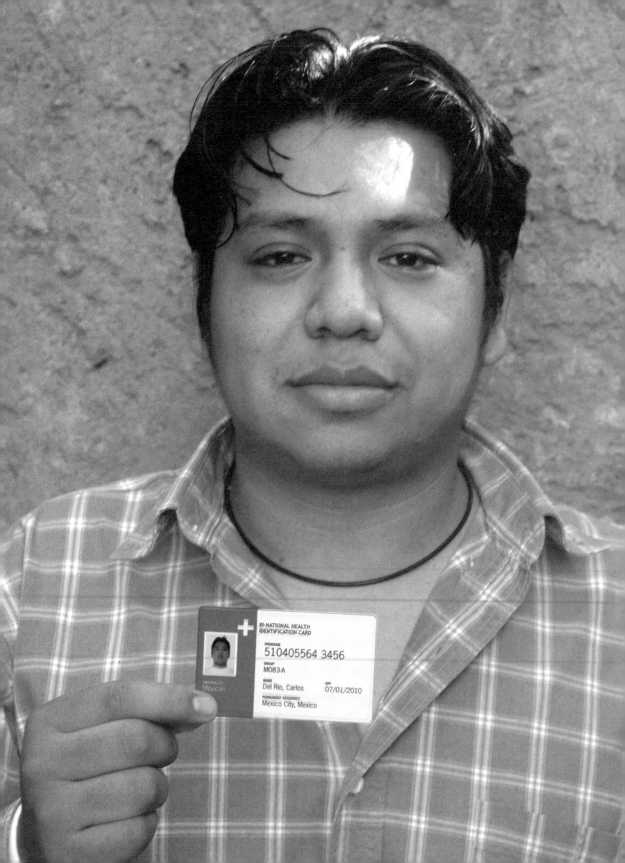

35

JUNE 12, 2025

Delta Health Lines? Heavily Discounted Travel Packages Available for Residents of the U.S. to Receive Medical Attention in Mexico

American health insurance companies are encouraging patients to get medical attention in Mexico instead of the U.S. With Medicare and Medicaid now valid south of the Rio Grande, and given the large gap between the costs of medical treatment and prescription drugs in both countries, it has become more cost-effective for the state and insurance companies to partially finance the patients' travel expenses than to cover their health care in the U.S. Incentives include reduced airfares and trips to beaches, pre-Hispanic ruins, and colonial cities. Private and public hospitals that recruit as much as 35% of Mexico's health professionals have been booming in border cities such as Tijuana and Ciudad Juárez for over a decade. Border cities have become the most popular health tourism destinations for those who need an affordable yearly physical as much as a weekend getaway.[32]

Carlos, a seasonal agricultural worker from Mexico, shows his binational health card that allows him to receive basic medical care in the United States.

Downtown Tijuana near the international boundary. The border region is expected to double its population by 2020 (growing from 12 million today to 25 million). Currently, over 90% of the border region's population lives in one of the fourteen sister cities. The sister cities of El Paso and Ciudad Juárez are expected to run out of water in ten to twenty years. The ability of border cities to absorb the growing migration from the interior of Mexico and provide for water, roads, and other city services will determine the quality of life for the region's residents.

15. URBANIZATION

As the border population is expected to double by the year 2020, addressing urbanization in the region will require sustainable growth. Installing sewage and water infrastructure between sister cities, attracting new talent to border communities, improving the use of public space and funds for a higher standard of living, and creating binational housing plans should be integral parts of the future urban development processes at the border.

> "The city belongs to the 21st century more than the nation. I think that the national is sinking whereas the city is coming back."
>
> —Saskia Sassen[1]

MIGRATION HAS CONTRIBUTED TO RAPID POPULATION GROWTH

Throughout history, urbanization has been a phenomenon experienced globally. 150 million people lived in cities in 1900. One hundred years later, that number increased nineteen-fold, reaching 2.9 billion. In 2007, over 50% of the world population will be living in cities, making the human race an urban species.[2]

Since the implementation of NAFTA, rural-to-urban migration has experienced a steep increase, especially in Mexico. Out of the 2,446 Mexican municipalities, the population in 1,048 of them, or about 24 million people, migrate internally, while those in the remaining 492 municipalities migrate abroad, mainly to the United States.[3] It is estimated that about 90% of the border population lives in one of the fourteen sister cities. In 2000, 6.3 million people were living on the U.S. side of the U.S.–Mexico border, and 5.5 million were living on the Mexican side of the border. This population continues to grow and is expected to double by 2030, reaching nearly 20 million.[4] The introduction of NAFTA has made a lasting impression on the agricultural sector as many farmers were put out of work due to their inability to compete with U.S. imports. While the maquiladoras have provided some jobs for unskilled workers, migration to border cities has become an alternative for many rural Mexicans.

Border counties are experiencing population growth at rates much faster than their state averages. An example of this is Cameron County, Texas, just south of Corpus Christi, which experienced population growth of 25.5% in the 1990s, while the state's average growth was just 16.3%.[5] The U.S. border population is growing three times faster than the rest of the country,[6] and massive migration to border cities has led to problems that communities cannot plan for on the scale at which they are happening. Suitable land for farming, water, energy, and biological resources necessary for sustaining border communities continue to be a challenge.

THE INEFFICIENCY OF HORIZONTAL CITIES

In both U.S. and Mexican border cities, urban areas are dealing with rapid population growth by expanding their cities outward. While in the United States city growth has resulted in middle/upper-class suburbs, Mexican city centers have come to be engulfed by slums due to rapid rural-to-urban migration. Simultaneously, worldwide slum populations are growing by 25 million a year, causing urban problems such as pollution and the destruction of cities' environmental support systems.[7]

Carlos Gutiérrez Ruiz of the National Commission of Housing Promotion (CONAFOVI), the country's biggest housing credit provider, declared that the way in which Mexican cities are horizontally designed is inefficient. The absence of a Department of Urban Planning contributes greatly to current circumstances. CONAFOVI asserts that existing city-planning problems are the fault of local authorities that have set the standards for urban development plans.[8] Although 75% of Mexico's population lives in urban regions, 20% are considered to be living in slums.[9] The housing shortage in 2000 was estimated at over 4.3 million units, 1.8

SEPTEMBER 10, 2017

Pay Them to Stay: Mexican Government's Taxation of Migration to Urban Centers Stirs Opposition

In an effort to control the record high influx of migrants to already exceedingly overpopulated cities, the Mexican government is to impose a tax on a portion of its citizens that already is burdened by a crushing lack of opportunities in the countryside. Officials argue that these taxes will fund the development of rural areas and will eventually generate jobs for the millions of unemployed whose only opportunity for survival is to flood cities and work in the informal sector. Critics point out the difficulties in collecting such a tax, and as an alternative, propose that the government devise a way to give out monetary incentives for people to remain in rural areas.

million of which required new construction, while the remaining 2.5 million needed to be improved to meet the standards involving maximum occupancy per unit and materials quality defined by the United Nations Center for Human Settlements. The greatest housing needs for Mexico as for the United States are located in their respective southern states.[10]

As suburbs continue to grow in American cities, critics have contested that the growth of suburbs is an alternative with more negative than positive effects on urban society. As the middle classes slowly move to the suburbs, city centers are left without crucial economical support; agricultural land disappears along with open countryside; traffic is increased and large distances between buildings necessitates driving, adding to pollution and consequently health problems; and new, costly development plans arise. Single families occupy large plots of land and build expensive homes, with big yards requiring high maintenance costs and large water supplies. Fitting more people into less space, on the other hand, provides more economic opportunities. Higher concentrations of people in cities allow for business growth, as commercial operations and retailers are more attracted to the areas.

HOW DIFFERENT CITIES HAVE COME TO DEVELOP
Los Angeles and New York
Different cities across the United States and Mexico have followed different models for development, arriving at very diverse results. Los Angeles and New York are examples of two polar opposites. Like Mexico City (and many others), which has made sprawl a habit, Los Angeles has one of the lowest densities of the major U.S. cities—with 2,344.20 people per square mile. In contrast, New York County has one of the highest densities—fitting 66,940.10 people per square mile.[11]

Los Angeles and New York are two urban areas that demonstrate how a city affects the ways in which people go about their daily routine. Because of a city's nature to be crowded versus being divided by large distances, transportation options are predetermined. In New York, well over half (59.6%) of the population commutes by mass transit, and 22.8% walk or bike as their primary means of transportation; in Los Angeles, by comparison, only 6.6% of the population use public transportation, and just 3.6% commutes by walking or biking.[12]

Mexico City and Monterrey
The explosive growth of the Distrito Federal in previous decades merged Mexico's capital and the neighboring State of Mexico into what is commonly known as Mexico City's metropolitan region. Attracted to the region's economic clout, where a quarter of the country's GDP is generated in 0.2% of the country's territory,[13] the region's population grew six-fold from 3.5 million to 18.4 million between 1950 and 2000. Five years later, it stood at nearly 20 million. In Mexico's only megacity, only 14,192 people inhabit each square mile. The metropolitan region of Monterrey, one of Mexico's biggest urban conglomerations, has an even lower density rate of 2,832 people per square mile.[14] Such low densities in Mexican cities, a result of poor planning measures, complicate other matters of making effective transport and infrastructure feasible.

NOT ENOUGH (AFFORDABLE) HOUSING BEING CREATED
In Tijuana, housing shortages have been a growing concern for years. In 2000, around 45,000 housing units were in need, over half of which were in the form of substantial repairs to the many homes in the city that are informally self-built without property titles.[15]

On the other side of the border, in San Diego, affordable housing is lacking as prices have sky-rocketed while low-paying jobs have experienced an increase. According to the San Diego Association of Governments, around 13% of the workforce earn less than $8.35 an hour, but the average apartment rental is $1,254, up almost 100% from the average $643 in 1990.[16] This high cost of living has forced many migrant families who cannot afford to rent their own apartments to share with other families, packing two and sometimes three families under the same roof.[17]

POVERTY PREVALENT IN BORDER CITIES

While the border population continues to grow, problems of poverty also present themselves. The U.S. border, where poverty rates are higher than the national average, contains five of the seven poorest regions designated by the Metropolitan Statistical Areas; about 19% of the U.S. border population lives in poverty,[18] while in Texas that average is even higher, with 35% of the border population living in poverty.[19] In contrast, poverty in the Mexican border region is less than the national average,[20] benefiting from the proximity of the U.S. economy. In Tijuana, however, 50% of the population lives in poverty—and another 40% are classified as living in the "poverty threshold," meaning that although they make enough to not technically be categorized as poverty sufferers, they can barely afford their basic needs. Of the remaining households that are living above the poverty line, only 5% are able to meet their basic needs without experiencing difficulty.[21]

Colonias—rural communities located within 150 miles of the U.S.–Mexico border that gener-ally lack adequate infrastructure and basic ser-vices—have existed since the 1950s.[22] Because *colonias* typically experience high levels of pov-erty, residents cannot afford to contribute to the construction of basic necessities. These communi-ties are most common to the state of Texas, where they can be found in twenty-two of the 254 Texan counties. According to a June 2000 random survey by the Texas Department of Health, almost 50% of the ninety-six colonia households surveyed report-ed that they make less than $834 monthly.[23]

BORDER CITIES LACK INFRASTRUCTURE

Throughout borderland cities, more drainage and sewage systems are in dire need. Seasonal rains often flood many urban areas, polluting beaches as trash is flushed into the sea. 12% of border residents do not have safe drinking water,[24] mak-ing them more susceptible to contracting water-borne diseases. While infrastructure is lacking, many border communities east of El Paso depend on the water from the Rio Grande river for drink-ing, bathing, and cooking—water that receives 24 million gallons of raw sewage daily and that has been found to contain fecal bacteria counts at 22,000 bacteria per milliliter. California's New River and the Tijuana River are among some of the other water supplies experiencing dangerously high contamination rates, receiving 76 million and 46 million liters, respectively, of raw sewage on a daily basis.[25]

According to La Comisión de Cooperación Ecológica Fronteriza/Border Environment Coopera-tion Commission (COCEF/BECC), a binational orga-nization devoted to enhancing human health and the environment of the border region, many cities in Baja California lack paved roads. They report that paved roads account for 38% of roads in Ensenada, 44% of roads in Mexicali, 55% of Rosarito's and Tijuana's roads, and only 35% of Tecate's roads.[26]

The Texas colonias are among some of the worst border communities in terms of infrastruc-ture, where faulty or nonexistent urban develop-ments serve the people. Cameron County is a prime example of this somber situation: of ninety-nine

MARCH 12, 2016

Not American but Angeleno. Secession Movement Spreads Like Wildfire Across the Globe's Major Cities

At the turn of the nineteenth century it was national independence movements that led to the world's configuration in the twentieth century. Today, it is secession movements that are rippling across cities unwilling to continue to be the fiscal cash cows of their respective countries. With a disproportionately low political representation in contrast with the overwhelmingly dense populations within their confines, they seek to become autonomous zones separate from the rest of their nations. The movement intensified during the chaotic first decade of the twenty-first century, then gradually caught on in places as disparate as Los Angeles, Mexico City, São Paulo, Seoul, Shanghai, Tokyo, Bombay, and Delhi. City leaders are to meet with United Nations officials in New York on March 20th and are confident that some of the cities they represent could be granted autonomous status within the next five years.

colonias in Cameron County, 26% lack sufficient water service and 71% lack wastewater treatment. Results from a 2000 survey of Texan colonia residents showed that only 54% had sewer service while over 50% obtained drinking water from sources other than taps.[27]

As the population is expected to grow and water becomes scarcer every day, the San Diego–Tijuana area will demand more potable water over the next two decades. In 1996, the binational region of Tijuana–San Diego used about 683,000 acre-feet of water, 90% of which was used by San Diego while only 10% was used by Tijuana.[28] Water usage in the region is expected to increase to 848,000 acre-feet by 2010, and both nations will face great challenges in the future.

Failing sewage systems on both sides of the border are causing major problems for their populations. In the International Border Planning Area of Otay Mesa and Zona Centro, sewage is transported by a series of collectors that carry it to the main collectors in the Tijuana River Valley. However, frequent pipe failures and breaks has led to the contamination of the Tijuana River Valley in San Diego and the Tijuana River.[29] In fact, many parts of Tijuana are not even connected to the sewage system, making the challenge even greater. Although many works have been in progress to correct lacking infrastructure problems, expanding urban centers will complicate already existing inefficiencies. Improving cross-border infrastructural systems for the future will be necessary to sustain the growing border population. Binational cooperation to build a system that will accommodate the cities' unique infrastructural dependencies on one another will be important in designing fully functioning urban centers in the future. In the sister cities such as Nogales/Nogales, Laredo/Nuevo Laredo, and San Diego/Tijuana, binational sewage systems have already been created. However, the remaining border cities have yet to develop sustainable sewage systems.

ATTRACTING NEW TALENT TO BORDER COMMUNITIES

George Mason University professor Richard Florida has been both praised and criticized for his ideas surrounding urban strategies. According to Florida, a city's economic growth and success are based upon its ability to attract creative talent. Diversity—ethnic, sexual, and cultural—are essential for cities in order to experience a boost in their economy. In his book, *The Rise of the Creative Class,* Florida argues that thriving urban centers of today are no longer governed by traditional economic theory because they depend on the people that make them up. According to Florida, location really does matter. Creative workers, who start up new companies based on their innovative designs and original ideas, want to live in cities such as these—creating economic growth with a lifespan far longer than that of the standard development of things such as shopping centers that generate large numbers of jobs.[30]

Border communities' potential to attain economic growth through Florida's contemporary ideas of development in today's state is feasible. The border today is one where two cultures fuse and where diversity is the norm. Accepting its adversity is an important step in allowing a welcome environment for its evolution. In concurrence with Florida's theory, only then would the border region truly be able to attract and maintain individuals that would fuel the economies. In a similar way, improving the quality of life of cities in the interior of Mexico could also prove to be an effective strategy to prevent the "brain drain" (losing

highly educated people because of a lack of opportunity within Mexico) and migration to the U.S.

Improving the Use of Public Space and Funds for a Higher Standard of Living

From 1995 to 2000, Bogotá, Colombia, underwent major urban changes. Under the administration of Mayor Antanas Mockus and later Mayor Enrique Peñalosa, the city saw rapid planning that has led to large-scale improvements. With a series of events on his agenda, Mayor Peñalosa jumpstarted the betterment of urban conditions. Stressing the importance of roads, transportation, libraries, and parks, the mayor left office having created "The Defense of Public Space," through which 1,034 parks were restored, maintained, and improved.[31] In addition, public transportation was vastly improved, reducing the need for personal automobile use, with the intent to reduce pollution rates and traffic congestion. The TransMilenio bus system now moves 770,000 passengers daily at a low cost.[32] Similarly, close to a million Mexicans cross into the U.S. everyday to shop and work, returning at night to their homes in Mexico.[33] A binational cross-border transport system is required to meet the mobility needs of this considerable amount of people.

By focusing on improving the quality of life at the border through city plans such as those that Bogotá has implemented, high immigration rates to the U.S. could be greatly reduced. Temporary migrants that make the Mexican side of the border their home while waiting to cross the border would be given the opportunity to stay in a city that provides them with the necessary resources to live the quality of life that they hope the prosperity of the U.S. will bring. At the same time, in its improved stages, a border that would offer open parks, low pollution rates, formal work, and affordable housing and lifestyle would provide a handsome alternative for many—including those who are not considering migration as an option.

MAKING BINATIONAL HOUSING PLANS

The Colonias Monitoring Program is a database that allows the public to observe the activity of colonias. The initiative, through joint efforts of the Instituto Nacional de Estadística Geografía e Informática (INEGI), the U.S. Geological Survey (USGS), and the U.S. Department of Housing and Urban Development (HUD), is working to reach four pairs of sister cities including Eagle Pass/Piedras Negras, El Paso/Ciudad Juarez, Douglas/Agua Prieta, and Nogales/Nogales. The program works to promote development in the highly impoverished areas, monitoring such areas as low-income housing and urban growth. Through an internet database, one can access tools to estimate development costs of colonias, access binational data, and arraign geographic-analysis tools to help facilitate decision-making and planning measures by the county.[34]

In New York City, the New Housing Marketplace Plan is an agenda created by Mayor Michael Bloomberg in order to combat the fact that housing in all five boroughs of New York City has reached prices that make housing significantly less affordable. The plan is a ten-year initiative with four main goals to make and secure affordable housing: finding new land for affordable housing, creating incentives to develop housing for new populations, harnessing the private market to create affordable housing, and preserving government-assisted affordable housing. The program is expected to provide 500,000 affordable homes for New Yorkers by 2013.[35]

Both a pedestrian bridge, and cultural museum, this proposed structure would sit right on the border between El Paso, Texas, and Ciudad Juárez, Chihuahua. Projects such as this could help attract and retain talent to border cities.

MARCH 15, 2016

Illegal Immigration to the U.S. Expected to Decrease as Border Cities in the U.S. and Mexico are Granted Binational Status

As border cities such as El Paso-Cd. Juárez and San Diego-Tijuana are granted binational status, border crossings from one country to another will be expedited thanks to a joint police force and customs and immigration agency. Although residents of these cities will not be granted double citizenship, permits for anyone without a criminal record to work on either side of the border will be issued within the next six months. Workers who in the past might have wanted to enter the U.S. illegally are expected to settle in the Mexican areas of these cities and apply for binational work permits instead. Many workers may not even need to cross the border to seek employment, since the official recognition of the binational status of these border cities is expected to create at least ten thousand new jobs, mainly in the city services sector.

less than 3

3-5

5-10

10-20

20-30

30-45

Programs such as these can be instituted to develop long-term plans that will have drastic implications for the future of the many families that are victims of long inadequate housing along the border. Measures such as those taken by the Colonias Monitoring Program and the City of New York hold the potential to drastically change the housing crisis that exists along the border, while providing people the basic necessities needed to live under safe and sanitary conditions.

NOTES

1. CONTEXT

1. Joe Havely, "Korea's DMZ: 'Scariest Place on Earth,'" CNN, Aug. 28, 2003, http://edition.cnn.com/2003/WORLD/asiapcf/east/04/22/koreas.dmz/ (accessed Sept. 7, 2006).
2. Tyche Hendricks, "Border Security or Boondoggle: Walls Around the World," *San Francisco Chronicle*, Feb. 26, 2006.
3. "Israel, Palestine and the Occupied Territories: Land and Settlement Issues," Global Policy Forum, http://www.globalpolicy.org/security/issues/israel-palestine/occupindex.htm (accessed Sept. 7, 2006).
4. Hein De Haas, "Morocco: From Emigration Country to Africa's Migration Passage to Europe," *Migration Information Source*, Oct. 2005, http://www.migrationinformation.org/Profiles/display.cfm?ID=339 (accessed Sept. 7, 2006).
5. "Demographic Time-Bomb Ticking Under Europe," *Management Issues News: At the Heart of the Changing Workplace* (Mar. 18, 2005), http://www.management-issues.com/2006/8/24/research/85332-7055.asp (accessed Sept. 6, 2006).
6. Richard Bernstein, "The Aging Europe May Find Itself on the Sidelines," *New York Times*, June 29, 2003.
7. Clean Clothes Campaign, "Working Conditions in Morocco," May 2003 Report, http://www.cleanclothes.org/publications/03-05-morocco.htm (accessed Sept. 7, 2006).
8. Canadian Department of Foreign Affairs and International Trade, http://www.dfait-maeci.gc.ca/can-am/main/front_page/relationship-en.asp (accessed Sept. 7, 2006).
9. Joachim Blatter, "Cross Border Regions: A Step Toward Sustainable Development? Experiences and Considerations from Examples in Europe and North America," in Paul Ganster, ed., *Cooperation, Environment and Sustainability in Border Regions* (San Diego: San Diego University Press and Institute for Regional Studies of the Californias, 2001).
10. The Cascadia Institute, http://www.columbiana.org/cascadia_institute.htm (accessed Sept. 7, 2006).
11. Blatter, "Cross Border Regions."
12. "EuroAirport: The Bi-national Airport with a Tri-national Function" (press release, Apr. 2006), http://www.euroairport.com/EN/euroairport.php?PAGEID= 83&lang=EN (accessed Sept. 5, 2006).
13. Ibid.
14. UNAIDS and World Health Organization, "AIDS Epidemic Update," special report on HIV prevention (Geneva: UNAIDS, Dec. 2005), http://www.who.int/hiv/epi-update2005_en.pdf (accessed Oct. 17, 2006).
15. USAID, "Health Profile: Southern Africa Region," Dec. 2004, http://www.usaid.gov/our_work/global_health/aids/Countries/africa/southernafrica_04.pdf (accessed Sept. 7, 2006).
16. Ibid.
17. Ibid.
18. UNAIDS and World Health Organization, "AIDS Epidemic Update."
19. United Nations Office on Drugs and Crime (UNODC), *Opium Poppy Cultivation in the Golden Triangle: Lao PDR, Myanmar, Thailand*, United Nations Office on Drugs and Crime (UNODC), Vienna, 2006:45, http://www.unodc.org/pdf/research/Golden_triangle_2006.pdf (accessed Sept. 7, 2006).
20. Gulnoza Saidazimova, "Central Asia: Experts Say Region Should Look to 'Golden Triangle' to Combat Drug Smuggling," *Radio Free Europe* (Jan. 31, 2005), http://www.rferl.org/featuresarticle/2005/01/37d15755-5c22-4df6-a4a9-2ab9cc3ab944.html (accessed Sept. 7, 2006).
21. United Nations Office on Drugs and Crime (UNODC), *Alternative Development: A Global Thematic Evaluation. Final Synthesis Report*. New York, 2005, http://www.unodc.org/pdf/Alternative_Development_Evaluation_Dec-05.pdf (accessed Dec. 30, 2006).
22. ASEAN Secretariat and United Nations Office on Drugs and Crime, "Towards a Drug Free ASEAN and China 2015: Assessing ACCORD Progress 2000–2005" (report from the project Regional Cooperative Mechanism to Monitor and Execute the ACCORD Plan of Action, Oct. 2005), http://www.accordplan.net/file/122005/16/Assessing%20ACCORD%20Progress%202000-2005.pdf (accessed Oct. 30, 2006).
23. Matías Braun, Ricardo Hausmann, and Lant Pritchett, "The Proliferation of Sovereigns: Are There Lessons for Integration?," in Antonio Estevadeordal et al., ed., *Integrating the Americas: FTAA and Beyond* (Cambridge: Harvard University Press, 2004),105 and Ernesto López-Córdova and Mauricio Mesquita Moreira, "Regional Integration and Productivity: The Experiences of Brazil and Mexico," in Estevadeordal, *Integrating the Americas*, 599.
24. Michael Hirsh, "The Energy Wars: The Rise of a New Global Energy Elite Means High Oil and Gas Prices Are Here to Stay," *Newsweek* (May 3, 2006).
25. Ibid. Gary J. Schmitt, "Energy Security, National Security, and Natural Gas," American Enterprise Institute for Public Policy Research (Apr. 2006), http://www.aei.org/publications/pubID.24223/pub_detail.asp (accessed Sept. 7, 2006).
26. Gabe Collins, "Russia's Energy Weapon," *Global Events Magazine* (May 4, 2006), http://www.geostrategymap.com/docf_Guest_May04_2006.htm.
27. The American Friends Service Committee, "North American Free Trade Agreement (NAFTA)," http://www.afsc.org/trade-matters/tradeagreements/NAFTA.htm (accessed Sept. 7, 2006).
28. Sandra Polaski, "Jobs, Wages, and Household Income," in John Audley et al., ed., *NAFTA's Promise and Reality: Lessons from Mexico for the Hemisphere* (Washington, D.C.: Carnegie Endowment for International Peace, 2004): 24.
29. Alejandro Nadal, Francisco Aguayo and Marcos Chávez, "Seven Myths About NAFTA. Three Lessons for Latin America," Interhemispheric Resource Center. November, 2003 http://americas.irc-online.org/articles/2003/0311_7-myths.html (accessed Dec. 30, 2006).

30. Debbie Seidbend, " U.S. Wheat and Corn Exports to Mexico Thrive Under NAFTA—North American Free Trade Agreement," *AgExporter* (Jan. 2004), http://findarticles.com/p/articles/mi_m3723/is_1_16/ai _114328146 (accessed Sept. 5, 2006.)

31. Mark Stevenson, "Mexicans Angered by Spread of Genetically Modified Corn," Dec. 29, 2001, *Associated Press*, http://www.genet-info.org/genet/2001/Dec/msg00039.html (accessed Sept. 5, 2006.)

32. Ibid.

33. James Peach, "The Long-Run and the Energy Sector in the U.S.–Mexico Border Region," in David A. Rohy, ed., *The U.S.–Mexican Border Environment: Trade, Energy, and the Environment: Challenges and Opportunities for the Border Region, Now and in 2020*, SCERP monograph series no. 7. (San Diego: Southwest Center for Environmental Research and Policy, San Diego State University Press, 2003).

34. Alfredo Corchado and Tracy Eaton, "Is Mexico Turning Into Colombia?" *Dallas Morning News*, Oct. 16, 2005.

35. Ted Robbins, "Illegal Immigrant Deaths Burden Border Towns," *All Things Considered* (NPR News, Oct. 6, 2006), http://www.npr.org/templates/story/story.php?storyId=4948382 (accessed Sept. 5, 2006).

2. DATA ON THE HYPERBORDER

1. Central Intelligence Agency, "World Fact Book" https://www.cia.gov/cia/publications/factbook/ (accessed Mar. 25, 2007).

2–4. International Telecommunication Union, "Yearbook of Statistics," 2005, http://www.itu.int/ITU-D/icteye/Indicators/Indicators.aspx# (accessed Mar. 25, 2007).

5. nationmaster.com, "Media Statistics. Average cost of local call by country," http://www.nationmaster.com/graph/med_ave_cos_of_loc_cal-media-average-cost-local-call (accessed Mar. 25, 2007).

6–9. "World Fact Book."

10. nationmaster.com, "Media Statistics: Televisions per capita by country," http://www.nationmaster.com/graph/med_tel_percap-media-televisions-per-capita (accessed Mar. 25, 2007).

11–13. "Yearbook of Statistics."

14–22. "World Fact Book."

23. 2002 or latest year available. Organisation for Economic Co-operation and Development, "Factbook 2006—Economic, Environmental and Social Statistics," http://caliban.sourceoecd.org/vl=13136849/cl=30/nw=1/rpsv/factbook/07-01-02-g01.htm (accessed Mar. 25, 2007).

24. U.S. population as of 20:40 GMT (EST+5) Mar 25, 2007, U.S. Census, "Data Finders: Population Clocks," http://www.census.gov/; Mexico population as of 2005, Instituto Nacional de Estadística Geografía e Informática (INEGI),

"Población total según sexo: 1950–2005," http://www.inegi.gob.mx/est/contenidos/espanol/rutinas/ept.asp?t=mpob01&c=3178 (accessed Mar. 25, 2007).

25. U.S. data from U.S. Census 2000, "Table GCT-PH1-R. Population, Housing Units, Area, and Density (geographies ranked by total population), 2000," http://factfinder.census.gov/servlet/GCTTable?_bm=y&-geo_id=01000US&-_box_head_nbr=GCT-PH1-R&-ds_name=DEC_2000_SF1_U&-redoLog=false&-mt_name=DEC_2000_SF1_U_GCT-PH1R_US9S&-format=US-9S (accessed Mar. 25, 2007). Mexico data from INEGI, "Densidad de población por entidad federativa, 2000," http://www.inegi.gob.mx/est/contenidos/espanol/rutinas/ept.asp?t=mpob11&c=3188 (accessed Mar. 25, 2007).

26. "World Fact Book."

27. Department of Economic and Social Affairs, Population Division, "International Migration 2006, " United Nations, http://www.un.org/esa/population/publications/2006Migration_Chart/2006IttMig_chart.htm (accessed Mar. 25, 2007).

28–29. "World Fact Book."

30. U.S. data from Center for Disease Control, "Fast Stats A–Z: Deaths/Mortality," http://www.cdc.gov/nchs/fastats/deaths.htm (accessed Mar. 25, 2007). Mexico data for 2005, INEGI, "Estadísticas sociodemográficas," *Cuadro resumen*, http://www.inegi.gob.mx/est/contenidos/espanol/rutinas/ept.asp?t=mpob00&c=5262 (accessed mar. 25, 2007).

31. U.S. data from Pew Hispanic Center, "From 200 Million to 300 Million: TheNumbers behind Population Growth," Fact Sheet, Oct. 10, 2006: Mexico data from "World Fact Book."

32. The World Bank. "Data and Statistics: 2005."

33. Organisation for Economic Co-operation and Development, "OECD Factbook 2006—Economic, Environmental and Social Statistics."

34. "World Fact Book."

35. "OECD Factbook 2006"

36. Ibid.

37. "World Fact Book."

38–52. The World Bank, "Data and Statistics: 2005," GDP at current dollar prices.

53. International Energy Agency, "International Petroleum (Oil) Production: Top World Oil Producers, 2005 (Million Barrels per Day)," http://www.eia.doe.gov/emeu/cabs/topworldtables1_2.html (accessed Mar. 26, 2007).

54. Years for U.S. and Mexico data: 2002 and 2006 respectively, "World Fact Book."

55. International Energy Agency, "International Natural Gas Production: Natural Gas Production (Gross Production, Vented, Flared, Reinjected, Marketed Production, and Dry Gas Production), All Countries, 2003 (Billion Cubic Feet)," http://www.eia.doe.gov/emeu/international/iea2004/table41.xls (accessed Mar. 26, 2007).

56. Year for U.S. and Mexico data: 2005, "World Fact Book."

57. International Energy Agency, "Output of Refined Petroleum Products: All Countries, Year 2003," http://www.eia.doe.gov/emeu/international/iealf/table32.xls (accessed Mar. 26, 2007).

58. International Energy Agency, "International Coal Production: Tables, All Countries, 1980–2004: Total Primary Coal," http://www.eia.doe.gov/emeu/international/iealf/table25.xls (accessed Mar. 26, 2007).

59. The World Bank, "Data and Statistics: 2005."

60. International Energy Agency, "International Electricity Imports, All Countries, 1980–2004. Billion Kilowatthours," http://www.eia.doe.gov/emeu/international/iealf/tables1.xls (accessed Mar. 26, 2007).

61. International Energy Agency, "International Electricity Exports, All Countries, 1980–2004. Billion Kilowatthours," http://www.eia.doe.gov/emeu/international/iealf/tables3.xls (accessed Mar. 26, 2007).

62. International Energy Agency, "International Carbon Dioxide Emissions and Carbon Intensity: Million Metric Tons of Carbon Dioxide," http://www.eia.doe.gov/emeu/international/iealf/tableh1cco2.xls (accessed Mar. 26, 2007).

63. The World Bank, "Data and Statistics: 2005."

64. U.S. data from 2006. Numbers for 2005 = -766,560 billion dollars. TradeStats Express, National Trade Data, "Total All Merchandise–Balance with World," http://tse.export.gov/NTDChartDisplay.aspx?UniqueURL=peuzjz2ecqrfjc45xnznihbx-2007-3-26-20-45-42 (accessed Mar. 26, 2007); Mexico data from 2005. "Informe Anual 2005" (April, 2006), Banco de México, http://www.banxico.org.mx/publicadorFileDownload/download?documentId={5AA1E2B9-58FE-147D-C97B-6B9E7406630B} (accessed Nov. 1, 2006).

65. U.S. data from 2006. Numbers for 2005 = 1,670,940 billion dollars. TradeStats Express, National Trade Data, "Total All Merchandise–Balance with World"; Mexico data from 2005, "Informe Anual 2005."

66. TradeStats Express, National Trade Data, "HS Total All Merchandise–Imports to Mexico."

67. U.S. data from 2006. Numbers for 2005 = 904,379 millions of dollars; Mexico data from 2005. "Informe Anual 2005."

68. TradeStats Express, National Trade Data, "HS Total All Merchandise–Exports to Mexico."

69–70. "World Fact Book."

71–80. The World Bank, "Data and Statistics: 2005."

81. U.S. Department of Transportation; Barton-Aschman & La Empresa, 1997.

82. Southwest Center for Environmental Research & Policy, "Border 2012: Fact Sheet: Revised Projections for the Population of the U.S.–Mexican Border," http://www.scerp.org/population/factsheet.pdf

83–84. U.S. Census 2000.

85. All trade by all surface modes between all U.S. Ports and Mexico, January 2006–December 2006, http://www.bts.gov/cgi-bin/tbsf/tbdr/by_port_mex.pl; Bureau of Transportation Statistics, the Intermodal Transportation Database, http://www.transtats.bts.gov/Fields.asp?Table_ID=1358 (accessed May 12, 2007).

3. REACTIONS TO THE HYPERBORDER

1. Michele Waslin, "The New Meaning of the Border: U.S.–Mexico Migration Since 9/11" (Center for U.S.–Mexican Studies, University of California, San Diego, May, 2003), http://repositories.cdlib.org/cgi/viewcontent.cgi?article=1040&context=usmex (accessed Oct. 18, 2006).

2. Laura W. Murphy and Timothy H. Edgar, "ACLU Testimony on 'Immigration Enforcement Since September 11, 2001' Before the House Judiciary Subcommittee on Immigration, Border Security and Claims" (May 8, 2003), ACLU, http://www.aclu.org/SafeandFree/SafeandFree.cfm?ID=12566&c=206 (accessed Oct. 18, 2006).

3. Waslin, "The New Meaning of the Border."

4. Michele Waslin, "Counterterrorism and the Latino Community Since September 11," (Cambio de Colores/Change of Colors conference, University of Missouri-Kansas City, Mar. 12–14, 2003), http://www.cambiodecolores.org/Library/2003_Waslin_Counterterrorism.htm (accessed Oct. 18, 2006).

5. Nedra Pickler, "Bush Presides Over Soldiers' Citizenship," Associated Press, July 24, 2006, http://www.comcast.net/news/politics/index.jsp?cat=POLITICS&fn=/2006/07/24/440714.html

6. U.S. Department of Homeland Security, "U.S. Department of Homeland Security Announces Six Percent Increase in Fiscal Year 2007 Budget Request,"(fact sheet, Feb. 6, 2006), http://www.dhs.gov/xnews/releases/press_release_0849.shtm (accessed Oct. 29, 2006).

7. Waslin, "Counterterrorism and the Latino Community Since September 11."

8. Attorneys for MALDEF and Friendly House, quoted in Jerry Seper, "Legal Challenge to Arizona Law on Illegals Dismissed," *Washington Times*, Aug. 11, 2005.

9. "The Universal Declaration of Human Rights," The United Nations, Dec. 10, 1948. http://www.un.org/Overview/rights.html (accessed Dec. 26, 2006).

10. The Library of Congress, "Intelligence Reform and Terrorism Prevention Act of 2004," http://thomas.loc.gov/cgi-bin/bdquery/z?d108:SN02845:@@@L&summ2=m&#major%20actions (accessed Jan. 3, 2007); Office of the Press Secretary, "President Signs Intelligence Reform and Terrorism Prevention Act," (Washington, D.C., Dec. 17, 2004), http://www.whitehouse.gov/news/releases/2004/12/20041217-1.html (accessed Jan. 3, 2007).

11. Michele Waslin, "The Real ID Act in the Latino Community," National Council of La Raza, http://nclr.org/files/29652_file_REAL_ID_summary_for_Latinos_final_bill.pdf

12. Kim Zetter, "No Real Debate for Real ID," *Wired News*, May 2005. http://www.wired.com/news/privacy/0,67471-1.html?tw=wn_story_page_next1

13. Waslin, "The Real ID Act and the Latino Community."

14. Ibid.

15. The Library of Congress, "Sensenbrenner Bill-H.R. 4437. Border Protection, Antiterrorism, and Illegal Immigration Control Act of 2005. Sec. 202. Alien Smuggling and Related Offenses," http://thomas.loc.gov/cgi-bin/query/F?c109:4:./temp/~c109Le9MVI:e43647: (accessed Dec. 30, 2006).

16. Laura Carlsen, "Killing Guillermo Martinez: Bad Blood on the Border," *Counterpunch* (Feb. 4/5, 2006), http://www.counterpunch.org/carlsen02042006.html (accessed Dec. 26, 2006); Tom Barry, "What's FAIR got to do with it?," Right Web (Silver City NM, International Relations Center, Jan. 19, 2006), http://rightweb.irc-online.org/rw/3053 (accessed Dec. 26, 2006).

17. Michael A. Fletcher and Jonathan Weisman, "Bush Signs Bill Authorizing 700-Mile Fence for Border," *Washington Post*, Oct. 26, 2006.

18. Steven Smith, "'Operation Jump Start' Puts 2,500 Guardsmen on Southern Border in June," American Forces Press Service, June 6, 2006, http://www.defenselink.mil/news/Jun2006/20060606_5350.html (accessed Oct. 31, 2006).

19. Barbara Barrett, "N.C. Troops on Guard at Mexican Border," *Charlotte Observer*, July 28, 2006.

20. U.S. Customs and Border Protection (CBP) website, http://www.cbp.gov/xp/cgov/toolbox/about/mission/cbp.xml

21. Robert C. Bonner, "Remarks by Robert C. Bonner, Kansas City Chamber of Commerce, Kansas City, Missouri" (U.S. Customs and Border Protection, May 16, 2005), http://www.cbp.gov/xp/cgov/newsroom/commissioner/speeches_statements/archives/2005/05162005_kansas.xml (accessed Oct. 18, 2006).

22. Ibid.

23. U.S. Office of Management and Budget, "Budget of the United States Government FY 2006: Department of Homeland Security," http://www.whitehouse.gov/omb/budget/fy2006/dhs.html (accessed Oct. 18, 2006).

24. Timothy Dunn, *The Militarization of the U.S.–Mexico Border 1978–1992: Low-Intensity Conflict Doctrine Comes Home* (Austin: CMAS, University of Texas Press, 1996).

25. U.S. Office of Management and Budget, "Budget of the United States Government FY 2006: Department of Homeland Security."

26. Bonner, "Remarks by Robert C. Bonner."

27. U.S. Department of Homeland Security, "US-VISIT: How It Works," http://www.dhs.gov/xtrvlsec/programs/editorial_0525.shtm (accessed Oct. 18, 2006).

28. P. T. Wright, (opening remarks, First Annual North American Integration Conference: Hyperborder, El Paso, Texas, November 7, 2005).

29. Garance Burke, "U.S., Mexico Negotiating to Set Up Customs Port in Kansas City," Associated Press, Nov. 16, 2005, http://www.kcsmartport.com/sec_news/media/articles/AssociatedPressStory.htm (accessed Oct. 31, 2006).

30. "Humane Borders Water Stations," Humane Borders, http://www.humaneborders.org/about/about_wstations.html (accessed Oct. 31, 2006).

31. Gary Duffy, "County OKs $25K for Water Stations in Desert," *Tucson Citizen*, Sept. 7, 2005.

32. Associated Press, "Mexico Halts Border Maps Hand-Out," CBS News, Jan. 26, 2006, http://www.cbsnews.com/stories/2006/01/26/ap/world/mainD8FCH6M00.shtml (accessed Oct. 31, 2006).

33. Amy Argetsinger, "In Arizona, 'Minutemen' Start Border Patrols," *Washington Post*, Apr. 5, 2005.

34. Seth Sandronsky, "Interview with Two Anti-Minutemen Activists," *Z Magazine* (Nov. 9, 2005), http://www.zmag.org/content/showarticle.cfm? SectionID=30&ItemID=9077 (accessed Oct. 31, 2006).

35. Ibid.

36. Ibid.

37. Diego Cevallos, "El narcotráfico se ensaña y acalla," *Enkidu* (Feb. 2, 2006), http://www.enkidumagazine.com/art/2006/300106/E_041_300106.htm (accessed Oct. 18, 2006).

38. Ibid.

39. Jill Stewart, "Courageous Tijuana Journalist to get Daniel Pearl Award" (Los Angeles Press Club, 2005), http://www.lapressclub.org/awards/47honors.shtml (accessed Oct. 18, 2006).

40. Diego Cevallos, "Reporters Targeted by Drug-Related Violence," Inter Press Service News Agency, Feb. 7, 2006, http://www.ipsnews.net/news.asp?idnews=32067 (accessed Oct. 18, 2006).

41. International Press Institute, "Jesus Blancornelas, Mexico," IPI Global Journalist, "50 Press Freedom Heroes" (Jan. 5, 2000), http://www.globaljournalist.org/archive/Magazine/Blanc-20002q.html (accessed Oct. 31, 2006).

42. Eric Umansky, "The Vigilante," *Columbia Journalism Review* (June/July, 2005), http://www.cjr.org/issues/2005/4/umansky.asp (accessed Oct. 31, 2006).

43. Talli Nauman, "Mexico's War on a Free Press," *Counterpunch* (Jan. 10, 2005), http://www.counterpunch.org/nauman01102005.html (accessed Oct. 18, 2006).

44. Sauro González Rodríguez and Carlos Lauría, "Dread on the Border: Attacks Spark Fear, Self-censorship in Newsrooms of Drug-plagued Mexican City," special report (Committee to Protect Journalists, Feb. 24, 2006), http://www.cpj.org/Briefings/2006/nuevo_laredo/nuevo_laredo.html (accessed Oct. 18, 2006).

45. Ibid.

46. Reporters Without Borders, "Reporters Without Borders Hails Special Prosecutor to Fight Attacks on Journalists," report, Feb. 24, 2006, http://www.rsf.org/article.php3?id_article=16559 (accessed Oct. 31, 2006).

47. United States Government Accountability Office, "Border-Crossing Deaths Have Doubled Since 1995; Border Patrol's Efforts to Prevent Deaths Have Not Been Fully Evaluated," Report to the Honorable Bill Frist, Majority Leader, U.S. Senate, Aug. 15, 2006, http://www.gao.gov/new.items/d06770.pdf (accessed Oct. 31, 2006).

48. "John and Jane Doe Migrant: They End Up in an Anonymous Pauper's Grave" (press release, Stop Gatekeeper, Oct. 28, 2004), http://www.stopgatekeeper.org/English/press-041028.htm (accessed July 26, 2006).

49. Susan Carroll, "Migrant Bodies Crowd Border Morgues," *Arizona Republic*, Jun. 22, 2006.

50. U.S. Department of State, "U.S.–Mexico Partnership for Prosperity," fact sheet (Office of the Press Secretary, Mar. 22, 2002), http://www.state.gov/p/wha/rls/fs/8919.htm (accessed Oct. 18, 2006).

51. Ibid.

52. K. Larry Storrs, "Mexico–United States Dialogue on Migration and Border Issues, 2001–2005" (Congressional Research Service report for Congress, June 2, 2005), http://www.fas.org/sgp/crs/row/RL32735.pdf (accessed Oct. 18, 2006).

53. "The U.S. Federal Reserve System and Banco de México promoted a program called Directo a México through which participating U.S. banks charge two dollars to send money to Mexico, using the U.S. and Mexican central banks as intermediaries," Partnership for Prosperity, "Action Plan" (report to the Presidents, Mar. 2006), http://p4p.fox.presidencia.gob.mx/p4p_us.php?seccion=plan (accessed Dec. 26, 2006).

4. A STATE OF INTERDEPENDENCE

1. Nancy Gibbs, "A Whole New World: Along the U.S.–Mexican Border Where Hearts and Minds and Money and Culture Merge, the Century of the Americas is Born," *Time* (June 11, 2001).

2. Tim Padgett and Cathy Booth Thomas, "Two Countries, One City," *Time* (June 11, 2001).

3. Environmental Protection Agency, Secretaría del Medio Ambiente y Recursos Naturales. "Frontera 2012: Programa Ambiental México-Estados Unidos" (May 5, 2003), 5, http://www.epa.gov/r6border/pdf/2012_spanish.pdf (accessed Nov. 5, 2006).

4. Padgett and Booth Thomas, "Two Countries, One City."

5. Jesus Cañas and Roberto Coronado, "Cyclical Differences Emerge in Border City Economies," *Crossroads: Economic Trends in the Desert Southwest* (Federal Reserve Bank of Dallas) 1 (2005), http://dallasfed.org/research/crossroads/2005/cross0501a.html (accessed Oct. 18, 2006).

6. California Technology, Trade and Commerce Agency, http://commerce.ca.gov/state/ttca/ttca_homepage.jsp (accessed Sept. 7, 2006).

7. "Interview with Jorge Bustamante" (Framing the Future: Tomorrow's Border Economy conference, El Paso, TX, Nov. 19, 2004), Federal Reserve Bank of Dallas, http://www.dallasfed.org/news/research/2004/04future_bustamante.html (accessed Oct. 17, 2006).

8. Ibid.

9. Cañas and Coronado, "Cyclical Differences Emerge in Border City Economies."

10. Padgett and Booth Thomas, "Two Countries, One City."

11. Ibid.

12. Ibid.

13. Rachel McHugh, "Time's Come for Jointly Managing Border's Surface, Underground Water," IRC Americas Program (Silver City, NM: International Relations Center, May 9, 2005), http://americas.irc-online.org/commentary/2005/0505tbwater.html (accessed Oct. 18, 2006).

14. Aureliano Gonzalez Baz, "Manufacturing in Mexico: The Mexican In-Bond (Maquila) Program," University of Delaware, http://www.udel.edu/leipzig/texts2/vox128.htm (accessed Sept. 7, 2006).

15. Gerard Morales, Benjamin Aguilera, and David K. Armstrong, "An Overview of the Maquiladora Program" (U.S. Department of Labor: Bureau of International Labor Affairs, 1994), http://www.dol.gov/ilab/media/reports/nao/maquilad.htm (accessed Sept. 7, 2006).

16. Carolyn Said, "The Immigration Debate: Effect on Economy Depends on Viewpoint," *San Francisco Chronicle*, May 21, 2006.

17. Juan-Vicente Palerm, "Neighbors Interdependence Increases," *UC Mexus News* 39 (Fall 2002), http://ucmexus.ucr.edu/index.php?content=publications/n39Fa02/editorial.html (accessed Sept. 7, 2006).

18. Senate Democratic Caucus, State of California, "Senator Jackie Speier's Bill to Inform Consumers About Contaminated Meat Outbreaks Goes to Governor for Signature" (press release, May 11, 2006), http://democrats.sen.ca.gov/templates/SDCTemplate.asp?a=5644&z=155&cp=PressRelease&pg=article&fpg=pressreleases&sln=&sdn= (accessed Sept. 7, 2006).

19. Jorge Santibáñez, Rafael Fernández de Castro, and Rodolfo Tuirán, "Reforma Migratoria en Estados Unidos: Impactos y Retos para México" (seminar at Colegio de la Frontera Norte [COLEF], Mexico City, May 29, 2006).

20. José Diaz Briseño, "Falla control en empleos de migrantes sin papeles," *Reforma*, June 20, 2006.

21. Pedro Celis, "Social Security: A Tale of Two Problems" (Seattle: Washington Policy Center, May 2004), http://www.washingtonpolicy.org/Misc/PNCelisSocialSecurity05-04.html (accessed Sept. 7, 2006).

22. Jay Root, "Migration to the U.S. Emptying Much of Mexican Countryside," *San Jose Mercury News*, March 26, 2006. Instituto Nacional de Estadística Geografía e Informática (INEGI), "Población inmigrante y emigrante y saldo neto migratorio, por entidad federative según lugar de nacimiento, 2000" http://www.inegi.gob.mx/est/contenidos/espanol/rutinas/ept.asp?t=mpob58&c=3235 INEGI, "Población total por entidad federative según sexo, 2000 y 2005," http://www.inegi.gob.mx/est/contenidos/espanol/rutinas/ept.asp?t=mpob02&c=3179

23. Geri Smith, "Channeling the Remittance Flood," *Business Week* (Dec. 28, 2005).

24. "Informe Anual 2005" (April, 2006), Banco de México, http://www.banxico.org.mx/publicadorFileDownload/download?documentId={5AA1E2B9-58FE-147D-C97B-6B9E7406630B} (accessed Nov. 1, 2006).

25. Mario López Espinosa, "Remesas de los mexicanos en el exterior y su vinculación con el desarrollo económico,

social y cultural de sus comunidades de origen," Immigration Migration Paper (International Labor Organization) 59 (2002), http://www.oit.org.mx/pdf/remesas/remesas.pdf (accessed Nov. 1, 2006).

26. Jonathan Fox, "Mexican Migrant Civic Participation in the United States," (Social Science Research Council, Aug. 15, 2006), Border Battles: The U.S. Immigration Debates, http://borderbattles.ssrc.org/Fox/ (accessed August 21, 2006).

27. "Lloyd Mexican Economic Report," (June 2005), Mexico Connect, http://www.mexconnect.com/MEX/lloyds/llydeco0605.html (accessed Sept. 7, 2006).

28. Sergio Aguayo Quezada, *Almanaque México–Estados Unidos* (Mexico City: Fondo de Cultura Económica, 2005).

29. "U.S. Interim Projections by Age, Sex, Race, and Hispanic Origin," U.S. Census Bureau, 2004, http://www.census.gov/ipc/www/usinterimproj/ (accessed Nov. 1, 2006).

30. Ibid.

31. Patrick May, Mary Anne Ostrom, and Rodney Foo, "A Call for Rights: Call for Immigration Rights from S.F. to Salinas," *San Jose Mercury News*, May 2, 2006.

32. Eliseo Medina, "The Birth of a National Movement," *Los Angeles Times*, May 2, 2006.

33. The civil rights protest on August 28, 1963, the biggest U.S. march of the twentieth century, attracted participants estimated to range between 200,000 and 500,000. Note from Thomas Gentile, *March on Washington: August 28, 1963* (Washington, D.C.: New Day Publications, 1983).

34. Fox, "Mexican Migrant Civic Participation in the United States."

35. Gillian Flaccus, "One Million Immigrants Skip Work for Demonstration," *San Francisco Chronicle*, May, 2, 2006.

36. Santibáñez et al, "Reforma Migratoria en Estados Unidos."

37. Suzanne Gamboa, "Immigrants' Interest in Citizenship Surges," *Associated Press*, Apr. 19, 2006, http://www.comcast.net/news/national/index.jsp?cat=DOMESTIC&fn=/2006/04/19/370995.html (accessed Sept. 7, 2006).

38. Arlene Davila, *Latinos Inc.: The Marketing and Making of a People* (Berkeley: University of California Press, 2001).

39. "Hispanic/Latino Market Profile" (Magazine Publishers of America, 2004), www.magazine.org/content/Files/MPA-HispMktPro.pdf (accessed Sept. 7, 2006).

40. Mexico's GDP in 2004 was $676.8 billion. See Aguayo Quezada, *Almanaque México–Estados Unidos*.

41. "Hispanic/Latino Market Profile."

42. Phil Lempert, "Latin Food: It's Burning Up Your Supermarket" (NBC News, Apr. 27, 2004), www.msnbc.msn.com/id/4491418/ (accessed Sept. 7, 2006).

43. The Infoshop, "Market Trends: Hispanics and Food" (Global Information, Inc., June 2003), http://www.the-infoshop.com/study/pf14211_hispanic_food.html (accessed Sept. 7, 2006).

44. Malcolm Beith, "Latinos and Lucre: The Race Is On to Win America's Hispanic Consumers," *Newsweek International* (Nov. 22, 2004).

45. Travel Industry Association of America, 2004, http://www.tia.org/index.html (accessed Sept. 7, 2006).

46. Davila, *Latinos Inc.*

47. Ibid.

48. Secretaría de Economía de México, "Negociaciones Comerciales: The Hispanic Market in the United States," http://www.economia.gob.mx/index.jsp?P=2408 (accessed Sept. 7, 2006).

49. Davila, *Latinos Inc.*

50. Kevin G. Hall, "Mexican Oilfield Crucial to the U.S. Facing Decline," *Knight Ridder Newspapers*, March 16, 2006, http://www.myrtlebeachonline.com/mld/myrtlebeachonline/news/nation/14116129.htm (accessed Sept. 7, 2006).

51. Energy Information Administration, "Official Energy Statistics from the U.S. Government," http://www.eia.doe.gov/emeu/cabs/Usa/Oil.html (accessed Sept. 7, 2006).

52. Geri Smith, "Pemex May Be Turning From Gusher to Black Hole," *Business Week* (Dec. 13, 2004).

53. Hall, "Mexican Oilfield Crucial to the U.S. Facing Decline."

54. David Shields, *Pemex: La Reforma Petrolera* (Mexico City, Temas de Hoy, 2005).

55. Ibid.

56. "Informe Anual 2005"

57. Based on number of arrivals (in millions) in 2003; United States: 40.4; Mexico: 18.7. Travel Industry Association of America, "International Tourism Overview—World Tourism," http://www.tia.org/researchpubs/itnl_tourism_world.html (accessed Oct. 18, 2006).

58. U.S. Department of Commerce, ITA Office of Travel and Tourism Industries, "U.S. Resident Travel Abroad Historical Visitation—Outbound 1994–2004 (One or More Nights)" (July 2005), http://tinet.ita.doc.gov/view/f-2004-11-001/index.html (accessed Oct. 18, 2006).

59. Secretaría de Turismo, "México. Dónde Estamos y Hacia Dónde Vamos en Materia de Turismo," Oct. 2006, http://www.sectur.gob.mx/PDF/hacia_donde_vamos.zip (accessed Nov. 4, 2006).

60. Ibid.

61. ITA Office of Travel and Tourism Industries, "Mexican Air Visitation Estimates (Market Share). Visitation to Census States. Year 2005." California: 29.7%; Texas: 19.8%. http://tinet.ita.doc.gov/view/f-2005-147-001/index.html (accessed Nov. 4, 2006).

62. U.S. Department of Commerce, ITA, Office of Travel and Tourism Industries, "Total International Visitors Volume to and from the U.S. 1995–2005," http://tinet.ita.doc.gov/outreachpages/inbound.total_intl_travel_volume_1995-2005.html (accessed Nov. 4, 2006).

63. U.S. Department of Commerce, ITA, Office of Travel and Tourism Industries, "International Visitor Arrivals to the U.S. by Region of Residency 2003pr and 2002" (Mar. 2004, updated May 2005), http://tinet.ita.doc.gov/view/f-2003-200-001/index.html (accessed Oct. 18, 2006). Mexico total: 10,526,000, Mexico Air: 1,359,418.Combined data with ITA Office of Travel and Tourism Industries, "Monthly Tourism Statistics: Non-Resident Arrivals to the U.S. By World

Region/Country of Residence, 2003" http://tinet.ita.doc.gov/view/m-2003-I-001/table_1.html (accessed Oct. 18, 2006).

64. International visitors to Mexico, 2003, according to DataTur, Secretaria de Turismo, using data from Banco de México. See http://www.sectur.gob.mx/wb2/sectur/sect_Estadisticas_del_Sector (accessed Nov. 4, 2006).

65. See DataTur, Secretaria de Turismo, http://www.sectur.gob.mx/wb2/sectur/sect_Estadisticas_del_Sector (accessed Nov. 4, 2006).

66. Secretaría de Turismo, "La Inversión Privada en el Sector Turístico," 2006, http://www.sectur.gob.mx/work/resources/LocalContent/12903/5/FolletoInversion2001a2006.pdf (accessed Nov. 4, 2006).

67. Rough estimation made from comparing all Mexico–U.S. and U.S.–Mexico visits on a ten-year timeframe (1995–2005). For example, in 2005, 128.39 million exits were registered out of Mexico and 115 million of them were one-day border excursions to the United States. The same year, out of the 103.15 million visitors to Mexico, 74.52 million were one-day trips to the Mexican side of the border. Similar relationships are found in the previous ten years. DataTur, Secretaria de Turismo, http://www.sectur.gob.mx/wb2/sectur/sect_Estadisticas_del_Sector (accessed Nov. 4, 2006)

68. Ibid. 2005 is the year with highest revenues for the Mexican border ($2.2 billion spent by excursionists from the United States. On the other hand, $3.95 billion was spent by Mexican excursionists in the U.S. that year, more than half of all money spent by Mexicans abroad ($57.27 billion versus $31 billion between 1995–2005).

69. As of 2000, the population of the 80 municipios on the Mexican side of the border stood at 6.35 million and the population of U.S. border counties stood at 6.553 million. United States–Mexico Border Health Commission, "Healthy Border 2010: An Agenda for Improving Health on the United States–Mexico Border" (Oct. 2003), 8.

70. U.S. Department of State, Embassy of the United States, Mexico, "Travel Warnings and Warden Messages: Rising Level of Brutal Violence in Areas of Mexico" (Sept. 14, 2006), http://mexico.usembassy.gov/mexico/ew060914violence.html (accessed Oct. 18, 2006).

5. SECURITY

1. Deborah McCarthy, "Los Desafíos de la Inteligencia en el Mundo Globalizado" (lecture, Universidad de Chile, Santiago, Chile, May 8, 2006) http://www.inap.uchile.cl/cienciapolitica/destacado57b.html (accessed Nov. 16, 2006)

2. The White House, "The National Security Strategy of the United States of America" (Washington, D.C., U.S. Government Printing Office, Sept. 2002), http://www.whitehouse.gov/nsc/nss.pdf (accessed Nov. 16, 2006).

3. Centro de Investigación y Seguridad Nacional, "Seguridad Nacional. ¿Qué es Seguridad Nacional?," http://www.cisen.gob.mx (accessed Nov. 16, 2006).

4. Claudia Flores, "Se publica Ley de Seguridad Nacional," Noticieros Televisa, Jan. 31, 2005, http://www.esmas.com/noticierostelevisa/mexico/422404.html (accessed Nov. 16, 2006).

5. Felipe Moreno, "Una Frontera Inteligente," http://www.felipemoreno.com/unafronterainteligente.html (accessed July 14, 2006).

6. "Hay 130 puntos vulnerables en el país," Revista Vértigo, Feb. 22, 2003, http://www.revistavertigo.com/historico/22-2-2003/reportaje4.html (accessed Nov. 16, 2006).

7. "It may well have become more difficult for terrorists to get into the country, but, as thousands demonstrate each day, it is far from impossible. Immigration procedures have been substantially tightened (at considerable cost), and suspicious U.S. border guards have turned away a few likely bad apples. But visitors and immigrants continue to flood the country.... Terrorism does not require a large force. And the 9/11 planners, assuming Middle Eastern males would have problems entering the United States legally after the attack, put into motion plans to rely thereafter on non-Arabs with passports from Europe and Southeast Asia." John Mueller, "Is There Still a Terrorist Threat?" Foreign Affairs (Sept./Oct. 2006). After the House of Representatives approved on September 14, 2006 the construction of a 700-mile-long fence along the U.S.–Mexico border, Rep. Lloyd Doggett (D-Tex) accused Republicans of playing upon voters' fears to score political points, saying they were trying to confuse Americans into thinking "Osama bin Laden is heading north in a sombrero" Chicago Tribune and Associated Press, "House Votes to Make Border Fence Between U.S., Mexico 700 Miles Longer," Seattle Times, Sept. 15, 2006.

8. Charlene Porter, "United States To Use Better Technology for Security, Hospitality," The Bureau of International Information Programs, U.S. Department of State, http://usinfo.state.gov/gi/Archive/2006/Jan/17-781544.html (accessed Nov. 16, 2006).

9. Department of Homeland Security, "Securing Our Nation's Borders," (fact sheet, Jun. 29, 2006) http://www.dhs.gov/xnews/releases/press_release_0938.shtm (accessed Jan. 7, 2006).

10. Embassy of Mexico in the United States, "Law Enforcement, Fight Against Organized Crime and Border Security" (Aug. 11, 2006), http://www.embassyofmexico.org/images/pdfs/Law%20enforcement%20border%20security%20%2002%2003%202006.pdf (accessed Nov. 16, 2006).

11. Jorge Herrera, "¿Qué es el Plan Centinela?," El Universal, Aug. 10, 2006.

12. Security and Prosperity Partnership of North America, "Security Agenda," White House Office of the Press Secretary, March 23, 2005, http://www.spp.gov/security_agenda/ (accessed Nov. 20, 2006).

13. Embassy of the United States in Mexico, "United States and Mexico Announce Joint Action Plan to Combat Violence on Both Sides of the Border," Embassy of the United States, March 3, 2006, http://mexico.usembassy. gov/mexico/ep060303chertoffabascal.html (accessed Nov. 20, 2006).

14. The U.S. State Department provided three mobile inspection units that can search trucks and find smuggled goods and people. It is also assessing Mexican officers in their training, especially in Chiapas. José Antonio Román, "Apoyo de EU para evitar paso de migrantes a México," *La Jornada*, Aug. 24, 2006.

15. Michael Hedges, "Bush Budget Scraps 9,790 Border Patrol Agents. President Uses Law's Escape Clause to Drop Funding for New Homeland Security Force," *Houston Chronicle*, Feb. 9, 2005.

16. U.S. Customs and Border Protection, "SBInet: Securing U.S. Borders," (fact sheet, Sep., 2006), http://www.dhs.gov/xlibrary/assets/sbinetfactsheet.pdf (accessed Jan. 4, 2007).

17. Eilene Zimmerman, "Border Protections Imperil Environment; Last Wilderness Area South of San Diego Could be Damaged," *San Francisco Chronicle*, Feb. 27, 2006.

6. NARCOTRAFFIC AND CORRUPTION

1. USAID, "Central America and Mexico Gang Assessment, Annex 4: Southern and Northern Borders of Mexico," Apr. 2006, http://www.usaid.gov/ locations/latin_america_caribbean/democracy/gangs_assessment.pdf (accessed Dec. 31, 2006).

2. Instituto Tecnológico Autónomo de México, "La Corrupción en los Cuerpos de Seguridad Estadounidense," *México en el Mundo* vol. 2, no. 12 (Dec. 2005), 1, http://internacionales.itam.mx/docs/Mexico_Mundo_Num12_Vol2.pdf (accessed Nov. 21, 2006).

3. Donnie R. Marshall, "Drug Trafficking on the Southwest Border" (DEA Congressional Testimony before the U.S. House of Representatives Committee on the Judiciary Subcommittee on Crime, Washington, D.C., March 29, 2001) http://www.usdoj.gov/dea/pubs/cngrtest/ct032901. htm (accessed Nov. 20, 2006)

4. Transparency International, "Corruption Perceptions Index 2006," Nov. 6, 2006, http://www.transparency.org/policy_research/surveys_indices/global/cpi (accessed Nov. 21, 2006).

5. Transparency International, "Global Corruption Barometer 2005," Dec. 9, 2005, http://www.transparency.org/policy_research/surveys_indices/global/gcb (accessed Nov. 20, 2006).

6. "$111 in current US dollars as of 2005, equivalent to $166 Purchasing Power Parity US dollars." Transparency International, "Global Corruption Barometer 2005."

7. Bureau for International Narcotics and Law Enforcement Affairs, "Counternarcotics and Law Enforcement Country Program: Mexico" U.S. Department of State, Washington, D.C., Aug. 10, 2005 http://www.state.gov/p/inl/rls/fs/50972.htm (accessed Nov. 20, 2006).

8. Drug Policy Alliance, "Drug Policy Around the World: Drug Trafficking & Interdiction," http://www.drugpolicy.org/global/drugtraffick/ (accessed Nov. 20, 2006).

9. "More than 90% of the value added (gross profit) of cocaine and heroin is generated at the distribution stage of the illicit drug industry." Office of National Drug Control Policy, "What America's Users Spend on Illegal Drugs," Washington, D.C., Executive Office of the President, 2001, http://www.unodc.org/pdf/technical_series_1998-01-01_1.pdf

10. Drug Policy Alliance, "Drug Policy Around the World: Drug Trafficking & Interdiction."

11. United Nations Office on Drugs and Crime, "2006 World Drug Report: Volume 1: Analysis," http://www.unodc.org/pdf/WDR_2006/wdr2006_volume1.pdf (accessed Dec. 26, 2006).

12. Drug Policy Alliance, "Drug Policy Around the World: Latin America," http://www.drugpolicy.org/global/drugpolicyby/latinamerica/

13. Rolando Herrera, "Ven que impunidad genera más violencia: Pellizcan ganancias del narco," *Reforma*, Sept. 18, 2006.

14. Procuraduría General de la República, *Programa Nacional para el Control de Drogas, Acciones y Resultados* (Mexico City, Nov. 2005).

15. Juan Manuel Mejia Domínguez, "Carteles del Narcotráfico se pelean por el DF," *Vértigo* (Feb. 4, 2006), http://www.revistavertigo.com /historico/4-2-2006/reportaje4.html (accessed Nov. 27, 2006).

16. USAID, "Central America and Mexico Gang Assessment, Annex 4."

17. Statistics for this section come from Laurie Freeman, "State of Siege: Drug-Related Violence and Corruption in Mexico: Unintended Consequences of the War on Drugs. A WOLA Special Report," Washington Office on Latin America (June 2006), 11, http://www.wola.org/publications/mexico_state_of_siege_06.06.pdf (accessed Dec. 26, 2006).

18. United Nations Office on Drugs and Crime, "2006 World Drug Report: Volume 2: Statistics," http://www.unodc.org/pdf/WDR_2006/wdr2006_volume2.pdf (accessed Dec. 26, 2006).

19. Marshall, "Drug Trafficking on the Southwest Border."

20. "Of the total $12.4 billion requested in the 2006 National Drug Control Budget, $5.9 billion was requested for the Department of Homeland Security and Department of Justice combined, while $233 million was requested for the Department of Education." Office of National Drug Control Policy, "National Drug Control Strategy," Appendix A: National Drug Control Budget Summary (Washington, D.C.: Office of Government Printing, Feb. 2005), http://www.whitehousedrugpolicy.gov/publications/policy/ndcs05/index.html (accessed Nov. 20, 2006).

21. Combining federal and state expenses, roughly $40 billion is the amount spent annually to fight drug use and drug abuse in the United States. Office of National Drug Control Policy, "National Drug Control Strategy: FY 2006 Budget Summary," (Washington, D.C.: Office of Government Printing, 2005), http://www.whitehousedrugpolicy.gov/publications/policy/06budget/ (accessed Dec. 26, 2006); National Center on Addiction and Substance Abuse at Columbia University (CASA), "Shoveling Up: The Impact of Substance Abuse on State Budgets" (New York: National Center on Addiction and Substance Abuse at Columbia University, 2001), http://www.casacolumbia.org/pdshopprov/files/47299a.pdf (accessed Dec. 26, 2006).

22. Christopher J. Mumola, Jennifer C. Karberg, "Drug Use and Dependence, State and Federal Prisoners, 2004" (Bureau of Justice Statistics, U.S. Department of Justice, Oct. 2006), http://www.ojp.usdoj.gov/bjs/pub/pdf/dudsfp04.pdf (accessed Dec. 26, 2006).

23. Drug Policy Alliance, "Barriers to Re-Entry for Convicted Drug Offenders" (fact sheet, Apr. 2003, http://www.drugpolicy.org/library/factsheets/barriers/index.cfm (accessed Dec. 26, 2006).

24. Ethan Nadelmann, "U.S. Policy: A Bad Export," *Foreign Policy* 70 (1988): 83–108.

25. Drug Policy Alliance, "What's Wrong with the War on Drugs: Alternatives to Prohibition," http://www.drugpolicy.org/drugwar/alternatives/ (accessed Dec. 26, 2006).

26. Executive Office of the President, "The Economic Costs of Drug Abuse in the United States. 1992–2002" (Washington, D.C.: Office of National Drug Control Policy, Dec. 2004), http://www.whitehousedrugpolicy.gov/publications/economic_costs/economic_costs.pdf (accessed Nov. 20, 2006).

27. National Institute on Drug Abuse, "Monitoring the Future. National Results on Adolescent Drug Use," National Institutes of Health, U.S. Department of Health and Human Services (2005), http://monitoringthefuture.org/pubs/monographs/overview2005.pdf (accessed Nov. 20, 2006).

28. Drug Policy Alliance, "Reducing Harm: Treatment and Beyond," http://www.drugpolicy.org/reducingharm/ (accessed Dec. 26, 2006).

29. Associated Press, "Se Retracta Fox Sobre Ley de Drogas para Uso Personal," *El Universal*, May 3, 2006.

30. Ethan A. Nadelmann, "La guerra antidrogas, peor remedio que el mal. Las políticas de EU buscan más subyugar que erradicar el flagelo, el sentir en AL" [Reducing the Harms of Drug Prohibition in the Americas], *La Jornada*, Nov. 30, 2005.

31. Although a binational program to legalize narcotics has not yet been discussed, former president Vicente Fox mentioned in interviews with two Mexican newspapers that the only way to win the war against drugs was by legalizing them, thereby eliminating the profit-motive and violence attendant with illegal trafficking. See Mike Trickeyl, "Mexico's President Backs Drug Legalization," *Vancouver Sun*, Mar. 21, 2001. President Fox also proposed legislation to de-penalize small possession of narcotics, which was approved by the Mexican Congress, but after hearing concerns from the U.S. State Department, Fox suspended his proposal and made amendments.

7. INFORMAL SECTOR

1. 11.88 million people out of 44.4 million over 14 years of age who are economically active are considered to be working in the informal sector. Data from Sept. to Oct., 2006. Instituto Nacional de Estadística Geografía e Informática (INEGI). "Tasa de ocupación en el secor informal trimestral" and "Población de 14 años y más según condición de actividad, ocupación y disponibilidad (Nacional)." http://www.inegi.gob.mx/est/default.aspx?c=5213 (accessed Dec. 31, 2006).

2. Richard Jackson, "Building Human Capital in An Aging Mexico," Center for Strategic and International Studies (CSIS), July 4, 2005.

3. David Shields, *Pemex: La Reforma Petrolera* (Mexico City: Editorial Planeta Mexicana, 2005), II: 37.

4. Jenny Schuetz, Eric S. Belsky, and Nicolas P. Retsinas, "The State Of Mexico's Housing 2004," (Cambridge, MA: Joint Center for Housing Studies of Harvard University, 2004), vii–viii. http://www.jchs.harvard.edu/publications/international/som2004.pdf (accessed Oct. 18, 2006).

5. Jeffrey Passel, "Estimates of the Size and Characteristics of the Undocumented Population" (research report, Pew Hispanic Center, Mar. 21, 2005), http://pewhispanic.org/files/reports/44.pdf (accessed Aug. 7, 2006).

6. Luis Alonso Lugo, "Remittances are Mexico's Biggest Source of Income, Says Fox," *San Diego Union Tribune*, Sept. 24, 2003; and "Lloyd Mexican Economic Report" (June 2005), Mexico Connect, http://www.mexconnect.com/MEX/lloyds/llydeco0605.html (accessed Sept. 7, 2006).

7. Bruce Wright, "Dollars Cross Borders," *Fiscal Notes* (Nov. 2005), http://www.window.state.tx.us/comptrol/fnotes/fn0511/dollars.html (accessed Dec. 26, 2006).

8. "Immigration," *Frontera NorteSur* (Jan.–Mar. 2005), http://www.nmsu.edu/~frontera/Jan-Mar05/immi.html (accessed Sept. 1, 2006).

9. Carlos H. Mendez, "Barrio Chino," *Conozca Más* (Nov. 2005).

10. Ibid.

11. Ibid.

12. "Hu Signs Trade Pacts with Mexico's Fox," *China Daily*, Sept. 13, 2005, http://www.chinadaily.com.cn/english/doc/2005-09/13/content_477304.htm (accessed Dec. 26, 2006).

13. Dean Calbreath, "Mexico is China's Final WTO Membership," *San Diego Union Tribune*, Dec. 7, 2000.

14. "Hu signs trade pacts with Mexico's Fox."

15. Ibid.

16. Luz Adriana Santacruz Carrillo, "Millones de niños mexicanos trabajan," *Univision Online*, July 22, 2004, http://www.univision.com/content/content.jhtml?cid=427962 (accessed Sept. 1, 2006).

17. International Labour Organization (ILO), "Education as an Intervention Strategy to Eliminate and Prevent Child Labour," http://www.ilo.org/iloroot/docstore/ipec/prod/eng/2006_02_edu_goodpractices.pdf (accessed July 12, 2006).

18. LEK Consulting, LLC, "The Cost Of Movie Piracy: An Analysis by LEK for the Motion Picture Association" (2005), http://www.mpaa.org/press_releases/leksummarympa.pdf (accessed Dec. 26, 2006).

19. International Federation of Phonographic Industry (IFPI), "One in Three Music Discs is Illegal but Fight Back Starts to Show Results," June 23, 2005, http://www.ifpi.org/site-content/antipiracy/piracy-report-current.html (accessed Dec. 26, 2006).

20. D. A. Barber, "The 'New' Economy?" *Tucson Weekly*, Jan. 2, 2003.

21. Ibid.

22. U.S. Immigration and Customs Enforcement, "Immigration Fraud" (fact sheet, June 11, 2004), http://www.ice.gov/pi/news/factsheets/fraud061104.htm (accessed Sept. 4, 2006).

23. Ibid.

24. Jeffrey Passel, "Mexican Immigration to the U.S.: The Latest Estimates," *Migration Information Source* (Mar. 1, 2004), http://www.migrationinformation.org/feature/display.cfm?ID=208 (accessed Sept. 4, 2006).

25. Eduardo Porter, "Illegal Immigrants are Bolstering Social Security with Billions," *New York Times*, Apr. 5, 2005.

26. Johana Parra, interview with author, May 2006.

27. President Bush asked Congress in the 2006 State of the Union address to "reform our immigration laws so they reflect our values and benefit our economy. I propose a new temporary-worker program to match willing foreign workers with willing employers when no Americans can be found to fill the job. This reform will be good for our economy, because employers will find needed workers in an honest and orderly system. A temporary-worker program will help protect our homeland, allowing border patrol and law enforcement to focus on true threats to our national security." Jennifer and Peter Wipf, "The Guest Worker Program: Both Sides of the Issue, Political Stands," About.com, http://immigration.about.com/od/laborjobsissues/i/GuestWorkrIssue.htm (accessed Oct. 18, 2006).

28. See Hernando de Soto, *The Other Path: The Economic Answer to Terrorism* (New York: Basic Books, 2002), and *The Mystery of Capital: Why Capitalism Triumphs in the West and Fails Everywhere Else* (New York: Basic Books, 2003). See also CATO Institute, "Hernando de Soto's Biography," http://www.cato.org/special/friedman/desoto/index.html (accessed July 11, 2006).

29. CATO Institute, "Hernando de Soto's Biography."

30. Instituto Libertad y Democracia, *Evaluación preliminar de la economía extralegal en 12 países de Latinoamérica y el Caribe. Reporte de la investigación en México. Instituto Libertad y Democracia* (Lima, Perú, 2006).

31. Saul Hansell, "At Last, Movies to Keep Arrive on the Internet," *New York Times*, Apr. 3, 2006.

8. MIGRATION AND DEMOGRAPHICS

1. Mario López Espinosa, "Remesas de los mexicanos en el exterior y su vinculación con el desarrollo económico, social y cultural de sus comunidades de origen" (report: Organización Internacional del Trabajo, 2003).

2. Jeffrey S. Passel, "Estimates of the Size and Characteristics of the Undocumented Population" (research report, Pew Hispanic Center, Mar. 21, 2005), http://pewhispanic.org/files/reports/44.pdf (accessed Aug. 7, 2006).

3. Ibid.

4. "A Quick Look at U.S. Immigrants: Demographics, Workforce, and Asset-Building," The Immigrant Policy Project, National Conference of State Legislatures, June 17, 2004, http://www.ncsl.org/programs/ immig/immigstatistics0604.htm (accessed Aug. 7, 2006).

5. Rogelio Saenz, "Latinos and the Changing Face of America," Population Reference Bureau, Aug. 2004, http://www.prb.org/Template.cfm?Section=PRB&template=/ContentManagement/ContentDisplay. cfm&ContentID=11337 (accessed Aug. 8, 2006).

6. Based on Pew Hispanic Center tabulations of the Census Bureau's 2005 American Community Survey public use microdata file, Aug. 29, 2006. "A Statistical Portrait of Hispanics at Mid-Decade. Table 1: Population by Race and Ethnicity: 2000 and 2005" (Sept. 2006), http://pewhispanic.org/reports/middecade/ (accessed Dec. 26, 2006).

7. Saenz, "Latinos and the Changing Face of America."

8. Jeffrey S. Passel, "Size and Characteristics of the Unauthorized Migrant Population in the U.S." (research report, Pew Hispanic Center, Mar. 7, 2006), http://pewhispanic.org/files/reports/61.pdf (accessed Jan. 1, 2007).

9. "Modes of Entry for the Unauthorized Migrant Population" (fact sheet, Pew Hispanic Center, May 22, 2006), http://pewhispanic.org/files/factsheets/19.pdf (accessed Aug. 7, 2006).

10. Ibid.

11. Passel, "Estimates of the Size and Characteristics of the Undocumented Population."

12. "Modes of Entry for the Unauthorized Migrant Population."

13. Passel, "Estimates of the Size and Characteristics of the Undocumented Population."

14. U.S. Census Bureau, American Factfinder, "Census 2000 Demographic Profile Highlights. Population Finder. Selected Population Group: Mexican"

15. Ibid.

16. Passel, "Estimates of the Size and Characteristics of the Undocumented Population."

17. Jim Edgar, Doris Meissner, and Alejandro Silva, "Keeping the Promise: Immigration Proposals from the Heartland," Independent Task Force Report, (Chicago: Chicago Council on Foreign Relations, 2004).

18. Stephen H. Legomsky, "E Pluribus Unum: Immigration, Race, and Other Deep Divides" (Carbondale: Southern Illinois University Law Review,. 1996), 21:101

19. Ibid.

20. Ibid.

21. "Overall, barring sizable immigration-induced economies or diseconomies of scale, the most plausible magnitudes of the impacts of immigration on the economy are modest for those who benefit from immigration, for those who lose from immigration, and for total gross domestic product. The domestic gain may run in the order of $1 billion to $10 billion a year. Although this gain may be modest relative to the size of the U.S. economy, it remains a significant positive gain in absolute terms." James P. Smith and Bary Edmonston, "The New Americans: Economic, Demographic, and Fiscal Effects of Immigration" (panel on the demographic and economic impacts of immigration, Washington, D.C., National Research Council, 1997), 6.

22. Eduardo Porter, "Illegal Immigrants are Bolstering Social Security with Billions," *New York Times*, Apr. 5, 2005.

23. Ibid.

24. Ibid.

25. López Espinosa, "Remesas de los mexicanos en el exterior y su vinculación con el desarrollo económico, social y cultural de sus comunidades de origen."

26. Human Rights Watch, "Bush–Fox Summit" (Feb. 12, 2001), http://www.hrw.org/backgrounder/americas/mex0212.htm (accessed Dec. 26, 2006); Amnesty International Canada, "Crossing the Line: Human Rights Abuses on the US–Mexico Border" http://www.amnesty.ca/usa/border.php (accessed Dec. 26, 2006).

27. Passel, "Estimates of the Size and Characteristics of the Undocumented Population."

28. Ibid.

29. Jonathan Fox, "Mexican Migrant Civic Participation in the United States," (Social Science Research Council, Aug. 15, 2006), Border Battles: The U.S. Immigration Debates, http://borderbattles.ssrc.org/Fox/ (accessed Aug. 21, 2006).

30. Ibid.

31. Ibid.

32. Pew Hispanic Center, "Latinos and the 2006 Mid-term Election" (fact sheet, Nov. 27, 2006), http://pewhispanic.org/files/factsheets/26.pdf (accessed Nov. 27, 2006).

33. Toshiko Kaneda, "A Critical Window for Policymaking on Population Aging in Developing Countries," Population Reference Bureau, Jan. 2006, http://www.prb.org/Template.cfm?Section=PRB&template=/Content/ContentGroups/06_Articles/A_Critical_Window_for_Policymaking_on_Population_Aging_in_Developing_Countries.htm (accessed Aug. 21, 2006).

34. Ibid.

35. Ibid.

36. Ibid.

37. Richard Jackson, "Building Human Capital in an Aging Mexico," Center for Strategic and International Studies, July 4, 2005.

38. United Nations, Department of Economic and Social Affairs, Population Division, "National Trends in Population, Resources, Environment and Development: Country Profiles" (2005), http://www.un.org/esa/population/publications/countryprofile/mexico.pdf and http://www.un.org/esa/population/publications/countryprofile/usa.pdf (accessed Dec. 26, 2006).

39. United Nations, Department of Economic and Social Affairs, Population Division, "World Population Aging 1950–2050, Mexico," http://www.un.org/esa/population/publications/worldageing19502050/pdf/142mexic.pdf (accessed Dec. 12, 2006).

40. Jackson, "Building Human Capital in an Aging Mexico."

41. United Nations, Department of Economic and Social Affairs, Population Division, "World Population Aging 1950–2050, United States of America," http://www.un.org/esa/population/publications/worldageing19502050/pdf/207unite.pdf (accessed Dec. 12, 2006). Jackson, "Building Human Capital in an Aging Mexico."

42. Frank B. Hobbs, "The Elderly Population" (Washington, D.C.: U.S. Census Bureau, Jan. 18, 2001), http://www.census.gov/population/www/pop-profile/elderpop.html (accessed Dec. 26, 2006).

43. In the future, it is possible for migration patterns to be overseen by a global migration organization. France and Spain proposed the creation of a Global Migration Plan in 2006. "The proposal…will include guidelines for controlling borders along with ideas on how to help develop the sub-Saharan countries, the main source of illegal migrants [in Europe]." "Migration Crisis: France, Spain to Submit Joint Proposal," *Morocco Times*, Oct. 19, 2005, http://www.moroccotimes.com/paper/article.asp?idr=6&id=10414 (accessed Oct. 18, 2006). The nearest existing example of a Global Migration Plan is the United Nation's Report of the Global Commission on International Migration, *Migration in an Interconnected World: New Directions for Action* (Geneva, 2005).

44. California Rural Legal Assistance Foundation, "3 mil migrantes han muerto: ¿A alguien le importa?" (2004) http://www.stopgatekeeper.org/Espanol/index.html (accessed Feb. 3, 2007).

9. EDUCATION

1. Rodolfo Rosas Escobar, "Esfuerzos de la SEP para mejorar calidad en la educación pública en el 2005," Dec. 30, 2005, http://foros.fox.presidencia.gob.mx/read.php?29,165232 (accessed Dec. 13, 2006).

2. Ángel Hernández, "Retos de la Educación en México," *Revista Vértigo* (Jan. 15, 2005), http://www.revistavertigo.com/historico/15-1-2005/reportaje2.html (accessed Dec. 12, 2006).

3. Secretaría de Desarrollo Social, "Programa de Desarrollo Humano Oportunidades," http://www.sedesol.gob.mx/acciones/pasossedesol.pdf (accessed Dec. 11, 2006).

4. Organisation for Economic Co-operation and Development, "Education at a Glance 2006: Indicator A1; Educational Attainment of the Adult Population," http://www.oecd.org/document/6/0,2340,en_2649_37455_37344774_1_1_1_37455,00.html (accessed Dec. 12, 2006).

5. Rosas Escobar, "Esfuerzos de la SEP para mejorar calidad en la educación pública en el 2005."

6. Organisation for Economic Co-operation and Development, "Education at a Glance 2006: Highlights," 36, http://www.oecd.org/dataoecd/44/35/37376068.pdf (accessed Dec. 26, 2006).

7. Ibid., 14.

8. Organisation for Economic Co-operation and Development, "Education at a Glance 2005. Briefing Note for United States," http://www.oecd.org/dataoecd/41/13/35341210.pdf (accessed Dec. 26, 2006).

9. Organisation for Economic Co-operation and Development, "Education at a Glance 2006: Highlights," 30.

10. Organisation for Economic Co-operation and Development, "Education at a Glance 2005: Briefing Note for United States."

11. U.S. Department of Education, Office of the Secretary, "Answering the Challenge of a Changing World: Strengthening Education for the 21st Century," (Washington, D.C.: U.S. Office of Government Printing, 2006).

12. U.S. Department of Education, "Four Pillars of No Child Left Behind: Overview," http://www.ed.gov/nclb/overview/intro/4pillars.html (accessed Dec. 4, 2006).

13. Organisation for Economic Development and Co-operation, Centro de México, "Panorama de la Educación 2005. Breve nota sobre México," 2005, http://www.oecd.org/dataoecd/28/22/35354433.pdf (accessed Jan. 1, 2007).

14. Organisation for Economic Development and Co-operation, "Education at a Glance 2006: Highlights."

15. Richard Fry, "The Changing Landscape of American Public Education: New Students, New Schools" (Pew Hispanic Center, Oct. 5, 2006), http://pewhispanic.org/files/reports/72.pdf (accessed Dec. 12, 2006).

16. Institute of International Education, "Open Doors 2006," country fact sheets http://opendoors.iienetwork.org/?p=89245 (accessed Dec. 13, 2006).

17. Institute of International Education, "U.S. Sees Slowing Decline in International Student Enrollment 2004/2005," Nov. 14, 2005.

18. Ibid.

19. U.S. Department of Education, Office of the Secretary, *Answering the Challenge of a Changing World: Strengthening Education for the 21st century.*

20. The number of researchers in China increased by 77% between 1995 and 2004. The projections for China's R&D spending for the year 2006 were estimated at just over $136 billion, slightly more than Japan's forecasted $130 billion. The U.S., in comparison, was estimated to have spent just over $330 billion.
Organisation for Economic Co-operation and Development, "China Will Become the Second Highest Invest in R&D by the End of 2006, Finds OECD" (press release, Dec. 4, 2006), http://www.oecd.org/document/26/0,2340,en_2649_201185_37770522_1_1_1_1,00.html (accessed Dec. 4, 2006).

21. Organisation for Economic Development and Co-operation, "Education at a Glance 2006: Highlights," 27.

22. A precedent to this scenario is the Binational Migrant Education Program dating back to 1976 created to improve the education of students moving between border states and Mexico. U.S. Department of Education, "Strengthen Teacher Quality: Binational Migrant Education Program (BMEP)," http://www.ed.gov/admins/tchrqual/learn/binational.html (accessed Oct. 17, 2006).

23. Roger Lowenstein, "The Immigration Equation," *New York Times Magazine* (July 9, 2006): 39–41.

24. Study conducted between 1996 and 2001. Richard Fry, "Recent Changes in the Entry of Hispanic and White Youth into College" (Pew Hispanic Center, Nov. 1, 2005), http://pewhispanic.org/files/reports/56.pdf (accessed Dec. 26, 2006).

25. Roberto Suro, *Strangers Among Us: Latino Lives in a Changing America* (New York: Vintage, 1999), 15.

26. Graciela Orozco, Esther González, and Roger Díaz de Cossío, Las Organizaciones Mexico-Americanas, Hispanas y Mexicanas en Estados Unidos. (Mexico City, Fundación Solidaridad México-Americana: 2003), 20.

27. Katherine Leal Unmuth, "Bar is Low for Bilingual Teachers," *Dallas Morning News*, Nov. 27, 2006.

28. Secretaría de Educación Pública, "Maestros mexicanos bilingües impartirán clases en Texas" (press release, Feb. 9, 2006.), http://www.sep.gob.mx/wb2/sep/sep_Bol0330206 (accessed Dec. 13, 2006).

29. Notes from presentation, Alberto Arce, "Production Sharing competitive panel" (First Annual North American Integration Conference: Hyperborder, Ciudad Juárez, November 8, 2005).

30. Ibid.

10. ECONOMIC DEVELOPMENT AND TRADE

1. Kevin P. Gallagher and Lyuba Zarsky, "NAFTA, Foreign Direct Investment, and Sustainable Industrial Development in Mexico," Americas Program Policy Brief (Medford, MA: Tufts University, Jan. 28, 2004), http://ase.tufts.edu/gdae/Pubs/rp/AmerProgFDIJan04.pdf (accessed Dec. 25, 2006).

2. Campaña de Calidad Fronteriza de El Paso del Norte, et al., "Una Nueva Visión de Comercio a lo Largo de la Frontera México–U.S.A. Un Nuevo Sistema para Aumentar la Seguridad y Competitividad Fronteriza a través de Zonas de Manufactura Segura" (Dec., 2005), http://www.borderlegislators.org http://www.borderlegislators.org/PDF-Documents/Una%20Nueva%20Visión%20Fronteriza%2002-28.pdf (accessed Dec. 25, 2006).

3. Secretaría de Economía, "Negociaciones Comerciales," http://www.economia.gov.mx/index.jsp?P=2113 (accessed Dec. 1, 2006).

4. Jesus Cañas, Roberto Coronado, and Robert W. Gilmer, "Southwest Economy: U.S., Mexico Deepen Economic Ties," *Houston Business* (Federal Reserve Bank of Dallas) 1 (Jan.–Feb. 2006), http://www.dallasfed.org/research/houston/2005/hb0502.html (accessed Oct. 18, 2006).

5. Yves Engler, "Bush's Mexican Gambit: The Fallout from NAFTA," *Counterpunch* (Jan. 8, 2004), http://www.counterpunch.org/engler01082004.html (accessed Nov. 30, 2006).

6. Ibid.

7. Laura Carlsen, "The Strange Mission of Vicente Fox: Mexico's Ill-Conceived Push for Free Trade," *Counterpunch* (Dec. 8, 2005), http://www.counterpunch.org/carlsen12082005.html (accessed Nov. 30, 2006).

8. Robert E. Scott, "NAFTA's Impacts on the States," Economic Policy Institute, Apr. 2001, http://www.epinet.org/content.cfm/briefingpapers_nafta01_impactstates (accessed Oct. 17, 2006).

9. Ibid.

10. In an interview with Cuauhtémoc Cárdenas, one of Mexico's most prominent political figures, he expressed a favorable opinion for Mexico to join MERCOSUR and avoid subjugating agreements with the United States. "Entrevista a Cuauhtémoc Cárdenas," *Nueva Mayoria* (Apr. 20, 2004), http://www.nuevamayoria.com/ES/ENTREVISTAS/040420.html (accessed Dec. 25, 2006).

11. U.S. Census, "Top Trading Partners —Total Trade, Exports, Imports. October, 2006,"

12. Cañas, Coronado, and Gilmer, "Southwest Economy."

13. Border Trade Alliance, "Keeping the NAFTA Market Place Competitive," http://espanol.thebta.org/keyissues/NAFTACompetitiveness/NAFTACompetitiveness.cfm (accessed Dec. 25, 2006).

14. Lucinda Vargas, "Maquiladoras Impact on Texas Border Cities," *The Border Economy*, Federal Reserve Bank of Dallas (June 2001): 25.

15. Johanna Parra (PhD candidate, Centro de Investigaciones y Estudios Superiores en Antropología Social), in discussion with the author, May 22, 2006.

16. Engler, "Bush's Mexican Gambit."

17. TradeStats Express, National Trade Data, s.v. "U.S. Imports 2000–2005," http://tse.export.gov/MapFrameset.aspx?MapPage=NTDMapDisplay.aspx&UniqueURL=yxpj2a45si5rsb455ghey455-2006-12-1-21-6-14 (accessed Dec. 01, 2006).

18. U.S. Census, "Top Trading Partners—Total Trade, Exports, Imports. October, 2006," Year To Date Total, http://www.census.gov/foreign-trade/top/dst/2006/10/balance.html (accessed Jan. 1, 2007).

19. Some recent examples of Global Cities for Commerce along borders are the Special Economic Zones of China in cities like Shenzhen, Zhuhai, Shantou, and Xiamen. Another example are China's coastal cities designated for overseas investment: Dalian, Qinhuangdao, Tianjin, Yantai, Qingdao, Lianyungang, Nantong, Shanghai, Ningbo, Wenzhou, Fuzhou, Guangzhou, Zhanjiang, and Beihai. See "Special Economic Zones and Open Coastal Cities," China in Brief, http://www.china.org.cn/e-china/openingup/sez.htm (accessed Dec. 1, 2006).

20. The current account deficits (government deficit and accounts balance) in the United States make the U.S. dollar and economy vulnerable to international market fluctuations. Fred Bergsten, Director of the Institute for International Economics, explains: "The U.S. current account deficit has reached an annual rate of about $800 billion, about 7% of U.S. GDP. This is far beyond the traditional 'danger threshold' of 4–5% of GDP and almost double the previous U.S. record deficits in the middle 1980s—after which the dollar fell by 50% in two years."
C. Fred Bergsten, "The Dollar and the Twin Deficits," (summary of remarks in conference "The Top Ten Financial Risks to the Global Economy," Global Markets Institute, Goldman Sachs, New York, Sept. 22, 2005). http://www2.goldmansachs.com/our_firm/our_culture/corporate_citizenship/gmi/images/GMI_Panels/Bergsten_paper.pdf (accessed Dec. 26, 2006).

21. Engler, "Bush's Mexican Gambit."

22. Carlsen, "The Strange Mission of Vicente Fox."

23. According to SEDESOL, 47% of Mexicans were living with patrimony poverty, defined as the inability to meet one's health, clothing, food, education, housing, and public transportation with minimum daily wage of 41.8 pesos or less. Comite Técnico para la Medición de la Pobreza, "Medición de la Pobreza 2002–2004," Secretaría de Desarrollo Social, (Jun. 14, 2005) http://www.sedesol.gob.mx/prensa/comunicados/presentaciones/MediciondelaPobreza2002-2004.ppt
The World Bank reports 20.4% of Mexicans live on under $2 per day. The World Bank Group, "2006 World Development Indicators," http://devdata.worldbank.org/wdi2006/contents/Section2.htm (accessed Jan. 1, 2007).

24. Jesus Cañas, Roberto Coronado, and Robert W. Gilmer, "Trade, Manufacturing Put Mexico Back on Track in 2004," *Houston Business*, Federal Reserve Bank of Dallas (Mar. 2005), http://www.dallasfed.org/research/houston/2005/hb0502.html (accessed Oct. 17, 2006).

25. U.S. Department of State, "U.S.–Mexico Partnership for Prosperity" (Washington, D.C.: Office of the Press Secretary), http://www.state.gov/p/wha/rls/fs/8919.htm (accessed Oct. 18, 2006).

26. Marilyn Carr, in her article "Globalization and the Informal Economy: How Global Trade and Investment Impact on the Working Poor," WIEGO (May 2001), notes that "In

Latin America and the Caribbean 'modern' services are a fast growing export sector. The region also has a large well-educated female labor force. In fact, it is the only region where—in several countries—women's enrollments in schools outnumber those for men. In Jamaica and other Caribbean Islands, there are now many relatively prestigious and well-paid jobs for women in 'digiports' which focus for example on data entry for U.S. airlines companies." http://www.wiego.org/papers/carrchenglobalization.pdf#search=%22global%20trade%20cities%22 (accessed Oct. 17, 2006).

27. Trade corridors exist in North America, such as the Pacific corridor, the Central Western corridor, the Canamex corridor, the Central Eastern corridor, the Eastern corridor, and the NAFTA Super Corridor. Following the implementation of NAFTA, coalitions of interest have been formed in order to promote specific transport channels to develop the infrastructures of these channels and to propose jurisdictional amendments to facilitate the crossing of borders. These coalitions include businesses, government agencies, civil organizations, metropolitan areas, rural communities and also individuals, wishing to strengthen the commercial hubs of their regions. The North American trade corridors are bi- or trinational channels for which various cross-border interests have grouped together in order to develop or consolidate the infrastructures. The North American corridors are considered multimodal in the sense that they bring into play different modes of transport in succession. The infrastructures may include roads, highways, transit routes, airports, pipelines, railways and train stations, river canal systems and port facilities, telecommunications networks, and teleports. North American Forum on Integration, "The North American Corridors," http://www.fina-nafi.org/eng/integ/corridors.asp?langue=eng&menu=integ (accessed Oct. 18, 2006).

28. Augusto Lopez-Claros, "Executive Summary," in World Economic Forum, *Global Competitiveness Report 2006–2007* (New York: Palgrave Macmillan, 2006).

29. World Economic Forum, Global Competitiveness Report 2006–2007.

30. Jorge Herrera, "Prevé OCDE Focos Amarillos de México en Competitividad," *El Universal*, Mar. 16, 2006.

31. Ibid.

32. GDP growth for 2007 and 2008 is expected to grow 3.5% to 4% compared to 2006. Organization for Economic Co-operation and Development, "OECD Economic Outlook No. 80—Mexico" (Nov. 28, 2006), http://www.oecd.org/dataoecd/6/36/20213236.pdf (accessed Dec. 01, 2006).

33. Jorge Herrera, "Prevé OCDE Focos Amarillos de México en Competitividad."

34. In the interest of competitiveness, the first Bush Administration established the Council on Competitiveness, headed by Vice President Dan Quayle. The Council forced changes in the Environmental Protection Agency's regulations, among other things in order to protect the interests of U.S. businesses. When NAFTA was being devised, environmentalists succeeded in gaining certain provisions that protect the environment; however, ambiguous language and a lack of strong guarantees in the trade agreement make it possible for environmental standards to be overstepped in the name of efficient trade. Tom Barry, Harry Browne, and Beth Sims, "Free Trade: The Ifs, Ands and Buts," *The Great Divide: The Challenge of U.S.–Mexican Relations in the 1990s* (New York: Gross Press, 1994).

35. Some signposts for this scenario include the signing of the Security and Prosperity Partnership (SPP) that was publicly stated on March 23, 2005 by President Bush, President Fox, and Prime Minister Martin. Other signposts include the Independent Task Force for the Future of North America, part of the Council on Foreign Relations and the North American Forum on Integration in Montreal, Québec. Prominent authors writing on behalf of a North American Community include Robert A. Pastor and Andrés Rozental, among others.

36. Canada Border Services Agency, "The Free and Secure Trade Program," http://www.cbsa-asfc.gc.ca/import/fast/menu-e.html (accessed Dec. 26, 2006).

37. Ibid.

38. Bob Willard is a widely known consultant in sustainability strategies for corporations. He estimates a 46% increase in profits in five years. Bob Willard, "The Sustainability Advantage," http://www.sustainabilityadvantage.com/adv.html (accessed Jan. 1, 2007).

39. Steve Schueth, "U.N. Launches Principles for Responsible Investment," GreenBiz.com, http://www.greenbiz.com/news/reviews_third.cfm?NewsID=32753 (accessed Oct. 17, 2006).

40. Since the Dow Jones Sustainability North America Index was created in late 2005, the total return on investment has been 11.71%, representing a similar ROI than the Dow Jones Industrial Average annual total return of 11.97% since inception in 1991. Dow Jones Sustainability Indexes, "Dow Jones Sustainability North America Index. Fact Sheet," http://www.sustainability-indexes.com/djsi_pdf/publications/Factsheets/DJSI_NA.pdf (accessed Jan. 1, 2007), and Dow Jones Indexes, "Dow Jones Select Dividend Index Summary," http://averages.dowjones.com/mdsidx/downloads/Quarterly_Rpts/Select_Div_4Q2005.pdf (accessed Jan. 1, 2007).

41. Klaus Toepfer, "Editorial," *Our Planet* vol. 16., no. 4, "Renewable Energy," (2006): 3. http://www.ourplanet.com/imgversn/164/full_pdfs/Our_Planet_16.4_english.pdf (accessed Dec.1, 2006).

42. The Chicago Climate Exchange, "Background on GHGs and Global Warming," http://www.chicagoclimatex.com/environment/background.html (accessed Dec. 26, 2006).

43. Alana Herro, "Kyoto: Impossible Goal or Economic Opportunity?" Eye on Earth, http://www.worldwatch.org/node/4362 (accessed Dec. 1, 2006).

44. "James L. Connaughton, the chairman of the Council on Environmental Quality, and other administration officials said they are focused on obtaining practical commitments

industrialized countries can meet without damaging their economies. He said that although some G-8 countries are struggling to meet their goal of bringing greenhouse gas emissions down to 1990 levels by 2012, the United States is on track to fulfill its pledge to reduce its carbon intensity—how much emissions are rising relative to overall economic growth—18 percent by 2012." Juliet Eilperin, "Climate Plan Splits U.S. and Europe; Parties Dicker on Draft for G-8 Talks," *Washington Post*, July 2, 2005.

11. TRANSPORTATION

1. Asim Khan, "Urban Air Pollution in Megacities of the World," *Green Times* (Spring 1997), http://dolphin.upenn.edu/~pennenv/greentimes/spring97/air_asim.html (accessed Dec. 2, 2006).

2. U.S. Census Bureau, "Mean Time Travel to Work," 2000 Census of Population and Housing, Demographic Profile, http://quickfacts.census.gov/qfd/states/00000.html (accessed Dec. 26, 2006).

3. In 2001 there were 107.4 million households in the United States, of which nearly 98.9 million (92%) owned or possessed one or more vehicles, an increase of 1.8% per year from 1983, when 86%, or 72.2 million out of 84.4 million households, possessed one or more vehicles. Energy Information Administration, "Household Vehicles Energy Use: Latest Data & Trends" (report, Nov. 2005), http://www.eia.doe.gov/emeu/rtecs/nhts_survey/2001/ (accessed Dec. 26, 2006).

4. National Highway Research and Technology Partnership, "Highway Research and Technology: The Need for Greater Investment" (Apr. 2002), http://onlinepubs.trb.org/onlinepubs/rtforum/HwyRandT.pdf (accessed Dec. 26, 2006).

5. Laura Carlsen, "The Strange Mission of Vicente Fox: Mexico's Ill-Conceived Push for Free Trade," *Counterpunch* (Dec. 8, 2005), http://www.counterpunch.org/carlsen12082005.html (accessed Dec. 2, 2006).

6. In 2004, 318,000 vehicles were sold. CONAPO reported 160,000 new births in Mexico City. Univision Online, "Habrá Más Autos que Bebés en México" (2004) http://www.univision.com/content/content.jhtml;jsessionid=KV45TQ0KJOGIQCWIAA4SFFAKZAAGAIWC?cid=352672 (accessed Dec. 2, 2006).

7. While the mortality rates from transport accidents are similar in both countries as of 2002 (U.S.: 16.3 deaths/1,000 people; Mexico: 16.2 deaths/1,000 people), there are more transport-related deaths in the United States due to its higher vehicle ownership and population. The World Health Organization estimated that by the year 2020 "road traffic crashes would be the second leading cause of mortality and morbidity in developing countries. This is in contrast to higher-income countries where long-term development means that vehicle use evolves at a slower pace, allowing road safety efforts to evolve in parallel." The Pan American Health Organization (PAHO) reports that in the United States, the leading cause of death for Hispanics under thirty-four years of age is traffic accidents. PAHO, "World Health Day 2004: Road Safety," http://www.paho.org/english/dd/pin/whd04_features.htm (accessed Oct. 18, 2006); PAHO, "Regional Core Health Data Initiative: Table Generator System," http://www.paho.org/English/SHA/coredata/tabulator/newTabulator.htm (accessed Sept. 15, 2006).

8. César Sánchez, "Exporta México Más Autos," *Reforma*, June 9, 2006.

9. Alvin Toffler and Heidi Toffler, *Revolutionary Wealth* (New York: Knopf, 2006), 356.

10. 1,790,382 full rail containers, versus 8,666,091 full truck containers in 2004. U.S. Bureau of Transportation, "TransStats," http://www.transtats.bts.gov/Fields.asp?Table_ID=1358 (accessed Oct. 18, 2006).

11. The Atlantic Corridor's Continental location, from the North American Trade Corridors, has the aim of developing an international corridor for trade and tourism between Toronto, Ontario, and Miami, Florida. North American Forum on Integration, "The North American Corridors," http://www.fina-nafi.org/eng/integ/corridors.asp?langue=eng&menu=integ (accessed Oct. 18, 2006).

12. In 2004, the United States consumed 20.7 million barrels of oil/day, making it the biggest oil consumer in the world. China, Japan, Germany, and Russia followed with 6.5, 5.4, 2.6, and 2.6 mb/d, respectively. That year, 12.1 mb/d of oil were imported in the U.S. Energy Information Administration, "Top World Oil Tables," http://www.eia.doe.gov/emeu/cabs/topworldtables3_4.html (accessed Oct. 18, 2006).

13. Lester Brown, "Beyond the Oil Peak," in *Plan B 2.0: Rescuing a Planet Under Stress and a Civilization in Trouble* (New York: W.W. Norton & Company, 2006).

14. John B. Heywood, "Fueling Our Transportation Future," *Scientific American* (Sept. 2006): 36–39.

15. Brown, "Beyond the Oil Peak." (accessed Dec. 2, 2006)

16. Lester R. Brown, "Eco-Economy Update 2006–9," Earth Policy Institute (Oct. 4, 2006), http://www.earth-policy.org/Updates/2006/Update59.htm (accessed Dec. 2, 2006); Energy Information Administration, "Emissions of Greenhouse Gases in the United States 2005" (Nov. 2006), ftp://ftp.eia.doe.gov/pub/oiaf/1605/cdrom/pdf/ggrpt/057305.pdf (accessed Dec. 2, 2006).

17. International Energy Agency, "World Energy Outlook 2004" (2004), 58, http://www.iea.org/textbase/nppdf/free/2004/weo2004.pdf (accessed Dec. 26, 2006).

18. Brian Halweil, "Home Grown: The Case for Local Food in a Global Market.," (Worldwatch Paper 163, Worldwatch Institute, Washington, D.C., 2002), 6.

19. International Center for Technology Assessment, "The Real Price of Gasoline," (Washington, D.C., Nov. 1998).

20. Halweil, "Home Grown," 26–27.

21. In 2004, 835,832 empty rail containers and 2,622,197 empty truck containers entered the U.S. U.S. Bureau of Transportation, "TransStats."

22. A local congressman who fears it as a magnet for illegal immigrants and drug dealers has blocked a federal loan guarantee for the Metropolitan Transit Development Board, owner of the U.S. tracks. Transportation Equity Act for the 21st Century (TEA 21) contains $10 million to build a South Bay rail yard but nothing toward the $100 million-plus required to repair and modernize SD&AE. Nonfederal funding possibilities include the State Highway Accounts Fund or the State Infrastructure Bank. In Mexico, RailTex of San Antonio, which had a temporary concession to operate the tracks between Tijuana and Tecate, was outbid for the permanent concession by Grupo Murphy. However, the necessary private financing has not yet materialized, with the result that the privatization of the rail operation is in limbo and the bidding process will have to be reopened. Steven P. Erie, "Toward a Trade Infrastructure Strategy for the San Diego/Tijuana Region" (paper presented at San Diego Dialogue's *Fronterizo* Forum, San Diego, Feb. 1999), http://sandiegodialogue.org/pdfs/Infrappr%20doc.pdf (accessed Oct. 18, 2006).

23. There is still hope, however, that the governor of the State of Chihuahua may adopt the project and continue moving it forward. Institute for Transportation and Development Policy, *Sustainable Transport* 17 (Winter 2005), http://www.itdp.org/ST/ST17/ST17.pdf (accessed Oct. 18, 2006).

24. Paul Ganster, "Tijuana, Basic Information" (Institute for Regional Studies of the Californias, San Diego State University), http://www-rohan.sdsu.edu/~irsc/tjreport/tj1.html (accessed Oct. 18, 2006).

25. Martin Wachs, "A Quiet Crisis in Transportation Finance: Options for Texas," (RAND Corporation, Apr. 2006), http://www.rand.org/pubs/testimonies/2006/RAND_CT260.pdf (accessed Oct. 18, 2006).

26. Secretaría de Comunicaciones y Transportes, "Programa Sectorial de Comunicaciones y Transportes 2001–2006," (Mexico City, Dec. 2001) : 71 http://dgp.sct.gob.mx/fileadmin/user_upload/Documentos/Programas/Programa_Sectorial_2001-2006/CAP-04.pdf (accessed Jan. 1, 2007).

27. W. Brad Jones, C. Richard Cassady, and Royce O. Bowden, Jr., "Developing a Standard Definition of Intermodal Transportation" (National Center for Intermodal Transportation, University of Denver and Mississippi State University), http://www.ie.msstate.edu/ncit/NCIT_WEB_UPDATE/Final%20Report%20Developing%20a%20Standard%20Definition%20for%20Intermodal%20Transportation.htm (accessed Oct. 18, 2006).

28. Paul Stephen Dempsey and Theodore Prince, "Investing in America's Future: The Need for an Enlightened Transportation Policy" (Intermodal Transportation Institute, University of Denver, Sept. 2004), 9, http://www.du.edu/transportation/Resources/pdfs/ITIWhitePaper.9.2004.pdf (accessed Dec. 26, 2006).

12. ENERGY

1. Marion King Hubbert, "Nuclear Energy and the Fossil Fuels," *Drilling and Production Practice* 95 (June 1956): 24–25. See also Michael C. Ruppert, *Crossing the Rubicon: The Decline of the American Empire at the End of the Age of Oil*, ed. Jamey Hecht (British Columbia: New Society Publishers, 2004).

2. Mark Williams, "The End of Oil? There are Good Signs that Worldwide Oil Production is Declining. Best Hold on Tight," *Technology Review: An MIT Enterprise* (Feb. 2005), http://www.technologyreview.com/read article.aspx?id=14178&ch=biztech (accessed July 6, 2006).

3. Francis De Winter and Ronald B. Swenson, "Dawn of the Solar Era: A Wake-Up Call," *Solar Today* (Mar./Apr. 2006), http://www.solartoday.org/2006/mar_apr06/wake_up.htm (accessed July 13, 2006). Gary Stix, among other experts, contends: "Even if oil production peaks soon—a debatable contention given Canada's oil sands, Venezuela's heavy oil and other reserves—coal and its derivatives could tide the earth over for more than a century." Gary Stix, "A Climate Repair Manual," *Scientific American* (Sept. 2006): 24–27.

4. Bhushan Bahree and Chip Cummins, "El Mercado global del petróleo, camino a una nueva era de conflicto y escasez" *Wall Street Journal Americas*, June 12, 2006.

5. De Winter and Swenson, "Dawn of the Solar Era."

6. Frank Verrastro, "Energy Information Administration 2005 Annual Energy Outlook" (testimony before the Committee on Energy and Natural Resources, United States Senate, "Emerging Global Energy Trends and Their Implications for U.S. Energy Needs, Security and Policy Choices," Feb. 3, 2005), http://energy.senate.gov/public/index.cfm?FuseAction=Hearings.Testimony&Hearing_ID=1367&Witness_ID=3951 (accessed July 12, 2006).

7. Ibid.

8. Ibid.

9. Ibid.

10. Ibid.

11. Geri Smith, "Pemex May Be Turning From Gusher to Black Hole," *Business Week* (Dec. 13, 2004).

12. Kevin G. Hall, "Mexican Oilfield Crucial to the U.S. Facing Decline," *Knight Ridder Newspapers*, Mar. 16, 2006, http://www.myrtlebeachonline.com/mld/myrtlebeachonline/news/nation/14116129.htm (accessed June 26, 2006).

13. Ibid.

14. Private investment in PEMEX is a delicate political issue in Mexico. Many reforms to the energy sector were proposed in the 2004–2005 legislative year. Among those proposals to reform the funding-sources for the oil industry are those by Fayad-Hopkins (Pemex as a public interest organization); Genaro Borrego Estrada (A corporative government looking after the public's interest); Jorge Chávez Presa (Opening non-associated gas to private capital investment); Grupo Monterrey (Investment funds and natural gas reform); José Luis Alberro (A North American

energy fund). David Shields, *Pemex: La Reforma Petrolera* (Mexico City, Temas de Hoy, 2005).

15. "Mexico estimates, using geological studies, it has oil reserves yet to be discovered of fifty-four billion barrels that would add to the existing proven reserves of 11.8 billion barrels," stated Fernando Canales, Mexico's Energy Secretary. "The potential reserves had not been explored since the country had no need to find new oil sources." In 2004, however, the Cantarell oil field's production started declining, forcing the country to look for oil 4,000 meters deep in the ocean. Agence France-Presse, "México con Grandes Reservas de Crudo," *El Nuevo Diario* (July 25, 2006) http://www.elnuevodiario.com.ni/2006/07/25/ultimahora/1333 (accessed Dec. 2, 2006).

16. Verrastro, "Energy Information Administration 2005 Annual Energy Outlook."

17. Bahree and Cummins, "El Mercado global del petróleo, camino a una nueva era de conflicto y escasez."

18. Verrastro, "Energy Information Administration 2005 Annual Energy Outlook."

19. Odón de Buen Rodrígues and José A. González Martínez, "Energy Efficiency in the Northern Border States," in David A. Rohy, ed., *The U.S.–Mexican Border Environment: Trade, Energy and the Environment: Challenges and Opportunities for the Border Region, Now and in 2020* (San Diego: San Diego State University Press, 2003), 191.

20. "Energy Development on the U.S.–Mexico Border," Americas Program Issue Brief (Silver City, NM: Interhemispheric Resource Center, June 14, 2002). Adapted from the report "Conclusions and Recommendations of Border Institute III," by the Southwest Center for Environmental Research and Policy (SCERP), http://americas.irc-online.org/briefs/2002/0206energy_body.html (accessed July 11, 2006).

21. Alan Sweedler, Margarito Quintero Núñez, and Kimberly Collins, "Energy Issues in the U.S.-Mexican Binational Region: Focus on California–Baja California," in Rohy, ed., *U.S.–Mexican Border Environment*, 81.

22. Alan Sweedler, "Energy and Environment in Mexico: Focus on the U.S.–Mexico Binational Region" (Center for Energy Studies, San Diego State University), http://www.iamericas.org/events/materials/journalism/ Periodismo/Sweedler.pdf (accessed July 11, 2006).

23. Ibid.

24. Sweedler, Quintero Núñez, and Collins, "Energy Issues in the U.S.–Mexican Binational Region."

25. Sweedler, "Energy and Environment in Mexico."

26. "Energy Development on the U.S.–Mexico Border."

27. Verrastro, "Energy Information Administration 2005 Annual Energy Outlook."

28. David A. Rohy, "The Interdependence of Water and Energy in the U.S.–Mexico Border Region," in Rohy, ed., *U.S.–Mexican Border Environment*, 118.

29. Ibid., 109.

30. Ibid., 119.

31. Sweedler, "Energy and Environment in Mexico."

32. Ronald B. Swenson, "Can Solar Energy Replace Oil?" (International Solar Energy Society (ISES) at Hubbert's Peak Forum, 2005), http://www.ecotopia.com/ISES (accessed July 12, 2006).

33. Joseph Florence, "Global Wind Power Expands," Earth Policy Institute (June 28, 2006), http://www.earth-policy.org/Indicators/Wind/2006.htm (accessed July 12, 2006).

34. Ibid.

35. David Gram, "Cow Power: A Renewable Energy Resource," *Associated Press*, June 30, 2006, http://www.comcast.net/news/science/index.jsp?cat=SCIENCE&fn=/2006/06/30/424738.html (accessed June 30, 2006).

36. Shell International, "Exploring the Future: Energy Needs, Choices and Possibilities; Scenarios to 2050" (2001), 18, http://www.shell.com/static/media-en/downloads/51852.pdf (accessed July 5, 2006).

37. Ibid.

13. ENVIRONMENT

1. Comisión Nacional para el Conocimiento y Uso de la Biodiversidad (CONABIO), "Capital natural y bienestar social" (June 29, 2006), http://www.conabio.gob.mx/2ep/index.php/Capital_natural_y_bienestar_social (accessed Dec. 26, 2006).

2. Greenpeace México, "Bosques y Selvas," http://www.greenpeace.org/mexico/campaigns/bosques-y-selvas-de-m-eacute-x (accessed Jan. 1, 2007).

3. Greenpeace México reports a loss of $7.5 billion yearly, while CONABIO's president José Sarukhán reports losses of $6.5 billion annually. Considering Mexico's GDP in 2004 was about $157 billion, the average of $7 billion in ecological losses amounts to about 4% of the country's GDP. CONABIO's numbers are calculated based on an annual average between 1996 and 2003. See Greenpeace México, "La destrucción de México: Consecuencias económicas y sociales de la devastación ambiental" (June 5, 2006), http://www.greenpeace.org/raw/content/mexico/press/reports/la-destrucci-n-de-mexico-cons.pdf (accessed Jan. 1, 2007); José Sarukhán, "Capital Natural y Bienestar Social" (press conference at the Museo Nacional de Antropología, Mexico City, June 12, 2006).

4. Comisión Nacional para el Conocimiento, "Capital natural," 2007.

5. United Nations Environment Program, "GEO 3 Fact Sheets on Regions (North America). Past and Present: 1972 to 2002," http://www.unep.org/GEO/pdfs/GEO-3%20Fact%20sheet%20N%20America.pdf (accessed Jan. 1, 2007).

6. Carmen Maganda, interview with Alejandro Quinto for *Hyperborder*, Nov. 2005.

7. U.S. National Atlas, "Water Use in the United States," http://nationalatlas.gov/articles/water/a_wateruse.html (accessed Oct. 20, 2006). Latest year recorded is 2000.

8. Elizabeth Mygatt, "World's Water Resources Face Mounting Pressure," Eco-Economy Indicators (Earth Policy Institute, July 26, 2006), http://www.earth-policy.org/Indicators/Water/2006.htm (accessed Oct. 20, 2006).

9. Mexico water availability sources taken from Comisión Nacional para el Conocimiento, "Capital natural." Water scarcity defined by the United Nations Environment Programme is 1,000 to 1,700 cubic meters of water per person available each year. United Nations Environment Programme, "Definitions of Water Stress and Scarcity." http://www.unep.org/vitalwater/21.htm

10. Water demand is expected to increase from 17 million acre-feet in 2010 to 21.6 million acre-feet by 2060. Texas Water Development Board, "2007 Draft State Water Plan," http://www.twdb.state.tx.us/publications/reports/State_Water_Plan/2007/Draft_2007SWP.htm (accessed Oct. 20, 2006).

11. Water supplies refer to the amount of water that can be produced with current permits, current contracts, and existing infrastructure during drought. This decrease is due to the accumulation of sediments in reservoirs and depletion of aquifers. Texas Water Development Board, "2007 Draft State Water Plan."

12. Carmen Maganda, interview with Alejandro Quinto.

13. Agencies, "El Senado de EEUU Aprueba la Construcción de un Muro en la Frontera con México," *El Mundo*, May 18, 2006, http://www.elmundo.es/elmundo/2006/05/17/internacional/1147894654.html (accessed Nov. 20, 2006).

14. Zimmerman, "Border Protections Imperil Environment."

15. Considering water supplies in Ciudad Juárez and El Paso are expected to run dry, a potential solution to meet the water demands of the region and to pay back Mexico's water debts would be to import water. The problem of water shortages has been highlighted many times in the past. See, for instance, Diego Cevallos, "Sin agua al sur del Rio Bravo," *Tierramérica*, http://www.tierramerica.net/2001/0520/articulo.shtml (accessed Dec. 2, 2006): "Due to an eight-year drought, the region was 1,700 cubic meters of water in debt to the United States and must invest around 1.52 billion dollars in the next five years to avoid supply difficulties in both cities and rural areas. Problems will worsen, authorities claim, if water is not managed in a more efficient manner in the rural areas of the border region, where 80% of the region's consumption takes place."

16. See U.S. National Academy of Sciences, *Climate Change Science: An Analysis of Some Key Questions* (Washington, D.C.: The National Academies Press, 2001).

17. "Global Warming Basics" (Pew Center on Global Climate Change, Arlington, VA), http://www.pewclimate.org/global-warming-basics/ (accessed Aug. 9, 2006).

18. The figures released by the EPA show that while the U.S. economy expanded by 51% from 1990 to 2004, total U.S. greenhouse gas emissions increased 15.8% in the same period. Environmental Protection Agency, "Inventory of U.S. Greenhouse Gas Emissions and Sinks: 1990–2004" (Apr. 15, 2006), ES-3, http://www.epa.gov/climatechange/emissions/downloads06/06_Complete_Report.pdf (accessed Dec. 2, 2006). See also Environmental Protection Agency, "The Kyoto Protocol and the President's Policies to Address Climate Change: Trends in Greenhouse Gas Emissions," (July 1998), http://yosemite.epa.gov/OAR/globalwarming.nsf/uniqueKeyLookup/SHSU5BWJXD/$file/wh_full_rpt.pdf?OpenElement (accessed Dec. 26, 2006).

19. Energy Information Administration, "Emissions of Greenhouse Gases in the United States 2005" (Nov. 2006), ftp://ftp.eia.doe.gov/pub/oiaf/1605/cdrom/pdf/ggrpt/057305.pdf (accessed Dec. 2, 2006).

20. Comisión Nacional para el Conocimiento, "Capital natural."

21. According to the USDA, "farmer adaptations are the main mechanisms for keeping up world food production under global climate change. By selecting the most profitable mix of inputs and outputs on existing cropland, for example, farmers may be able to offset from 79 to 88 percent of the 19- to 30-percent reductions in world cereals (wheat plus other grains) supply directly attributable to climate change." Roy Darwin, et al., "World Agriculture and Climate Change: Economic Adaptations," Agricultural Economic Report No. 703 (U.S. Department of Agriculture, Natural Resources and Environment Division, Economic Research Service, Washington, D.C., 1995).

22. Lester R. Brown, "Global Warming Forcing U.S. Coastal Population to Move Inland," Earth Policy Institute, http://www.earth-policy.org/Updates/2006/Update57.htm (accessed Aug. 16, 2006).

23. Ibid.

24. The Central Bank of Mexico (Banxico) recorded in 2005 the first fall in agricultural production in thirteen years in their 2005 annual report. "Informe Anual 2005" (April, 2006), Banco de México, http://www.banxico.org.mx/publicadorFileDownload/download?documentId={5AA1E2B9-58FE-147D-C97B-6B9E7406630B} (accessed Nov. 1, 2006).

25. According to CONABIO, 65% of basic grains in Mexico are produced in the country. However, the National Farmers Chamber (Camara Cámara Nacional Campesina, CNC), reports 50% of all grains in Mexico are imported. Comisión Nacional para el Conocimiento y Uso de la Biodiversidad, "Capital natural y bienestar social."

26. Today, the four largest meatpacking companies in the United States—ConAgra, IBP, Excel, and National Beef—slaughter 84% of the nation's cattle. Eric Schlosser, *Fast Food Nation: The Dark Side of the All-American Meal* (New York: Houghton Mifflin, 2001), 137.

27. "Benefits of NAFTA" (PowerPoint presentation, U. S. Department of Agriculture, Foreign Agricultural Service, 2006), http://www.fas.usda.gov/itp/Policy/NAFTA/NAFTA_Overview_2006.htm (accessed Aug. 17, 2006).

28. Danielle Murray, "Oil and Food: A Rising Security Challenge," Earth Policy Institute (May 9, 2005), http://www.earth-policy.org/Updates/2005/Update48.htm (accessed Dec. 26, 2006).

29. Daniel Chacón (BECC, General Manager, Ciudad Juárez, Chihuahua), interview with Alejandro Quinto for *Hyperborder*, June 25, 2006.

30. Alma D. Cota Espericueta, et al., "Evaluación de 52 Sistemas Fotovoltaicos de Bombeo de Agua Instalados en México a Través del PERM" (Congreso Mundial de Energía Renovable, Centro de Convenciones, Guanajuato, Gto., México, Nov. 8–12, 2004), http://www.re.sandia.gov/en/pb/pd/alma%20ISES%20AR%2027-01.pdf (accessed Dec. 26, 2006).

31. United Nations Environment Program, "GEO 3 Fact Sheets on Regions (North America)."

14. HEALTH

1. Alvin Toffler and Heidi Toffler, *Revolutionary Wealth* (New York: Knopf, 2006).

2. Department of Health and Human Services, Centers for Disease Control and Prevention, "Chronic Disease Prevention," http://www.cdc.gov/nccdphp/ (accessed Aug. 23, 2006).

3. United States Department of Health and Human Services, "New Surgeon General's Report Focuses on the Effects of Secondhand Smoke" (press release, June 27, 2006), http://www.hhs.gov/news/press/2006pres/20060627.html (accessed Aug. 23, 2006).

4. University of Houston, "Sex Workers in Border Regions Potential Source for HIV/AIDS Spread; UH Study: Free Trade, Globalization May Be Factors in Spread of AIDS in Americas" (press release, Dec. 2, 2002), http://www.uh.edu/admin/media/nr/2002/122002/valdezaids12022002.htm (accessed Aug. 22, 2006).

5. Data from latest year available, 2004. Organisation for Economic Co-operation and Development, "OECD Health Data 2006" (June 2006), http://www.oecd.org/document/30/0,2340,en_2825_495642_12968734_1_1_1_1,00.html (accessed Sept. 13, 2006).

6. California Health Care Foundation, "Health Care Costs 101" (Mar. 2, 2005), http://www.chcf.org/documents/insurance/HCCosts10105.pdf (accessed Dec. 2, 2006).

7. David C. Warner, "Health Workforce Needs: Opportunities for U.S.–Mexico Collaboration," *Responding to Unmet Needs through International Collaboration for Health Professionals: The Case of the U.S. and Mexico* (Conference Proceedings and Background Papers, Center for Health and Social Policy, Lyndon B. Johnson School of Public Affairs, University of Texas at Austin, Nov. 2003).

8. Ibid.

9. The private health care system in Tijuana includes individual and group practices and clinics (800, including medical and dental); 133 private hospitals; 127 laboratories; and 651 pharmacies. The client base includes Tijuana residents who can afford to pay for the services as well as San Diego and other U.S. residents, who opt for services in Tijuana because of lower cost, Spanish-speaking health care providers, and/or availability of therapies or drugs not available in their home country. Paul Ganster, "Tijuana, Basic Information" (Institute for Regional Studies of the Californias [IRSC], San Diego State University), http://www-rohan.sdsu.edu/~irsc/tjreport/tj1.html (accessed Oct. 23, 2006).

10. Warner, "Health Workforce Needs."

11. Ibid.

12. Ibid.

13. Jennifer Eldridge, "Health Care Access for Immigrants in Texas" (working paper from the Policy Research Project on Expanding Health Care Coverage for the Uninsured, the Lyndon B. Johnson School of Public Affairs, University of Texas at Austin, May, 2002).

14. Ibid.

15. National Center for Chronic Disease Prevention and Health, "U.S.–Mexico Border Diabetes Prevention and Control Project," http://www.cdc.gov/DIABETES/projects/border.htm (accessed Dec. 26, 2006); Secretaría de Salud, "Salud: México 2001–2005," 120 http://evaluacion.salud.gob.mx/saludmex2005/SM-2001-05cap2.pdf (accessed Dec. 26, 2006); National Institute of Diabetes and Digestive and Kidney Diseases, "National Diabetes Statistics," http://diabetes.niddk.nih.gov/dm/pubs/statistics/index.htm#7 (accessed Dec. 2, 2006).

16. United States–Mexico Border Health Commission, "Border 2010: An Agenda for Improving Health on the United States–Mexico Border" (Oct. 2003), 24, http://www.borderhealth.org/files/res_63.pdf (accessed Dec. 2, 2006).

17. Lester R. Brown, "Obesity Epidemic Threatens Health in Exercise-Deprived Societies," Earth Policy Institute (Dec. 19, 2000), http://www.earth-policy.org/Alerts/Alert11.htm (accessed Dec. 2, 2006).

18. Pan American Health Organization, "Prevalence of Overweight among Adult Population (20–74 years)," Table Generator System, http://www.paho.org/English/SHA/coredata/tabulator/newTabulator.htm (accessed Dec. 2, 2006). Based on country information. Data for Mexico: 1999; data for United States: 2001. See also "U.S. People Getting Fatter, Fast," BBC News (Aug. 25, 2005), http://news.bbc.co.uk/2/hi/health/4183086.stm (accessed Oct. 23, 2006).

19. "Redefining and Reforming Health Care for the Last Years of Life" (research brief, RAND Corporation, 2006), http://www.rand.org/pubs/research_briefs/2006/RAND_RB9178.pdf (accessed Oct. 23, 2006).

20. The President's Council on Bioethics, "Taking Care: Ethical Caregiving in our Aging Society" (Washington, D.C., Sept. 2005), http://www.bioethics.gov/reports/taking_care/taking_care.pdf (accessed Aug. 23, 2006).

21. Luis Miguel Gutiérrez Robledo and Emilio José García Mayo, "United Nations Expert Group Meeting on Social and Economic Implications Of Changing Populations Age Structure" (Salud y Envejecimiento de la Población en

México, Mexico City, Aug. 31–Sept. 2, 2005), http://www.aarp.org/research/international/map/facts/a2004-03-19-globalaging-map-mexico.html (accessed Aug. 22, 2006).

22. Ibid.

23. American Hospital Association, "Trends Affecting Hospitals and Health Systems," Trendwatch Chartbook 2002 (Washington, D.C.: The Lewin Group, Nov. 2002).

24. Warner, "Health Workforce Needs."

25. Toffler and Toffler, Revolutionary Wealth.

26. "Redefining and Reforming Health Care for the Last Years of Life."

27. Warner, "Health Workforce Needs."

28. Seguro Popular, "El Seguro Popular beneficia ya a 4 Millones de Familias" (press release, Aug. 25, 2006), http://www.seguro-popular.gob.mx/contenido.php?ntc_id=10 (accessed Dec. 26, 2006).

29. Secretaría de Salud, "Iniciativa de Saludo México-California," http://www.saludmigrante.salud.gob.mx/acciones/inica1i.htm (accessed Dec. 2, 2006).

30. "Health Highlights: June 21, 2006," (Forbes.com), http://www.forbes.com/forbeslife/health/feeds/hscout/2006/06/21/hscout533380.html (accessed Oct. 23, 2006).

31. Organisation for Economic Co-operation and Development, "OECD Health Data 2006."

32. Dr. David C. Warner at the LBJ School of Public Affairs, University of Texas at Austin, has dedicated many years of research to the topic of health insurance portability across borders—the potential of Medicare to be used by Americans in Mexico, which could benefit the many Americans who have retired in Mexico as well as binational residents who commute across the border on a daily basis.

15. URBANIZATION

1. Saskia Sassen, interview with Blake Harris (June 1, 1997), http://www.govtech.net/magazine/story.php?id=95352&issue=6:1997 (accessed Dec. 3, 2006).

2. Lester R. Brown, "Designing Sustainable Cities," in Plan B 2.0: Rescuing a Planet Under Stress and a Civilization in Trouble (New York: W.W. Norton & Company, 2006)

3. Romeo S. Rodríguez Suárez and Carlos Esponda Velásquez, "Programa Vete Sano. Regresa Sano," http://www.saludmigrante.salud.gob.mx/acciones/vesano.htm (accessed Dec. 3, 2006).

4. James Peach and James Williams, "Population Dynamics of the U.S.–Mexican Border Region, 2003" (San Diego: SCERP/SDSU Press, forthcoming), http://www.scerp.org/population.htm (accessed Dec. 26, 2006).

5. Ariel Cisneros, "Texas Colonias: Housing and Infrastructure Issues," The Border Economy (Federal Reserve Bank of Dallas, June 2001), http://www.dallasfed.org/research/border/tbe_cisneros.html (accessed Aug. 15, 2006).

6. Ibid.

7. Mike Davis, "Slum Like It Not," Grist Magazine (Mar. 29, 2006), http://www.grist.org/news/maindish/2006/03/29/davis/ (accessed Aug. 15, 2006).

8. Carlos Gutiérrez Ruiz, "Debe privilegiarse el desarrollo vertical de las ciudades para desalentarse el crecimiento difuso," Consejo Nacional del Fomento a la Vivienda (press release, Oct. 18, 2006), http://www.conafovi.gob.mx/prensa/boletines/Octubre19_1_2006.htm (accessed Dec. 26, 2006).

9. United Nations Human Settlements Programme, "Global Report and the State of the World's Cities Report 2001" (Compendium of Human Settlement Statistics, Statistical Annex, Table 1: Population of slum areas at mid-year, by region and country 2001), http://hq.unhabitat.org/programmes/guo/documents/Table1.pdf (accessed Dec. 26, 2006).

10. Comisión Nacional del Fomento a la Vivienda, "Rezago Habitacional 2000," http://www.conafovi.gob.mx/Publicaciones/REZAGO.pdf (accessed Dec. 3, 2006).

11. Mark Ginsberg and Mark Strauss, "New York City: A Case Study in Density After 9/11," Principles for the Rebuilding of Lower Manhattan (Boston Society of Architects/AIA, Sept. 2003), http://architects.org/emplibrary/C6_b.pdf (accessed July 16, 2006).

12. Ibid.

13. 21.8% and 9.5% of Mexico's GDP is produced in Distrito Federal and State of Mexico, respectively. Instituto Nacional de Estadística Geografía e Informática, "Producto interno bruto por entidad federativa: Participación sectorial por entidad federativa 2004," http://www.inegi.gob.mx/est/contenidos/espanol/rutinas/ept.asp?t=cuna14&c=1669 (accessed Dec. 3, 2006).

14. Data for urban areas, population, and density comes from the following sources: United Nations, Department of Economic and Social Affairs, "Urban Agglomerations 2005" (2006), http://www.un.org/esa/population/publications/WUP2005/2005urban_agglo.htm (accessed Dec. 26, 2006); Virgilio Partida Bush and Carlos Anzaldo Gómez, "Escenarios demográficos y urbanos de la zona metropolitana del valle de México" (Consejo Nacional de Población, 2003), http://www.conapo.gob.mx/publicaciones/2003/04.pdf (accessed Dec. 26, 2006); Comisión Ambiental Metropolitana, "La zona metropolitana del valle de México," in Programa para mejorar la calidad del aire ZMVM 2002–2010 (Mar. 2003) http://www.paot.org.mx/centro/libros/proaire/cap02.pdf (accessed Dec. 26, 2006); Instituto Nacional de Estadística, Geografía e Informática, "Estadísticas del Medio Ambiente de la Zona Metropolitana de Monterrey 2001" (2001), http://www.inegi.gob.mx/prod_serv/contenidos/espanol/bvinegi/productos/integracion/sociodemografico/medioambmty/2001/emazmm01.pdf (accessed Dec. 26, 2006).

15. Comisión Nacional del Fomento a la Vivienda, "Rezago Habitacional 2000."

16. San Diego Housing Commission, "Housing Statistics," http://www.sdhc.net/giaboutus2.shtml (accessed Aug. 16, 2006).

17. Robert L. Bach and Richard Kiy, "Shared Destiny: Shaping a Binational Agenda for Health Priorities," International Community Foundation (May 2006), http://www.icfdn.org/shared-destiny/05_cross-border.htm (accessed Aug. 16, 2006).

18. "U.S.–Mexico Border Health," (U.S. Department of Health and Human Services, Bureau of Primary Health Care, May 2005), http://bphc.hrsa.gov/bphc/borderhealth/ (accessed July 13, 2006).

19. New Mexico Border Health Commission, "Demographic Profile of U.S.–Mexico Border" (New Mexico State University, Las Cruces, Aug. 28, 2000), http://www.nmsu.edu/~bhcom/bhcomm-demog.html (accessed Aug. 15, 2006).

20. John B. Anderson, "Trends in Quality-of-Life Indicators in U.S. and Mexican Border Regions, 1950–1990," in Paul Ganster, ed., *Cooperation, Environment, and Sustainability in Border Regions* (San Diego: San Diego State University Press and Institute for Regional Studies of the Californias, 2001), 123.

21. Alejandro Canales, "Industrialization, Urbanization, and Population Growth on the Border," *Borderlines* 58, no. 7 (1999), http://americas.irc-online.org/borderlines/1999/bl58/bl58dev_body.html (accessed Aug. 16, 2006).

22. U.S. Department of Housing and Urban Development, "¿Qué son las Colonias?" (2000), http://espanol.hud.gov/groups/frmwrkcoln/whatcol.cfm?&lang=es (accessed Aug. 16, 2006). See also Cisneros, "Texas Colonias."

23. Cisneros, "Texas Colonias," and Jennifer Eldridge, "Health Care Access for Immigrants in Texas," (working paper, Policy Research Project on Expanding Health Care Coverage for the Uninsured, The Lyndon B. Johnson School of Public Affairs, University of Texas at Austin, 2002), http://www.utexas.edu/lbj/faculty/warner/uninsured/2002_papers/immigrants.pdf (accessed Aug. 16, 2006).

24. Oliver Bernstein, "Walking the Line: What Mexican Activists can Teach the Planet about Poverty and the Planet," *Grist Magazine* (Mar. 7, 2006), http://www.alternet.org/envirohealth/33968/ (accessed Aug. 21, 2006).

25. New Mexico Border Health Commission, "Demographic Profile of U.S.–Mexico Border."

26. Daniel Chacón (BECC, General Manager, Ciudad Juárez, Chihuahua), interview with Alejandro Quinto for *Hyperborder*, June 25, 2006.

27. Cisneros, "Texas Colonias."

28. Nan Valerio, Paul Gagliardo, and Ana María Lemus, "Map 4: Water Infrastructure" (Institute for Regional Studies of the Californias, San Diego State University), http://www-rohan.sdsu.edu/~irsc/atlas/text/wateng.html (accessed Aug. 24, 2006).

29. Dean J. Gipson and Ana María Lemus, "Map 5: Sewage Infrastructure," (Institute for Regional Studies of the Californias, San Diego State University), http://www-rohan.sdsu.edu/~irsc/atlas/text/seweng.html (accessed Aug. 28, 2006).

30. Richard Florida, *The Rise of the Creative Class* (New York: Basic Books, 2002).

31. Ricardo Montezuma, "The Transformation of Bogota, Colombia, 1995–2000:_ Investing in Citizenship and Urban Mobility," *Global Urban Development Magazine* (May 2005), http://www.globalurban.org/Issue1PIMag05/Montezuma%20article.htm (accessed Aug. 28 2006).

32. Jonas Hagen, "The World Learns from Bogota," Urban City, http://www.urbanicity.org/FullDoc.asp?ID=441 (accessed Aug. 28, 2006).

33. Pia M. Orrenius, "Illegal Immigration and Enforcement Along the Southwest Border," *The Border Economy* (Federal Reserve Bank of Dallas, June, 2001) 30, http://www.dallasfed.org/research/border/tbe_issue.pdf (accessed Jan. 1, 2007).

34. U.S. Geological Survey, "Monitoring Colonias along the United States–Mexico Border" (fact sheet 2004-3070, Aug. 2004), http://erg.usgs.gov/isb/pubs/factsheets/fs307004.html (accessed Aug. 28, 2006).

35. The City of New York Department of Housing Preservation and Development, "The New Housing Marketplace: Creating Housing for the Next Generation 2004–2013," http://www.nyc.gov/html/hpd/downloads/pdf/10yearHMplan.pdf (accessed July 18, 2006).

GLOSSARY OF TERMS

Amerindian: derived from American Indian, Amerindian is a broad term used to identify the indigenous peoples of the Americas whose ancestors inhabited the land before the arrival of the Europeans.

Amero: common currency proposed for the Americas, like the Euro of the European Union.

Amexica: an emerging term used to define the border region; Amexica stands for the blending of culture, language and economic conditions along the U.S.–Mexico border.

Banda music: a traditional form of Mexican music that originated in the border state of Sinaloa in the 1930s but became extremely popular throughout Mexico in the 1990s. Since the banda explosion, the brass-based music has become increasingly present among immigrant and Mexican-American communities in the United States.

BECC: Border Environment Cooperation Commission.

Borderlands: area or region defined by the presence of a border.

Bracero: a person who worked as a guest worker for the Bracero Program in the agricultural sector of the U.S. during the World War II and post-war period until the mid-1960s, when the program was terminated and many of the workers and their families were deported to Mexico.

Chicano/a: a term that is used to refer to the identity and cultural patterns of certain people of Mexican descent living in the United States. Often times chicanos are second or third generation Mexican-Americans who have a sense of ethnic pride or consciousness for being both Hispanic or Latino and American.

Cholo/a: a term that is sometimes considered derogatory in the U.S. context and refers to Mexican, Mexican-American, or Chicano "gangsters." Cholos are often identified by their style of dress, which may include baggy pants, flannel shirts (usually with just the top buttoned), sleeveless shirts (commonly known as "wife-beaters"), black-ink tattoos, hairnets and bandanas.

Clicka: a slang word for gang.

Colonias: neighborhoods and irregular settlements characterized by poor infrastructure and services along the U.S.–Mexico border.

Corrido: a narrative song that usually originates in the mestizo Mexican cultural area, which includes the South Western United States. Corridos originally served as a method of communication and education and are sometimes referred to as poetry.

Coyote: a person who helps undocumented migrants cross into the U.S., almost invariably for a high price. Coyotes are also known as polleros, human smugglers, or human traffickers.

Cultural Assimilation: a process in which ethno-cultural groups (such as immigrants and minorities) give up or lose customs that formerly set them apart as "different" from the conventional social norm in order to become integrated and absorbed by the greater established society.

El Norte: a term used by Mexicans that refers to the United States, the country north of Mexico to which many people migrate.

El Otro Lado: a term used by Mexicans to refer to the United States and when people migrate to the other side of the border.

El Paso del Norte: a part of the border region that includes the cities of Monterrey, Ciudad Juárez, El Paso, Santa Teresa, NM, and Tucson, AZ.

Femicide: a term used in reference to the murders of female factory workers in Ciudad Juarez. According to sociologist Julia Monarrez, the word femicide is applied to any type of abuse—murder, torture, rape, and mutilation—that is aimed at the elimination of women.

Gabacho: a term used in Mexico to refer to a White American person.

Green Card: the document that proves one's Permanent Legal Resident status in the United States.

Gringo: a sometimes-derogatory nickname for Americans that is used in Mexico and other parts of Latin America. Although the word's origins are disputed popular belief is that the term dates back to the Mexican-American War and the Mexicans' resentment of the green-uniformed U.S. army presence, which prompted people to demand that the "greens go," from which the word gringo derived.

Gringolandia: a term that refers to the United States, where gringos live.

Grupo Beta: a group of border workers dedicated to protect the rights and well being of migrants in the border region.

Hispanic: the classification Hispanic refers to people whose culture and/or heritage ties to Spain, thus rendering it controversial for some as it does not clearly indicate a connection with Latin American backgrounds. The term first showed up on the U.S. census in 1980.

Hispanic Challenge: a term coined by Samuel Huntington that refers to the cultural threat that Hispanics and particularly Mexicans pose on American culture.

Latino/a: derived from the Spanish word latinoamericano, the term Latino refers to inhabitants of Latin America and their descendents living outside the region. In the U.S. context it is used to socially and ethnically differentiate people. Many people of Latin American backgrounds prefer Latino to Hispanic, yet the term is still controversial as some claim that it excludes the indigenous peoples of the region and many prefer to be referred to by their national heritage instead of a broad, all-encompassing term that ignores the vast differences in the backgrounds and histories of groups who descend from different Latin American nations.

Maquiladora: an industrial company owned in part or total by foreign or multi-national corporations. The main output product must be exported out of Mexico, receives special tax exemptions and the companies are permitted to import foreign parts. The majority of Mexico's maquiladoras reside along the U.S.–Mexico border.

Melting Pot: a metaphor that describes a theory of how homogenous societies develop and is often associated with the United States. The melting pot suggests that distinct cultural, ethnic, and/or religious identities are lost when people of different groups mix and instead a new, common identity that is understood to be different from the original components is formed.

Mestizo: a Spanish origin term, mestizo is used in the context of the Americas to describe a person of mixed European and indigenous ancestries.

Metroplex: an urbanized, multi-city region.

Mexamerica: a term from Joel Garreau's book, *The Nine Nations of North America* that refers to the American Southwest and Mexico combined as one of the nine nations of North America.

Mica: the word for green card in Spanish.

Minutemen: see Vigilante Groups.

Mojado: see Wetback

Mulatto/a: in the present day context this term is used primarily in Latin America to describe people of both African and European ancestry and/or African and Latino ancestry.

Municipio: zoned regions inside Mexican states. The American counterpart to a municipio is a county, also known as municipality.

NADBANK: North American Development Bank.

NAFTA: North American Free Trade Agreement.
Neoliberalism: a structural adjustment policy, which according to its supporters is meant to help developing nations manage foreign debt and become reoriented toward the world market

economy. It is a political-economic philosophy that is strongly supported by the United States and global financial institutions like the International Monetary Fund and the World Bank. Neoliberalism emphasizes the shrinking of the state, minimal or no government intervention in the economy, fiscally responsible governments, the establishment of attractive environments for foreign investment (which usually implies the dismantlement of state regulations, such as labor laws and environmental standards), and open markets. It is considered controversial and is a practice that is often criticized.

Oaxacalifornia: often referred to as a transnational space, Oaxacalifornia is an emerging term that pertains to the large presence and increasing influence of primarily indigenous migrants from the Mexican state of Oaxaca in California.

Pollo: a person who is in the process of being smuggled to the U.S. by a pollero.

Pollero: a human smuggler or human trafficker. Polleros are also commonly referred to as coyotes.

Shared Responsibility: a term used by president Fox to refer to the way border security and migration should be handled between the United States and Mexico.

Smart Border: a new security model for borders where crossings are expedient and safe.

Spanglish: a term used to refer to speech that in some shape or form mixes the English and Spanish languages. It is considered a product of bilingual communities and the uniting and integration of different cultures.

TexMex: a cultural term referring to the mix of Mexican and Texan cultures. This term is widely used in other countries to refer to Hispanic or Mexican cultures in general.

Transnationalism: pertains to the significant interconnectivity found between peoples around the world and suggests a loosening of nation-state boundaries in order to foster deepened cooperation across borders, regions, and continents. The concept has advanced due to developments in telecommunication—particularly the Internet—immigration, and globalization. Transnational coalitions, organizations and networks often begin at the grass-roots level with the aim of taking action or provoking change at the binational or transnational level.

Vigilante Groups: groups of people who for a specific cause take the law into their own hands if they feel official authorities are not handling issues properly or effectively. The term became popularized in 2005 when the Minutemen Project began. The Minutemen are a controversial group in the United States who has begun patrolling the U.S.–Mexico border in an effort to curb undocumented immigration. W

Wetback: a derogatory term for an undocumented immigrant who crosses the Rio Grande to enter the U.S. Historically, people would arrive by boat to the American coasts as well, often getting wet.

Whole Enchilada: an expression used by Jorge Castañeda—former foreign relations officer of Mexico—that referred to the establishment of a complete migration agreement between Mexico and the U.S.

Zetas: a group of ex-military workers who are now in compliance with the Cartel del Golfo, a powerful drug cartel in Mexico. *Zeta* is also the name of a weekly newspaper in Tijuana that reports on the narcotrafficking, corruption and other sensitive issues. Jesus Blancornelas, the director of *Zeta*, survived a 1997 assassination attempt for his exposés on corruption and drug trafficking in Mexico, and has lost several of his colleagues and staff members to violent murders as well. He was chosen to receive the 1999 UNESCO/Guillermo Cano World Press Freedom Prize.

ILLUSTRATION SOURCES

6-7. World Migration patterns. Source: United Nations, International Migration, 2006.

8. Estimate for the U.S.–Mexico border from 2003 projection to 2030 by J. Peach and J. Williams. 2003. "Population Dynamics of the U.S.-Mexican Border Region." Unpublished, forthcoming SCERP Monograph. San Diego: SCERP/SDSU Press.
Other countries estimates from 2006 World Population Datasheet. Population Reference Bureau.

11. Top 10 Migration Countries, 1970–1995. Source: World Migration Report, 2003. International Organization for Migration.

22-23. UN Millennium Development Goals. Progress Report, 2006. Source: The United Nations. The Millennium Development Goals Report. Statistical Annex, 2006.

24-25. International Comparisons Among G-20 Countries. . Unless otherwise noted, all sources from World Bank, Data and Statistics.
Control of Corruption, Percentile Rank: No data available for European Union. Kaufmann, Daniel, Kraay, Aart and Mastruzzi, Massimo, "Governance Matters V: Governance Indicators for 1996-2005" (September 2006). Available at SSRN: http://ssrn.com/abstract=929549
Net Migration Rate, 2000-2005: United Nations.International Migration, 2006.
Expenditure on R&D as a % of GDP, 2004: No Data for E.U., and Saudi Arabia. UNESCO, "Statistics. Country/Regional Profiles." http://www.uis.unesco.org/profiles/selectCountry_en.aspx

27. West Bank map. Based on a map published in the London Times, 5 May 2006, in an article called Truth in Mapping,

32. Cascadia map. David McCloskey, Cascadia Institute.

40-41. Proposed Priority Axes for Natural Gas Pipelines. INO-GATE. 2003.

46. Tri-lateral Trade in North America 1993–2006. Sources: Secretaría de Economía. Balanza comercial de México con Canadá. http://www.economia.gob.mx/?P=2261#
U.S. Census Bureau. Trade in Goods (Imports, Exports and Trade Balance) with Mexico. http://www.census.gov/foreign-trade/balance/c2010.html
U.S. Census Bureau. Trade in Goods (Imports, Exports and Trade Balance) with Canada. http://www.census.gov/foreign-trade/balance/c1220.html

80. U.S. Border patrol sectors and Mexican

82-83. Migrant Deaths, Water Stations, and Rescue Beacons, FY 2000-2004. Source: Humane Borders. Fronteras Compasivas. Migrant Death Data for U.S. Government Fiscal Years: October 1,1999-September 30, 2004. Migrant Death Data Sources: U.S. Border Patrol (Tucson & Yuma Sectors), Mexican Consulates, County Medical Examiners: Cochise, Maricopa, Pima, Pinal, Santa Cruz, and Yuma Counties. Spatial Data Sources: Arizona Land Resource Information System, Southern Arizona Data Services Program, Surface Management Data Published, 1988.

98. Understanding the Border's Conditions. Source: International Community Foundation, "Blurred Borders. Transboundary Issues and Solutions in the San Diego/Tijuana Border Region," San Diego-Tijuana: Comparative Advantages and Challenges, http://icfdn.org/publications/blurredborders/12ComAdvtgChallenges.htm

101. As of March, 2005, unauthorized Mexicans in the U.S. represented," Source: own calculations based on Jeffrey S. Passel's "The Size and Characteristics of the Unauthorized Migrant Population in the U.S.," March 7, 2006. Pew Hispanic Center.

103. Farmworkers in the U.S., Data does not always add up to 100% because of rounding. Source: U.S. Department of Labor, "Findings from the National Agricultural Workers Survey (NAWS) 2001 - 2002. A Demographic and Employment Profile of United States Farm Workers."

105. Remittances to Latin America, 2006. Source: Inter-American Development Bank.

142. The Size of the Global Illicit Drug Market. Source: United Nations Office on Drugs and Crime.

143. Major drug cartels in Mexico and main drug entry points into the U.S. Source: Procuraduría General de la República, Programa Nacional para el Control de Drogas, Acciones y Resultados. (Mexico City, Nov. 2005).

172. Hispanic and Mexican population in the U.S. as percentage of total population, 2005. Sources: Estimates from 2005 American Community Survey, U.S. Census; Jeffrey S. Passel, "The Size and Characteristics of the Unauthorized Migrant Population in the U.S.," Pew Hispanic Center, March 7, 2006. http://pewhispanic.org/files/reports/61.pdf (accessed Apr. 29, 2007); Pew Hispanic Center, "Estimates of the Unauthorized Migrant Population for States based on the March 2005 CPS," Apr. 26, 2006, http://pewhispanic.org/files/factsheets/17.pdf (accessed Apr. 29, 2007); Pew Hispanic Center, "Hispanics. A People in Motion," Jan. 2005, http://pewhispanic.org/files/reports/40.pdf (accessed Apr. 29, 2007).

178. Mexican-born ppopulation in U.S. Source: Jeffrey S. Passel, "Unauthorized Migrants: Numbers and Characteristics," Pew Hispanic Center, June 14, 2005. http://pewhispanic.org/files/reports/46.pdf (accessed May 16, 2007).

205. Mexican Products Status in U.S. Source: Reforma, August 23, 2004.

225. Potential Congestion Points in U.S. Roads by 2020. Source: U.S. Department of Transportation. Battelle, February 25, 2002. Estimated Average Annual Daily Truck Traffic, 2020. Source: U.S. Department of Transportation, Federal Highway Administration, Office of Freight Management and Operations, Freight Analysis Framework.

227. North American Trade Corridors. Source: North American Forum on Integration.

231. Based on the Oil and Gas Liquids, 2004 Scenario, by Colin J. Campbell.

232. Urban Settlements and Oil Fields in the Gulf of Mexico. Source: Oilwatch Sudamérica.

238. World Solar Radiation. Source: estimates using data from the National Renewable Energy Laboratory, NREL. Potential solar development in Mexico's northern states. Source: Own calculations.

239. U.S. Solar Radiation. Source: NREL, the Electric & Hydrogen Technologies & Systems Center. May, 2004. Model estimates: http://www.nrel.gov/gis/il_solar_pv.html

281. Hispanic Home Ownership Rate. Source: 2005 American Community Survey; U.S. Census.

PHOTO CREDITS

10. Courtesy Alfonso Caraveo. El Colegio de la Frontera Norte (COLEF).

12. David McNew, Getty Images.

18. Sandy Huffaker, Getty Images.

28. AP Photo/Oded Balilty.

30. AP Photo/Arturo Rodriguez.

31. AP Photo/Arturo Rodriguez.

36. AP Photo/Elizabeth Dalziel. Caption source: United Nations Office on Drugs and Crime. "Opium Poppy Cultivation in the Golden Triangle 2006." Executive Summary. http://www.unodc.un.or.th/Executive_summary/Executive_Summary_Golden_Triangle_Opium_Survey_2006.pdf

43. Courtesy Alfonso Caraveo, COLEF.

45. Dirck Halstead/Time Life Pictures/Getty Images.

48. Courtesy Alfonso Caraveo, COLEF.

70. Scott Olson/Staff, Getty Images.

77. Top right: Alfonso Caraveo, COLEF.

77. Bottom right, bottom left, top left: Gerald L. Nino.

77. Middle left: James Tourtellotte.

78. Top: James Tourtellotte, Courtesy CBP.

78. Bottom: AP Photo/Gregory Bull.

79. Top: James Tourtellotte, Courtesy CBP.

79. Bottom left, bottom right: CBP, U.S. Customs and Border Protection.

81. Courtesy David Maung/Humane Borders.

84. Courtesy Alfonso Caraveo, COLEF.

86. AP Photo/Khampha Bouaphanh.

87. Top: AP Photo/Khampha Bouaphanh.

87. Bottom: Scott Olson/Staff, Getty Images.

88. Courtesy Alfonso Caraveo, COLEF.

89. Top: AP Photo/Reed Saxon.

89. Bottom: Courtesy Ramón T. Blanco Villalón/Zeta.

92. Phillippe Diederich/Stringer, Getty Images.

96. AP Photo/Milenio-Rocio Vazquez.

97. Courtesy Alfonso Caraveo, COLEF.

98. Top, bottom: Courtesy Alfonso Caraveo, COLEF.

99. Visible Earth, NASA; Border photographs courtesy Alfonso Caraveo, COLEF.

102. David Turnley/Staff. Getty Images.

105. Glenn Frank. istockphoto.com.

107. AP Photo/Matt Warnock.

110. Claudia Arias.

111. Claudia Arias.

112. 1: U.S. Department of Justice.

112. 2: New York World-Telegram & Sun Collection, Prints and Photographs Division, Library of Congress.

112. 3: U.S. House of Representatives.

112. 6: Frédéric de la Mure (French Ministry of Foreign Affairs - Photographic Service).

112. 7: U.S. Department of Commerce.

112. 8: U.S. Department of the Treasury.

112. 9: U.S. Department of State.

112. 10: U.S. Senate.
112. 11: U.S. Department of Energy.
112. 12: U.S. Customs and Border Protection.
112. 14: U.S. House of Representatives.
112. 15: U.S. Department of Energy.
112. 16: University of California Riverside.
112. 17: Iowa State University.
112. 18: Library of Congress.
115. Ann Summa/Contributor. Getty Images.
120. AP Photo/Ron Edmonds.
123. Mauricio Daniel Serna Murais.
124. Erik S. Lesser/Stringer. Getty Images.
128. Top: AP Photo/Rich Pedroncelli.
128. Bottom: Gary Williams/Stringer. Getty Images.
129. Gerald Nino, U.S. Customs and Border Protection.
130. Left: AP Photo/The Sun, Benjamin Hager.
130. Right: Gary Williams/Stringer. Getty Images.
132. Claudia Arias.
134. Omar Torres/Staff. Getty Images.
141. Gerardo Magallon/AFP/Getty Images.
143. Top, bottom: AP Photo/Denis Poroy.
147. Patti McConville. Getty Images.
148. Mauricio Daniel Serna Murais.
150. Courtesy Pablo López.
156. Top right, middle right, middle left, top left: Devon
     McLorg.
156. Bottom left: Steve Dibblee. istockphoto.com.
156. Bottom right: Courtesy Frank Van Kalmthout.
158. LAR/Fernando Romero.
159. Courtesy Pablo López.
160. Mauricio Daniel Serna Murais.
163. Claudia Arias.
164. Courtesy Bárbara Miranda.
166. Jeff Hutchens/Contributor. Getty Images.
170. Alejandro Quinto.
174. Courtesy Louis Hock.
175. AP Photo/Denis Poroy.
178. AP Photo/Reed Saxon.
188. Courtesy Fred Lonidier.
194. Claudia Arias/Peter Ty.
196. Courtesy Paul Maxwell, Binational Sustainability Labo-
     ratory and Sandia National Laboratories.
198. Omar Torres/Staff. Getty Images.
204. Edward Burtynsky.
207. Top, bottom: LAR/Fernando Romero.
209. Mauricio Daniel Serna Murais.
213. LAR/Fernando Romero.
216. Sandy Huffaker/Stringer. Getty Images.
223. LAR/Fernando Romero.
228. Courtesy James Corner/Field Operations.
241. Peter Ty.
242. Courtesy SEMARNAT.
252. Courtesy Carlos A. de la Parra.
255. Top: Rafal Swidzinski, Stock.XCHNG.
255. Bottom: LAR/Fernando Romero.
256. Courtesy Jacobo Kupersztoch.

263. Catherine Ledner. Getty Images.
266. LAR/Fernando Romero.
268. Courtesy Alfonso Caraveo, COLEF.
276. Top left, top right: Courtesy Alfonso Caraveo, COLEF.
276. Bottom: Courtesy Pablo López.
278. Top, bottom: LAR/Fernando Romero.
318. AP Photo/Denis Poroy.

INDEX

Page numbers in *italics* refer to illustrations. Page numbers in **boldface** refer to the future scenarios discussed in the book. Page numbers in **black** refer to illustrations in future scenarios.

E

and piracy of consumer products, 154, 157, 159
and property rights, 158–59
street vendors in, *156*, 158, **164**
inSite_05, *175*, *188–89*
Intelligence Reform and Terrorism Prevention Act, 74
interdependence, between U.S. and Mexico
and consumer market/economic influence, 108–111
and labor, 100–104, 106–108
and *maquiladoras*, *97*, 97, 99, 100, 201, 202, 235, 252, 271
and oil industry, 113
and politics, 112, *112*
and remittances, 104, *105*, 106, 201
in sister cities, 95–97
and tourism, 113–14
International Boundary and Water Commission, 245
International Energy Agency (IEA), 231
International Monetary Fund (IMF), 39, 157, 201
Internet use, *22*, *25*, 109, 111
Iran, as oil exporter, 231, 232, 235
Israel–Palestine border, 26, *27–29*, 29

J

journalists, and exposure of narcotraffic/corruption, *89*, 88–90, 140, 142
just-in-time manufacturing, 219
"Just Say Know" anti-drug campaign, 144–45, 264

K

Korea, North and South, border between, 26
Kunming, China, *36–37*
Kyoto Protocol, 210, 213, **253**

L

labor, Mexican, *92–93*, *102*
in agricultural sector, *92–93*, 100, 103, 173, **176**
exodus of, and effect on Mexico, 101, 104, 177
and guest workers (scenario), **162–63**, **176**
in informal sector, 152–65
in *maquiladoras*, 42, *97*, 97, 99, 100, 201, 271
national boycott by, 106, *107*, 108
and Social Security system, 158, 175, 177
undocumented, 100–101, 108, 157–58, **160–61**, **162–63**, 173
Laos, 35, 36
La Paz Agreement, 69, 251
Laredo, Texas, 95, *99*, 219, 277
Latin America, 104, *105*, **170**
Latinos, 106, **170–71**. *See also* Hispanics
Legal Permanent Residents (LPRs), 73, 108
Los Angeles, 157, 158, 178, 273
Lujan, Manuel, Jr., 112, *112*

M

Mahony, Roger M., *47*
El Mañana (newspaper), 140
maquiladoras, 42, *97*, 196, 201, 271
and deaths of women workers, 99, *134–35*
growth of, as caused by NAFTA, 97, 100, 201, 202, 235
toxic wastes produced by, 236, 252
marijuana, 145, **146–47**, **148–49**
Marin, Rosario, 112, *112*
Martin, Paul, 126
Martinez, Mel, 112, *112*
McAllen, Texas, 95, *99*
Menendez, Robert, 112
Mercosur (Southern Cone Common Market), *38*, 39, **203**
"metroplex." *See* Ciudad Juárez; Ciudad Juárez-El Paso "metroplex"; El Paso
Mexicali, 13, 95, *99*, 125, 247
residential energy use in, 235
Silicon Border industry park in, 196
tires dumped in, as reclaimed, *242–43*, 252
Mexican American Legal Defense and Educational Fund (MALDEF), 74
Mexican Americans
as consumer market, 109
organizations of, and political influence, 178–79
population of, 169, *172*, 178
Mexico, 9, 25, 30. *See also* border, U.S.–Mexico; interdependence
biodiversity of, 245
border security sectors, *80*
as compared to U.S., *24–25*, 52–57, *58–59*. *See also specific topics*
customs facility of, in U.S., 80
foreign direct investment in, 110, 202
and future scenarios, **212–13**, **214–15**, **253**, **262–63**, **267**
indigenous communities in, 245
oil exports by, 104, *105*, 113
poverty in, 201–202, 204–205
and relations with U.S., key events in, 68–69, 91
remittances to, 104, *105*, 106, 110, 201
Mexico City
drug trade/turf wars in, 140
informal housing in, *150–51*, *159*, *276*
informal sector in, *156*
metropolitan region of, **212**, **240**, 273
as southernmost hub of "NAFTA highway," 219–20
Tepito marketplace in, *156*, **161**, 202
water access in, 247
Michoacán, 106, 110, 140
micro electro mechanical systems (MEMS), 196, *196*
migrants, deaths of
attempts to prevent, 81, *81–83*, 84, 177
and Border Patrol involvement, 177
costs associated with, 81, 84, 177
as marked by crosses, *84*, 87
and Mexican identification program, 91
under Operation Gatekeeper, 181–87

W

Z

Dave "Cannonball" Smith flying over the U.S.–Mexico border from Tijuana to San Ysidro, California on August 27, 2005. The event "One Flew Over the Void," is an art piece by artist Javier Téllez, and was part of the inSite_05 festival.